DRAGOONS AND DRAGOON OPERATIONS IN THE BRITISH CIVIL WARS, 1638-1653

Andrew Abram

'This is the Century of the Soldier', Fulvio Testi, Poet, 1641

HELION & COMPANY

Helion & Company Limited
Unit 8 Amherst Business Centre
Budbrooke Road
Warwick
CV34 5WE
England
Tel. 01926 499 619
Email: info@helion.co.uk
Website: www.helion.co.uk
Twitter: @helionbooks
Visit our blog http://blog.helion.co.uk/

Published by Helion & Company 2023
Designed and typeset by Mary Woolley, Battlefield Design (www.battlefield-design.co.uk)
Cover designed by Paul Hewitt, Battlefield Design (www.battlefield-design.co.uk)

ISBN 978-1-804511-95-4

British Library Cataloguing-in-Publication Data.
A catalogue record for this book is available from the British Library.

For details of other military history titles published by Helion & Company Limited contact the above address or visit our website: http://www.helion.co.uk.

We always welcome receiving book proposals from prospective authors.

Contents

List of Illustrations

List of Tables

List of Abbreviations

AA	*Archaeologia Aeliana*
A&O	*Acts and Ordinances*
BCA	Birmingham, City Archives
BL	British Library
BLB	*Brereton Letter Books*
Bod Lib.	Bodleian Library
BRO	Berkshire Record Office
CJ	*Journals of the House of Commons*
CRO	*Cheshire Record Office/Cheshire Archives*
CSPD	*Calendar of State Papers Domestic*
DRO	Derbyshire Record Office
DM	*Derbyshire Miscellany*
DWL	Dr Williams Library
ECWNQ	*English Civil War Notes & Queries*
ECWT	*English Civil War Times*
EHR	*English Historical Review*
ERA	East Riding Archives
ERO	Essex Record Office
FRO	Flintshire Record Office
GA	Gloucestershire Archives
HJ	*Historical Journal*
HLRO	House of Lords Record Office
HMC	Historical Manuscripts Commission
HR	*Historical Research*
IHS	*Irish Historical Studies*
JAAS	*Journal of the Arms and Armour Society*
JCA	*Journal of Conflict Archaeology*
JRRIL	John Rylands Research Institute and Library
JSAHR	*Journal of the Society for Army Historical Research*
LA	Lancashire Archives
LincsA	Lincolnshire Archives
LCL	Lichfield Cathedral Library

LJ	*Journals of the House of Lords*
LRO	Lancashire Record Office
LRRO	Leicestershire and Rutland Record Office
MH	*Midland History*
MS	Manuscript
MSS	Manuscripts
NA	Nottinghamshire Archives
NAM	National Army Museum
NLW	National Library of Wales
ODNB	*Oxford Dictionary of National Biography*
P&P	*Past & Present*
ROP	*Royalist Ordnance Papers*
SA	Shropshire Archives
SCJ	*Sixteenth Century Journal*
SofA	Society of Antiquaries
SRMML	Scottish Rite Masonic Museum & Library
SRO	Staffordshire Record Office
SuffolkRO	Suffolk Record Office
SomersetA	Somerset Archives
TGM	*The Gentleman's Magazine*
THSLC	*Transactions of the Historical Society of Lancashire and Cheshire*
TLCAS	*Transactions of the Lancashire and Cheshire Antiquarian Society*
TNA	The National Archives
TPMLAA	*Transactions and Proceedings of the Modern Language Association of America*
TRHS	*Transactions of the Royal Historical Society*
TSANHS	*Transactions of the Shropshire Archaeological and Natural History Society*
TT	Thomason Tracts
ULSP	University of Leeds, Special Collections
WA	Worcestershire Archives
WarksA	Warwickshire Archives
WH	*War in History*
WSHC	Wiltshire and Swindon History Centre
WSL	William Salt Library
WYA	West Yorkshire Archives
WYHC	West Yorkshire History Centre
YML	York, Minster Library

Acknowledgements

In completing this book, I would like to thank the staff of various archives for their ready assistance. I would also like to thank Gary Ashby for sharing his knowledge of Sir Thomas Aston's regiments of horse and dragoons, and Charles Singleton of Helion & Co. for his continued advice and encouragement throughout this and other projects.

The Series Editor would like to acknowledge and thank Mike Chetham for his generous donation of the front cover background image to the book.

Explanatory Notes and Conventions

Although dates prior to 1752 are recorded with the year beginning 25 March, modern dating is used throughout, with the New Year being taken to start on 1 January. Spellings in contemporary manuscripts and printed sources (which varied considerably during the seventeenth century) have been modernised, while where appropriate, current forms of punctuation have been added to period accounts. The contemporary monetary, measurement and weights values, following the Imperial system, have been quoted throughout.

Monetary values are 12 pennies (12d) = 1 shilling (1s); 20 shillings = one pound sterling (£1); thus £1 = 240d.

Lengths and distances are given in inches, feet, yards, ells and miles, 12 inches (in) = 1 foot (ft); 3 feet = 1 yard (yd), 1,760 yards = 1 mile (mi), 22 inches = 1 ell.

Weights are in pounds and ounces 16 ounces (oz) = 1(lb), 112lb = 1 hundredweight (cwt), 20cwt = 1 ton.

Introduction

The following book examines in depth the concept, raising, equipping, composition, organisation, and operational role of dragoons during the British Civil Wars (1638–1653). By its definition and scope, this study can never claim to be definitive, especially as many contemporary records providing information about these troops no longer exist. Various general studies of the wars and their wider context cover, to one extent or another, the subject of dragoons, but they do so often merely within the context of broader military campaigns and forces.

Civil war dragoons are well served by contemporary sources (both in manuscript and printed form), although much of this material has received little attention or has remained unknown to researchers. Probably the most important are the various military documents among the Commonwealth Exchequer Papers in the National Archives, principally SP28, but also War Office records (WO) and Exchequer Papers (E). Additionally of use have been several collections in the British Library and Bodleian Library, in addition to other national and regional archives, including the National Library of Wales, are particularly relevant. Various documents, such as pay warrants, muster rolls, records of the issue and receipt of equipment and ammunition, officer's commissions and certificates of service, disbursements by army treasurers, corporations, and sequestration committees, depositions, letters, newsbooks, petitions, and quarter sessions papers have proved invaluable. In terms of printed material, government records, such as *Royalist Composition Papers*, *Royalist Ordnance Papers*, and *Acts and Ordinances of the Interregnum* are especially relevant, as is the wide range of contemporary newsbooks and tracts. Equally important are the printed transcriptions of civil war documents preserved in the *Historical Manuscripts* series, which include a large quantity of now lost manuscript material. Added to this, military manuals offer a valuable insight into how the role, arming and nature of dragoons was perceived in contemporary theory and practice, while highlighting how this arm helped shape the complexion of the mid-seventeenth century battlefield

If one problem with studying the Parliamentarians is that there is a relative abundance of material, the opposite is true of the Royalists. Although they probably kept detailed administrative records, very few of these have survived. This is partly because the Royalists did not have a comparable body to the Committee for Taking Accounts of the Whole Kingdom, although there were Royalist committees that examined accounts at county level. As P. R. Newman asserts, for the northern armies 'Rank and file study is impossible.

Muster rolls are rare for the army of the Parliament, and virtually nonexistent for the northern Royalist forces. This is due, partly to destruction of records, but we cannot suppose that accurate and consistent details were always kept, anyway.'[1] The most significant set of Royalist records applicable to this book are those pertaining to the Royalist Ordnance Office at Oxford. The surviving papers of the Ordnance Office are divided between the various classes of WO papers in The National Archives, alongside those of the Parliamentarian Ordnance Office.[2] Like the Parliamentarian Ordnance Papers, there are further volumes in the British Library and Bodleian Library.[3] These papers have been examined in detail by Ian Roy, and an edited selection of them published by the Oxfordshire Records Society in two volumes. The other major source for the Royalists comes from the papers of Sir Edward Walker, the King's secretary, deposited in the British Library. These contain notes on the proceedings of the Royalist Council of War, along with drafts of official correspondence with commanders and other records relating to Royalist administration.[4]

Various regiments of dragoons and autonomous companies (referred to also in the seventeenth century as troops) were recruited by both sides, although some came and went, and several units remain obscure, both in their origins and their history. Some companies were attached to regiments of horse, following the Continental practice, which was particularly adopted by professional soldiers such as Prince Rupert and Sir Arthur Aston. Their mounted role also allowed for some reorganisation into and redeployment as cavalry formations. Often this was indicative of battlefield attrition and operational requirements, but losses (particularly amongst officers and non-commissioned officers) and the hazardous nature of their duties, were also responsible for a level of interchangeability among regiments and minor units. During the early months of the English Civil War, sizeable numbers of dragoon regiments were raised and maintained by the Parliamentarian armies.

In November 1642, Charles I, lacking the resources of London, complained to the Earl of Newcastle, 'I want dragoons, which is the rebels' strength, their foot not liking winter marches.'[5] Nevertheless, at Edgehill a Royalist brigade of around 1,500 dragoons cleared the hedges and ditches 'with great courage and dexterity' on both flanks of the King's army.[6] Such was the usefulness of this arm that in July 1644 the Parliamentarian commander Sir William Waller proposed to convert his entire Parliamentarian army to dragoons but was prevented by a lack of suitable horses. Dragoons were used widely by the Royalist forces operating along the Welsh borders in 1643, though with varying success. Given the nature of much of the style of dragoon

1 P. R. Newman, 'The Royalist Army in Northern England, 1642–45', PhD thesis (University of York, 1978), I, p.33.
2 TNA, WO 49/79; WO 55/424; WO 55/457; WO 55/459; WO 55/1661.
3 BL, Ms Add 34325; Bod Lib., Ms Rawlinson D395.
4 BL, Mss Add 36913–19, 6804, 6851–2; Mss Harley 18980–1.
5 BL, Ms Harley 6988, f.76r.
6 *A Relation of the Battel fought between Keynton and Edgehill, by His Majesty's Army and that of the Rebels* (Oxford: 1642). TT, E126[24].

operations, fighting in the regions was suited to these soldiers. In 1642, various Royalist gentlemen in North Wales were commissioned to raise regiments and companies, some of which joined Charles I's Oxford Army. Like some of their Royalist counterparts, between 1642 and 1646 Sir William Brereton's Parliamentarian dragoons in Cheshire developed into a flexible and experienced fighting force that was habituated to warfare.

Some authors have suggested that civil war dragoons were a fighting elite – versatile and highly specialised troops accustomed to hazardous service – who were often commanded by professional soldiers and recruited from veterans of other conflicts.[7] There is some truth in this, although there are various examples of inexperienced, and poorly equipped and officered dragoon units during the early stages of the wars. Nevertheless, some military experience is evident from the opening stages of the fighting in England, when some Royalist dragoons seemed better trained and disciplined than others of Charles I's armies. For the Parliamentarians, many recruits were obtained in London from returning veterans and foreign professionals. Among Brereton's dragoons, some of his captains were commissioned in the capital, and in 1642 most of the recruits enlisted there, possibly in part from Dutchmen or from British soldiers returning from abroad.[8] Moreover, Colonel Fraser's Covenanters were built around 'four complete companies' returned from Continental service, whilst the regiment was considered the 'stoutest' in the army.

7 Barratt, John, *Cavaliers: The Royalist Army at War 1642–1646* (Stroud: Sutton, 2000), pp.50–3; Andrew Abram, "Sufficiently Different to the Rest of the Army': The Cheshire Parliamentarian Dragoons in the First Civil War', *JSAHR*, 98 (2020), pp.220–38.

8 Andrew Abram, *More Like Lions than Men: Sir William Brereton and the Cheshire Army of Parliament, 1642–46* (Solihull: Helion & Co., 2020), pp.142–3 & 347–8; 'The Influence of Military Professionals and Trained Band Officers in Lancashire and Cheshire during the British Civil Wars', *TLCAS*, 112 (2020), pp.113–34.

1

The Origins and Role of Dragoons

Dragoons were an essential component of seventeenth century armies, even if some contemporaries reflected uncertainties about their precise function, which developed over time. During the Thirty Years' War (1618–48), heavily armoured lancers and cuirassiers had become increasingly obsolete, although the medium harquebusiers and the mounted foot – known as dragoons – continued to evolve. One contemporary, Thomas Digges, noted 'it is now to small purpose to wear arms, seeing the fury of the fire shot is such, as no armour is able to hold it out.'[1] The practice of mounting infantry armed with arquebuses (short, smoothbore firearms) probably originated with the French Huguenot armies of the late 1500s. King Henri IV appreciated the fundamental role of his mounted forces in warfare and heightened its battlefield effectiveness. Thus, he made extensive and original use of a comparatively new kind of soldier, the *arquebusiers-à-cheval* or mounted infantrymen. These acted as an effective, mobile, and potentially potent force against their more numerous and better-provided enemy.[2] The term 'dragoon' (or according to some contemporary descriptions, 'dragooner') seems to derive from the use of this type of soldier in the Dutch army of the period. The term was taken from the dragoon's primary weapon – the 'dragon', a short large-bore flintlock firearm (originally perhaps with its muzzle decorated with a dragon's head), slung from a broad leather belt, and hanging from his side so he could ride unencumbered.

Sir James Turner, who served under King Gustav II Adolf (Gustavus Adolphus) of Sweden on the Continent during the 1630s, wrote 'we may suppose we may borrow their name from Dragon, because a musketeer on horseback, with his burning match riding at a gallop, as many times he doth,

1 *Foure Paradoxes, or Politique Discourses: 2 concerning* militarie discipline, written long since by Thomas Digges Esquire. 2 of the worthinesse of warre and warriors, by Dudly Digges, his sonne (London, 1604), p.61.

2 Archer Jones, *The Art of War in the Western World* (New York: Oxford University Press, 1987), pp.207–10; Ronald S Love, '"All the King's Horsemen": The Equestrian Army of Henri IV, 1585–1598', *Sixteenth Century Journal*, 22 (1991), pp.511–33.

may sometimes resemble that beast, which naturalists call a Fiery Dragon.'[3] The origin of the word *tragons* is Dutch, and was used to describe mounted infantry. In the army of the States General, commanded by Maurice, Prince von Nassau-Siegen, the infantry on horseback were described as *trachonzoder muskutirer zu pferdt* ('pferdt' meaning horse, thus, mounted musketeers) or *tragons*.[4] Throughout this period then, they were essentially mounted infantry who rode, rather than marched to the battlefield. Even so, these increasingly multi-purpose troops formed a distinct combat arm, combining the firepower of infantry with the mobility of cavalry, and capable of undertaking their own specialist, small-scale operations. In December 1602, during the so-called Long War (Turkish) of 1591–1606, Archduke Matthias of Austria ordered the mobilisation of four companies of 100 dragoons of Tilly's regiment (*draconische pferd*), recruited from among Walloon mercenaries. These rode 'good horses' and were armed with a sword, a long wheel-lock musket on a shoulder strap, bandolier, and a pistol in a belt or on their saddle. As a formation lighter than the harquebusiers, such dragoons appear to have been the ideal support for the heavy cavalry during combat.[5]

Johann Jacobi von Wallhausen (Open source)

Providing an accurate description of dragoons, based on contemporary definitions, has proven difficult, however. In 1616 the German soldier, and one of the leading military theorists and writers of the day, Johann Jacobi von Wallhausen, divided cavalry into four kinds: lancers, cuirassiers, carabineers, and dragoons. He stated that although the latter rode on horseback, they fought on foot.[6] Though not considered to be true cavalry, the dragoon was another form of mounted soldier. According to John Cruso, writing in 1632, 'The dragoon was invented for special services to assist the cavalry as infantry; considering there be many exploits which cannot be effected by the cavalry alone.'[7] This opinion was shared by Turner, who wrote 'seldom there is any occasion of service against an enemy, but wherein it is both fit and necessary to join some foot with the horse, dragoons then go not only before to guard passes (as some imagine) but to fight in open field.' However, he insisted that dragoons were part of the cavalry and came under the

3 Turner, *Pallas Armata*, p.230.

4 Werner Hahlweg, *Die Heeresreformder Oranier, Das Kriegsbuch des Grafen Johann von Nassau-Siegen* (Wiesbeden: Selbstverlag der Historischen Kommission, 1973), pp.314, 317.

5 Joseph Kelenik, 'The Military Revolution in Hungary', Dávid Géza and Pál Fodor (eds), *Ottomans, Hungarians, and Habsburgs in Central Europe* (Leiden: Brill, 2000), pp.117–62, (pp. 133–4).

6 Johann Jacobi von Wallhausen, *Kriegskunst zu Pferd* (Frankfurt: 1616), pp.16–17.

7 Cruso, *Militarie Instructions*, p.44.

command of the generals of horse.[8] Wallhausen's dragoons, like the infantry of the early seventeenth century, consisted of both musketeers and pikemen, usually in equal parts:

> For dragoons you will take half musketeers, the other half pikemen, each equipped with appropriate arms as is depicted in *The Military Art for Infantry* [the first volume of his work], which they will use as infantrymen since they are more related to infantry than cavalry. However, since they are always mounted and stationed likewise in the cavalry lines, I wanted to discuss the matter here. Their arms, then, are the musket or the pike.[9]

Similarly, Cruso, in a chapter entitled 'Of the arming of the dragoon' stated:

> The dragoon is of two kinds: pike and musket. The pike is to have a thong of leather about the middle of the pike, for the more commodious carrying of it. The musketeer is to have a strap or belt fastened to the stock thereof, almost from one end to the other, by which (being on horseback) he hangeth it at his back, keeping his burning match and the bridle, in the left hand His horse is of the least price, the use thereof being but to expedite his march, alighting to do his service.[10]

Wallhausen recommended that entire regiments, comprising musketeers and pikemen, should be mounted as dragoons, although on the battlefield several companies were deployed as one unit of pikemen, while the musketeers of the same companies formed another. Accordingly, a company of dragoons should muster 200 men: 100 pikemen, who were to form up 10 ranks deep, and 100 musketeers divided into two bodies of 50 and also drawn up in 10 ranks of 5, and placed on each flank of the pikes.[11] Wallhausen's work – which caused some uncertainty during the 1620s and 1630s as to how dragoons should be armed – were nevertheless read widely by soldiers of many nationalities, and widely copied in British military manuals. Even so, one problem with some published military writers of this period is that they mixed actual drills, formations, and troop types with their theories. Wallhausen did this in most of his works, particularly in *Kriegskunst zu Fuß*, published in 1615.[12] However, there are several surviving examples of pikemen and musketeers being temporarily mounted on horseback, in practice dragoons were mounted musketeers. Laurence Spring argues that during the Continental wars of the period, the existence of various dragoon units 'gained popularity as the war progressed.' He states further, 'Whether there were any dragoons armed with pikes in the Bavarian Army is not known, but in 1634 there

8 Turner, *Pallas Armata*, p.236.
9 Wallhausen, *Kriegskunst zu Pferd*, pp.16–17.
10 Cruso, *Militarie Instructions*, p.31.
11 Wallhausen, *Kriegskunst zu Pferd*, pp.55, 98–9.
12 David R. Lawrence, *The Complete Soldier: Military Books and Military Culture in Early Stuart England, 1603–1645 (Leiden: Brill, 2008), pp.8–9.*

were sixteen companies, total of 1,080 men, although five companies were attached to cavalry regiments, leaving just two regiments of dragoons.'[13]

The arming of such soldiers with pikes in a more deliberate manner might have been a fad in European armies of the 1620s. There is some evidence that the British were, at least as far as mounted infantry is concerned, aware of the concept of dragoons and were encouraging the county militias to develop them during the early decades of the seventeenth century. In May 1626 a letter from the Privy Council to the Lord Lieutenant of Norfolk, regarding the state of the trained bands recommended 'That the proportion of pioneers after the rate of 100 to 1,000 soldiers be provided, with carts, carriages and a convenient number of nags to mount shot upon.' Though slightly puzzling, this might refer to horses for soldiers (possibly dragoons) who might be detailed as a guard for the pioneers. However, a further entry relating to the Norfolk trained bands from 1635, entitled 'Orders for the general uniformity of all sorts of arms both horse and foot' states, 'That there may be order, that in case of occasion of service the pikes may be mounted on nags as well as shot, which being mounted are rightly called dragoons.'[14] In 1638 the Cambridge Trained Band contained 1,000 foot and 80 mounted soldiers, the latter being 30 harquebusiers and 50 dragoons. With other East Anglia militia formations, they were selected for service in the First Bishops' War in Sir Simon Harcourt's regiment of foot, and in June 1640, they were transported to Newcastle for service against the Scots.[15]

With the disappearance of the light horseman or lancer in early seventeenth century England and Wales, it became commonly accepted that there were three types of mounted troops: the cuirassier, the harquebusier and the dragoon. In 1623, the Privy Council's *Instructions for Musters*, notable as the first endeavour to classify national standards for militia training, portrayed the harquebusiers and dragoons as similar kinds of troops, who used the harquebus or carbine on the battlefield.[16] The 1623 *Instructions* also defined the weapons and accoutrements of each, but even here, there was doubt about the variations between the two. Some English dragoons were raised and mustered for service in the Bishops' Wars – two conflicts resulting from Charles I's attempt to impose Anglicanism on the Scottish Church or Kirk, which began the struggles known collectively as the Wars of the Three Kingdoms in England, Scotland and Ireland. In April 1639 Sir Thomas Fairfax's Yorkshire Trained Band company of dragoons assembled at York, and by the following month 160 soldiers were mustered, besides commissioned and non-commissioned officers. These were probably part of the Earl of Holland's brief mounted incursion across the Scottish border, the

13 Laurence Spring, *In the Emperor's Service: Wallenstein's Army, 1625–1634* (Solihull: Helion & Co., 2019), pp.32, 48–9.

14 W. Wrye (ed.), *State Papers Relating to Musters, Beacons, Ship-money, &c. in Norfolk from 1626 chiefly to the beginning of the Civil War* (Norwich, 1907), pp.126, 202.

15 John Rushworth, *Historical Collections of Private Passages of State* (London: D Browne, 1721), III, pp.1085–6.

16 *Instructions for Musters and Armes, and the use thereof by order from the lords of his Maiesties most honourable Privy Counsayle* (London: 1623); Lawrence, *Complete Soldier, p.286.*

first military action of the conflict.[17] Moreover, during the Second Bishops' War the English garrison at Berwick-upon-Tweed was supplemented by way of a warrant, dated 10 January 1640, for the raising, payment, arming and equipping of 600 Cumberland dragoons in six companies under the command of Colonel Francis Trafford, 200 of who were the tenants of the Earl of Northumberland.[18] On 27 February 1640, Trafford had informed Sir Henry Vane, Charles I's secretary:

> Perceiving that great preparations are made and the superior officers already pricked, while I am not mentioned or assured of any command, this emboldens me to acquaint you with what is necessary for the King's service. That the 600 dragoons now lying in Cumberland may be so settled as to render them useful upon all occasions, for being as they are now, they can do little good, seeing that Sir Richard Gream and others have, and still do endeavour to render them useless. That the Lord General will give me order and commission for levying 400 dragoons in Wales to make the regiment of 1,000 complete, each trooper to be armed with a Scotch pistol, besides musket and sword. The 600 Cumberland dragoons to remain for their country's defence upon their own border, for that is their desire. The 400 Welsh to be disposed of wheresoever the Lord General shall think fit.[19]

This regiment, envisaged as 1,000 dragoons in 10 companies of 100 men each, occupied the town's citadel for a period of eight months as part of the rapidly expanding English garrison.

Writing in the 1670s the Englishman Thomas Venn suggested that pike-armed dragoons remained a very fashionable (though, it seems, impractical) concept. He stated, 'Dragoons are but foot, (to be) on horseback and are so mounted for the expedition of their march, who are to have large leather belts, for the more easy carriage of their pikes and muskets, in some extraordinary service, for making good of passes, lining of hedges, and other ambushments.'[20] To some extent, for political, economic and geographical reasons Britain's military development at the end of the Elizabethan and beginning of the Stuart period was slower than its Continental role models. At the commencement of the civil wars, therefore, the military machine in Britain, which bred various armies, fought to catch up. Although the Three Kingdoms experienced periods of peace, ever since the 1580s, British soldiers had learned the military science and developments of warfare during their service abroad. Four Scots and four English regiments were in the pay of the Dutch United Provinces, and there were also officers and men serving in French, German, Dutch and Spanish armies. Moreover, the methods

---

17 Rushworth, *Historical Collections*, III, p.910; Andrew Hopper, *'Black Tom': Sir Thomas Fairfax and the English Revolution* (Manchester: Manchester University Press, 2007), p.17.

18 *CSPD 1639–40*, pp.317–8; Rushworth, *Historical Collections*, III, pp.930–1; Mark Fissel, *The Bishops' Wars, Charles I's campaigns against Scotland 1638–1640* (Cambridge: Cambridge University Press, 1994), pp.43–4.

19 *CSPD 1639–40*, pp.491, 549–50.

20 Thomas Venn, *Military and Maritine [sic] Discipline in Three Books* (London: E. Tyler, et al., 1672), pp.8–9.

of Gustav II Adolph had given British troops a high regard for Swedish innovations in the art of war.

The early seventeenth century was a period of considerable development in military tactics. Professionals, or veterans with military experience, were primarily those English, Scottish, Welsh and Irish gentry who had served as commissioned officers for pay overseas prior to 1642, although there were also significant numbers of ordinary soldiers in regiments. Though their numbers have been underestimated, in 1639 nearly 200 officers and gentlemen were listed as having served on the Continent and thus available for Charles I's army in the First Bishops' War.[21] Among other native-born soldier-authors was Francis Markham, a veteran of 'thirty and odd years', and author of some authority concerning the Dutch Wars in which he participated between 1590 and 1610. In his *Five Decades of Epistles of Warfare* published in 1622, he provided a soldier's insight into the structure and organisation of contemporary armies of the day. As part of his observations on mounted warfare, he wrote, 'To these Low Countries have produced another sort of horsemen …. and they call them dragoons which I know not whether I may return them foot-horsemen, or horse-footmen.'[22]

Similarly, in his *Soldier's Accidence*, published in 1625, his brother, Gervase Markham described dragoons accordingly:

> The last sort of which our horse troops are compounded, are called dragoons, which are a kind of footmen on horseback, and do now indeed succeed the light horsemen, and are of singular use in all of the actions of war; their arms defensive are an open headpiece with cheeks, and a good buff coat with deep skirts; and for offensive arms, they have a fair dragon fitted with an iron work, to be carried in a belt of leather, which is buckled over the right shoulder, and under the left arm, having a turnell of iron with a ring through which the piece runs up and down; and these dragons are short pieces of 16 inches, the barrel, and full musket bore, with firelocks or snaphaunces: also a belt, with a flask, priming box, key, and bullet bag and a good sword: the horse shall be armed with a saddle, bridle, bitt, petrel, crupper, with straps for his sack of necessaries, and the horse himself shall be either a good lusty gelding, or a nimble stoned horse. These dragoons in their marches are allowed to be eleven in a range or file, because when they serve it is many times on foot, for the maintenance or surprising of strait ways, bridges or fords, so that when ten men alight to serve, the eleventh man holds their horses: so that to every troop of a hundred, there is a hundred and ten men allowed[23]

In 1629, Robert Ward stated, 'the dragoons are no less than a foot company, consisting of pikes and muskets, only for their quicker expedition they are mounted upon horses, they are of great use for the guarding of passages and fords, in regard to their swiftness they may prevent the enemy foot, and

21 Lawrence, *Complete Soldier*, pp.1–10; Barbara Donegan, 'Halcyon Days and the Literature War: England's Military Education before 1642', *P&P*, 147 (1995), 65–100, (p. 71).

22 Francis Markham, *Five Decades of Epistles of Warre* (London: Augustine Matthews, 1622), pp.2, 83.

23 Gervase Markham, *The Soldier's Accidence* (London, 1625), p.42.

gain places of advantage to hinder their passage.'[24] He also urged that pikes should be carried, albeit with 'a thong of leather' to keep the soldier in the saddle. J.B. in his book, *Some Brief Instructions for the Exercising of the Horse-Troops*, provided an effectual view of the use of such weapons, not only while mounted, but in seizing key features such as passes and bridges. He based his work on his personal experiences of warfare in the British Isles:

> The other arming of the cavalry used in these our modern times, known by the name of dragoons (being only foot mounted) is a sword (all) and some muskets, and some pikes, both having leather thongs fixed to them, whereby they may be the easier carried; his lighted match and bridle in his left hand, having his right hand at liberty for the better ordering of his pike or musket in their march, and as occasion shall require. Yet in these our English wars, it was observed that the dragoons seldom used any pikes, and of late times most snaphaunce locks; they being chiefly to secure passes, and to line hedges, if occasion require, either to secure the other cavalry with whom they marched, or to offend the enemy.[25]

Increasingly, the role of these troops in supporting the cavalry in battle, by providing fire support and extra mobility, came to be regarded as a distinct characteristic. Thus, the dragoons became invaluable for raiding expeditions where musketry provided the horse with a distinct advantage, either as support for cavalry combat or for assaults on enemy garrisons. Wallhausen had advocated those dragoons were 'devised so that the infantry or a portion

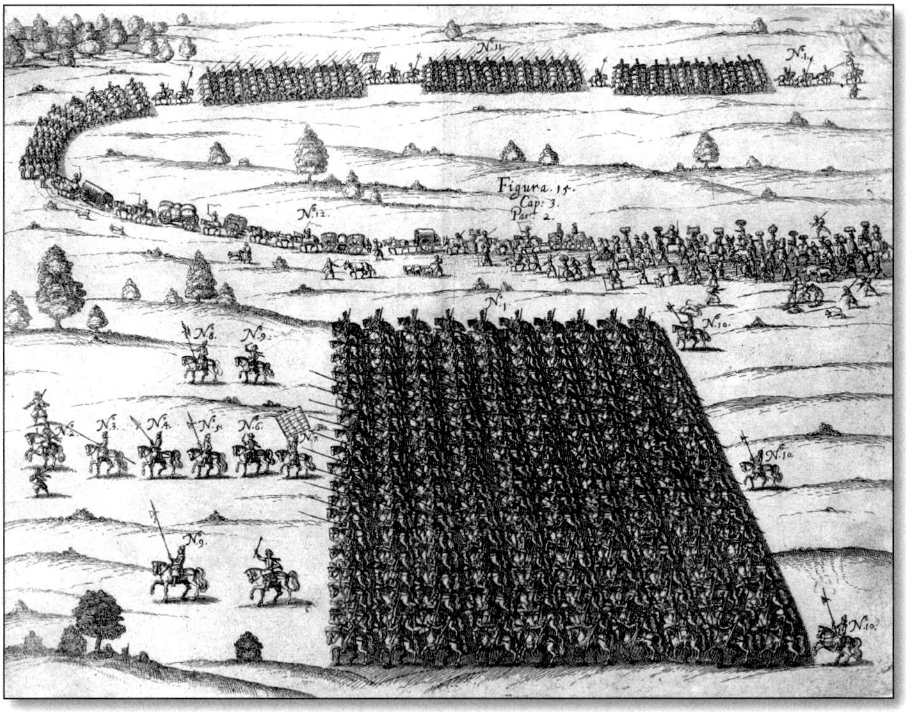

Wallhausen, *Kriegskunst zu Pferd*, Dragoon files on the flanks of regiment of lancers. (Open source)

24 Robert Ward, *Animadversions of Warre* (London: John Dawson, 1639), pp.294 & 302–3.
25 J. B., *Some Brief Instructions for the Exercising of the Horse-Troops* (London: 1661), p.28.

of it mounted on horse (since there [are] a number of deeds which cannot be accomplished by cavalry alone), may promptly and rapidly come to the aid of the cavalry.'[26] Of the dragoons' general role, Francis Markham commented:

> their march is for the most part, upon the swiftest gallop; their place in scouts, foraging, and upon all needful discoveries; and the effect of their principal service is to defend and make good all passages over rivers, as fords, bridges, mill-dams, and the like, all strait ways, hills, valleys, and other places of retreat, they may upon occasion alight from their horses and serve on foot, spoiling all foragers and pillagers, assailing troops in their lodgings, and when they find themselves drawing into any inconvenience, they may presently mount again and retire into their safety.[27]

As previously mentioned, in the Bavarian Army during the 1630s five dragoon companies were attached to cavalry regiments.

With regards to their training and battlefield application, Cruso specified that since dragoons operated as infantry and there was an 'abundance' of books dealing with this arm it was unnecessary for him to write anything.'[28] Moreover, Ward wrote 'As for the dragoons, their service and use of arms doth so nearly correspond with the postures of the infantry, to which postures I altogether refer them', whereas John Vernon, author of *The Young Horse-man*, added that the dragoon 'must perform his service on foot.'[29]

Even though they often acted with the cavalry, Sir John Turner maintained that the operational role of the dragoons was that of the infantry, although:

> Dragoons are musketeers mounted on horses, appointed to march with the cavalry, in regard there are not only many occasions, wherein foot can assist the horse, but that seldom there is any occasion of service against an enemy, but wherein it is both fit and necessary to join some foot with the horse, dragoons then go not only before to guard passes (as some imagine) but to fight in open field; for if an enemy recounter with a cavalry in a campaign or on open heath, the dragoons are obliged to alight, and mix themselves with the squads of horse, as they shall be commanded; and their continued firing, before the horse comes to the charge, will, no doubt, be very hurtful to the enemy. If the encounter be in a close country, they serve well to line hedges, and possess enclosures, they serve for defending passes and bridges, whether it be in the advance, or retreat of an army, and for beating the enemy from them.

To this, he added:

> Their service is on foot and is no other than that of musketeers; but because they are mounted on horseback, and ride with the horse, either in the van, or behind in

26 Wallhausen, *Kriegskunst zu Pferd*, p.16.
27 Markham, *Five Decades*, p.167.
28 Cruso, *Cavalrie*, p.44.
29 Ward, *Animadversions*, p.302; John Vernon, *The Young Horse-man, or, The honest plain-dealing cavalier* (London: 1644), p.9.

> the rear of an army, they are reckoned as a part of the cavalry, and are subordinate to the general, lieutenant-general, or major-general of the horse, and not to those of the foot. And being that sometimes they are forced to retire from a powerful and prevailing enemy, they ought to be taught to give fire on horseback, that in an open field they may keep an enemy at a distance till they get the advantage of a closer country, a straight, a pass, a bridge, a hedge, or a ditch, and then they are bound to alight, and defend that advantage, that thereby (though perhaps with the loss of the dragoons themselves) the cavalry may be saved

In *Some Brief Instructions*, the writer, J. B., considered they were 'invented for special services, to assist the cavalry as infantry.'[30] What might be termed 'dragoon work' – rapid, effective scouting and skirmishing in advance of an army – was a recent development in European warfare, but not yet utilised in Britain due to long periods of peace. Experienced proponents of this kind of soldiering on the Continent included returning professionals such as Sir Arthur Aston and Sir George Lisle on the Royalist side, and Colonels James Wardlaw and John Middleton in the Parliamentarian army.

A more common description of most seventeenth century dragoons was presented by Charles Ogier, secretary to the French ambassador, about Polish dragoons in Prussia in 1635. He remarked, 'they are poor men, as they are facing the enemy without armour and helmets, riding on small and mediocre horses.'[31] The narrative of Captain Edward Wogan, an officer in Colonel John Okey's New Model Army regiment, which covers the entire campaign from 1645 to 1646, commences with his view that the dragoons 'were always counted the best men of the army.'[32] By contrast, in the 1670s the British professional soldier, Roger Boyle, Earl of Orrery characterised dragoons as 'commonly the briskest, and daringst of the private soldiers, so they are also the least sober.'[33] The involvement of dragoons during the British Civil Wars in combined arms warfare was an important aspect of their development and continuing innovation as mounted troops, somewhat away from their supposed role as merely mounted infantry. Though anecdotal in nature, there survives abundant evidence from contemporary reports of battlefield tactics and fighting promoted by some of the leading proponents of mounted warfare, such as Prince Rupert and Sir Arthur Aston of Charles I's Oxford Army, Colonel John Middleton of Essex's forces and Lieutenant-Colonel Michael Jones, the commander of the horse of Sir William Brereton.

Turner specified that the function of the dragoons was to advance or retreat before the rest of the army, to secure lines of communication and key points, while in close contact with the enemy they were expected to occupy hedges and ditches. According to him, it was just in open combat when they were required to dismount and deliver musket fire alongside cavalry

30 J. B., *Some Brief Instructions*, p.26.

31 Charles Ogier, *Dziennikpodróży do Polski, 1635–1636* (Gdańsk: BibliotekaMiejska, 1950), p.120.

32 Thomas Carte, *A Collection of Original Letters and Papers, concerning the affairs of England, from the year 1641 to 1660, found among the Duke of Ormonde's Papers* (London: 1735), I, pp.126–42.

33 Roger Boyle, Earl of Orrery, *A Treatise of the Art of War dedicated to the King's Most Excellent Majesty* (1677), p.35.

formations. Turner further recommended that the service of the dragoon was on foot but said that they should be instructed to give fire on horseback so they could resist an enemy until they could retire to a secure position. He directed dragoons on foot to fire in one of the three methods employed by musketeers: by introduction, where firing was used 'to move a division towards and enemy while seeking to inflict continual injury upon him to break his resolve to stand'; by extraduction, used 'to withdraw a division away from the enemy while seeking to inflict continual injury upon him to hinder or break his resolve to advance'; and by doubling the half-files to bring six ranks into three to deliver the *salvee*, intended to 'do great execution upon to enemy and to shatter his resolve.' As Turner described:

> Next, firing by three ranks at a time, should not be practiced, but when either the business seems to be desperate, or that the bodies are so near, that the pikemen are almost come to push of pike, and then no other use can be made of the musket but of the butt-end of it. I say then that this manner of six ranks to fire at two several times is not at all to be used; for if it come to extremity, it will be more proper to make them all fire at once, for thereby you pour as much lead in your enemy's bosom at one time as you do the other way at two several times, and thereby you do them more mischief, you quail, daunt, and astonish them three times more, for one long and continued crack of thunder is more terrible and dreadful to mortals than ten interrupted and several ones, though all and every one of the ten be as loud as the long one.[34]

At Piercebridge, near Darlington, on 1 December 1642, the vanguard of the Marquess of Newcastle's army emulated the Scots' all-arms tactics employed at Newburn by clearing the town of Parliamentarian troops and storming the medieval bridge, the main crossing over the River Tees. The combined assault of dragoons, foot and artillery continued for several hours, although Colonel Thomas Howard, leading his regiment of dragoons, was killed, though they and the supporting infantry overpowered Sir John Hotham's forces, causing them to withdrawal south towards Knaresborough.[35]

If Captain William Stewart's account is to be believed, at Marston Moor on 2 July 1644 the Scottish Covenanter dragoons assisted Cromwell's 'Ironsides' by clearing Royalist musketeers out of a ditch and later towards the end of the battle they advanced on Newcastle's foot 'and by their shot made a way for the horse to enter and put them to the sword.'[36] Moreover, on 18 September 1645 as Charles I, with a force of around 3,000 cavalry marched towards Denbighshire and Chester, from where Sir John Byron had petitioned him for assistance, troops from Sir William Brereton's forces began shadowing him. Nathaniel Lancaster, chaplain to Brereton's regiment

34 *Ibid.*, p.237.

35 *A Most True Relation of the Battell fought by Capt. Hotham against the Earl of New-Castle, neer Tollerton in Yorkshire* (London: 3 December 1642). TT, E129 [9]; Rushworth, *Historical Collections,* III, p.78.

36 *A Full Relation of the Victory on Marstam-Moor [sic.]. By Captain William Stewart* (2 July 1644). TT, E54 [19].

of horse and 'official' historian to the army, mentioned that in countering the King's movements the Cheshire foot were deployed 'to secure the garrisons from surprise', and that Lieutenant-Colonel Michael Jones, with 400 cavalry and dragoons rode into the south of the county 'to fall upon the rear of the enemy, and to fight if occasion should require.'[37]

In his *Anima'dversions of Warre*, Ward provides a further glimpse of the role of dragoons in all-arms tactics. Of 'the excellent service which may be performed by the dragoons here in England,' he wrote:

> As for the dragoons, their service and use of arms doth so nearly correspond with the postures of the infantry, to which postures I altogether refer them. They were invented for special services, to assist both the cavalry and infantry, for there are many exploits which cannot be affected by the cavalry alone. The musketeers are to exercise themselves to give fire on horseback, in the same fashion as the harquebusiers ought to do. Being come to guard a passage or to do any other the like service, they are to alight and demean themselves as infantry, as in diverse places in this book you may read, only here by the way I will show how necessary it were, to breed and train up certain companies of them in this our Kingdom .... Now these troops of dragoons being well exercised and practiced as they ought, let any sensible man judge if they shall not prove in time of need most useful in regard of their speedy march.[38]

Similar points were made by General George Monck, a professional soldier who began his military career in 1625 and served in the Dutch War of Independence until 1638, and then throughout the British Civil Wars, who recommended that an army have as many troops of dragoons as regiments of horse (i.e., from one-fifth to one-quarter the strength of the horse).[39] Hence, some of the leading military writers of the day envisaged that as specialist mounted soldiers the prime tactical purpose of the dragoons was the delivery of effective musket fire in support of, and together with the cavalry. Cruso explicitly recommended that dragoons should dismount before firing:

> The dragoon was invented for special services to assist the cavalry as infantry, considering they may be exploits which cannot be affected by the cavalry alone. The musketeer [dragoon] must exercise himself to give fire on horseback, as the harquebusier. Being come to guard a passage, or to do any other the like service, they are to alight, and to demean themselves as infantry. Whereof it shall be needless here to enlarge, seeing that we have books in such abundance upon that subject, as they are able rather distract, than instruct the reader ... Being so alighted to do their service (as abovesaid) every of them is to cast his bridle over the neck of his sideman's horse, in the same order as they marched, keeping them so together, by help of such as are thereunto especially appointed[40]

---

37 John Lewis (ed.), *The Siege of Chester: Nathaniel Lancaster's Narrative* (Nottingham: Raider Books, 1987), p. 17.
38 Ward, *Anima'dversions of Warre*, pp.302–3.
39 George Monck, *Observations upon Military and Political Affairs* (London: 1671), p.28.
40 Cruso, *Military Instructions*, p.44.

In taking this further, Orrery described the role of dragoons in supporting cavalry formations in combat. This suggests a more frequently practised method of dismounting before deploying their firepower:

> the seventh troop [in every cavalry regiment] should be of firelocks, or dragoons, whose duty should be to guard the quarter of the regiment; to secure passes with celerity; to force passes possessed by the enemy; to assist the horse when they fight in enclosed countries; and in battles, to alight; and marching up in the outermost flank of the regiment, should in two ranks, the first kneeling, the second standing, a little before the squadrons charged, fire upon the enemy, their guns loaded with pistol bullets, which I have sometimes practiced, and found it attended with great success; every tenth man while the rest were on such service, was to hold the horses of those who were thus employed; and if the enemy were routed, they were all to mount again, and to follow the execution.[41]

How such horse management was achieved under these conditions during the British Civil Wars is not entirely clear, however. Akin to Cruso and Gervase Markham, Ward recommended,

> any horse if he be swift will perform this service in regard they alight and do their service a foot; so that when ten men alight, the eleventh holdeth their horses, so that to every troop of 120 there is 132 men allowed.'[42]

To Turner, 'then they alight, they cast their bridle reins over the necks of their side-man's horses, and leave them in that same order as they marched. Of ten dragoons, nine fight, and the tenth man keeps the ten horses.'[43] Though Markham and Ward suggest, respectively, that troops or companies should be 100 and 132 men strong, pay warrants and muster rolls indicate that during the British Civil Wars dragoon sub-units often fielded (in some cases significantly) lower numbers, something that might have affected how many horses were held by riders during dismounted combat.

Nevertheless, the action of dismounting and passing animals to designated 'horse holders' under battlefield conditions is likely to have been challenging, while dragoon horses would have required some level of training. The application of this did not always go well. Having recently arrived in Cheshire from London, a party of Sir William Brereton's (Parliamentarian) dragoons under the command of Captains Bramhall and Goldegay (which had been largely recruited in the capital) engaged in a confused night action at Nantwich against Sir Thomas Aston's troops, which included Sir Vincent Corbet's Shropshire dragoon regiment. According to one Parliamentarian source, following the discharge of a case of drakes, 'Captain Goldegay dismounted his dragooners, and turned his horses upon them, which

41 Orrery, *Treatise*, pp.33–35.
42 Ward, *Anima'dversions*, p.302
43 Turner, *Pallas Armata*, p.232.

brought them into confusion, and charged upon them very sore.'[44] During the action, Goldegay was wounded, and his lieutenant and two soldiers were killed. This episode has been taken to mean that the dragoons, showing their inexperience, neglected to leave anyone to hold their mounts, which were mistaken by the startled Royalists for charging cavalry.

Orrery's advice to the dragoons, 'to alight, and marching up in the outermost flank of the regiment, should be in two ranks, the first kneeling, the second standing,' sounds comparable to the Swedish method of doubling ranks and firing one volley (*salvee*) at the last possible moment, a method that became increasingly common during the British Civil Wars. This conflicts with Turner's recommendation of a 'rolling' fire – 'their continued firing, before the horse comes to the charge, will, no doubt, be very hurtful to the enemy.'[45] The dragoons, according to Orrery, were positioned ahead of their army's horse lines, both to afford a better field of fire, and to avoid startling their own mounts. The disadvantage of this tactic was probably that if the combination of firepower and countercharge failed to halt the enemy horse, any bodies of dragoons or musketeers would have been left dangerously exposed. At Lansdowne in July 1643, musketeers belonging to Sir Ralph Hopton's army were ordered to threaten the flank of the oncoming Parliamentarian horse. One account of the fighting described how:

> Those that came upon the rear used most diligence and, having left their dragoons in the end of the lane towards the field charged very gallantly, and routed two bodies of their [Royalist] horse, where of the last was, by Prince Maurice his command to Sir Ralph Hopton winged by Cornish musketeers, who (poor men) though the horse were routed between them kept their ground and preserved themselves till the Earl of Carnarvon's regiment of horse was drawn up to them.

On this occasion, however,

> the Earl of Carnarvon with his regiment and the aforesaid musketeers charged the enemy's horse and totally routed them. Presently after this appeared two great bodies of the enemy's horse advancing towards their flank, which induced a good charge of two bodies of the King's Horse, and some volleys of musketeers before they broke, but at last were routed and chased.[46]

Nonetheless, at Winceby in Lincolnshire on 11 October 1643, a relatively small, but important battle was fought predominantly with mounted units. The Royalist forces under Sir William Widdrington, who were attempting to relieve the siege of nearby Bolingbroke Castle, were confronted by a combined force of cavalry and dragoons led by Colonel Oliver Cromwell of the Eastern

44 *Cheshire's Successe since their pious and truly valiant Colonel, Sir William Brereton, Baronet, came to their rescue, &c.* (London, 20 March 1643). TT, E94 [6].

45 Turner, *Pallas Armata*, p.236.

46 Alan Wicks (ed.), *Bellum Civile: Sir Ralph Hopton's Memoirs of the Campaign in the West, 1642–1644* (Leigh-on-Sea: Partizan Press, 1988), pp.53–4.

Association Army and Sir Thomas Fairfax, of the Northern Association army, advancing to intercept them. According to a Parliamentarian source:

> the enemy that morning drew their whole body of horse, and dragoons into the field, being 74 colours of horse and 21 colours of dragoons, in all 95 colours. We had not many more than half so many colours of horse and dragoons, but I believe we had as many men.[47]

Following a small action, fought on the previous evening, during which a detachment of Royalist cavalry defeated an enemy scouting force, the forlorn hopes of both armies – consisting of dragoons – commenced a sharp firefight. These troops had been deployed ahead of their lines allowing the horse time to deploy in battle formation. The Royalist dragoons fought effectively, but they were rendered powerless when their supporting horse routed, thus forcing them to surrender. As the same author wrote:

> It was about twelve a clock, ere our horse and dragoons were drawn up, after that we marched about a mile nearer the enemy, and then we began to descry him by little and little coming towards us; until this time we did not know we should fight, but so soon as our men had knowledge of the enemy's coming they were very full of joy and resolution, thinking it a great mercy that they should fight with him ... both they and we had drawn up our dragoons, who gave the first charge, and then the horse fell in. Colonel Cromwell fell with resolution upon the enemy, immediately after their dragoons had given him the first volley, yet they were so nimble, as within half pistol shot they gave him another his horse was killed under him at the first charge ... Truly this charge was so home given that the enemy stood not another but were driven back upon their own body that was to second them, and put them into disorder, our men charged all in with him, and then they ran for it, leaving all their dragoons which were now on foot behind them.

It was Cromwell's initial cavalry charge that did most of the damage, however. Fairfax concluded the battle by attacking the Royalist left flank. Sir William Widdrington, the Royalist commander, would report to the Marquess of Newcastle:

> We have in a manner totally lost our foot and dragoons that were there, being near 800 horse, extremely dispersed, but no great number cut off ... Their horse are very good, and extraordinarily armed; and may be reported to be betwixt 50 and 60 Troops, being very strong. I do not know the number of their foot; but we believe them to be about 1,500, or betwixt that and 2,000. Their foot was not come

47 *A True Relation of the Late Fight Betweene the Right Honourable The Earle of Manchester's Forces, and the Marquesse of Newcastles Forces, 11 Oct., neere Home Castle in Lincolnshire* (London: 11 October 1643). TT, E.71 [5].

> up to their horse; and the ground they had chosen would not admit of above three divisions of horse to charge at once.[48]

This tactic – the use of the *salve* – more usually employed by divisions of shot in foot regiments, followed the method developed further during the Thirty Years' War by the Swedish army of King Gustav II Adolf, and usually delivered by bodies of 30 men in six ranks. Gustav II Adolf had sought to increase the firepower of his infantry to compensate for the inferiority of the Swedish cavalry, whereby the ranks of musketeers were reduced from eight to ten men deep to six. Gustav added the tactic of 'doubling files', thus transforming a six-rank formation into three ranks. The front rank would kneel, the second rank crouch, and the third rank would stand. All three ranks would then fire simultaneously to deliver a devastating *salvee*. As David Blackmore observes in his study of British firepower:

> During the English Civil War, a particularly aggressive way of fighting based upon the close-range delivery of overwhelming firepower followed by an immediate advance to hand-to-hand combat was developed in England and Scotland, and used by all protagonists. This was not something found in drill books and although it was similar to the Swedish *salvee* developed by Gustavus Adolphus there were important differences, primarily in the manner of its application.[49]

The Swedish methods of warfare were recognised in Britain before the beginning of the civil wars in 1638. They were described in some detail by the Scottish professional soldier Robert Monro, who served as an officer in the Swedish army between 1630 and 1634. In explaining the process for firing three ranks together by divisions of shot, he wrote:

> When you would command the body of your musketeers to give fire in a *Salve*, as is ordinary in battle, before an enemy join, or against horsemen; then you command the bringers up or rear to double the front to the right hand, and to make ready, having the match cocked and their pans well-guarded, having closed the three ranks, though not the files, the officers standing in equal front with the foremost rank, betwixt two divisions, he commands to give fire, one *Salve*, two or three, and having charged again, and shouldered their arms, they retire to the left hand again, every man falling behind his own leader.[50]

This method was adopted during the British Civil Wars, and it is possible to conclude that aside from skirmishes, it was the main type of delivering musket fire. The 'official' Royalist account of the Battle of Edgehill, fought on 23 October 1642, described how the King's right wing was 'in some confusion',

48 John Rushworth, *Historical Collections of Private Passages of State* (London: D Browne, 1721), V, p.282.

49 David Blackmore, *Destructive and Formidable: British Infantry Firepower, 1642–1765* (Frontline Books: London, 2014), p.35.

50 William S Brockington, Jr., (ed.) *Monro, His Expedition with the Worthy Scots Regiment Called Mac-Keys* (Westport CT: Praeger, 1999), p.316.

the cavalry on that portion of the field having routed their Parliamentarian counterparts. But, faced with the threat of enemy horse and foot, advancing 'in good order', the writer stated, 'ours made a stand and soon rallied together, having some dragoons [evidently of Sir Arthur Aston's brigade] with them, and so advancing, made the dragoons give them a volley or two of shot, which made the rebels instantly retire.'[51] The Royalist Captain John Gwyn related that at Brentford on 12 November 1642 the King's foot, 'after once firing suddenly … advance up to push of pikes and the butt-end of muskets.'[52] Likewise, Colonel Walter Slingsby, writing sometime after the event, recalled the tactics employed by the infantry at the Battle of Cheriton on 29 March 1644:

> Upon this success the enemy resumes their first courage, which prompted them to try a field with us, or rather a better than that, which made them resolve to beat us; and so with a strong body of horse charges our foot on the left wing, on that part which my Lord of Brainford was pleased to make your servants charge, then the enemy's horse was repulsed with loss. They immediately tried the second charge in which Captain Herbert of my Lord Hopton's Regiment was slain, with a fresh body and were again repulsed, and so again the third time, the foot keeping their ground in a close body, not firing till within two pikes' length, and then three ranks at a time, after turning up the butt end of their muskets, charging their pikes, and standing close, preserved themselves, and slew many of the enemy.[53]

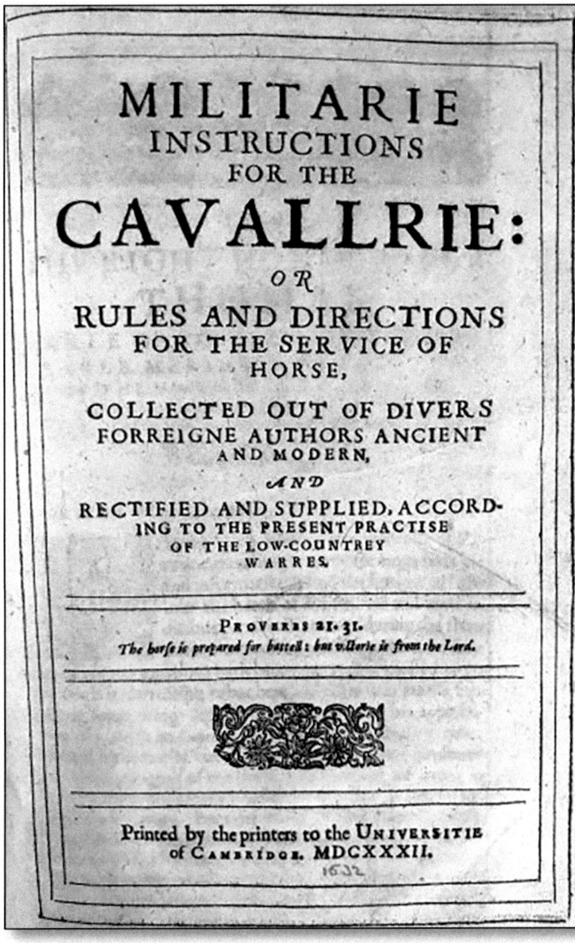
MILITARIE
INSTRUCTIONS
FOR THE
CAVALLRIE:
OR
RULES AND DIRECTIONS
FOR THE SERVICE OF
HORSE,
COLLECTED OUT OF DIVERS
FORREIGNE AUTHORS ANCIENT
AND MODERN,
AND
RECTIFIED AND SUPPLIED, ACCORD-
ING TO THE PRESENT PRACTISE
OF THE LOW-COUNTREY
WARRES.

PROVERBS 21. 31.
The horse is prepared for battell: but victorie is from the Lord.

Printed by the printers to the UNIVERSITIE
of CAMBRIDGE. MDCXXXII.

John Cruso, *Militare Instructions for the Cavallrie* (1632) (Open source)

Documentary and archaeological evidence indicates that similar tactics, and especially the *salvee*, were employed by both armies at Naseby on 14 June 1645. Of the opening phases of the infantry action Sir Edward Walker, the King's secretary recorded,

> The foot on either side hardly saw each other until they were within carbine shot, and so made only one volley; ours falling in with sword and butt end of musket

51 *A Relation of the Battel fought between Keynton and Edgehill, by His Majesty's Army and that of the Rebels* (Oxford: 1642). TT, E126 [24].

52 Peter Young and Norman Tucker (eds), *Military Memoirs of the Civil War: Richard Atkyns and John Gwyn* (London: Longmans, 1967), p.46.

53 Hopton, *Bellum Civile*, pp.99–100.

Wallhusen, *Kriegskunst zu Pferd*, Dragoons on horseback (Open source)

> did notable execution; so much as I saw their colours fall, and their foot in great disorder.[54]

This firefight is corroborated to an extent by scatter patterns of musket bullets in parts of the southern area of the battlefield. As Glenn Foard states,

> The relative lack of musket balls on the slope down into Broadmoor might be consistent with the firing of just one volley as the two bodies closed and then, because the troops rapidly became engaged in hand-to-hand fighting, they will not have produced a distribution of musket balls.[55]

Later in the battle, after Charles I's infantry reserve had been deployed, Sir Thomas Fairfax began to attack a still intact brigade-sized formation – Prince Rupert's 500-strong 'bluecoats'. Few sources describe the fighting in any detail, but they agree that cavalry units of the New Model Army alone were involved in charging them from the front, side and rear. Joshua Sprigge described:

> the remaining business was with part to keep the enemy's horse from coming to the rescue of their foot, which were now all at mercy, except one tertia, which with the other part of the horse we endeavoured to break, but could not, they standing with incredible courage and resolution, although we attempted them in the flanks, front and rear, until such time as the general called up his own

54 Sir Edward Walker, *Historical Discourses upon Several Occasions* (London: W. B., 1705), p.115.
55 Glenn Foard, *Naseby: The Decisive Campaign (Barnsley: Pen & Sword, 2004 edn), p.262.*

> regiment of foot (the lieutenant-general being likewise hastening of them) which immediately fell in with them, with butt-end of muskets (the general charging them at the same time with horse) and so broke them.[56]

None of these events are reported in detail in Royalist sources, though a passage in Rupert's diary mentions, 'Lindsey commanded the Guards and Russell Rupert's regiment of foot. After the reserves were beaten, Rupert faced again with his horse but the men were not in condition to do much.'[57] Although there is no mention of a firefight, a dense concentration of musket balls on the lower slope of Dust Hill close to where the Naseby-Sibbertoft road now runs (where Rupert's would have been if it had advanced slightly forward of its position given in Robert Streeter's tableau), might suggest that Fairfax's musketeers fired at least one volley before falling on with their musket butts

After deploying along the Sulby Hedges on the left flank of the New Model Army at the start of the battle and pouring musket fire into Prince Rupert's Horse as it charged past, Colonel John Okey's regiment of dragoons was for some time separated from the rest of the army, and fully expected to be defeated in detail by the attacking Royalists. But as Okey, who had for more than an hour resisted all attempts to dislodge him witnessed the consolidated regiments of foot drive back the King's infantry, he ordered his regiment to attack the now exposed Royalist right flank.

Describing the closing stages of the fight at Naseby, Sprigge wrote:

> our dragoons having already begun to fire upon their horse, they not willing to abide a second shock upon so great disadvantage as this was like to be, immediately ran away, both fronts and reserves, without standing one stroke more. Our horse had chase of them from that place, within two miles of Leicester (being the space of fourteen miles) took many prisoners, and had the execution of them all that way.[58]

The final rout and pursuit of Charles I's army is well described by Okey himself:

> I perceiving (after one hour's battle) caused all my men to mount and to charge into their foot, which accordingly they did, and took all their colours, and 500 prisoners, besides what we killed, and all their arms. After this the King drew his horse up into a body again. And then I drew up my dragoons, and charged the King's regiment of horse, and they faced about and run away, and never made any stay till they came to Leicester, and we pursued them within three miles and a half of Leicester, which was about 15 miles from the place where we fought. We took, as near as we can guess, between 4 and 5,000 men, with many horses, all their

56 Joshua Sprigge, *Anglia Rediviva or England's Recovery* (London: 1647), pp.38–9.

57 WSHC, 413/444/Ai, f.70r.

58 Sprigge, *Anglia Rediviva*, pp.39–40.

> ordnance, bag and baggage; and there was as we were informed, but two foot men went into Leicester; the King himself very hardly escaped[59]

It has generally been assumed from the specific comments by Sprigge ('our dragoons having already begun to fire upon their horse'), and Okey ('I … caused all my men to mount and to charge into their foot,' and 'I drew up my dragoons, and charged the King's regiment of horse') that the New Model dragoons participated in the army's counter-attack on its left wing by remounting and charging as pseudo-cavalry.[60] Thus, Peter Young, writing in 1985, expressly stated:

> The charge of Okey's dragoons at the end of the day calls for comment. In those days dragoons were supposed to act simply as mounted infantry. They were not encouraged to regard themselves as the equal of horse. It may be that Okey's was the first mounted charge made by a dragoon regiment. Certainly, no other episode of the sort occurs in the annals of our civil war.[61]

Such conjectures can be questioned, however. Barry Denton has asserted:

> Surely what is being described [by contemporary remarks] is the New Model's use of firepower, not a cavalry action. Okey's men would have ridden to within 200 yards of the enemy, dismounted, and charged forward firing every 50 yards or so to build up a firefight. In support, the horse would prevent a counter charge, and within two or three minutes the shot from the dragoon weapons would force a fall back if not a full-scale retreat.[62]

Thus, Okey's 'mounted charge' seems likely to have been one of repeated dismounts and remounts to deliver a series of salvees. Rather than simply mounting up as cavalry, this would be entirely in keeping with the practice of combined arms mounted operations employed by armies of the British Civil Wars, which included units of dragoons being officially or informally attached to cavalry regiments. This provided additional firepower and assisted movement, particularly during the opening and closing phases of combat, harassing operations and the covering of retreats. Some of the musket fire from Okey's men may have been directed at the remnants of Rupert's returning cavalry, but its main target must have been the King's Lifeguard of Foot, which had deployed as part of Charles I's infantry reserve with Rupert's regiment of foot. A concentration of musket balls at and adjacent to the northeast corner of Sulby Hedges is near to where Streeter and Bernard de Gomme located this unit at the start of the battle.[63]

---

59 *More Particular and Exact Relation*, p.6.

60 Peter Young, *Naseby 1645: The Campaign and the Battle* (London: Century, 1985), pp.275–6; Foard, *Naseby, p.277; Ronald Hutton, The Making of Oliver Cromwell (New Haven and London: Yale University Press, 2021), p.263.*

61 Young, *Naseby*, pp.275–6.

62 Barry Denton, *Naseby Fight* (Leigh-on-Sea: Partizan Press, 1988), p.50.

63 Foard, *Naseby, p.276.*

A second scheme, known as the 'Dutch model', also prevailed in British military thinking as many professionals had considerable experience serving with the Dutch, and consequently it was normal for their system to become dominant during the civil wars. Previously employed among the English and Welsh county militias, the method depended on lines of deployment with pikes in the centre and musket divisions on the flanks, in files 8 to 10 deep, with, according to the semi-anonymous writer Edmondes, and comprising leaders and bringer-ups who were 'experienced, wise and valiant'.[64] The exercising of pike and shot was to be carried out in battalias – according to the usual Dutch practice approximately 500 men. Hence, the first rank of musketeers would fire, before retiring to the rear to reload, the intention being that there would be a constant harassing fire and the divisions of shot were protected from attack. Nevertheless, compared to the Swedish system, this method consumed considerable quantities of ammunition, as well as the requirement for large numbers of musketeers.[65] Both the Dutch and Swedish applications of firepower could be used in combination. At Edgehill, both sides seem to have adopted both methods, although with generally poor results. Exactly which tactics were employed at Hopton Heath in Staffordshire between opposing units of dragoons remains unclear. On 19 March 1643, the Royalist forces commanded by the Earl of Northampton encountered around 1,400 Parliamentarians brought together by Sir William Brereton and Sir John Gell. During the opening phase of the battle, a dragoon action developed between three Cheshire companies and a combined body of 300 of their counterparts, some of whom were from Yorkshire and Shropshire.[66] Of the firefight and aftermath, Brereton wrote that the Parliamentarians:

> came on with great resolution and boldness, and in very good order … there were five companies of dragoons, whereof I brought three, some of which did extraordinary good service. There were near one hundred of the dragoons slain in the place where the dragoons skirmished, and I cannot discern that we lost more than two or three. And yet they fought so long, and so fiercely, until all their powder and bullet was spent. Afterwards they joined, and fell to it pell mell, one upon another, with the stocks of their muskets These were Captain Bramhall's men, who behaved themselves well at Brentford, and also at Middlewich, upon Monday 13 March.[67]

In his broadsheet *Military Instructions, or the Soldier tried for the use of the Dragoon*, published in June 1644, Nathaniel Burt, begins by referring the reader to particular sections of Cruso's *Militarie Instructions* and William Bariffe's *Young Artillerie Man*, and reasoned that they should have an

64 Observations Upon the Five First Bookes of Caesars Commentaries (London: 1604), p.130.

65 Stuart Reid, *All the King's Armies: A Military History of the English Civil War 1642–1651* (London: History Press, 2007), p.9.

66 *Certain Informations*, 20 March–3 April 1643; T. J. Brighton, *Royalists and Roundheads in Derbyshire* (Bakewell: Bakewell and District Historical Society, 1981), pp.44–5.

67 Greenslade, M. W. and Baugh, G. C. (intro.), *The History and Antiquities of Staffordshire, by Stebbing Shaw* (East Ardsley: E. P. Publishing, 1976), I, pp.80–1.

enhanced role on the battlefield. Thus, he called for the employment of dragoons in attacking withdrawing enemy troops, stating:

> Suppose the enemy retreating, and their horse facing while they draw off their great guns, and baggage, marching away with their infantry, they losing ground, retreat entire, together, with their cornets on the head of their troops, they being on a hill, having a deep and dangerous dale, to friend, fit to lay ambuscadoes in, besides the night approaching to help them.[68]

Despite the clear stress placed upon service on foot in contemporary military manuals, Ward noted that dragoons should also 'exercise themselves to give fire on horseback, in the same fashion as the harquebusiers ought to do.'[69] Cruso advocated that this was to be done by ranks[70] For service on foot Burt recommended the manual written by Barriffe, yet felt that the dragoon:

> may do better service, firing on horseback, than the cuirassier, the way being dubitable, by advancing slowly after them, following them about musket shot, the cuirassier being within such distance as is needful, to relieve them, if that the enemy should seem to charge, or attempt it.

The writer additionally proposed that those dragoons should discharge their muskets while mounted:

> for the better performance thereof, they are to fire by introduction, on horseback; which is a passing through, or between the files, the files being at open order: the first rank having given fire, by the commanders' direction, let the bringer-up pass through the files, which is commonly to the left, placing themselves before their leaders, in the front, and then giving fire, the rest of the ranks acting the same successively, till such time as they shall receive order to the contrary, or to close their files I am loath to form their place of march upon such occasions, but the van, or flanks, is most advantageous, and necessary for them, because from thence they can command, and send farthest, and make the best use, to line the hedges, or to beat up their ambuscadoes, if need require: but not knowing the situation of the place, or the form of the enemy, which they may pursue, I leave it to the wisdom of the commander.

When applied against a retreating enemy this method offered two advantages; dragoons that had fired could reload without needing to move, while at the same time the unit continued to advance. If the dragoons were retreating on horseback, Burt advised:

> as their occasion requires, or the ground will permit, the last rank sometimes facing about, and firing upon the enemy, then wheeling off to the right, or left,

68 Nathaniel Burt, *Military Instructions, or the Soldier tried for the use of the Dragoon* (London: 1644).
69 Ward, *Animadversions of Warre*, pp.302–3.
70 Cruso, *Cavalrie*, p.98.

> as the ground best affords I would advise them (herein) to keep their files close, and place themselves before their leaders in the front, till they receive order to the contrary.

There are a few examples of dragoons engaging the enemy while mounted during the British Civil Wars. In his report to the Cambridge Committee of the battle fought at Gainsborough on 28 July 1643 Cromwell stated:

> It hath pleased the Lord to give your servant and soldiers a notable victory, now, at Gainsborough. I marched, after the taking of Burleigh House, upon the Wednesday, to Grantham, where I met about 300 horse and dragoons of Nottingham; with these by agreement with the Lincolners, we met at North Scarle, which is about ten miles from Gainsborough, upon the Thursday in the evening, where we tarried until two of the clock in the morning, and then with our whole body advanced toward Gainsborough. About a mile and half from the town, we met a forlorn hope of the enemy, of near 100 horse, our dragoons laboured to beat them back, but not alighting from their horses, the enemy charged them, and beat some four or five of them off their horses; then our horse came up and charged them, and made them retire into their main body.[71]

The implication in this is that the Parliamentarian dragoons attempted to oppose the horse while on horseback – perhaps firing from the saddle – but were beaten off before they could deploy on foot. Moreover, although Cromwell's horse routed the enemy at Grantham, the impact made by the Lincolnshire troops may have been rather limited. However, when Cromwell stormed Faringdon, one of the satellite garrisons of Oxford on 30 April 1645, he reportedly 'fell upon the sconce on the southwest side with four troops of dragoons and the Abingdon foot, carrying ladders.'[72] The participation of four dragoon units was confirmed in a letter of Sir Edward Nicholas to Prince Rupert the following day.'[73]

As far as other military duties of dragoons were concerned, Burt recommended:

> The dragoons having been sent forth for the taking some bridge, or stopping some passage, the enemy having possessed himself of it before them, and advancing towards their quarters, whether in field or garrison, and being too strong for them to encounter with, having retreated as before to their quarters, or some place of advantage, where they may secure their horses in the way, they being acquainted therewith before, and what scouts the enemy hath out, may give the enemy an unexpected volley of shot from some secret and unexpected place, which may offer itself to their view, which having performed, to mount suddenly again, for better and sooner expedition.

71 John Vickers, *God's Ark overtopping the World's Waves* (London: 1646), pp.9–10.
72 Rushworth, *Historical Collections*, VI, p.237.
73 Eliot Warburton, *Memoirs of Prince Rupert and the Cavaliers* (London: S & J. Bentley and Henry Fley, 1849), III, p.79.

Various contemporary writers provided reasons for the training and exercising of mounted troops on a regular basis. Turner wrote:

> Another part of the military exercise consists of teaching the soldiers both of horse and foot to fight orderly and readily with an enemy, and this is that which properly we call training and drilling. It consists of two parts, the first is to teach them their offensive arms (whatsoever they be) handsomely, readily and dexterously, and this is ordinarily called the postures. The second is to make them, when they are in a body, to cast themselves in such a figure or order as shall be commanded them, and this is commonly called the motions or evolutions[74]

Few contemporary training manuals provide a sense of how these were to be put into practice, however. Henry Hexham, an English military writer who had served in the Low Countries, recommended that captains of a troop of horse:

> ought also above all things to be religious, fearing God, temperate, moderate, just, continent, wise, and discreet, curious in the choice of his men, and horse, and to see that they be well managed, ready, and his troup well exercised, that they carry themselves valiantly upon service, in the face of the enemy, and to be careful, and vigilant upon their watch.[75]

As no specific instructions for the exercising of dragoon mounts seem to have been forthcoming, Cruso wrote of the handling of cavalry horses:

> Concerning the horse (presupposing him to be of sufficient stature and strength, nimble of joints, and sure of foot, etc.) he must (of necessity) be made fit for service, so as you may have him ready at command to pace, trot, gallop, or run in full career; also to advance, stop, retire, and turn readily to either hand, and all with alacrity and obedience. Now, to bring him to this ready turning, he is to be ridden the ring, and figure eight, first in a great compass, and so in a less by degrees, first upon his pace, then on the trot, and so to the gallop and career. These things he may be taught by using the hand, leg, and voice. For the hand (observing not to move the arm, but only the wrist) if you would have him to face to the left, a little motion of the little finger on that rein, and a touch of the left leg (without using the spur) doth it: if to face (or turn) to the left about, a harder, etc. If you would have him to trot, you are to move both your legs a little forward; for the gallop, to move them more forward; and for the career to jerk them most forward, and to move the body a little forward with it. After every motion performed, it were good to keep him a while in that motion, as when you bid him stand, to stand a while, etc. Also it were not amiss, after everything well done, to give him some bread or grass as a reward For the voice, you may use the words, advance, hold, turn, or the like; but because the voice cannot always be heard, it were good to use him chiefly to the motions of the hand and leg. It

74 Turner, *Pallas Armata*, p.209.

75 Henry Hexham, *The First Part of the Principles of the Art Military practiced in the Warres of the United Netherlands* (Delft: 1642), p.3.

> will also be very useful to teach him to go sideways: this he may be brought unto by laying his provender somewhat far from him in the manger and keeping him from turning his head towards it. He must also be used to the smell of gunpowder, the sight of fire and armour, and the bearing of shot, drums and trumpets, etc. but by degrees and with discretion. When he is at his oats (at a good distance from him) a little powder may be fired, and so nearer to him by degrees. So may a pistol be fired some distance off, and so nearer: in like manner a drum or trumpet may be used. The groom may sometime dress him in armour, and he may be used (now and then) to eat his oats from the drumhead. It will be very useful sometime to cause a musketeer to stand at a convenient distance, and both of you to give fire upon each other, and thereupon to ride up close to him: also to ride him against a complete armour, so set upon a stake, that he may overthrow it, and trample it under his feet: that so (and by such other means) your horse (finding that he receives no hurt) may become bold to approach any object. He may also be used to mountainous and uneven ways, and be exercised to leap, swim, and the like.[76]

Considerable numbers of officers and soldiers from the British Isles who fought in the British and Irish civil wars were veterans of Continental religious and dynastic conflicts.[77] Thus, numerous Royalist and Parliamentarian leaders employed military professionals to train, organise and lead their regiments and sub-units. The Parliamentarian commander in Derbyshire, Sir John Gell, served as a Captain of trained bands between 1624 and 1634, and owned a copy of Thomas Styward's *The Pathwaie to Martiall Discipline* (1582). Surviving in the Derbyshire Archives, his copy is badly worn and bloodstained, suggesting that it was used during the civil wars. It is also plausible that Gell reportedly served 'two years in the borders of France under the late duke of Buckingham.'[78] Similarly, officers of considerable military experience on the Continent, such as Sir Arthur Aston and Colonel John Middleton raised and commanded dragoon formations from early in the wars. In June 1642 instructions for the raising of cavalry under the command of the Earl of Essex stated that those able to 'find and maintain' horse and horseman were to be paid 2s 6d a day. Volunteers were to go to the Guildhall in London and provide their addresses. When 60 troopers were enrolled, a committee was authorised to appoint officers for the troop, 'to command, train, and exercise them.'[79] By this model about 75 troops of horse and five companies of dragoons were recruited, thus providing Parliament with a token strength of 5,000 mounted soldiers. Officers' commissions sometimes authorised them, among other things, to train their officers and soldiers.

Early in the conflict the Royalist governor of Shrewsbury, Sir Francis Ottley established a company of dragoons, 'to be employed in his Majesty's

76 Cruso, *Militarie Instructions*, pp.15–16.

77 Roger B. Manning, *An Apprenticeship in Arms: The Origins of the British Army, 1585–1702* (Oxford: Oxford University Press, 2006), pp.160–61; Charles Carlton, *Going to the Wars: The Experience of the British Civil Wars, 1638–1651* (London: Routledge, 1992), pp.19–20.

78 DRO, D3287/1043/4, D252/60/26c.

79 *LJ*, V, p.142.

special service for the defence of this town.'[80] Ottley's commission, dated 7 September 1642, empowered him to:

> take the said company of volunteers into your charge, and them to command, train, discipline, and exercise, as their captain and leader, willing and commanding the said soldiers to be obedient, and ready to receive and accomplish the directions, commandments and summons, of you, their captain, and of the officers you shall appoint under you in all things which shall concern, and be for the preservation of Our said town, and Our good subjects inhabiting there.[81]

The commission issued by the King to Sir Thomas Aston on 3 October 1642 authorised him to 'impress, raise, enroll, and retain one regiment of 500 horse as Colonel of them to command, arm, discipline, train, and order in warlike manner.'[82] In similar fashion, Captain John Brooke, commanding a company of foot in Sir William Brereton's forces, issued a warrant on 13 December 1643 to the constables of Aston and Aston Grange to ensure that all trained soldiers they were liable to maintain within their townships should muster fully armed, and 'to find there to be equipped and trained in martial discipline.' Likewise, on 16 March 1644 Brooke instructed the Aston constables 'to appear upon Monday next, being the 18th day of this present March, before me, at Norton Hall with their complete arms and also everyone that is charged to find arms who are not yet listed. And they to be received and trained according to the discipline of war.'[83]

On 29 August 1642, Oliver Cromwell wrote in a letter to the Suffolk Committee, 'I beseech you be careful of what captains you choose, what men be mounted; a few honest men are better than numbers. Some time they must have for exercise.'[84] However, he provided no indication of the nature of that exercise, though given the relative straightforwardness of cavalry drill it seems likely that a substantial amount of training occurred once units were completed and deployed into the field. When Colonel John Seaton's Parliamentarian regiment of dragoons left London in early September 1642 Captain Wilson, commanding one of the companies, 'marched from Uxbridge and quartered at Amersham, and in that afternoon drew his men into a body, and exercised them.' On the 10th they continued to Aylesbury, 'and there in the way met divers cavaliers that were conveyed up in carts towards London, being taken in the north, and guarded up by the High Sheriff's men of Buckinghamshire.' Wilson, however:

> hearing that they were coming drew up his men into a broad place in the road that so they might have room to pass by his troop; and passing on further he drew up his men in battalia in a great cornfield on this side [of] Wendover, and

80 SA, 6000/13294; 'Ottley Papers' (1895), p.266.

81 'Ottley Papers' (1894), pp.42–3.

82 SRMML, USM 009.

83 Aston, unlisted warrants dated 13 December 1643 and 16 March 1644.

84 W. C. Abbott (ed.), *Writings and Speeches of Oliver Cromwell* (Oxford: Clarendon Press, 1988), I, p.256.

> so exercised his men on horseback, to see how his men could do execution on horseback if they should be set upon in a place that might be disadvantageous to them on foot.

Eventually, as the regiment continued its progress,

> in a plain field Sir John commanded them to be drawn up in one body, and gave them some instructions which he would have them observe, and so marched forward with them, to Oxford.[85]

Commonly in contemporary descriptions of armies, broad numbers of 'foot, horse and dragoons', 'horse and dragoons' or 'foot and horse' are given or imagined. But sometimes, where dragoons are unmentioned, they were often part of cavalry regiments or formations, including brigades (in modern terms, battle groups). Some companies were directly attached to regiments of horse, either permanently or occasionally, following the Continental practice, which was also adopted by the Scottish armies. As Stephen Ede-Borrett, in his study of the origins of Okey's New Model Army dragoons observes:

> This non-regimenting of dragoon companies was not unusual, and it is probable that during the English Civil Wars more dragoons served in independent companies, or as part of regiments of horse, than truly served in established and formalized regiments of dragoons.'[86]

Their mounted role allowed for some reorganisation into and redeployment as cavalry formations. Often this was indicative of battlefield attrition and operational requirements, but losses (particularly amongst officers and non-commissioned officers), and the hazardous nature of their duties, were also responsible for a level of interchangeability amongst regiments and minor units.

Although by the circumstances of its survival and availability for researchers surviving evidence is far more plentiful for the Parliamentarian forces during the British Civil Wars, it is apparent that many dragoon formations were characterised by their flexibility, as well as their interchangeable and diverse nature. They, like their Royalist counterparts, were ideal for participation in small-scale operations, including raiding and 'beating up' operations, that is, an unexpected foray against enemy quarters. In May 1644 Colonel Richard Bagot, Royalist governor of Lichfield reported to Prince Rupert the recent arrival of Lord Denbigh in Tamworth 'with eighteen colours of horse and at most 1,500 foot.' He added that the Parliamentarian commander had sent to Leicester for further troops and had with him forty wagons of arms and ammunition, eight cannon, and at least £30,000. Bagot consequently advised Rupert, that the Prince's troops 'will have good sport in beating up

85 *True Relation of the late proceedings of the London Dragoneers, sent down to Oxford, consisting of foure Companies under the command of Sir John Seaton* (London: 1642). TT, E118 [39], pp.3–5.

86 Stephen Ede-Borrett, 'Some Notes on the Raising and Origins of Colonel John Okey's Regiment of Dragoons, March to June, 1645', *JSAHR*, 87 (2009), pp.206–13, (p. 206).

his quarters, and if they quarter of this side [of] Stafford they shall have very little rest.'[87] On 16 May 1645 during the siege of Chester, Lieutenant-Colonel Michael Jones, the commander of the Cheshire horse, informed Sir William Brereton, 'dragoons and not foot are proper for the beating up of quarters. Were there but eight troops of horse and four of dragoons I would engage myself – and never trouble the foot – that no enemy should lie quietly in Cheshire, or near it.'[88]

Such opportunist raids might also have been the result of a dearth of resources experienced by some formations. The semi-independent Parliamentarian garrison at Edgbaston House, near Birmingham was established in October 1643 by Colonel John Fox, an unusual and rather maverick individual nicknamed 'Tinker' by the Royalist press owing to his social origins. He had probably served as a Captain of horse and was seemingly leading an independent company of dragoons when he took control of Edgbaston. Sometime before February 1644, the Earl of Denbigh, commander-in-chief of the West Midlands Association, commissioned Fox as Colonel of a regiment comprising six troops of horse and two companies of dragoons, which he raised in the Black Country. The dragoon companies were led by Captain John Johnson and Captain Williams. At its peak in late 1644 the formation probably retained three or four cavalry troops and two companies of dragoons.[89] Musters in 1645 and 1646 show a general reduction in the size of the garrison of Edgbaston, however. In September 1645 there was a single troop of horse commanded by Colonel Fox, comprising five officers and 35 troopers; a company of dragoons under Commissary Humphrey Tudman with three officers and 16 men; a foot company led by Captain Johnson, mustering three officers and 26 soldiers; and nine garrison officers.[90]

From September 1645 to April 1646 part of Captain Robert Colemore's Warwickshire foot company served at Edgbaston, probably part of a move to gain more control of the garrison.[91] The surviving accounts are too chaotic to be precise, but all the signs are that very little pay was received from either the Earl of Denbigh or the Warwickshire Committee, which opposed the Earl's authority. In April 1644 Fox complained to his commander tellingly of 'the extreme want of money not only to pay my soldiers but to buy victuals for the maize, and hay and oats for horses … it needs no enemies to destroy us for this garrison will destroy itself.'[92] Two months later a muster of Colonel Fox's troops revealed that barely 74 of the 256 dragoons, horse and scouts recorded possessed complete arms and mounts.[93] Consequently, Fox and his soldiers plundered and exacted contributions as far as Bewley and Evesham, and even held meticulous watch on local roads to harry merchants heading

87 WSL, Ms Salt 482.

88 BL, Ms Add 11331, f.119r; *BLB*, I, 555.

89 WA, CR 2017/C9/54; TNA, SP28/37, f.509r; *CJ*, III, pp.515, 523; Andrew Hopper, "Tinker' Fox and the Politics of Garrison Warfare in the West Midlands, 1643–50', *MH*, 24 (1999), pp.98–113.

90 TNA, SP28/34/1, ff.64r–64v.

91 TNA, SP28/123/2, ff.289r.–291r.

92 WA, CR 2017/C9/76A.

93 TNA, SP28/204, unfol.

towards Royalist garrisons. Things may not have improved substantially during the following year, going by a list of garrison troops' muster rolls (documents upon which pay was calculated) for 25 April, 28 May, 12 July, 19 August and 27 September were submitted to the County Committee.[94]

Even so, Fox's forces also carried out extensive scouting and operated an effective system of intelligence gathering, which benefitted the Parliamentarian war effort throughout the Midlands and elsewhere.[95] The predatory activities of Fox and his men in the Midlands was not confined to the Parliamentarian forces, however. In his study of the financial accounts of the Royalist garrison of Lichfield, Ian Atherton suggests that in May 1643 the money-raising efforts of its governor, Colonel Richard Bagot, should be regarded as press *Brandtschatzung* (burning money) or the 'fire-raid' as undertaken by Continental armies during the Thirty Years' War. Additionally, he asserts 'the image of Bagot the rob carrier, preying on the traffic of the region's roads, attacking the trade of Coventry and pillaging Birmingham,' may be a fairly accurate one.[96]

Though acting upon different motives, another semi-independent force in the Midlands was the Staffordshire Moorlanders, a rough-hewn force of men (800 foot and 200 dragoons) raised in the rugged uplands of the north-eastern part of the county around Leek. This terrain was described by the Royalist Richard Symonds as 'a woody enclosed country all the way, except the moors on top of the hills; a black earth where they dig and cut a heathy turf; a rebellious place.'[97] From their inception in November 1642, the Moorlanders opposed plundering by Sir Francis Wortley's troops and all Royalist infiltrations into the area.[98] By early 1643, the Royalists had established small garrisons in Staffordshire at Lichfield, Wolverhampton, Tamworth and Stafford, and the Moorlanders represented the only effective military force opposing them. With little outside aid they grouped together under their leader, whom they referred to as the 'Grand Juryman'. They armed themselves with an assortment of weapons, while two local captains provided them with some rudimentary training. Early in February the Moorlanders demanded not only that Royalists at Stafford withdraw, but they attempted to assault the town.[99] Their resolve was only weakened when reinforcements placed under the authority of the Sheriff of Staffordshire, William Comberford, arrived to strengthen the Royalist garrisons in the region. On 28 November 1643 a force of 2,000 Moorlanders was attacked by Royalist mounted forces, and after a bitter struggle lasting two hours they were defeated and their base at Leek taken.

---

94 TNA, SP28/34/1, ff.64r.-v.

95 WA, CR 2017/C9/55; CR 2017/C9/58; CR 2017/C9/64; CR 2017/C9/70; BL, Ms Add 11331, ff.82r, 85r, 107r–107v, 121r; *BLB*, I, 475–6, 489, 539, 543.

96 Ian Atherton, 'Royalist Finances in the English Civil War: The Case of Lichfield Garrison, 1643–5', *MH*, 33 (2008), pp.43–67, (p. 61).

97 C. E. Long (ed.), *Diary of the Marches of the Royal Army during the Great Civil War; kept by Richard Symonds*, Camden Society, Old Series, 74 (1859), p.176.

98 SA, QS/R, Special Sessions 1642, f.10r.

99 HMS, *Hastings*, II, pp.88–90; *Ottley Papers*, VI, pp.75–6.

The Moorlanders, however, regrouped and remained active in northern Staffordshire. On 2 December, they successfully countered the operations of Colonel Henry Hastings's troops, as one Parliamentarian source reported:

> Colonel Hastings, that eminent rob-carrier, we hear for certain by letters to the House of Commons, upon a design to relieve Tutbury Castle in Staffordshire, which is kept against the Parliament, marching from Ashby-de-la-Zouch unto Staffordshire, was set upon by valiant Moorlanders, who made a miserable route of his troops, killed about 100, took about 150 horses, 100 arms, all their baggage, many prisoners, whereof most of his captains and officers (all but one) some say himself very narrowly escaping, and is gone back to Ashby to bemoan his bad success.[100]

The various changes of personnel evident in dragoon units seem to have been predominantly due to battlefield attrition, promotion, lack of adequate pay and reorganisations among fighting forces, but also the rather ad hoc circumstances of the beginnings of some regiments and companies. Additionally, some might come and go or transmute into other formations. This is detectable amongst officers and non-commissioned officers more often than amongst common soldiers, although the latter are generally more difficult to identify in documents and thus their movement between different units remains problematical. In Brereton's Parliamentarian forces, Ralph Burroughs, the original lieutenant to Captain Bramhall's dragoon company, seems to have left the unit by March 1643 when an officer of that name first appears in pay warrants for Brereton's own troop of horse, until his commission ended on 31 July 1644.[101] John Turner began as sergeant in the same unit, but muster rolls indicate that by 20 May 1643 he had been promoted to cornet. After Turner's capture and release as prisoner-of-war in late 1643 or early 1644, he became a lieutenant, serving later in that rank under Captain Godfrey Gimbert in the Cheshire army, and receiving pay until at least July 1647.[102]

Some military officers held commissions in multiple units of dragoons, cavalry and infantry, either contemporaneously or at different times. Consequently, these individuals are therefore difficult to tie down with a great deal of certainty, especially given the fragmentary or contradictory records of their service. This is especially prevalent among various Royalist officers, for whom negligible evidence survives. According to the petition of Captain Robert Rowell of Skipton, dated 11 December 1673, he was:

> very constant and loyal in serving our late King, and more to manifest the same, he bore the title of officer upon all occasions, as follows: he was captain under Colonel Lamplough at Hessay Moor battle, cornet under Colonel Grey [in his regiment of dragoons] at Edgehill, lieutenant of horse under Colonel Bradshaw at Leeds when Selby was taken and lieutenant of foot under Colonel Sir Michael

100 *Perfect Diurnall*, 29 November–6 December 1643.
101 TNA, SP28/152/7, ff.5r., 7v., 9v.
102 TNA, SP28/124/1, ff.72r.–78r., 114r.

> Woodhouse at Stoke House. It pleased God that he was delivered without much harm by wounds, yet the bad usage he had from the enemy, being several times taken prisoner.[103]

In August 1642 the Parliamentarian, Sir Walter Earle, raised a troop of horse and was at the siege of Sherborne, but he also possessed a small dragoon force, of uncertain status. The latter may have disbanded and reformed in January 1643, however, and was perhaps reduced into Francis Sydenham's company of dragoons by the summer.[104]

Robert Greville, 2nd Baron Brooke recruited foot in Warwickshire in August 1642 and brought up troops from London to the county to lift the Royalist siege of Warwick Castle. In her study of the civil wars in the county, Ann Hughes discovered no evidence of Parliamentarian impressment in Warwickshire, and suggests that all those who served in the county forces were volunteers.[105] According to one newsbook, as an incentive for enlistment at the Militia Ordinance musters in Warwickshire, Brooke provided 'wine and strong drink' for all the trained bands and volunteers.[106] He also raised a regiment of foot, clad in purple coats, for the Earl of Essex's army in London, and which fought at Edgehill. After this was disbanded in December 1642, Brooke was appointed commander-in-chief for the Associated counties of Warwick, Stafford, Leicester, and Derby on 7 January 1643. He thus began raising new regiments of horse, foot and dragoons in the Midlands with commissioned officers largely recruited in London.

Captain Anthony Otway's financial accounts record that he served as Captain of foot under Lord Brooke in Warwickshire between 27 January 1643 to 6 April 1643; as Captain of dragoons from 6 April to 3 June 1643; as Captain of horse in the regiment of Colonel William Purefoy between 3 June 1643 and 2 May 1645; in the same regiment, but under Colonel William Colemore from May 1645 to August 1646; and under Sir Thomas Fairfax's command from 3 May to 20 June 1646. Captain Otway's dragoons were raised in part through the contributions of Warwickshire ministers, but they were converted into a troop of horse after two months' service.[107] Although the Warwickshire County Committee planned to disband the troop in May 1646, it served with the New Model Army until June. Otway served in Ireland under Colonel Michael Jones from 1648 and died there in 1650. In January 1644, Otway's troop mustered 10 commissioned and non-commissioned officers, 42 troopers, and a chaplain, Nathaniel Macham. Otway claimed that his men were 30 weeks in arrears for their service between May 1643 and June 1646, and had, in any case, only received the sum of 12s 0d per week, rather than

103 WYAS, QS1/13/4/6/8.

104 HMC, *Fifth Report*, pp.42–3, 83.

105 Ann Hughes, *Politics, Society and Civil War in Warwickshire, 1620–1660* (Cambridge: Cambridge University Press, revised edn, 2002), p.120.

106 *A True Relation of the Lord Brooke's Settling of the Militia in Warwickshire* (London: 1642). TT, E669 [50].

107 TNA, SP28/136/33, unfol. ; SP28/332, examinations of Otway's troopers

the usual 17s 0d. In his will, Otway claimed personal arrears of £1,500 for his English service.[108]

Kenilworth Castle had been garrisoned by its governor, Captain Hastings Ingram, in January 1643, however, he was implicated in a plot to betray Warwick to the Royalists and put under armed guard in early April.[109] Albeit briefly, a dragoon company, commanded by Captain Samuel Hill served as part of the garrison. In January 1646 he wrote to the Committee of Accounts:

> I am very ready to render an account of my employment [in Warwickshire], particularly at Kenilworth, though it more properly belongs to Captain Ingram, who was governor of the Castle, and from whom I received orders and did nothing otherwise. It is true that, being commanded by him, I fetched in divers malignants with whom he compounded and received their money, and what I had to pay my dragoons I had from him, which when I can call to mind I will inform you. I never received any myself from any of them, but left it wholly to him, who commanded in chief. If any horses were taken from any upon groundless information of their malignancy, they must not blame the messengers, but him who sent them.[110]

Another officer in the Midlands forces of Parliament was a Captain Lynch. A note inserted into the second accounts of Colonel John Barker, both governor of Coventry and Colonel of Coventry-based forces, mentions that Lynch was 'to be lieutenant of a company of dragoons from 27 January 1643 in the service of Colonel Barker; commissioned Captain of dragoons on 20 February 1643 in the service of Lord Brooke; and another to be Captain of a troop of harquebusiers from 16 February 1644 by the Earl of Essex's commission.'[111] Similarly, Captain Thomas Hunt of Coventry – one of the 'comparatively obscure men' described by the unfavourable *Mercurius Aulicus* as 'a broken mercer' – was commissioned by Colonel John Bridges, the Parliamentarian governor of Warwick Castle to command 40 dragoons and foot in February 1643, and Captain of horse in February 1644.[112] Hunt's dragoon company was part of Colonel William Purefoy's regiment of horse. A list of the regiment, undated but from early 1644, records the presence in Captain Hunt's command of a lieutenant, a cornet, two sergeants, two corporals, one drummer and 59 dragoons.[113]

Hunt had served previously as a lieutenant of dragoons in Lord Brooke's Association army and throughout much of 1644, he was nominally the commander of two separate forces: dragoons serving at Tamworth, and horse at Astley where he was governor. From August 1644, the forces at Astley were effectively commanded by Hunt's brother, Lieutenant Goodere Hunt, while the company of dragoons was converted to a cavalry troop under his

108 TNA, SP28/136, Otway's accounts; Prob. 11/215, f.30r.

109 TNA, SP28/37, ff.126r & 126v; SP28/139/3, f.10r; *The Last Weeks Proceedings of the Lord Brooke* (London: 1643). TT, E91 [19].

110 *CSPD 1645–7*, p.310.

111 TNA, SP28/136/20, f.9r.

112 *Mercurius Aulicus*, 19–26 April 1644.

113 Warks A, CR2017/9, f.40r; Peter Leadbetter, 'Extracts From The Earl of Denbigh's Letter Book', *Arquebusier, XXXVIII/II* (2022), pp.22–28.

own direct control.[114] Various quantities of horses, saddles and tack were supplied to Captain Hunt for himself and his dragoons by the inhabitants of Bailey Lane Ward, Bishop Street, Gosford Street and Jordan Well Wards of Coventry, while (among other things) Thomas Woodard of Beauchamp in Alcester Parish claimed 9s 0d 'paid in free quarter to six red coats under the command of Captain Hunt for 36 meals.'[115]

114 TNA, SP28/253B, unfol. , examination of Captain Thomas Hunt; HMC, *Eighth Report, App. I*, p.596.

115 TNA, SP28/185, ff.11r–12v & 15r; SP28/201/3, f.1r; SP28/201/5, ff.1r, 15r; SP28/201/2, f.5r.

2

Combined Arms Tactics and Specialist Operations

The involvement of dragoons during the British Civil Wars in combined arms or all-arms combat – the mutual deployment of the fighting components of an army on the battlefield – and resulting concepts of manoeuvre warfare was an increasingly essential aspect of their role as mounted soldiers. Some contemporary military writers made it implicit that the conflicts in Britain prompted a rethinking of cavalry tactics. Although Cruso's manuals, which embraced both infantry and cavalry drill based on the Dutch model, made no mention of combining the two arms on the battlefield, he mentioned, 'The occasions for the combat of the cavalry are many and frequent. Sometime by a sole company, sometime by more troops, other while by all the horse together.'[1]

Similarly, the Englishman, Hexham included a key section on the presence of cavalry squadrons in supporting the first line foot in which he portrays engaging:

> Battalions of horse, interlaced, and placed betwixt the intervals, and distances of the foot, as the ground necessity may require. For, if an enemy's Horse should be ranged between his battalions of foot, it is needed then, that the other side should observe the same form likewise, and have Horse to encounter Horse, lest they should break in upon the foot divisions.[2]

By 1644–5, most armies possessed well-trained and effective mounted troops (the cuirassier having been largely phased out in the early stages of the fighting). Hence, the dragoons played an increasingly vital part in the conflict. Various examples of combined operations involving the deployment of dragoons with the horse, in which they dismounted to provide firepower can be found in some campaign accounts. At Edgehill in October 1642, and the First Battle of Newbury on 20 September 1643, two brigades of dragoons

1 Cruso, *Military Instructions*, p.38.
2 Hexham, *Principles*, p.58.

cleared the hedges in advance of the King's cavalry forces, even though they suffered significant losses[3]

By implication, fighting in enclosed countryside involved the high expenditure of ammunition from protracted and intense musket fire. This is reflected in the order made in the immediate aftermath of the fighting at the First Battle of Newbury for 'fifty barrels of powder with match and bullet proportionable' to be supplied immediately to the King's army from the Royalist magazine at Oxford due to shortages caused by the intense nature of the firefight.[4] In February 1644 at Stamford Bridge, near York, local Royalists attacked the river crossing, defended by a breastwork on the eastern bank and possibly a newly fitted drawbridge. According to Sir Henry Slingsby, who commanded the King's forces, Colonel 'Throckmorton commanded the party, and falling upon [them] by the time it was light day, placed his dragoons to play hotly upon him from the bridge, while he passed his Horse over at the ford. So the enemy without any more dispute quit the town and shift every man for himself.'[5]

The Royalist cavalry officer Richard Atkyns, who wrote a lively account of his part in the 1643 campaigns in the West with Prince Maurice, recounted two instances when dragoons supported the Horse by providing frontal firepower or flanking fire to disrupt an enemy attack. Whenever possible, they made use of hedges and enclosures to offer protection from enemy cavalry and infantry. Atkyns claimed to have received a commission 'for raising a regiment of dragoons in mid–1643,' though other evidence of the unit's existence seems lacking.

In similar fashion, when in May 1643 Arthur, Lord Capel, the Royalist commander in Shropshire was ordered by Prince Rupert to relieve the garrison of Warrington in Lancashire, he later reported,

> having supplied Halton Castle (which will be likely their next attempt) with some powder, I made my retreat, and brought off with me six or seven of the rebels' scouts; the rebels had stolen some dragoons through a woody ground to lie near our way to march covertly, and at the going off of the pieces fired upon us, but were, with a party of horse attending them, repulsed by our Welsh without any loss to us, or them, for ought we come to know.[6]

Such dragoons are likely to have been Captain Richard Littler's company of Sir William Brereton's Parliamentarian army. Hence, the superior mobility of dragoons, on occasion seconded by cavalry, could provide an advantage over musketeers and other soldiers. Nevertheless, lacking the support of pikemen, they could only stand against horse or foot if they possessed the benefit of terrain or cover.

3 Symonds, *Diary*, pp.64–6; Christopher Scott, *The Battles of Newbury – Crossroads of the English Civil War* (Barnsley: Pen and Sword, 2008), pp.44–5.

4 *ROP*, II, p.291.

5 Daniel Parsons, *The Diary of Sir Henry Slingsby* (London: Longman, 1836), p.93.

6 'Ottley Papers' (1895), pp.325–6.

Hence, the Royalist commander Sir Thomas Aston recalled that prior to the battle at Middlewich on 13 March 1643, 'On our passage to the enemy, a party of dragoons and horse, under Captain Spotswood's command, was ordered to give them an alarm at Northwich (though with more caution than it was executed), the lieutenant imprudently engaging himself, which was expressly forbidden.'[7] By contrast, in his report of the fight Aston's opponent, Sir William Brereton led or sent out cavalry and dragoon units from Northwich, where he was then based, 'and gave them an alarm there, but without any intention to assault them in their quarters – they being very strong on foot and well-armed, and we had no foot at all there then.'[8]

At Lansdowne on 5 June 1643, following indecisive skirmishing lasting two hours, Sir Ralph Hopton began to withdraw, but the Parliamentarian commander, Sir William Waller ordered his cavalry and dragoons against the Royalist's rearguard, which they put to flight. In describing this action, Atkyns wrote:

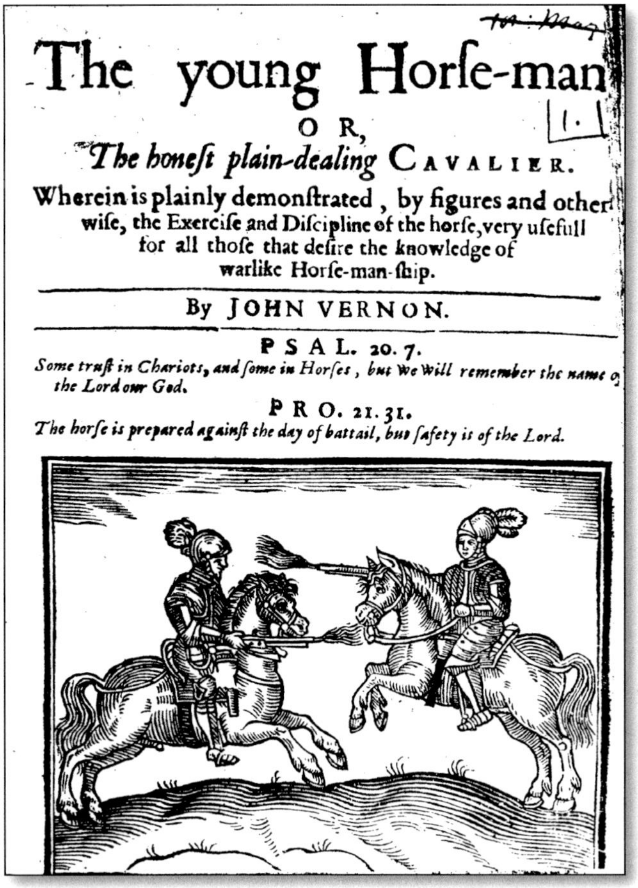

The young Horſe-man
O R,
The honeſt plain-dealing CAVALIER.
Wherein is plainly demonſtrated, by figures and otherwiſe, the Exerciſe and Diſcipline of the horſe, very uſefull for all thoſe that deſire the knowledge of warlike Horſe-man-ſhip.

By JOHN VERNON.

PSAL. 20. 7.
Some truſt in Chariots, and ſome in Horſes, but we will remember the name of the Lord our God.

PRO. 21. 31.
The horſe is prepared againſt the day of battail, but ſafety is of the Lord.

John Vernon, *Young Horseman* (1644) (Open source)

> About three of the clock they (seeing their advantage) sent down a strong party of Horse, commanded by Colonel Burrell, Major Vantruske and others, not less than 300, and five or six hundred dragoons on both sides of the hedges, to make way for their advance, and to make good their retreat. And this was the boldest thing I ever saw the enemy do, for a party of less than 1,000 to charge an army of 6,000 Horse, foot and cannon in their own ground, at least a mile and a half from their body. Our Horse being placed before our foot and cannon, we commanded off troop by troop, and being within half musket shot of the hedges lined both sides by their dragoons, several horses were killed, and some of our men; their muskets playing very hard upon our Horse, made us retreat so disorderly, that they fell foul upon our foot, and indeed there was not room enough for us to retreat in order unless we had gone upon the very mouths of their muskets I suppose the stratagem was to draw on their party of horse upon our foot and cannon, the better to rout them and then our horse to fall in upon them to do execution, for the dragoons making their way by pioneers, were not discovered till they were shot.

7 BL, Ms Harley 2135, f.93r.

8 *Cheshire's Successe.*

Of the part played by dragoons in combined mounted operations during the Royalist assault on Chewton Mendip, located about five miles from Wells, on 10 June 1643 Atkyns recounted:

> When we came within twenty score of the enemy, we found about 200 dragoons half musket shot before a regiment of horse of theirs in two divisions, both in order to receive us. At this *punctilio* of time, from as clear a sunshine day as could be seen, there fell a sudden mist, that we could not see ten yards off, but we still marched on; the dragoons amazed us with the mist, hearing our horse come on, gave us a volley of shot out of distance and disordered not one man of us, and before we came up to them they took horse and away they ran, and in the mist immediately vanished. We then had less work to do, but still we had enough; for there were six troops of horse in two divisions, but about three or four hundred dragoons more, that they lined the hedges on both sides of their horse when we came within six score of them, we mended our pace and fell into their left division, routing and killing several of them. The dragoons on both sides, seeing us mixed with their own men that they could not fire at us, but they might kill their own men as well as ours, took horse and away they ran also. In this charge I gave one Captain Kiteley quarter twice, and at last he was killed The Lord Arundel also took a dragoons colours[9]

A further example of such fighting occurred at Cheriton on 29 March 1644, where the Royalist Lord Hopton, retreating with his army through Alresford:

> thereupon went, and commanded his own regiments of horse and dragoons, that were advanced about half a mile before, to make all the speed with any convenience they could, to get into the town, and as soon as they recovered the town, the dragoons to alight, and make good the barricades towards the enemy, and the horse to stand together in a body in the market place to second them, as there should be occasion.[10]

Similarly, as the fighting began at Marston Moor on 2 July 1644 Colonel Hugh Fraser's dragoons from the Earl of Leven's Covenanter army cleared a cross ditch of musketeers in front of Cromwell's Ironsides on the left wing of the Parliamentarian horse, enabling them to charge and rout the Royalist cavalry to their front. According to one report, 'By the good management of Colonel Fraser, they acted their part so well that at the first assault they beat the enemy from the ditch, and shortly after killed a great many.' Following a brief respite, Fraser's men joined the attack on the Marquess of Newcastle's white-coated foot regiments, who resolved to die rather than surrender. Consequently, 'a Scots regiment of dragoons commanded by Colonel Fraser, with two others, was brought to open them upon some hand, which at length they did; when all their ammunition was spent, having refused quarter everyman fell in

9 *Vindication of Richard Atkyns, Esq., as also a Relation of several Passages in the Western War* (London: 1669), pp.24, 26–7, 30–1.

10 Hopton, *Bellum Civile*, p.79.

the same order and rank wherein he had fought.'[11] It is certain that Fraser's dragoons were armed with matchlock muskets because on 19 February 1644, after fighting at Corbridge, they received 50lbs of powder, 50lbs of match and 50lbs of bullets. On 25 March the regiment was issued with 300lbs of powder, 100lbs of match and 100lbs of musket balls.[12]

The retreat of the Earl of Essex's horse under Lieutenant-General Sir William Balfour from Lostwithiel on 30 August 1644 was covered by a fighting retreat by Captain Jeremiah Abercrombie's dragoons. As the fugitives neared the safety of Saltash the dragoons, left behind as part of the rearguard, occasionally making a stand, firing a volley, and then retreating.[13]

Similarly, at Winceby on 11 October 1643, when on the second day of the battle a combined force of cavalry and dragoons of the Eastern Association Army engaged the Royalists in a firefight. As one Parliamentarian newsbook reported:

> we had drawn up our dragoons, who gave the first charge, and then the horse fell in. [Whereby] the enemy stood not another but were driven back upon their own body that was to second them, and put them into disorder, our men charged all in with him, and then they ran for it, leaving all their dragoons which were now on foot behind them.[14]

Given that the core of Colonel Okey's regiment was drawn from the Earl of Manchester's dragoons, they would have been used to this way of fighting, and are likely to have operated in this fashion during the New Model Army's counter-attack at Naseby and the pursuit of the remnants of the King's troops towards Leicester.[15]

As with other kinds of troops, the hard usage of mounted units, including dragoons during the British Civil Wars could also severely limit their effectiveness. This was especially so during continuous campaigns and harsh weather conditions. In November 1645, Colonel Robert Mainwaring, in command of the London Brigade, a kind of expeditionary force raised from the City Trained Bands and the City Auxiliaries, which had operated in the Newbury campaign of the autumn of 1644, and was currently boosting the Parliamentarian forces in the East Midlands, explained to Sir William Brereton:

> I have had hard marches and hard duty since my coming from London. [On] 5 November I received orders from Colonel-General Poyntz to march with his brigade unto you. The ways I find very hard and the dragoons' horses very weak

11 James Somerville, *Memorie of the Somervilles* (Edinburgh: James Ballantyne and Co., 1815), II, pp.315, 348.

12 C. S Terry (ed. & intro.), *Papers Relating to the Army of the Solemn League and Covenant 1643–1647 I*, (Edinburgh: Scottish History Society, 1917), pp.127–30.

13 Rushworth, *Historical Collections*, II, p.702; Walker, *Historical Discourses*, pp.67–8.

14 *A True Relation of the Late Fight Betweene the Right Honourable The Earle of Manchester's Forces, and the Marquesse of Newcastles Forces, 11 Oct., neere Home Castle in Lincolnshire* (London: 11 October 1643). TT, E.71 [5].

15 Sprigge, *Anglia Rediviva*, p.331.

> in regard of our hard marches and duty. Our dragoons' arms are much broken and many unfit in regard of the storming and taking in of Shelford House. Many of our horses tire which doth retard my march. I desire that you will be pleased to give order for my quarters that so we have a little refreshment that we may be better able to do our duty.[16]

On 8 September 1645, Parliament had ordered the raising of 500 horse and 500 dragoons to form the London Brigade. The dragoons were commanded by Colonel William Webb, a grocer of Cornhill, London, who had served under Colonel John Venn in March 1643, then as Captain and Sergeant-Major in the Green Auxiliaries

During October 1645, 500 horse and 500 dragoons raised from the reorganised London Brigade, currently operating in the Midlands, participated in the Parliamentarian storming of Shelford House, near Newark, garrisoned for the King by Colonel Philip Stanhope. Between 1 and 3 November 1645 the attacking troops (under the direct leadership of Colonel John Hutchinson) filled the moat with faggots of wood, which they climbed over and then used their scaling ladders against the heavily defended walls. The ladders were too short, however. Some of the Brigade's units, tasked with assaulting the West ramparts were initially beaten back, but after 30 minutes of bitter close quarters fighting with a determined enemy, they succeeded in taking the eastern ramparts, albeit incurring heavy casualties.[17] Webb's dragoons appear to have been closely engaged. In his account of the action Colonel-General Sydenham Poyntz reported, 'The London Brigade behaved themselves very faithfully in this service; the rest wanted no courage.'[18] The petition of Robert Boulter, presented to the Nottingham Quarter Sessions on 1 July 1646, testified that he 'served for a corporal under Captain John Wilson, under the command of Colonel Webb, being dangerously shot at the going on at Shelford House and having lain at great charges so long as my money lasted. But now all is gone and I am indebted, and know not how to relieve myself unless your Honours take pity of me.'[19] On 5 November Poyntz ordered the Londoners to assist Brereton's forces besieging Chester, yet before Mainwaring's troops could reach them they were redirected to Leicestershire.

Operating in a mobile, mounted role, alongside units of cavalry, the dragoons of Sir William Brereton's army in Cheshire were central to the Parliamentarian victory at Denbigh Green on 1 November 1645. The official Parliamentarian report described how:

> The forlorn hope, forty out of every regiment, was commanded by Captain Otter, captain of the reformadoes, a gallant soldier, and Captain Edwards, a Cheshire

16 BL, Ms 11332, f.62r; *BLB*, II, 843.

17 *A full Relation of the Desperate charge of the malignants for the betraying of Monmouth, also how Lieut.-Col. Kyrle fell into the enemy's quarters near Hereford, likewise a copy of Col. Sandys' letter of the manner of taking Shelford House* (London: 4 November 1645). TT, E308 [19].

18 *LJ*, VII, p.678.

19 TNA, SP28/241/1, f.310r.

> captain and well deserving gentleman. Coming to Whitchurch, a mile from Denbigh, they were in a lane flanked by the enemy's horse and dragoons, so that they were forced to make good that pass with the forlorn hope and Cheshire dragoons, under the command of Captains Finch and Holt, stout and resolute men. These with the forlorn hope behaved themselves gallantly and maintained the pass until the foot came up, the most part of which with the Warwickshire and Derbyshire horse, commanded by Majors Saunders and Hawkesworth, seconded the forlorn hope and bore the burden of the day, whiles the reformadoes, Cheshire horse and 400 Lancashire foot were intended for a greater service.[20]

Brereton's dragoons operated in a variety of roles throughout the First Civil War, including the seizing of bridges and strongholds, raiding, reconnaissance, patrolling, pursuing retreating enemy troops, foraging and intelligence gathering, specialist siege operations, direct assaults and providing covering fire for both the horse and foot. During 1643 they undertook surprise raids, often at night, and on 9 November 'three or four companies of country dragoons' led a desperate assault of Farndon Bridge, the gateway into North Wales:

> by placing ladders to the top of the drawbridge and cutting the ropes. Which being done and the [draw]bridge falling down we had access to the gates and casting over some hand grenades amongst the Welshmen – which struck such terror into them as that they all run away and could not be obtained to relieve. Whereby we had a very fair opportunity to force open the gates: which being done, the enemy was without much difficulty beaten from their double works within the gates[21]

In 1645, when the Cheshire forces and other auxiliary regiments were besieging Chester, Captain Gimbert's company undertook siege operations against Beeston Castle, an important part of the Parliamentarian leaguer of Chester.[22] Listed in charge of 60 firelocks (dragoons) in April 1645, he also commanded 'Fort Royal' – the blockhouse situated opposite the fortress's outer gates. On 19 September, a Parliamentarian body of 500 horse, 700 foot and 200 dragoons left its assembly point at Beeston and executed a probing attack on the riverside mount at Boughton, part of the defences of the city of Chester. During that night, carrying scaling ladders, Gimbert's men spearheaded a fast-moving assault that took the defenders entirely by surprise. As Nathaniel Lancaster, the army's historian, related:

> Captain Gimbert was the first that entered, his ladder being too short, he lifted up his man to the mount (near the riverside) from the top of it, his man drew him

---

20 *A True Relation of a Great Victory obtained by the Parliament Forces in Cheshire, under Sir William Brereton, against the King's Forces, under the command of Sir William Vaughan, near Denbigh, November 1. 1645* (London: 5 November 1645). TT, E.308 [14]; BL, Ms Add 11332, ff.76r–76v; *BLB*, II, 801.

21 HMC, *Thirteenth Report, App.*, I, p.151.

22 TNA, SP28/196/1, f.13r.; SP28/152/7, f.8v.

> up by the hand and then they cried 'a town, a town', immediately they cleared that mount, slew Lieutenant Aldersley, the captain of the watch, and put the rest, about six men, to flight. Then others set to their ladders, possessed themselves of all the mounts of that side of the city, and with the instruments we brought with us, broke open the gates: then all the horse entered, with the remainder of the foot, with loud shouts, which utterly daunted the enemy. The next work was to take the Barra, being the fortification for the Forest Street, which was affected speedily, by entering at the back of some houses, not far from the gate. So we fell upon that guard in the rear, who fled in all haste into the city. That while our men opened the gate into the Forest Street, which we entered with a full body of horse and foot, and some close pursued the guard, that they were near entering the city with them. Master Mayor very difficultly got into the city, but made such haste, that he left the sword and mace at his house in the suburbs.[23]

During the comparative quiet of 21 September, the Parliamentarians placed a gun battery near St John's Church, to the immediate east of Chester, and the following day began heavy bombardment on its walls aimed at forcing a breach. That evening 500 troops, including two companies of dragoons, stormed through. In the ensuing close-quarter fighting the dragoons – leading the assault – sustained the greatest of the casualties. Captain Simon Finch and some of his soldiers were wounded, while Gimbert and his lieutenant also fell. A muster roll of Captain Gimbert's company, dated 21 November 1645, records the cost of three days' bitter fighting. Besides the captain, lieutenant, one sergeant, two corporals, two drummers and 51 soldiers listed present, there were ten soldiers listed either as 'absent upon wounds' or 'wounded', and three more described as 'wounded and discharged'.[24] As testament to this unit's virtually continuous exposure to combat during this period, a warrant issued to the army's treasurer, James Croxton, and dated 15 October 1645, instructed him 'to pay Captain Gimbert's soldiers wounded in the service, their month's pay.'[25]

Sir William Waller's forces – the smallest and least reliable of the major Parliamentarian armies – in the West in 1643 were reported that, 'there is in this army ... no more than 500 foot, and two regiments of horse and dragoons.' The same source related, in response to Waller's march to Worcester to besiege the city, 'His Majesty gave present order for three regiments of horse and dragoons to be sent speedily away to relieve the same.'[26] Likewise, in Sir Ralph Hopton's second Royalist army, raised in September 1643 'for the clearing of Dorsetshire, Wiltshire and Hampshire, and to point forward as far as he could to London,' his own regiment and that commanded by the Earl of Crawford were joint formations of cavalry and dragoons.[27] The suggestion here, is that what was being described were combined 'regiments' of horse and

23 Lewis (ed.), *Siege of Chester*, pp.17–18.

24 TNA, SP28/224/1, ff.72r–74v.

25 TNA, SP28/224/1, f.28r.

26 *Mercurius Aulicus*, 7–14 March, 3–11 June 1643.

27 Hopton, *Bellum Civile*, p.61; Laurence Spring, *The Armies of Sir Ralph Hopton: The Royalist Armies in the West 1642–46* (Solihull: Helion & Co., 2020), p.147.

dragoons, partly perhaps on an ad hoc basis. Combined regiments were also a feature of Parliamentarian armies. On 6 March 1643, Robert, Earl of Essex, as Captain General of the Parliamentary Army, appointed William Purefoy to be Colonel of a regiment of horse and dragoons raised in Warwickshire 'for defence of the King, Parliament, and Kingdom'.[28]

In terms of the deployment of combined arms tactics, a fierce encounter occurred at Bowdon Hill, near Sunderland, on 24 March 1644, following the crossing into northern England by the Earl of Leven's Scots Covenanter Army. The confrontation lasted most of the day, until Royalist musketeers were sent forward to line the hedges and ditches breaking up the ground between both sides, and thus preventing any deployment of horse. Having faced a steady but ineffective bombardment from the Royalist artillery for more than an hour, the Scottish dragoons rode forward, dismounted, and began firing, the engagement being disputed amidst the enclosed ground in the darkness until around midnight. According to one report:

> our dragoons began the play, and then the musketeers in the hedges upon both sides, our bodies of foot advancing at all quarters to the hedges, the enemy's cannon discharging upon them an hour and a half with very small hurt ... many officers who have been old soldiers did affirm they had never seen so long and hot service in the night time.[29]

Another added, 'What the event of this meeting will be I do not know, nor will not guess; hitherto hath the Lord helped us. Our men are cheerful, our hopes good.'[30]

In 1642 and early 1643 sizeable numbers of dragoon regiments were raised and maintained by the Royalist and Parliamentarian armies, although the effectiveness of some units – sometimes raised quickly and disbanded after campaigns, was blunted by the lack of available horses and suitable equipment. Although during the autumn of 1642 the King probably had plenty of cavalry, there is some evidence that he was short of dragoons. By 10 September 1642, Charles was reported to have assembled an army of less than 2,000 horse, but the strength of his infantry (about 1,200) and its state were described as unable to 'encourage a temperate man.' Less than half were armed and eighty of them had been hired for 1s a man a day, a sum considerably higher than the standard rate of pay of the rival armies. The rumour was that the King might not 'have any infantry at all and would [make] his foot into dragoons, which yet he may do, if foot come in no faster.'[31] When he commenced his march at Bridgnorth for London on 13 October, his forces reportedly consisted of

28 *CSPD 1641–43*, p.449.

29 C. S Terry, 'The Scottish Campaigns in Northumberland and Durham between January and June 1644', *AA*, 2nd Series, 21 (1899), pp.146–79, (p. 172).

30 *A True Relation of the Proceedings of the Scottish Army, from 12th March to the 25th, dated from his Excellency the Lord Generall Lesley's Quarters, neare Sunderland, 25 March 1644* (Edinburgh, 1644).

31 *A continuation of our weekly intelligence from His Majesties Army* (London: 16 September 1642), p.4.

roughly 6,000 infantry, upwards of 2,000 horse and 1,500 dragoons.[32] Some commissions were clearly issued for the raising of Royalist dragoon units before this, as Charles I had 800 at Uttoxeter on 14 September. Sir Edward Duncombe, one of the King's dragoon colonels, had been the Lieutenant-Colonel in Sir Robert Strickland's trained band foot which had attended the King at York. Duncombe's dragoons seem to have been recruited extremely hastily, and the regiment's constituent parts raised independently. Given that, according to one report, the unit was exactly 500 strong, at full strength in other words, at Edgehill, various individually raised companies might have been brought together to form one specific regiment.[33]

Colonel Edward Grey's regiment of dragoons, like that of Duncombe's, appeared early in the war, but vanished after only a few months. On 20 July 1642, this unit was engaged in one of the first acts of hostility in Yorkshire, when numbering 300 dragoons it burned and ransacked the outbuildings of Great Houghton House, near Barnsley. One newsbook, reporting from York on 19 September, related:

> Now the fair pretences of the Cavaliers appears, that t'was fire and sword they meant, they have lately plundered Sir Edward Rodes his house, burnt all his out houses and taken away £600 worth of goods, slain one of his servants, and violently used others, it was done by Captain Grey's regiment, a Northumberland gentleman, who hath the command of 500 dragooners, most of them consisting of Papists and popish commanders, though to this worthy knight it was a sad accident, yet it hath put courage into our West Riding, for on a sudden 1,500 men were in arms to take these cavaliers, and being on their march, the cavaliers got notice, and by a still march in the night, escaped to Mansfield in Nottinghamshire.[34]

It was also reported that 'on Tuesday last, the King advanced with his whole army to Derby, consisting of 7,000 horse and foot, thither Colonel Grey of Wark repaired unto him, with 500 dragoons.'[35]

Another early northern Royalist regiment was that commanded by Colonel Sir Thomas Gower, who joined the King at the first siege of Hull in July 1642. It was reported that Gower was commissioned to raise 1,000 dragoons – virtually two regiments – on 22 August, although informed the Royalist MP Sir Richard Leveson on 5 August 1642, 'Five regiments of horse are raising for the King, besides two of dragoons.' He continued, 'I have command to raise 1,000 dragoons, Colonel Heron 600, others 400.'[36]

---

32 BL, Ms Harley 6851, f.211r; Arthur Collins (ed.), *Letters and Memorials of State* (London: T. Osborne, 1746), II, p.667.

33 *A Most True Relation of the Present State of His Majesties Army: Wherein Also the Truth of that Declaration Published by the Parliament, of Their Happy Victory in the Battaile at Keynton, is Both Justly Asserted and Abundantly Proved, Humbly Presented by the Author who was Personally Present, to the Honourable the Lords and Commons in Parliament Assembled* (London: 3 December 1642). TT, E244 [2].

34 *Special Passages*, 13–20 September 1642.

35 *England's Memorable Accidents*, 19–26 September 1642.

36 *True Proceedings from York, and a True Relation of the Manner of his Majesties setting up of his standard at Nottingham* (London: 22 August 1642). TT, E115 [4]; HMC, *Fifth Report*, I, p.191.

Moreover, he described a sortie that had been led by Sir John Meldrum from the besieged town of Hull against the King's arsenal in Anlaby on 27 July. It was this reversal that forced Charles to lift the siege and retreat to York. Gower wrote:

> Parliamentarian troops sallied by night … they came three miles from Hull, and making a stand with 40 horse and some 200 foot, they fell into the town of Anlaby, wherein Lieutenant Colonel Duncombe and Major Frankland lay with their [dragoon] companies, and letting alone the *corps du guard*, took all the rest between sleeping and waking, beat up the quarter, surprised the sentinels (whom they slew), hurt some others, and carried twelve or thirteen prisoners away. They also fired a barn wherein their ammunition lay (being half a barrel of powder), and frightened the regiment so abominably, that the next day at noon the highways were filled with runaways, and in three companies they could not muster fifteen men.

On 5 October 1642 he claimed that he alone was opposing Hotham's raids from Hull, writing, 'I have a mighty burden upon my shoulders being now to oppose orders of Parliament (for oath binds me to maintain the country in peace so far as I can) and this without money or means, but the bare assistance of the people which I cannot make a foundation upon.'[37] What became of Gower's own dragoons remains unclear, but they may have been absorbed into his cavalry regiment, which was also present at the siege. Sir Thomas Hanmer, a Flintshire gentleman, had also been commissioned by Charles I at Nottingham on 7 September 1642 to raise a dragoon regiment of 200 men from North Wales.[38] These probably acted as part of the garrison of Chirk Castle. Nonetheless, as Sir Richard Bulstrode, who served at Edgehill in the Prince of Wales' regiment of horse, remarked, 'Our chief want was arms; for most of the regiments, which were raised in Wales, were very ill-armed. However, they were brave and resolute to serve their King, with such arms as they had, or could get in their march, and our army increased daily, by many coming to us from all parts, as we marched.'[39]

On several occasions, the Parliamentarian commander Sir William Waller mounted his musketeers to assist strategic operations, and such was the usefulness of these troops that his own regiment of foot was reformed as a second regiment of dragoons, with over 500 soldiers mustering in London in September 1643.[40] Raised in 1642 from various companies from Essex's army, Waller's first regiment served in his campaigns of 1642 and 1643, but after the defeat at Roundway Down – where the Parliamentarian army in the West was practically wiped out – the unit was returned to strength. On 30 March 1644 Parliament passed an Ordinance 'for raising and maintaining

37 HMC, *Fifth Report*, I, p.193.

38 NLW, Ms Bettisfield 111; John Lord Hanmer, *Memorial of the Parish and Family of Hanmer in Flintshire* (London: Chiswick Press, 1877), pp.64–5.

39 Richard Bulstrode, *Memoirs and Reflections upon the reign and government of King Charles the 1st and K. Charles the 2nd* (London: N. Mist, 1721), p.75.

40 Laurence Spring, *Waller's Army: The Regiments of Sir William Waller's Southern Association* (Pike & Shot Society, 2007), p.150.

3,000 foot, 1,200 horse, and 500 dragoons to be commanded by Sir William Waller as Serjeant-Major-General of the forces under the Earl of Essex and of all other forces in the Associated counties of Southampton, Surrey, Sussex, and Kent.'[41] A few months later Waller's old regiment of dragoons passed to Major-General James Holborne. In August Sir William Waller asked the Committee of Both Kingdoms for 50 guidons (10 to a regiment), 100 dragoon drums, 5,000 belts for their muskets and 2,000 swords for the second regiment of dragoons.[42] His plans, however, were thwarted by a lack of suitable horses. On 6 June the Committee of Both Kingdoms ordered the Committee of Kent to dispatch 100 dragoons and a troop of horse for the Oxford campaign. Perhaps in response to this, on 1 July Sir Arthur Haselrig, Waller's then second in command, reported the problems encountered by mounting infantrymen for escort duties to the Committee of Both Kingdoms:

> Yesterday the money was conveyed safe to Leighton, where we found Major General Browne; but there being certainly informed that Sir William Waller's forces were disputing passes with the King, and that the King's forces are between us and Waller, also that the foot here is not tried and no horse at all, I sent the money to Aylesbury, where it now is, and the governor takes great care of it. Waller's commissary is there, and I appointed those few Kentish horse and dragoons to be at Aylesbury till they receive further orders, conceiving it will cause a rumour of new forces brought into the town … I hear the gentlemen of Essex say that if their ordinance had passed when desired there had been three regiments of horse ready at this present, and that they are now very diligent in raising horse, so that I apprehend a kind letter may draw out some horse for the preservation of their foot. They sent 1,000 of their foot [as] mounted pikes and musketeers, such a sight as pikes to march mounted I never saw, and should we have had an alarm our mounted pikes would have made rout sufficient. To dismount the pikes and not musketeers would discontent the pikes, which caused Major General Browne to send back all their horses[43]

The county of Kent seems not to have raised any regiments of dragoons, although there were several independent companies. It was reported that 120 dragoons accompanied Sir Michael Livesey's Kentish regiment of horse at Farnham in November 1643 and various units participated in the Parliamentarian siege of Arundel Castle. From Farnham on 2 September 1644 Sir William Waller reported to the Committee of Both Kingdoms, 'On this day a company of dragoons under Captain Butler arrived out of Kent, and I expect three companies of the new Kentish regiment tonight or tomorrow. All these poor men have brought their mouths with them, and my Abingdon blades, they are the pictures of famine and poverty, and I fear the money still at London will not amount to three weeks' pay.'[44] Captain Nathan Butler also commended a company of foot in the Sutton at Hone Lathe Kent Trained

41 *LJ*, VI, pp.496–7; *A&O*, I, pp.413–18.
42 *CSPD 1644*, p.460.
43 *Ibid.*, pp.211, 297.
44 *CSPD 1644*, pp.468–9.

Sir William Waller (c1597-1668) From *A Survey Of Englands Champions*, Josiah Ricraft (London 1647) (Stephen Ede-Borrett collection)

Band regiment. Among other dragoon units were those led by Captain William Skinner, Captain Robert Smith and Captain Phillips. Skinner's was in existence by June 1644, while the latter two were referred to on 30 November as 'captains of dragoons drawn out from Colonel [Ralph] Weldon's regiment.' Moreover, between 2 June and 2 September Captain Smith had received pay for his company for a captain, a lieutenant, an ensign, a quartermaster, four sergeants, eight corporals, one drummer and 114 private sentinels.[45]

In November 1642, 1cwt of powder, match and bullet was issued to Colonel Ralph Dutton's Royalist regiment of foot from the Oxford magazine. In order to safeguard the convoy delivering these items, 80 horses were brought to Reading, which as the governor reported, 'I am to mount musketeers upon there, 1lb of powder, with match and shot [provided to each soldier] accordingly.'[46] Following the ambush of Royalist troops at Sourton Down on 25 April 1643, captured documents revealed Charles I's order to Sir Ralph Hopton to rendezvous with the army from Oxford, and to 'use your best diligence to horse all your foot, both musketeers and pikes, as dragoons that they may march to us with more ease, speed and safety.'[47] According to Richard Symonds – who enlisted in the King's Lifeguard towards the end of 1643, and participated in, and was thus able to write about, various campaigns – on 13 August, Sir Thomas Glenham's foot 'were made dragoons in Brecknockshire, and to march too with us,' although conversely, some dragoon units (often chronically understrength through battlefield attrition and desertion) were converted to infantry.[48] In similar fashion, the Parliamentarian politician, Bulstrode Whitelock, reported that during the relief of Basing House in September 1644 the Royalist commander, Colonel Henry Gage possessed 'about 1,500 of the King's foot out of several garrisons mounted for dragoons.'[49]

The tactical and combat value of dragoons was remarked upon by several contemporary soldiers and commentators. Writing in 1622 about his experiences in Ireland, Francis Markham recommended that:

> the colonel is to foresee that in the composition of his regiment, the dragoons be chosen from the ablest, nimblest, and most active men that can be got, being of that dexterity and quickness of spirit that they may be able to vault to and from

45 TNA, SP28/130/3, f.147v–148r.
46 TNA, WO55/423, f.142v.
47 *A Perfect Diurnall*, 1–8 May 1643.
48 Symonds, *Diary*, p.223.
49 Whitelocke, *Memorials*, p.99.

> their horses at pleasure, and to carry their pieces so close guarded in their left hands, that in performing of any of these sudden actions there may be found neither trouble nor hinderance.[50]

Audacity in military operations is often accompanied by the act of surprise. Thus, prior to the storming of Lowestoft by Eastern Association troops on 14 March 1643:

> The Colonel [Oliver Cromwell] summoned the town, and demanded, if they would deliver up their strangers, the town and their arms, promising them no favour, if so; if not, none. They yielded to deliver up their strangers, but not to the rest. Whereupon our Norwich dragoons crept under the chain before mentioned, and came within pistol-shot of their ordnance, proffering to fire upon their cannoneer, who fled; and so they gained two pieces of ordnance and broke the chain [drawn across the entrance to deter cavalry], and they and the horse entered the town without more resistance.[51]

The Cheshire commander, Sir William Brereton, was drawn into the war in Staffordshire in mid–1643. In a tactical method that he would develop a reputation for, during the early hours of 16 May, he oversaw the nocturnal assault of the Royalist town and castle of Stafford. His own troop of horse and Captain John Bramhall's dragoons, seconded by companies of Staffordshire foot, 'took the town by *scalado*, with the loss of very few men on both sides, some sentinels only excepted, for the cavaliers in the town seeing themselves too desperately and suddenly surprised, had not the power to make any opposition.' Prisoners to the number of 300 were reportedly taken, besides arms, horses and '42 were men of note and quality.'[52] Brereton now capitalised on his success by capturing Wolverhampton, employing the same tactics he had used at Stafford, 'about three o'clock in the morning without any opposition or resistance.'[53] The same daring was in evidence in November 1643 in an attack on Parliamentarian-held Chillington House in Staffordshire, the former home of the recusant Peter Giffard. According to one source:

> Lieutenant Carter with his sixteen dragoons went to the gate, and knocked until a soldier came and opened it, on whom the lieutenant seized, and with a pistol set to his breast, commanded him to be silent until his dragoons were all come up, and then forced the soldier to show them the direct way through the back quarters, which the soldier promised, but when he came near the hall door, he broke loose, and ran in crying 'Arm, arm, we are all betrayed', which caused the

50 Markham, *Five Decades*, pp.167–8.

51 W. C. Abbott (ed.), *Writings and Speeches of Oliver Cromwell* (Oxford: Clarendon Press, 1988), p.219.

52 *Certaine Informations*, 18 May 1643; James Hall (ed.), *Memorials of the Civil War in Cheshire and the adjacent counties by Thomas Malbon, of Nantwich, Gent., and Providence improved by Edward Burghall*, Lancashire and Cheshire Record Society, 19 (1889), pp.54–5.

53 M. W. Greenslade and G. C. Baugh (intro.), *The History and Antiquities of Staffordshire, by Stebbing Shaw* (East Ardsley: E. P. Publishing, 1976), I, p.55.

> lieutenant to shoot the soldier that he fell dead in the hall, where 110 soldiers were sat at dinner, whom the lieutenant and his dragoons suddenly assaulted, and with discharging two of his muskets made them all fly into the upper rooms, their arms being at the other end of the house.[54]

Such was the value of these troops that on 28 April 1645, during the blockade of Oxford, Cromwell lamented, 'It is a great pity we want of dragoons, I believe most of their [the Royalists'] petty garrisons might have been taken in and other services done, for the enemy is in huge fear.'[55] During the New Model Army's march to Naseby in June 1645 Colonel John Okey's companies rode in the vanguard and occupied the village after the Royalist departure the night before the battle, while other dragoon units were attached to regiments of the Associated Horse.[56] Although they showed their initiative and skill at Torrington, Exeter and elsewhere, a particularly ingenious and audacious use of the New Model's dragoons occurred on 29th July 1645, when Okey's men initiated the seizure of Bath without firing a shot by crawling across the bridge to the town gate, where they seized the muzzles of the guards' muskets. They called on the defenders to accept quarter, whereupon the latter dropped their weapons and ran away. The dragoons then blew open the gate, and the garrison quickly surrendered.[57]

A particularly ingenious plan was put into effect at Hereford, a Royalist garrison that had been relieved by the King's appearance in September 1645. At dawn on 18 December, in bitter winter conditions, soldiers under the command of Colonel Thomas Morgan, the governor of Gloucester, who were disguised as labourers from outside the city reported for the daily duty of breaking ice on the city ditch and river. They quickly overpowered the guards and opened the gates for waiting troops. The next day, Hungerford, wrote to the Shropshire Committee:

> I presume mine was the first to you concerning Hereford, which being doubtful, this may the first that may assure you of the taking of it and the manner. Yesterday morning before the bridge was let down, in the time of the great fog, six men with bills as countrymen came to the gates and said they had come all night with their contribution money for fear of the Roundheads. Upon which they let down the bridge and, undiscovered by reason of the fog, three or four companies of dragoons, surprised all the guards and were soon seconded. Many got over the walls as when we took Shrewsbury, whereof the governor [Sir Barnabas Scudamore] was one who escaped to Ludlow. The last night late I heard this was Lieutenant General Cromwell's stratagem, to which God gave a happy issue.[58]

A contemporary pamphlet testified that help was given to the Parliamentarians by an unnamed reformado officer and accomplices among the garrison, but

54 *Mercurius Aulicus*, 23–30 November 1643.
55 Abbott (ed.), p.396; HMC, *Sixth Report*, p.57.
56 Foard, *Naseby, pp.192, 208.*
57 Sprigge, *Anglia Rediviva*, p.76.
58 BL, Ms Add 11333, f.48v; *BLB*, II, 1056.

also noted that 'Captain Howarth and one of Colonel Birch his captains commanded the firelocks to the priory' [St Guthlac's Priory, some 300 yards from the city walls], and added 'Captain Howarth and 150 firelocks possessed the gate.'[59] That these soldiers were indeed dragoons is confirmed by a letter from the Shropshire Committee to Sir William Brereton on 23 December 1645, in which it wrote:

> Out of the several relations we have heard and conference we have had with those that have received it from the governor of Hereford his own mouth since they came to Ludlow, we conceive the truth to be that Colonel Morgan, governor of Gloucester, with a party of horse and dragoons, drawn out of Gloucester, Monmouth, Canon Frome and other of the Parliamentarian garrisons, laying hold of the opportunity now that so many of the Hereford forces were drawn out for the relief of Chester and others sent to Raglan upon an unknown design, and making most of the mist upon Thursday morning, marched all night and, early in the morning upon the letting down of the bridge, a small party first rushed upon the sentinels, and the rest came up presently and with speed rushed upon the main guards[60]

Some modern authors have suggested that civil war dragoons were something of a 'fighting elite', who were often commanded by professional soldiers and recruited from veterans of other conflicts. There is some truth in this, although there are some examples of inexperienced, and poorly equipped and officered dragoon units, especially during the early stages of the wars. The notion that at least some dragoons were 'specialist' in their nature and effectiveness places these soldiers within the modern military-theoretical concept of 'asymmetrical warfare', a byword used to describe disparity in power between opposing forces, customarily for conflicts that involve guerrilla tactics or paramilitary units.[61] Some Royalist dragoons, at times drawn from, or bolstered by, experienced officers and foreign professionals were better trained and disciplined than most of the King's army. For the Parliamentarians, many commissioned officers had served on the Continent, and a significant quantity of recruits were obtained in London from returning veterans and foreign professionals. The Welsh soldier, Thomas Morgan of Llangattock, Monmouthshire went abroad when very young and gained considerable experience fighting in the Low Countries under Bernard of Saxe-Weimar. Morgan returned to England at the beginning of the First Civil War to serve as a Captain of dragoons in Ferdinando, Lord Fairfax's Parliamentarian army in Yorkshire, and was particularly noted for his skills

59 *A new tricke to take townes: or, The just and perfect relation of the sudden surprisall of Hereford; taken December 18. 1645* (London: 1645), printed in John and T. W. Webb (eds), *Memorials of the Civil War Between King Charles I and the Parliament of England, as it Affected Herefordshire and the Adjacent Counties* (London: Spottiswoode, 1879), II, pp.402–3.

60 BL, Ms Add 11333, f.58r; *BLB*, II, 1089.

61 Andrew Mack, 'Why Big Nations Lose Small Wars: The Politics of Asymmetric Conflicts', *World Politics*, 27 (2) (1975), pp.175–200; Michael Roberts, 'The Military Revolution, 1560–1660', Clifford J. Rogers (ed.), *The Military Revolution Debate: Readings on the Military Transformation of Early Modern Europe* (Boulder: Westview Press, 1995), pp.13–35.

in siege warfare. His dragoons formed part of the forlorn hope at Adwalton Moor on 30 June 1643, and the following year served at Nantwich and Marston Moor, as well as operations in Lincolnshire. In March 1645, Morgan was promoted Colonel of dragoons in the regiment formerly commanded by Sir William Constable, then Sir William Fairfax. He succeeded Colonel Edward Massey as commander-in-chief of all the forces in Gloucestershire and governor of Gloucester on 18 June 1645.[62]

Professionals, or career officers with military experience, were predominately those English, Scottish, Welsh and Irish gentry who had served for pay overseas prior to 1642. Their numbers have been underestimated, but in 1639 almost 200 officers and gentlemen were listed as having served on the Continent and thus joined the King's army in the First Bishops' War.[63] Many of these also served in Royalist, Parliamentarian and Covenanter forces from 1642 onwards. At the beginning of the conflicts in Britain the expertise of professional soldiers was much sought after, although some were offered inducements to prevent them from taking up arms for their adversaries. In his 1598 treatise, *The Theorike and Practike of Moderne Warres*, the soldier Robert Barret, who had spent much of his life in the profession of arms among the French, Dutch, Spaniards and Italians, wrote of officers 'such as have seen wars, and borne office in the same, I mean honest and valiant men, not tapsterly praters, and ale-bench braggers, who know no point of soldiery in the world.'[64] A significant quantity of commissioned officers who later commanded dragoon units had served on the Continent and Ireland. These included among the Parliamentarians Sir John Seaton, Colonel John Middleton, Colonel James Wardlaw and some captains of the Earl of Essex's army.

In Sir William Brereton's Cheshire forces some of his captains were commissioned in London, and in 1642 many of the recruits who enlisted in their companies were probably Dutchmen or British soldiers returning from abroad. Likewise, Captains Gwilliam Goldegay and Godfrey Gimbert were probably professionals, while Captain Simon Finch came over to England with the Royalist army from Ireland in November 1643 as an officer in Sir Michael Darnley's regiment of foot. He was captured on 25 January 1644 following the defeat at Nantwich, and consequently joined the forces of Parliament under Brereton.[65] These were highly skilled and valued officers, who distinguished themselves on several occasions.

Notable among the King's armies were Sir Arthur Aston and Colonel James Ussher. Aston, who was Colonel-General of Dragoons and commander of a company of dragoons in the Oxford Army, had been in the service of Sigismund III, King of Poland and other commanders during the Thirty Years' War. At the beginning of the Scottish rebellion in 1639, Sir Arthur returned

62 Basil Morgan, 'Sir Thomas Morgan', *Oxford DNB* (2004); *CJ*, IV, p.323; *LJ*, X, p.228.

63 Barbara Donegan, 'Halcyon Days and the Literature War: England's Military Education before 1642', *Past & Present*, 147 (1995), 65–100, (p. 71).

64 Robert Barret, *The Theorike and Practike of Moderne Warres discoursed in dialogue wise* (London, 1598), p.5.

65 BL, Ms Harley 2135, ff.69v–71r; BL, Ms Add 11331, f.137r; *BLB*, I, 1.; Abram, "Sufficiently Different', pp.220–38; 'Military Professionals, pp.113–34.

to Britain with as many soldiers of note as he could bring with him.[66] He was commissioned Sergeant-Major-General of the King's forces at Newcastle upon Tyne in April 1640, and of the trained bands of Yorkshire and sundry other companies in September 1640.[67] Similarly, James Ussher was an Anglo-Irish officer who had served effectively in the Bishops' Wars and was killed during the storming of Lichfield by Royalist troops on 20 April 1643.

Nonetheless, like other civil war troops, some dragoons (rightly or wrongly) drew criticisms for plundering and acts of ill-discipline. These soldiers fought in all the major armies of the Thirty Years' War, gaining a distasteful reputation amongst some observers. In his book on the history and art of war, the Duc de Rohan considered that 'they have ruined the infantry, every man desiring to have a nag so that he might be fitter to rob and to pillage.'[68] Similarly, Jacob von Grimmelshausen made it clear in his rollicking, probably semi-autobiography that dragoons serving in Germany were looked down upon, particularly by 'proper' cavalry, and did little to dispel the impression that these soldiers were disreputable.[69] Such distain was shared by the former Royalist Thomas Lacy, who remarked in his satire *The Old Troop*, 'Rascals, did I not know you at first to be three tattered musketeers, and by plundering a malt-mill of three blind horses, you then turned dragooners.'[70]

All the dragoons in the Earl of Stamford's Parliamentarian army in the West (including Sergeant-Major Balfour's and Captain Edward Freeman's companies, the latter having served as part of the Gloucester and Tewkesbury garrisons) were stood down during the armistice of 28 February 1643. Though this may have been for organisational purposes, on 15 April Stamford reported to the Speaker, 'of dragoons none at all, for I have found that they serve their own turns by plundering and robbing, but do little service or serve at all.'[71] When in April 1643 troops of the Eastern Association Army (principally Sir Miles Hobart's regiment of foot) under the command of Colonel Oliver Cromwell arrived in Peterborough *en route* to besiege the Royalist garrison of Crowland its cathedral was despoiled and the vandalising of religious images, tombs, books and medieval stained glass, deemed to be 'popish' continued for some days.[72] The promotion of Puritan iconoclastic practices, with ordinances introduced throughout 1643, for the purging of such images, was common among the Eastern Association. Hence, when the city of York was seized by the following year by the Parliamentarians, following their triumph at Marston Moor, Sir Thomas Fairfax proclaimed

66 BRO, R/Z10/9/1–3 – Passports and safe conduct for Sir Arthur Aston: Passport to travel to Germany, 3 March 1635; General safe conduct, 29 March 1641; Passport to travel to Holland, 10 April 1645.

67 BRO, R/Z10/1–2.

68 Henri, Duc de Rohan, *The Complete Captain* (London: 1631), p.10.

69 J. A. Underwood (trans), Johan Jakob Christoffel von Grimmelshausen, *The Adventures of Simplicius Simplicissimus* (Harmondsworth: Penguin, 2018), pp.81–4, 205.

70 Thomas Lacy, *The Old Troop, or, Monsieur Raggou: as it was acted at the Theatre-Royal* (London: 1672), p.2.

71 HMC, *Thirteenth Report, App. 1*, p.703.

72 *Speciall Passages and Certain Informations*,18–25 April 1643; *Mercurius Aulicus*, 26 April–1 May 1643.

there was to be no ransacking or destruction of the city's churches, and the stained glass and other treasures of the Minster remained intact.

Soon after the first attacks on Peterborough Cathedral (others occurred again in July 1643) Parliamentarian patrols continued to frequent local churches. On 10 June soldiers from Captain Richard Beaumont's company of the Earl of Manchester's dragoon regiment appeared in the village of Yaxley in Huntingdonshire, four miles south of Peterborough, where they broke into St Peter's Church, and according to one account, did 'piss in the font, and then baptise a horse and mare, using the solemn words of baptism, and signing them with the sign of the Cross.'[73] In early 1644, Colonel John Pickering's dragoon regiment was among the Eastern Association troops besieging Hillesden House in Buckinghamshire. In February, Parliamentary forces retreated before a Royalist attack, and the King's troops occupied and fortified the late medieval mansion. On 4 March Cromwell and Sir Samuel Luke led 2,000 men against it, overrunning the trenches and expelling a small Royalist outpost from the church. Though the governor surrendered the house as Cromwell was preparing to storm it, the place was ransacked in search of treasure and burnt to the ground. Pickering's dragoons, amongst other Parliamentarian soldiers, were accused of indiscipline and described by a member of the Royalist Verney family as 'a rude multitude, most of them pressed into service'.[74]

As specialist mounted troops, the work of civil war dragoons, apart from their regular roles of reconnaissance, battlefield operations and siege-work, was wide and various. In December 1642, a force of volunteer Parliamentarian dragoons was established in Norfolk to 'keep the county from plundering', and arms were bought 'for the defence of the county.'[75] Escorting convoys of arms, ammunition, clothing, and provisions to field units and garrisons was common. In July 1643, a munitions convoy bound for Hopton's Cornish foot became caught up at Devizes. To alleviate the situation the King ordered Sir John Heydon, Lieutenant-General of the Ordnance, 'to send to the army under Lord Marquis of Hertford,' 15cwt of match, powder and musket shot 'on horseback by dragoons in bags behind them for the more speedy expedition, for that it much imports the safety of that Our army to hasten it with all possible diligence.'[76] As part of the relief column dispatched to relive Gloucester, on 21 March 1644 1,000 Parliamentarian cavalry and dragoons were stated to be at Stratford-upon-Avon 'as a convoy to carry in their knapsacks and on spare horses, powder and provisions into [the town]'.[77] Likewise, on 28 September the Committee of the Militia was instructed to supply 40 dragoons to escort wagons carrying arms and clothes for the Earl of Essex's army from London to Godalming. The next day, the Committee of Kent ordered Captain Sir John Browne with 70 horse and dragoons to be

---

73 Jack Higham (ed.), Simon Gunton, *History of the Church in Peterborough* (Peterborough and Stamford: Clay Books, 1990), p.335.

74 HMC, *Seventh Report*, pp.446–7; Frances P. Verney, *Memoirs of Verney Family during the Civil War* (London: Longmans, Green & Co., 1892), II, pp.196–7.

75 Bodl. Lib., Ms Tanner 64, ff.99r & 101r.

76 TNA, WO55/495, ff.347r.–49r.; Bod Lib., Ms Rawlinson D395, ff.36v–37r.

77 *CSPD 1644*, p.64.

in Southwark the following night to convoy provisions for Essex's forces to Arundel, and from here they were to accompany another convoy.[78]

Dragoons were also called upon for escort duties in support of the New Model Army. On 10 June 1645, Parliament ordered the provision of '100 dragoons to convoy the money to be sent to Sir Thomas Fairfax's army, and that they shall be paid for the same.' Additionally, parties of dragoons conveyed recruits and accompanied convoys of provisions and money from London, St Albans and Reading to the New Model in the West Country, and other Parliamentarian forces during the winter of 1645–46.[79] In October 1645, during the Parliamentarian siege of Chester, Sergeant-Major Jerome Zankey, the officer commanding Sir William Brereton's own cavalry troop was authorised to 'go out speedily with a significant army of horse and dragoons to fetch out of Wales so many cattle' for the provisioning of the besieging troops. This was advantageous because he also gained intelligence about a Royalist force of around 1,000 horse and some foot near Ruthin, where they were recruiting.[80] Such operations could be discovered and countered by enemy troops, however. On 9 May 1643 it was reported by a Royalist newsbook:

> It was advertised also out of Staffordshire, that his Majesty's forces garrisoned in Tamworth Castle, having notice of 200 foot and dragoons, that were sent from Coventry to carry provisions and supplies to some of their accomplices in Maxstoke Castle (not far from Coleshill, in the county of Warwick) met them in the way, and fell so unexpectedly upon them, that they killed 25 in the place, took 18 of their horses, with their arms and weapons, put all the residue to flight, and hindered the designed supply from going forwards[81]

Intelligence gathering, scouts and scouting patrols often supplied seventeenth century military commanders with timely and accurate information about enemy troop dispositions, strengths, and movements. Cruso, an authority on cavalry tactics placed great emphasis on operational intelligence, writing:

> Every good commander must have these two good grounds for his actions: 1. The knowledge of his own forces, and wants (knowing that the enemy may have notice of thereof and therefore must always be studying for remedies, if the enemy should come suddenly upon him). 2. The assurance of the condition and estate of the enemy, his commodities and necessities, his councils and designs, thereby begetting divers occasions, which afterwards may bring forth victories[82]

Cavalry and dragoons were the customary sources of reconnaissance because of their capacity to cover a wide area and report back quickly. Moreover,

78 *Ibid.*, pp.290–2 & 538–9.
79 *CSPD 1644–45*, pp.151, 196, 253, 267–8, 306, 359, 402, 434, 584.
80 BL, Ms Add 11332, ff.31v–32r, 47r; *BLB*, II, 676, 774–5.
81 *Mercurius Aulicus*, 9–16 May 1643.
82 Cruso, *Militarie Instructions*, p.81.

dragoons were particularly experienced in operating as detached mounted formations covering a wide variety of tasks.

Amongst larger armies the responsibility for scouting was typically assigned to the Lieutenant-General of Horse. Cruso (among others) advised that spies (scouts) should be 'choice men, valiant, vigilant and discreet.' Sir Samuel Luke, MP for Bedford and Captain of horse was employed as Scoutmaster-General to the Earl of Essex's army in January 1643, with the governorship of what became the major Parliamentarian garrison at Newport Pagnell. Thus, Luke possessed interests in, and frequently contributed to, Parliamentarian operations over a wide area of the south and east Midlands. He was by provided with funding for 24 men and horses 'who were employed daily as spies into the enemy's armies and garrisons.'[83] Luke was a vigilant and painstaking intelligence officer who, valuing the importance of loyalty, recruited his scouts in the early part of the conflict from soldiers of his own cavalry troop and regiment of dragoons. His Parliamentarian colleague, Sir William Brereton, effectively utilised a network of intelligencers throughout Cheshire and the Midlands, which reported vital information on the movements and numbers of enemy troops, as well as the presence of key commanders, such as Prince Maurice.

Additionally, one of Brereton's dragoon captains, William Wright, testified that upon his commission, dated 11 April 1644, he was sent 'to quarter in Aston [in Cheshire] and maintain a force, to prevent the enemy from making incursion into safe places.'[84] Thus, his company seems to have been tasked with the patrolling of river crossings into, and the internal security of the vitally important parts of the county between the Rivers Mersey and Weaver. These dragoons were maintained and supplied by local townships. Two undated warrants relate to the provision of mounts and food. Captain Richard Littler instructed Thomas Woollett, one of the constables of Aston township (the home of the Royalist, Sir Thomas Aston), 'to provide Sergeant Hall [with] two horses, one of your own, the other from George Guest, for scout horses this night for our safeties and the safety of this township.' Additionally, the constables of Bucklow Hundred charged those of Aston and Aston Grange with bringing each day two horse load of oats to Great Budworth, presumably for the dragoon horses. The township of Aston was also responsible for finding pay for Littler's soldiers. A warrant issued by Colonel Henry Brooke on 2 September 1643 informed the officials:

> I formerly sent out several leys to them for collecting of moneys for the dragoons and as you are, as appears, behind with your payment. These are henceforth to charge and command you that you are besides with and withal four weeks' pay more at 6s 6d per week, which you to supply at Norton before 7 [September] 1643 to my clerk.[85]

---

83 TNA, SP28/23, f.8r; I. G. Philip (ed.), *Journal of Sir Samuel Luke* (Oxford: Oxfordshire Record Society, 1950), I, p.xi.

84 TNA, E121/351, ff.63r–63v; BL, Ms Harley 2128, f.166r.

85 Aston, unlisted warrants, dated 20 November 1643 x 2 February 1644, 2 September 1643.

When attached to field armies, dragoons were often placed on picket duty, often making use of the firelock muskets at night, when the glow of a match could advertise the positions of military units. Colonel John Okey's regiment of the New Model Army was detailed to perform all picket duties during the 1645–46 campaign, even though the cavalry carried carbines. Similarly, during the Parliamentarian siege of Chester, detachments from Sir William Brereton's dragoon companies were often co-located with troops of horse in the most remote and vulnerable areas on the Welsh side of the River Dee.

Mounted forces of all armies were also engaged in punitive expeditions and tax collecting raids. When Parliament's weekly and monthly assessments began in the winter of 1642–3, the £3,000 monthly levy rapidly proved unpopular in Worcestershire. Thus, from March 1643 onwards it became necessary to employ mounted troops to collect arrears.[86] While quartered in Wiltshire in January 1644 Prince Rupert authorised Sir Thomas Aston, 'Colonel of one regiment of horse and one regiment of dragoons in his Majesty's army':

> for the accommodation and subsistence of your regiments you are from time to time to receive levy, take and fetch your maintenance for the same out of the aforesaid hundreds according to the number of your effective officers and soldiers, and his Majesty's allowance in the last establishment for the maintenance of his horse forces and dragoons … And in the interim, you must strictly command all your officers to by no means transgress or exceed your aforesaid directions or suffer any oppression to be enforced on any of the inhabitants of these towns, parishes, and places in the hundreds aforesaid from which you shall receive your maintenance for your said regiments of horse and dragoons by any soldiers under your command. And if at any time any town, towns, parishes or places in these said hundreds, which by agreement shall be to allow you maintenance for your said regiments of horse and dragoons shall neglect the punctual payment or delivery for your due maintenance to such your troops as they shall be to maintain, immediately after the same shall become due it shall then become lawful for you from time to time to levy all and every their arrears by such parties of horse as you shall think fit.[87]

A few months later, Aston sanctioned Captain William Ratcliffe of his own cavalry regiment, 'to send out troops from Westbury hundred to various townships, to collect contributions for the week 25 February to 5 March.'[88] Periodically, however, such activities could prove hazardous to the soldiers involved, especially when faced with the opposition of reluctant civilians. The accounts of the collectors for Bucklow Hundred in Cheshire include the sum of 6s 'paid to Captain John Brooke's soldiers distraining upon John Laughton's goods at two several times and carrying them to Daresbury.'[89] Moreover, on 5 May 1645 Brooke (temporarily commanding the cavalry

86 Bodl. Lib., Ms Rawlinson D924, f.152r.

87 WRO, X3/119/AC/1.

88 WRO, X3/119/AC/17.

89 BL, Ms Harley 2166, f.130r; 2136, f.39v; 2128, f.119r.

troop of his brother, Colonel Henry) reported that a corporal of his, having been

> 'sent over into Cheshire out of Wales to collect pay, as well as for some soldiers in his squadron as for myself' was set upon by locals from the township, whereupon 'Mr Daniell himself run violently to have stabbed him with a knife, which by God's providence fortuned upon a belly-piece on his doublet, otherwise he had either slain him or much endangered his life, being just opposite to his heart.'[90]

Such attacks on troops and local Parliamentarian officials were not uncommon, especially during the latter stages of the conflict. There were anti-excise riots in Warrington in 1645 and in southwest Lancashire in 1649. In April 1645 Colonel John Moore was ordered to dispatch troops to the town to settle taxes and punish defaulters.[91]

90 BL, Ms Add 11331, f.79v.; *BLB*, I, 457.
91 TNA, SP24/15/8; SP24/74.

3

Organisation and Composition of Dragoon Units

As seventeenth century dragoons were, in their basic role, mounted foot, in most cases they were organised along the same lines as infantry regiments, with their officers and non-commissioned officers holding similar ranks, except the cornet, who carried the guidon or colour. But although they were formed into companies, some – mostly those attached to cavalry regiments – in their operational roles were akin to troops of horse. It was more usual for dragoon regiments to consist of five or six companies or troops. Although some managed to come close to this, especially during the early months of the First Civil War, other regiments never reached that number and were often no more than large companies. The establishment for civil war dragoon regiments was 1,000 men in 10 companies of 100 dragoons each, besides officers, but this was rarely achieved in practice. Similarly, the establishment for the New Model Army's only regiment of dragoons, that commanded by Colonel John Okey, was projected in December 1644 to be 1,500 men, besides commissioned and non-commissioned officers, although this was revised by the Commons on 11 January 1645 to 1,000 dragoons in 10 companies.[1] During the first half of 1645 numbers in Okey's regiment remained significantly lower and it remains unlikely that the establishment figure was ever reached.

On 1 November 1641, the English Parliament received news of a Catholic Confederate rebellion in Ireland. Initially, an army of 2,000 horse and 6,000 foot was to be raised to suppress it, but later it was enlarged to 10,000 with an appeal to the Scots for a similar number for the defence of Ulster.[2] Although this force was placed under the authority of Robert Sidney, Earl of Leicester, he remained in England throughout the emergency and command in Ireland was given to James Butler, Earl of Ormond who had been appointed Lieutenant-General. Ormond's first task was to select the forces to be sent in response to Charles I's orders. These were a mix of existing regiments, which were mostly shipped to Ireland from Chester, Neston and Liverpool during

1 *CSPD 1644–1645*, p.205; *CJ*, IV, pp.16–17.

2 *CJ*, II, pp.300–13; *LJ*, IV, pp.412, 421, 438, 486.

the early months of 1642.[3] At the start of the insurrection the only forces in Ireland were the 39 infantry companies and 14 cavalry troops of the Old Standing Army, spread across the provinces of Leinster, Munster, Connaught and Ulster. Three independent companies of dragoons were raised by the English Parliament in 1641–2 for service with Ormond's army. To enable the maintenance and equipping of these units the Commons agreed on 17 December 1641:

> That £179 4s 0d, being for one month's pay, shall be paid to the officers of the 300 dragoons, in three companies. That £5 0s 0d a horse shall be allowed for the 300 dragoons, and for the 33 horses for the officers, allowing to every company eleven horses, for the levying of them, and bringing them upon the place of muster in Ireland; and then to enter into pay. Owen O'Connell be, from this House, recommended to the Lord Lieutenant of Ireland, to have the command of one of the companies of dragoons.[4]

Thus, money was levied for the soldiers' pay in January 1642, and in April they, in company with five troops of horse, received a month's pay.[5] Thus, Captain Radcliffe Duckenfield's company of 100 dragoons, besides commissioned and non-commissioned officers, temporarily under the command of Cornet William Crofton, was paid the sum of £274 17s 4d; Captain Nathaniel Moyle's and Captain Adam Paite's equally sized commands received the same, although a different set of payments lists the latter as mustering 180 dragoons. Moreover, the sum of £4 4s 0d was disbursed to John Mercer, described as 'surgeon to the three troops of dragoons.'[6] All three companies were shipped from Chester to Dublin in April 1642. According to a list of 'money paid to several owners of ships for transportation of the regiment of troopers, carbines and dragoons at 2s 0d per man and 12s 0d per horse,' Captain Duckenfield's soldiers and their horses were transported in five different vessels, at a cost to the State of £69 12s 0d; Captain Moyle's aboard four ships at a cost of £75 8s 0d; and Captain Paite in three at a cost of £51 12s 0d.[7]

On 23 January 1643, Lord Inchiquin had informed Speaker Lenthall that 'the lightness of the Irish foot requires us to have a regiment of dragoons and boldly desire Lieutenant Colonel Mynne may have the command of them.'[8] Nicholas Mynne, an experienced officer, had previously served in Sir Charles Vavasour's regiment of foot in Ireland. Parliament, however, was already in

3 See, for example, disbursements made by the mayor and aldermen of Chester for pay and provisions to various military officers and units, including the Lord Lieutenant's regiment of horse and Captain Thomas Sandford's company of firelocks between January and April 1642 prior to their embarkation for Ireland (CRO, DCC/14/3–78; DCC/47/22–40; HMC, *Fifth Report, App.*, pp.349–52).

4 *CJ*, II, pp.348, 360.

5 TNA, SP28/1B, ff.323r–327v; Bod Lib., Ms Carte 10, f.603v; Ian Ryder, *An English Army for Ireland* (Leigh-on-Sea: Partizan Press, 1987), p.37.

6 TNA, SP28/147/1, f.1r; SP28/1B, f.325v; HMC, *Fourteenth Report, App. VII*, p.124.

7 TNA, SP28/147/1, ff.8r–9v.

8 *Special Passages*, 24–31 January 1643; *CJ*, II, p.949.

the process of raising such a regiment of dragoons. On 8 December 1642 an order had been issued:

> for levying dragoons in Somersetshire and Cornwall. Resolved, upon the question, that 1,000 dragoons be levied, in Somerset, Devon, and Cornwall; 500 at the officers' own expense, upon adventure for land in Ireland; and 500 to be taken up upon ticket, upon Papists, commissioners of array, non-contributors, and delinquents; and those dragoons to be employed in the service of the western parts till the latter end of March next, and then to be sent into Ireland, for the service of that Kingdom; and that £1,000 be advanced unto them upon account; and likewise ready money to provide arms and 1,000 saddles; and that the said £1,000, and money for arms and saddles, shall be repaid out of the plate raised in the county of Devon and Cornwall upon the Propositions. And that all his Majesty's officers and well-affected persons, who value the Protestant religion, and the safety of their lives and estates, in the peace of the Three Kingdoms, be obliged to assist Captain James Chudleigh, and the other officers of Colonel Mynne's regiment, in the speedily levying of these dragoons; and that all officers and soldiers of the said regiment be required (in absence of their colonel) to obey the said Captain Chudleigh, their officer-in-chief, according to the discipline of war.[9]

Chudleigh was duly commissioned Colonel of the regiment, but after serving with it in the West Country, in 1643 he defected to the King's army and his seemingly collection of dragoon companies disbanded.

Various independent dragoon units of sub-regimental or company strength are known to have been raised and operated during the wars. Sir William Constable's regiment – ostensibly a company under Captain John George – operated in the East Riding of Yorkshire from September 1643 until April 1644. In early 1644 the unit passed to Sir William Fairfax and participated in the relief of Nantwich.[10] Also, the dragoon company raised in 1642 by Sir Thomas Norcliffe of Langton, in the East Riding of Yorkshire, took part in the storming of Leeds by Parliamentarian forces in January 1643, but during the September they converted to cavalry. Norcliffe led his dragoons from 12 December 1642 to 18 September 1643. On the latter date he was commissioned captain of horse, and fought at Winceby and Nantwich, so the dragoons might have been upgraded as part of Sir Thomas Fairfax's Regiment of horse. On 22 May 1644, Sir Thomas Norcliffe was commissioned Colonel of his own cavalry regiment, and was at the siege of York, the fight at Marston Moor and the siege of Pontefract.[11]

Regiments of dragoons and individual companies (also referred to as troops in some documents) were recruited by both sides, although some came and went, and several units remain obscure, both in their origins and

9 *LJ*, V, p.482.

10 TNA, SP28/247/3, ff.64v–66r; Jennifer Jones, 'The War in the North: The Northern Parliamentary Army in the English Civil War, 1642–1645', PhD thesis (York University, Toronto, 1994), pp.375–6.

11 TNA, SP28/41, ff.125r–126v; SP28/266/1, f.95r; BL, Ms Add 11331, ff.41v & 56r; *BLB*, I, 392–3.

history. Thus, a remarkably small quantity of surviving documents shed light on the commissioning of dragoon commanders in the Royalist army, and the strengths of their units, although some letters, muster rolls, pay warrants and some anecdotal material provide information on the origins of specific units. Further records, in the form of testimonials and petitions, often regarding outstanding arrears of pay are more plentiful for the Parliamentarians, and especially commissioned officers. Thus, in the Cheshire forces commanded by Sir William Brereton, the certificate of service of Captain John Lea records that his company was raised in London in autumn 1642, and that he was in actual service from 7 November 1642 until 12 November 1643, being some 370 days.[12] The testament of Captain William Wright, dated 12 August 1647, states that he received his commission as captain of dragoons on 11 April 1644, serving in command of his company until 30 September 1644.[13] Equally, Jane Castlon petitioned the Warwickshire Committee on 15 March 1645 that her husband, Ralph, had served as Captain and Sergeant-Major of dragoons under Lord Brooke in Staffordshire from 27 January 1643 to 1 October 1644, at which point he became Captain-Lieutenant to Colonel Thomas Mytton's troop of horse.[14]

Dragoon units in the Earl of Newcastle's army in the north were few, while evidence for their existence is slight and often dependent on oblique references to officers' names. Sir Edmund Duncombe's regiment was recruited hurriedly in August-September 1642, before fighting at Edgehill with the Oxford Army, where it was described being '500 strong'.[15] This was possibly a rounded-up figure, however, as there are suggestions that various individual troop formations were combined into one specific regiment, which later participated in the Royalist attack on Cirencester (where it probably sustained heavy losses) before returning to its native Yorkshire.[16] On 17 May, Sir Samuel Luke, Scoutmaster-General to the Earl of Essex, reported, 'Colonel Duncombe, who lay about Faringdon with 500 men, which he had a long time maintained at his own charge, for want of money to pay them, both himself, and 40 of his officers and 80 of his soldiers are gone quite away, and the rest were either lost, killed or run away before.'[17] P. R. Newman suggests that survivors of the regiment 'might have been combined into Lord Belasyse's (Northern) Regiment of foot after Selby, and stayed in York rather than fighting at Marston Moor.'[18]

12 TNA, SP28/252/1, f.184v; SP28/265/1, ff.68r–68v & 70r.

13 BL, Ms Harley 2128, f.166r; TNA: SP28/208, f.33v; E121/351, ff.63r–63v.

14 TNA, SP28/247, f.7r.

15 *A Most True Relation of the Present State of His Majesties Army: Wherein Also the Truth of that Declaration Published by the Parliament, of Their Happy Victory in the Battaile at Keynton, is Both Justly Asserted and Abundantly Proved, Humbly Presented by the Author who was Personally Present, to the Honourable the Lords and Commons in Parliament Assembled* (London: 3 December 1642). TT, E244 [2].

16 BL, Ms Harley 6851, f.237r; Peter Young, *Edgehill 1642: The Campaign and the Battle* (Kineton: Roundwood Press, 1967), pp.85 & 187.

17 Luke, *Letter Books*, p.77.

18 P. R. Newman, 'The Royalist Army in Northern England, 1642–45', PhD thesis (University of York, 1978), II, p.498.

The genesis of Sir Thomas Gower's regiment is puzzling in that on 22 August 1642 he was commissioned to raise 1,000 dragoons, effectively two regiments. He could have kept one and given the other to Colonel Duncombe.[19] What became of Gower's dragoons is uncertain, but they might have been absorbed into his cavalry regiment. By contrast, Colonel Francis Carnaby's dragoons appear to have formed a single company, raised in Northumberland in 1642.[20] Again, the history of the formation is obscure, though it might have been attached to Carnaby's regiment of horse as an extra troop, or simply absorbed by it. Commissioned to raise a regiment of 500 dragoons in January 1643, Sir Thomas Aston initially recruited 220 men divided into four companies. Some of the dragoon officers were Chester men and there were links with the 'city regiment'. Captain Thomas Newland brought in his '60 foot part raised and armed' to form one troop. Aston's dragoon formation seems to have been included as part of the main 'regiment' of horse, with which it frequently served.[21] The King's nephew, Prince Rupert, commissioned John Warcup as Lieutenant-Colonel in Aston's regiment of dragoons on 5 January 1644.[22] A muster of Sergeant-Major Michael Mason's cavalry troop taken in mid–1645, includes the last of Aston's dragoons, being the survivors of Captain Thomas Newland's dragoon company, which had been formed nearly three years earlier, and newly converted to horse under Michael Mason, another dragoon officer.

An additional troop list, undated but probably made up about the same time (given that two of the commissioned officers had been promoted and the same names of the troopers appear), includes annotations in Sir Thomas Aston's hand, appearing to denote deficiencies of military equipment and clothing amongst 25 members of the transformed unit, or at least his plan to convert the dragoons into horse.[23] These soldiers would appear to have been formerly dragoons:

Richard Foster – helmet, carbine
George Mason – helmet, pistol
John Moss – helmet, carbine
Gerard Burne – helmet, carbine, boots
Thomas Carter – helmet
Abraham Nobbs – helmet, carbine
William Francis – boots
William Chad – helmet, carbine
James Hargreave – helmet, carbine, sword
Marmaduke Corke – helmet, carbine, boots
Ellis Burkett – helmet, carbine, sword
Thomas Chevers – helmet, carbine, sword

19 *True Proceedings from York, and a True Relation of the Manner of his Majesties setting up of his standard at Nottingham* (London: 22 August 1642). TT, E115 [4]; HMC, *Fifth Report, App. I*, pp.191, 193.
20 Newman, 'Royalist Army', II, p.495.
21 BL, Ms Add 36913, ff 88r–94v, 101v, 105r, 107r–108v; BL, Ms Harley 6853, ff.149r–151v.
22 SofA, Ms 138, f.130r.
23 BL, Ms Harley 6852, ff.151r–2v.

Martin Edwards – boots
Robert Leigh – helmet, pistol
William Bennett – boots, stockings
Roger Parker – helmet, carbine
George Shepard – helmet, carbine, pistol
John Perry – helmet, carbine, pistol
John Clarkson – helmet, carbine
Thomas Baker – helmet, pistol, shirt
John Stanley – helmet, carbine
John Stone – helmet, carbine, pistol, boots
John Carter – boots
Robert Strong jnr – helmet, carbine, sword

The early happenings of Sir Vincent Corbet's dragoons in Shropshire were somewhat precarious. In December 1642 it was agreed that 'up to a thousand or at least 600 dragoons' be procured by the subscriptions of thirty-three Royalist gentry.[24] Corbet's commission as Colonel of dragoons was authorised, 'for the defence of his Majesty and that county'.[25] The arrangement for raising these soldiers was extended to provide for their maintenance by a general tax on the county. Yet by the following month most of the subscriptions had failed to materialise. At their first muster, the dragoons numbered 60 men, and by January 1643 less than 300 men had been recruited. Sir Vincent's hastily raised and inexperienced men joined Sir Thomas Aston's troops as they returned to Cheshire from their quarters in Reading in January 1643. However, they were overwhelmed at Nantwich by Sir William Brereton's Parliamentarian forces. Brereton later described that during the action the 50 dragoons of Corbet's regiment were ordered to occupy the town, but they 'were presently disordered and many of them ran away without ever giving fire.'[26] John Harrington, a relative of the Royalist leader in Shropshire, Sir Francis Ottley, wrote, 'I was heartily sorry to see Sir Vincent Corbet so poorly furnished with raw soldiers and young commanders.'[27] These dragoons continued to operate in and around Cheshire, Shropshire and the Welsh borders until 1646.

In army pay warrants the sub-regimental units of dragoons were generally referred to as 'companies', and occasionally 'troops', doubtless because of their association with equestrian formations. Moreover, owing to their often independent and specialist roles, and the specific circumstances of their origins, it was common to find independent, unregimented dragoon units in Royalist and Parliamentarian forces, as well as the Army of the Solemn League and Covenant. On 1 November 1642, Parliament ordered that Captain William Hill of Tewkesbury receive money from the collectors

---

24 WA, CR2017/C176;HMC, *Tenth Report, App. IV*, pp.403–4.

25 BL, Ms Harley 6851, ff.236r & 248r; SA,6000/13291.

26 *Cheshire's Successe since their pious and truly valiant Colonel, Sir William Brereton, Baronet, came to their rescue, &c.* (London, 20 March 1643). TT, E94 [6]

27 William Phillips, 'The Ottley Papers relating to the Civil War', *TSANHS*, 2nd Series, VI (1894), pp.27–78, (p. 69).

in Gloucester for the raising and pay of 100 dragoons and officers in Sir William Waller's Southern Association Army. He received the sum of £320 for forming a company, but whether he attracted the required 100 recruits is unclear. On 24 March 1643 Captain Hill received a gratuity for his service at Highnam House.[28] This officer served in the same army as Captain of horse from 28 March to 11 December 1643, then as Captain-Lieutenant in the foot regiment of Colonel Christopher Potley between 14 March and 10 September 1644. He retained that command until the regiment was reduced in April 1645.

On 23 October 1646 Nathaniel Hill, 'brother and administrator to Captain William Hill, deceased' petitioned Parliament:

> That his brother, holding a commission from the Earl of Essex to raise a troop of dragoons in county Gloucester, borrowed several sums of him, being then under-sheriff of that county, to furnish his troop, upon promise of repayment. His brother for two years having faithfully and valiantly conducted himself in the Parliament's service, at length came to London sick and wounded, and died, leaving the sums of money so borrowed wholly unsatisfied. Now that it has pleased God to give the Parliament victory over their enemies, whereby men may now quietly come to London, the petitioner is required to pay in the money he received when sheriff, but which he lent to his brother, so that he is not able to do as required, and is likely to be ruined, unless some speedy course be taken whereby he may receive his brother's arrears [of pay], amounting to about £1,000, of which no penny has yet been received[29]

Captain Robert Allan led his independent company of dragoons to Beverley on 30 June 1643 to defend it against Royalist forces commanded by Sir Hugh Holley. The unit was perhaps later integrated into Sir William Constable's regiment of dragoons.[30] Likewise, Colonel John Hilton recruited a single company of dragoons (under the command of Captain Francis Jackson) in County Durham in late 1642, which was associated with his own infantry regiment in the north.[31]

Because of their sometimes-piecemeal nature, garrison forces tended to include a variety of troop types, and they could either contain a proportion of dragoons or were made up entirely of such soldiers. In his study of the Royalist army in the North of England, Newman found that garrisons 'tended to blur the normal distinctions between horse, foot and dragoons'.[32] More generally, commissioned dragoon officers could serve both in units of horse and dragoons (sometimes contemporaneously), as well as fluctuate between various dragoon units. This often confuses their appearance and dates of service in surviving pay warrants and other documents. On 6 December 1642, Parliamentarian justices ordered 'the raising of a body

28 *CJ*, II, p.829; *LJ*, V, p.437; Peachey and Turton, *Fall of the West*, VI, p.631.
29 *CSPD 1645–7*, p.481.
30 Jones, 'War in the North', p.367.
31 Newman, 'Royalist Army', II, pp.495, 506.
32 *Ibid.*, p.373.

of dragoons to garrison the town of Cirencester', and soon afterwards, horses and pay were provided for the four companies duly recruited.[33] The Royalists regarded this garrison, like that of Marlborough, as a threat to their domination of the region around Oxford. Thus, when the Marquess of Hertford reinforced the Royal capital with 2,000 Welsh levies in January 1643, he advised the King that while Cirencester stayed in enemy hands, his forces 'could not long subsist, the stores of all places (where they were masters), being near spent and exhausted.'[34]

Such dragoons were encountered by the Royalist commander, Sir John Byron, during an attempt to resupply Hertford's troops in the Cotswolds. As the Royalist newsbook *Mercurius Aulicus* reported on 1 January 1643:

> On Friday being the 30th day of December, Sir John had order to march with his whole regiment to Burford (a town about 12 miles from Oxford) to convey thither two cart loads of ammunition for the Lord Marquess of Hartford, who was expected the next day at Stow, with all his forces. Being arrived at his quarter, his first enquiry was what forces the rebels had at Cirencester, or any other place adjoining. In which when as he could receive no satisfaction from the townsmen there, he sent a party of horse that night towards Cirencester, who went within a mile and a half of the town, and brought word, that there were not above 500 dragoons there quartered, the horse which had been there being marched to Tetbury. The next day being Saturday there was little news, more than the day before had yielded. But about seven of the clock at night, a party that had been sent forth towards the enemy, brought word, that about two miles from the town in the way to Cirencester they had discovered four dragoons with light matches, who so soon as they made towards them, rode back so fast that they could by no means overtake them. Sir John imagining by this discovery that there might be some design that night upon his quarter, commanded Captain St John to ride towards Cirencester with 40 horse; and that the whole regiment should be in a readiness[35]

In South Yorkshire the Royalist gentry fortified their manor houses against the vigorous activities of the Parliamentarian forces commanded by the Fairfaxes in late 1642. The unpopular Sir Francis Wortley garrisoned his home at Tankersley with 150 dragoons, while the constables of ten local townships received orders from the Crown to contribute to the maintenance of the garrison. In the October he was described as one of the 'chief cavaliers that bear sway in the city of York.'[36] The following month Wortley

33 GA, D2510/11–12.

34 John Washbourne (ed.), *Bibliotheca Gloucestrensis: A Collection of Scarce and Curious Tracts Relating to the County and City of Gloucester* (Gloucester, 1825), p.178.

35 *Mercurius Aulicus*, 1–7 January 1643.

36 *True Proceedings from York, and a True Relation of the Manner of his Majesties setting up of his standard at Nottingham* (London: 22 August 1642). TT, E115 [4]; *Terrible News From York sent in a letter to London* (London, 1642), ML, CWT, 42-04-08.

led a raid through Derbyshire and Staffordshire, recruiting, according to a Parliamentarian newsbook, 'miners and other base shag-raggs' as he went.[37]

The Royalist garrison of Skipton contained dragoon companies among its numbers. In February 1643 Sir John Mallory's 700-strong 'regiment' at Skipton include 150 dragoons under Captain William Prideaux, although a later petition of the maimed soldier, Samuel Constantine of Kettlewell, mentions that he was 'first listed by Captain Cuthbert Wade, Esquire, in his troop of dragoons under the command of Sir John Mallory.'[38] Sir Thomas Hanmer's Royalist dragoons, originally raised in September 1642, served predominantly in the Chirk garrison following the seizure of the castle from the Parliamentarian leader Sir Thomas Myddelton.[39]

Skipton Castle (author's photo)

Captain Edward Freeman commanded an independent company of dragoons in the West Country as part of the Parliamentarian garrisons of Hereford, Gloucester and Tewkesbury between 27 September 1642 and 16 March 1643, at which point he took a commission in the Earl of Stamford's regiment of Horse, perhaps taking his men with him.[40] Also in the West Country, Colonel Nicholas Devereux, who had been a Captain and Lieutenant-Colonel of dragoons, maintained such troops as part of the

37 *England's Memorable Accidents*, 31 October–7 November 1642, p.67; HMC, *Ninth Report*, II, p.387.

38 WYL150/5810 (T/32/46); WYHC, QS, 1/14/5/6/1; Richard T. Spence, *Skipton Castle in the Great Civil War 1642–1645* (Skipton Castle, 1991), p.25; Newman, 'Royalist Army', II, p.38.

39 NLW, Ms Bettisfield 111; Hanmer, *Memorial*, pp.64–5.

40 TNA SP28/258, ff.290r–290v; Stuart Peachey and Alan Turton, *The Fall of the West* (Bristol: Stuart Press, 1994), VI, p.632.

garrisons of Malmesbury and Great Chalfield.[41] On 21 August 1643, Sergeant-Major Michael Searle left Colonel William Strode's regiment of foot, which had been raised in Somerset and was serving in the West under Sir William Waller's control, and was recruited into the foot regiment of Sir William Gould in the garrison of Plymouth. Searle was subsequently commissioned Colonel of a regiment of dragoons on 29 June 1644. This remained in the garrison until 30 September 1644, however, between 8 October 1644 and 5 April 1645 his soldiers came under the authority of the Earl of Essex.[42] It is possible that Searle's dragoons were drawn from the disbanded dragoon regiment of Colonel Chudleigh, but also the 150 men drawn from Gould's foot regiment who were immediately mounted, and the remains of the Cornish Horse, which had returned from their mauling at Roundway Down on 13 July 1643. Besides, many of the dragoons in Waller's army had previously served in the Plymouth area.[43] According to pay warrants, Captains Richard Wynch, Nicholas Haywood, and Henry Potter commanded dragoon companies in Searle's regiment from 29 June to 30 September 1644 and in Essex's Army between 8 October 1644 and 5 May 1645. Captain Thomas Cottrell, who had previously served as a company commander in Colonel James Carr's regiment of foot, served under Searle from 29 June to 30 September 1644.[44]

When on 28 July 1643 Oliver Cromwell was made Governor of the Isle of Ely, the Cambridgeshire Trained Bands were summoned to garrison the city. This was probably an auxiliary regiment, which served until 1647. Cromwell commanded some 'loose troops of dragoons' as Lieutenant-General of the Eastern Association Army, a term which might have referred to this Cambridgeshire trained band unit, or other more temporary and less recognised dragoon units, which are known to have been under him. In 1638 the Cambridge Trained Band comprised 1,000 foot and 80 mounted soldiers, the latter consisting of 30 harquebusiers and 50 dragoons. With other militia units from East Anglia, they were selected for service in the First Bishops' War in Sir Simon Harcourt's foot regiment, and in June 1640 they were shipped to Newcastle for service against the Scots.[45] In common with other garrison formations the numerous dragoon units under the auspices of the Eastern Association were led by various officers at different times. Captain Francis Underwood, who is known to have commanded a company of foot by 1 April 1644, also led the dragoons within the garrison of Ely and during Parliamentarian operations against Crowland Abbey.[46] Other companies were led by Captains Henry Cannon and William Miller.[47]

41 TNA, SP28/138/1, f.29r.; J. H. P. Pafford (ed.), *Accounts of the Parliamentary garrisons of Great Chalfield and Malmesbury, 1645–1646*, Wiltshire Archaeological and Natural History Society, Records Series, 2 (Brussels: J. Adam, 1966), pp.65–6.

42 TNA, SP28/253A, 24v; SP28/175, unfol.

43 Peachey and Turton, *Fall of the West*, III, p.360; IV, 447–50; V, pp.556–9.

44 TNA, SP28/253A, ff.2r & 57r; SP28/266/3, f.4v; SP28/267/1, f.114r.

45 Rushworth, *Historical Collections*, III, pp.1085–6.

46 TNA, E121/2/10; Spring, *Eastern Association*, p.70.

47 BL, Ms Harley 427, f.146r; TNA, E121/2/2; E121/3/4; E121/4/1/130; Malcolm Wanklyn, *Reconstructing the New Model Army Volume 1: Regimental Lists April 1645 to May 1649* (Solihull: Helion and Co., 2015), pp.44 & 63.

The Parliamentarian garrison of Aylesbury contained both cavalry and dragoons. The latter, under Captain Edmund Phipps (who claimed pay as captain of a company of dragoons between 3 August 1643 and 13 May 1644) numbered 59 soldiers, besides officers on 16 November 1643.[48] In a similar light, the Parliamentarian garrison at Windsor possessed immense strategic value as the western bulwark for London, but it was also a major distribution centre for supplying goods to the garrisons of the Thames Valley, in addition to the southwest of England and the Midlands.

Equally, from the beginning of the war, Windsor Castle acted as the headquarters for the Parliamentarian armies under both the Earl of Essex and Sir Thomas Fairfax. Windsor's garrison mostly consisted of a regiment of foot, commanded by the governor, Colonel John Venn. Soon after the garrison was established in October 1642 however, Parliament disbursed money for 'the raising of dragoon horses employed under the command of the Lord General at Windsor and elsewhere', with money for meat and pad-saddles for the horses.[49] The garrison accounts mention the purchase, in November 1643, of horse tack, such as bridles, girths and halters, and also state that a number of saddles had been sent for mending.[50] There appears to have been roughly 50 dragoons in the garrison. The dragoon unit was primarily employed in patrolling the hinterland about Windsor and the Thames Valley area.

Similarly, in the Midlands dragoons formed an integral if transitory part of Parliamentarian garrisons under the control of the county forces belonging to Warwickshire and Staffordshire. Though it is difficult to provide an accurate picture of the Edgbaston garrison, because it never acquired a stable organisation, as it was independent of the Warwickshire Committee, the list of units present in July 1644 gives three troops of horse commanded by Colonel Thomas Fox, his brother Sergeant-Major Rheingold Fox, and his brother-in-law Captain Humphrey Tudman. Two companies of dragoons – under Captains Williams and Johnson – made a combined total of 25 commissioned and non-commissioned officers, and 256 soldiers and scouts. However, barely 74 of these dragoons possessed complete arms and mounts. Musters in 1645 and 1646, demonstrate a significant diminution in the size of the garrison: in September 1645 the cavalry troop commanded by Colonel Fox comprised five officers and 35 men; a formation of dragoons under Captain Tudman with three officers and 16 sixteen men; and a company of foot under Captain Johnson, mustering three officers and 26 soldiers, most of whom were ill-equipped.[51]

Given the ad hoc nature of some military garrisons, and circumstances occasioned often by increasing shortages of men and horses, some Royalist cavalry doubled up as dragoons and foot. Colonel Sir Hugh Cholmley's cavalry formed the Parliamentarian garrison of Scarborough until March 1643, when it defected to the Royalists. In 1644 the troopers substituted

48 TNA, SP28/253A, ff.106r–106v; SP28/266/1, f.73r.; SP 28/219, f.182r.; SP 28/220/6, f.121r.

49 *CSPD, 1642*, p.451.

50 TNA, SP28/126/1, f.28v.

51 TNA, SP28/204, unfol.

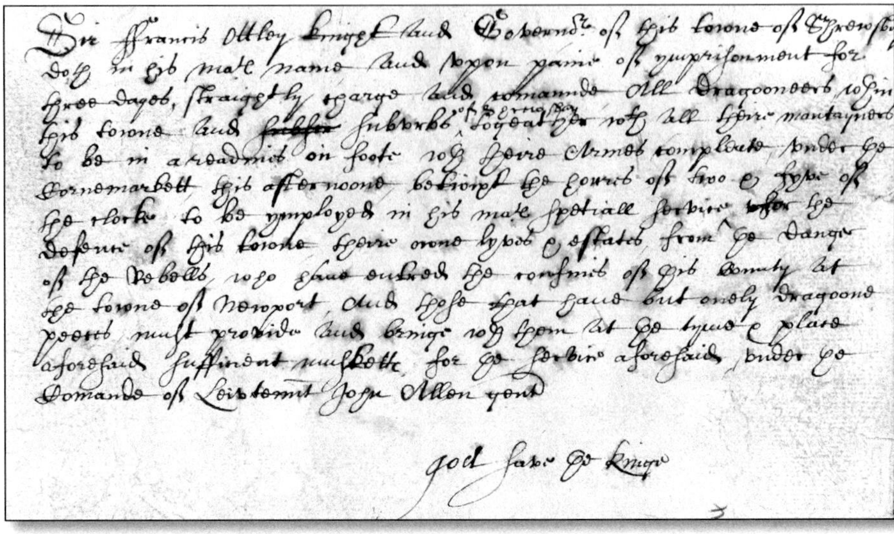
Sir ffrancis Ottley knight and Governor of this towne of Shrewsb[ury] doth in his Ma[jes]t[ie]s name and upon paine of imprisonment for three dayes, straightly charge and commaunde All Dragooneers within this towne and suburbs togeather with all shire-maintayners to be in a readiness on foote with theire Armes compleate under the Cornemarkett this afternoone betwixt the houres of two & three of the clocke to be ymployed in his Ma[jes]t[ie]s speciall service for the defence of this towne theire owne lyves & estates from the danger of the Rebells who have entred the confines of this County at the towne of Newport, And those that have but onely dragoone horses must provide and bringe with them at the tyme & place aforesaid sufficient musketts for the service aforesaid, under the Commande of Leivtennant John Allen yonge

God save the Kinge

Commission of Sir Francis Ottley, Shropshire Archives 6000/13294 (courtesy of Shropshire Archives)

as foot and dragoons.[52] As Newman suggests, with most garrison forces, it is difficult to say with certainty that anything near a regimental structure among the formation was achieved.[53] When the Royalist garrison of Carlisle surrendered in 1645, Sir Thomas Glenham's diminutive regiment of foot, described on 6 August as the 'King's Lifeguard', was ordered to Cardiff, where, according to Richard Symonds, they 'were made dragoons … and march with us.'[54] One reference to the Skipton Horse (possibly including the dragoons), dated 19 January 1644, gives 88 soldiers in the garrison – being 40 in the colonel's troop; 20 in the lieutenant-colonel's; and three captains' troops of 12, 12 and 13 respectively; no sergeant-major's troop is listed, although most of the garrison's horses had been sent to York.[55]

Rather than garrisons, other dragoon units were raised and maintained specifically for the security of local areas, especially during the early part of the war. In late 1642 a company of Royalist dragoons was raised in Shrewsbury for the defence of the town and its environs, under the command of the governor, Sir Francis Ottley, and captained successively by him, and two local officers.[56] Likewise, on 17 October, a troop of horse and 100 dragoons was ordered to be recruited in Devon, 'for the quiet of that county, to answer all alarms, to bring up to Parliament delinquents, and to do other service, as they shall be enjoined by one or both Houses of Parliament.' Both units were to be raised at the charge of the county, and to be paid out of the contribution money of the city of Exeter, where they were to be billeted. To arm the dragoons, 100 snaphaunce muskets were dispatched from London.[57] In a similar fashion, in

52 M. Y. Ashcroft (ed.), *Scarborough Records, 1641–60* (Northallerton: North Yorkshire Record Office, 1991), p.20; Jack Binns, *A Place of Great Importance: Scarborough in the Civil Wars, 1640–60* (Lancaster: Carnegie, 1996), pp.18–20.

53 Newman, 'Royalist Army', II, pp.37–8.

54 C. E. Long (ed.), *Diary of the Marches of the Royal Army during the Great Civil War; kept by Richard Symonds*, Camden Society, Old Series, 74 (1859), p.223.

55 WYA, WYL150/5810 (T/32/46).

56 SA, 6000/13294;'Ottley Papers' (1895), pp.266, 311 & 355–6.

57 *CJ*, II, pp.812, 830.

February 1643, an Ordinance was passed for the establishment of two troops of horse, and a regiment of dragoons in Hampshire, 'for the defence of that county and for raising of monies for the maintenance of those forces', while Parliament further commanded the 'raising of 500 dragoons in the county of Surrey, under the command of Nicholas Stoughton, for the defence of the said county.'[58]

In Sir William Brereton's Cheshire forces, which contained a substantial dragoon element, one company was recruited for the purpose of local or internal security. The Parliamentarian governor of Northwich, Lieutenant-Colonel Gerard, in 1643 raised a unit of three officers, two sergeants, three corporals and 36 dragoons under the command of a local officer, but likely a professional, Captain Richard Littler. Recruited in northwest Cheshire (and more specifically, Northwich town and Hundred), the company's role included patrolling duties in the strategically important area of the Weaver Valley, extending northwards to the garrisons of Halton and Norton, as well as the vital roads and crossings over the River Mersey.[59] Similarly, on 5 August 1650 Thomas Rippon, former Captain in Colonel Ralph Assheton junior's regiment of horse in Lancashire and governor of Lancaster, was authorised to raise four companies of dragoons, 'to be admitted to pay for three months, to be employed in keeping open the passages between Berwick and the army in Scotland.'[60]

As a reflection of the increasingly valuable role of dragoons in mounted warfare, they operated for most of their service in conjunction with the mounted formations of most armies, a feature that followed Continental practice. Orrery recommended that each regiment of horse should consist of six troops of cavalry troopers and one company of dragoons, as he believed that 'dragoons thus annexed to the horse, are much better than they are, when regimented entire, and by themselves.' He gave some practical reasons for this on the basis that the cavalry commanders would be:

> more careful to them, and will not needlessly harass them by extraordinary and unequal duty, and the horse officers knowing all their dragoons by name, and they knowing all the horse officers, they are the more likely to fight cheerfully for them, or not to escape unpunished if they be remiss; for every one being known, none can escape by ignorance; the contrary to which is often experimented [experienced] in commanded parties, when the officers are unknown to the soldiers, and the soldiers to the officers[61]

Orrery left another practical reason until last, as he wrote that 'to omit many other particulars, some have observed that as the dragoons are commonly the briskest, and daringst of the private soldiers, so they are also the least sober', and 'tis likelier to wean them from the fault, when they are but a

58 *Ibid.*, pp.960 & 964.

59 TNA, SP28/224/1, f.40v; Abram, 'Sufficiently Different', p.225; *More Like Lions*, pp.355–6.

60 TNA, E121/3/1; SP 28/252/298; *CSPD 1650*, pp.271, 276 & 334–5.

61 Orrery, *Treatise*, p.24.

seventh part of the regiments, then when they are an entire regiment, and all birds of one feather.'[62]

The reasoning behind either formally including companies or troops of dragoons in cavalry regiments, or attaching dragoons to mounted forces, seems to have been that they provided additional firepower and aided movement, particularly during the initial phases of combat, harassing operations and covering withdrawals. In the long run, however, such associations served only to blur the distinction between the two. Wallhausen, writing in 1632, noted:

> Dragoons are as good as cavalry as they are as infantry to surprise the enemy in camp. The pikemen are very useful to stop enemy cavalry in woods and other places. This sort of cavalry comes in well in battles of columns. For if engaged with the enemy, the advance guard will find it advantageous to order the dragoons to advance against the enemy's formations and troops either on the flank or from the rear. And from the fact that you understand how to employ them, their usefulness, their character and their effect, you will not hold them in contempt but will consider them of great consequence as an innovation and as cavalry.[63]

He did not explicitly state whether he expected these dragoons to dismount, nor even to engage the enemy with musketry, but the notion of combined operations tactics seems implicit.

Various cavalry regiments and mounted formations during the British Civil Wars encompassed both horse and dragoon elements. Captain Thomas Armstrong commanded a regiment of horse and dragoons that served in Ormond's army in the Confederate Wars in Ireland. It was established in Leinster in 1641–2 with 60 harquebusiers and 40 dragoons, and on 4 May 1642 there were mustered 12 officers, 54 troopers and 42 dragoons, besides 1 man absent, 2 in prison and 6 sick. Some independent dragoon companies were raised by Protestant officers in Ireland at the onset of the Irish revolt. Sir Charles Coote commanded 60 dragoons, who were based at Naas in County Kildare in 1642, and later garrisoned Taulagh. Furthermore, Captain Trevor's dragoons were newly raised (seemingly as an independent command) intended to support the Scots Covenanters in Ulster in 1642, although there is a possibility that the company was attached to Colonel Arthur Hill's cavalry regiment, in which Trevor was an officer.[64]

In the English Midlands the Royalist commander, Henry Hastings (Lord Loughborough) originally established his regiment of horse on 1 August 1642 by virtue of a warrant to raise 400 men, and when the King arrived in Oxford in November he was authorised to raise a further 500 dragoons.[65] Whether this many dragoons were ever mustered remains uncertain, given the lower numbers achieved by other Royalist colonels, though Hastings did have some

62 *Ibid.*, p.35.

63 Wallhausen, *Kriegskunst zu Pferd*, p.17.

64 HMC, *Fourteenth Report, App. VII*, pp.135–6; Ryder, *English Army for Ireland*, pp.37–8.

65 HMC, *Hastings*, II, pp.85, 87; *ROP*, II, 264n.

of these soldiers with him during his foray into Cheshire in February 1643.[66] Given that just one dragoon unit has been traced in connection with Hastings, that of Colonel Devereaux Wolseley, it is possible that it was of company size and commonly attached to either his own regiment of horse (or that commanded by Wolseley himself).[67]

A similar Parliamentarian regiment of horse and dragoons was that raised and led by Colonel Richard Cole, the son of a Bristol merchant family. His regiment, probably stationed mainly in the city, existed briefly between February and July 1643, although Cole lapsed into Royalism or neutrality, and obtained Charles I's pardon in early 1644, even though he had begun the war as a member of the Somerset Committee. Captain James Harrington appears to have been variously placed with Cole's dragoons, and the probably combined regiment of cavalry and dragoons commanded by Colonel Alexander Popham, a local unit serving in the West Country and based at Bath.[68]

The continued employment of substantial quantities of dragoons among units of horse is evident from a list of Sergeant-Major Thomas Lilburne's cavalry troop, which mustered on 9 June 1646.[69] Of Offerton, County Durham, Thomas was first cousin to his fellow Parliamentarian officers Robert, John and Henry Lilburne. He was commissioned Captain in Colonel Robert Lilburne's newly raised regiment of horse on 25 May 1644 and continued to serve in Lord Fairfax's Northern Association forces until the end of the First Civil War. In 1648 Thomas Lilburne commanded a reformed troop in Colonel Robert Lilburne's regiment at Preston and Winwick.[70] According to a muster roll of June 1646, his troop contained a lieutenant, a cornet, a quartermaster, one clerk, three trumpeters, four corporals, five reformadoes and two sergeants of dragoons (Richard Bull and Edward Crawley). Of the 160 soldiers listed, 45 were described as dragoons, whereas 143 soldiers were stated to be mounted and 17 others unmounted. However, the latter figures do not differentiate between troopers and dragoons.

Colonel Gerard Croker's cavalry regiment served with the Oxford Army in 1644 and with Lord Goring in 1645, with a company of dragoons on its establishment under the command of Captain Erasmus Sacheverell.[71] In December 1642 the sum of £170 was disbursed to Captain Gibbons for his company of dragoons as part of the mounted component of the Earl of Warwick's reserve army, which was subsumed into Essex's field forces at various stages of the First Civil War. Gibbons' command may have been composed either partially or wholly of veterans who had returned from Dutch service. Warwick's units were in 1642–3 under the authority of Colonel James Holborne, a Scots professional with Continental experience, whilst Captain Lukeman's troop belonging to this formation was 'called the Dutch

66 BL, Ms Add 36913, f.125r.

67 LRRO, QS6/1/2/1.

68 Peachey and Turton, *Fall of the West*, V, pp.560–2.

69 TNA, SP28/123/2, ff.239r–241v.

70 *Perfect Occurrences of every daies Iournal*, 24–31 March 1648. TT, E522 [10]; Rushworth, *Historical Collections*, IV, p.847.

71 TNA, WO55/423, f.139v.

troop'.[72] Likewise, John Fiennes – third son of William Fiennes, 1st Viscount Saye and Sele, brother to Colonel Nathaniel Fiennes and MP for Oxfordshire – recruited a troop of harquebusiers in Essex's army in July 1642. He served in the West Country with his brother, but after the fall of Bristol his troop was disbanded on 3 August 1643. On 20 June 1644, however, John received a commission as Colonel of a regiment of horse raised in North Oxfordshire. This served mainly in the Oxfordshire area, most notably besieging Banbury between 27 August and 25 October 1644, until the Royalists raised the siege. Payments made in the September include one to Captain Henry Wheeler 'for himself and his troop of dragoons'.[73] Wheeler later served as a reformado in Fiennes' regiment of horse in the Oxfordshire area.

Even though it was not a New Model regiment, Colonel John Fiennes' horse fought as part of the right wing of the army at Naseby, breaking the King's regiment of foot, and capturing his own and fourteen other colours. The dragoon company commanded by Captain Wheeler may have been with it. Following the defeat of the King's forces, Colonel Fiennes' regiment, along with the Suffolk horse, was tasked by Cromwell to accompany the captured Royalist prisoners and trophies to London.[74] In addition to Rossiter's and Fiennes' dragoons, other dragoon units are mentioned as being present among the Associated Horse on both flanks of the New Model at Naseby (that is, separate to Okey's regiment). Arriving in time to participate in the battle, the Suffolk horse and dragoons under the command of Colonel Brampton Gourdon, numbering between 300 and 400, were divided into two bodies, one to each wing of cavalry.[75] In describing the initial deployment of Sir Thomas Fairfax's army, George Bishop, likely an intelligence officer embedded in the force, wrote:

> In our right wing of horse were the General's (sometime Lieutenant-General Cromwell's), Colonel Whalley's, Colonel Pye's, Colonel Rossiter's, Colonel Fiennes' and Colonel Sheffield's regiments. In the left wing were Colonel Ireton's […], Colonel Fleetwod's, Colonel Rich's, Colonel Butler's, Colonel Vermuyden's, and the Suffolk regiments, dragoons equally divided on both parts.[76]

Bishop's account differs in other respects from Streeter's illustration in Josiah Sprigge's *Anglia Rediviva*, however that does not make it faulty.

Captain Walter Scott led a company of dragoons in the Earl of Denbigh's cavalry regiment between 11 December 1643 and 30 March 1645.[77] During the relief of Gloucester in September 1643 the dragoon regiments of the

72 TNA, SP28/144/1, f.9v.

73 TNA, SP28/139/19, ff.205r, 207r, 209r; SP28/147, unfol.

74 Luke, *Letter Books*, pp.579, 581; *The Manner how the Prisoners are to be brought into the City of London* (London: T.F. and J.Coe, 1645). TT, E288 [45]; *Kingdom's Weekly Intelligencer*, 17–24 June 1645.

75 'Receipt of 16 days' pay as Colonel to Naseby at 39s 0d', quoted in Alfred Kingston, *East Anglia and the Great Civil War* (London: 1897), p.201.

76 *A More Particular and Exact Relation of the Victory obtained by the Parliament's forces under the command of Sir Thomas Fairfax* (London: Richard Cotes, 1645). TT, E288 [38]

77 TNA, SP28/131/12, ff.14r.–14v.

Earl of Essex's army were dispersed, with some companies going to Waller's forces in the West, and the rest attached to regiments of horse in Essex's forces. One company was commanded by Captain George Dundas, lately an officer in Colonel Wardlaw's dragoons in the same army, while another, led by Captain Jeremiah Abercrombie, a Scots professional officer, remained in Essex's forces.[78] In a clear example of combined arms tactics, it was reported by a Parliamentarian observer that during an attack on the King's army on 4 September 1643 by Essex's troops:

> Sergeant Major General Skippon with only 200 musketeers and two pieces bravely advanced, assisted by Sir Philip Stapleton and Lord Grey's horse, and 40 dragoons under Captain Abercrombie. This small force (his Excellency being there in person to the great encouragement of the party) marching directly upon the enemy, and skirmishing with them, made their whole body to retreat; and though they still appeared before us, we marched on, and drove them seven miles[79]

The following August, during the final phase of the Royalist encirclement of Essex's horse at Lostwithiel, Abercrombie's dragoon company – consisting of one lieutenant, one cornet, one quartermaster, three sergeants, three corporals, three drummers and 64 dragoons – was almost wiped out while fighting a bitter rearguard action, during the escape of Balfour's horse, against Sir Thomas Aston's cavalry and dragoons, and other Royalist Horse among hedgerows 'on two rising grounds'.[80] Captain Abercrombie and some of his men then barricaded themselves into a house, bringing the Royalist pursuit to a halt. They were forced to surrender when the enemy stormed it, but by then the Parliamentarian horse had reached the safety of Saltash and the following day was ferried across the River Tamar to Plymouth.[81] Described as being captured with Abercrombie was Cornelius Shibborne, Captain of a company of dragoons in the Earl of Essex's army, which had fought at the First Battle of Newbury.[82]

In May 1644, Captain Abercrombie had also received a commission from the Earl of Essex as Captain of a troop of cavalry to be attached to the Lord General's own regiment of horse. About 15 May, he was paid the sum of £126 10s 0d 'for the recruit of his troop'.[83] As Sir Samuel Luke's letter books illustrate, during this period the Parliamentarian garrison of Newport Pagnell, which he commanded as governor, experienced severe problems in obtaining finance and provisions from the Buckinghamshire area. Accordingly, the previous December, Luke brought in all the beans, peas, wheat and cattle from around Buckingham rather than allow them to fall into Royalist hands. According to one newsbook, in January 1645

78 TNA, SP28/5, ff.205v–206r., SP28/7; ff 320r, 452r; SP28/191, f.177v.
79 Washbourne (ed.), *Bibliotheca Gloucestrensis*, p.239.
80 Sir Edward Walker, *Historical Discourses upon Several Occasions* (London: W. B., 1705), p.64.
81 Rushworth, *Historical Collections*, II, p.702; Walker, *Historical Discourses*, pp.67–8.
82 TNA, SP28/149, ff.147v, 162r.; John Wilson, *Buckinghamshire Contributions for Ireland 1642 and Richard Grenville's Military Accounts 1642–1645* (Buckinghamshire Record Society, 1983), pp.113 & 127–8.
83 TNA, SP28/149, ff.148v, 162v; Wilson, *Buckinghamshire Contributions*, pp.114 & 128.

Captain Abercrombie, who had established a small garrison at Addington, three miles southeast of Buckingham, exacted levies on the local area and issued warrants to the constables of Brackley, demanding the sum of £40 or he would 'not leave a cock to crow among you'.[84] Soon afterwards, he took from the recently captured Hillesden House £60 0s 0d, with victuals for 200 soldiers and horses for two days.[85] The constables' accounts for various Buckinghamshire townships record exactions and free quarter to Essex's forces and some New Model Army units. Thus, Abercrombie obtained large quantities of provisions from Adstock, while in May 1646 Cuddington had to provide quarter for 240 horses and 60 soldiers of Captain Daniel Abbot's dragoons from Colonel Okey's New Model regiment, for which the inhabitants were recompensed.[86]

By late 1644, Captain Abercrombie commanded what remained of Colonel James Wardlaw's regiment which had served at Edgehill.[87] From his quarters at Addington on 5 March 1645, Abercrombie wrote to Essex, describing his involvement in military operations in the Buckingham area:

> The Sunday following, I sent out a small party commanded by Hugh Campbell, my cornet, who met with a party of the enemy at Bicester taking up contribution money, skirmished and took four of the enemy prisoners. The next Tuesday being the 27 February, I went out and took good store of provision going to Boston guarded by some musketeers who ran into a wood so could not be had. On Wednesday next at night, the 28 February, I went to Nook with my own horse and dragoons, leaving my dragoons at Islip Bridge for our safe retreat. We entered the house and took some arms with other things necessary for men and horses – belonging to the enemy – out of the house. We pursued the enemy through the house to the leads, where there was a narrow trap and a double door, so we could go no further. I did not stay long, it being day before I came to Nook, I retreated close by the King's troops, losing but two horses, which was nothing in respect of what we got. Sunday 2 March, I borrowed from Sir Samuel Luke 100 horse and that same night marched towards Kidlington where the King's troops quartered. We made our passage over the river with faggots at Islip Mill with the one half of the party commanded by myself to get betwixt them and Oxford, so that I was in the village before they knew. The rest of the party I sent to Casworth Bridge – commanded by one of Sir Samuel's captains – to break open a chain with a lock, and a turn-pick with another very strong lock which was the way of our retreat. This troop consisting all of gentlemen were quartered at Oxford. Some of them gone that afternoon before I came thither, leaving their servants and horses at their quarters. We took six or seven prisoners with one of his Majesty's commissaries betwixt 30 and 40 horses with many pistols [and] carbines; we gave them a strong alarm at Oxford, and all the country round where the enemy are quartered. Colonel Palmer – one of the enemy – with his regiment made a show of

84 *Mercurius Aulicus*, 28 February–5 March 1645.

85 Frances P. Verney, *Memoirs of Verney Family during the Civil War* (London: Longmans, Green & Co., 1892), I, p.34; II, pp.189–207; Luke, *Letter Books*, pp.623–8.

86 TNA, SP28/4, ff.268r–270r; SP28/149/1, f.41v; SP28/149/4, unfol.

87 Symonds, *Diary*, p.73.

> pursuing us, but at very great distance. There is one of the enemy, a sergeant, came to me out of Bletchingdon House, another yesternight out of the King's troop who affirmed the enemy to be very feared so that they are gone from Nook to Bletchingdon House, since we beat their quarters up at Nook. There is eight score of the enemy in Bletchingdon House which if it were under the command of the Parliament – being thought a very considerable place – who ever should be in it were able to do good service commanding all for the most part betwixt Oxford, Winslow and Banbury.[88]

Captain Jeremiah Abercrombie was killed in action on 9 March 1645 and his command was reduced at Luton on 11 April alongside Sergeant-Major Robert Hamilton's cavalry troop of the Earl of Essex's regiment.[89] Receiving fourteen days' pay with Abercrombie's former unit, amounting to £27 3s 8d, was Lieutenant John Platt, Cornet Hugh Campbell, Quartermaster William Hall and Corporal Middleton Rogers. On 4 April Sir William Campion, the commander of the Royalist garrison of Boarstall House, fortified in late 1643 to protect the King's headquarters at Oxford, sent a list of Parliamentarian prisoners for exchange to Sir Samuel Luke at Newport Pagnell. He stressed especially that 'If it be not inconvenient leave unnominated those of Captain Abercrombie's troop, for the Governor of Oxford has desired that they might be exchanged for some of his men now prisoners in Abingdon.'[90]

On 5 April 1645 the Committee of Both Kingdoms ordered that 'the horse, foot, and dragoons lately under the command of Captain Abercrombie do repair forthwith to High Wycombe, there to be in readiness to serve the garrison of Henley-on-Thames upon order from its governor, and that Sir Thomas Fairfax be acquainted with this order, and that it was ordered formerly by the Lord General [Essex] at the desire of this Committee.' Two weeks later another order was issued to 'the commander of the dragoons lately Captain Abercrombie's. The Lord General has already sent you orders to march with the company of dragoons under your charge to Henley, but we are informed that you have not yet started, and therefore write to order you to march at once to Henley, where you will receive further orders from the governor of that garrison.' The apparent tardiness of the unit is likely to have been related to a lack of pay because the dragoons remained unpaid on 20 March.[91]

According to the petition presented by the widow of Edward Nethercotes to the Nottinghamshire Quarter Sessions on 6 April 1657, her husband 'served Parliament as a captain of dragoons under the command of Colonel Francis Thornhaugh', during which service he was killed. Thornhaugh raised a regiment of horse in late 1642 or early 1643, and going by this entry he appears also to have had dragoons under his command, probably attached to, or as an official part of his cavalry. Though based at Nottingham, the regiment fought under Cromwell at Gainsborough in 1643, the relief of

88 HMC, *Thirteenth Report*, *App. I*, p.214.
89 TNA, SP28/43, f.658r.; SP28/29/2, f.419r.
90 Luke, *Letter Books*, 1205.
91 *CSPD 1644–5*, pp.341, 360, 386, 418.

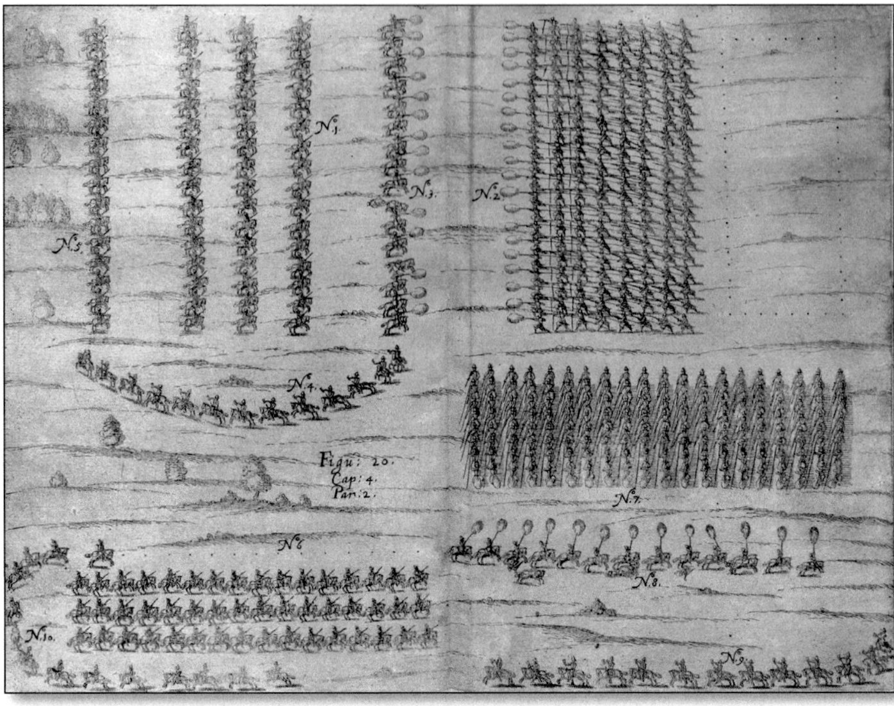

Wallhausen, *Kriegskunst zu Pferd*, harquebusiers or mounted dragoons maneuvering (Open source)

Newark in March 1644, and joined Colonel-General Sydenham Poyntz's Northern Army in 1645 and 1646.[92]

Elsewhere, Sir Thomas Myddelton, appointed by Parliament as Sergeant-Major-General of the counties of North Wales in 1643, claimed pay as a Colonel of a regiment of dragoons and Captain of a company of dragoons from 30 August 1644 to 15 June 1645. Alexander Elliot served as captain of dragoons under him from 24 June to 22 November 1644 and as Sergeant-Major of dragoons from 22 November 1644 to 24 May 1645.[93] His men were presumably among the defenders of Hawarden Castle, who negotiated its surrender in early December 1643 to local Royalist forces and reinforcements from Ireland. Elliott was still serving in Myddelton's brigade when it entered Montgomeryshire in September 1644, and was located there the following January, when his company mustered 39 men, including officers. He is suggested by R. N. Dore to be one of Sir Thomas' English officers recruited during 1643 from the London area, although given his surname, Elliott could have been a Scotch professional soldier.[94]

Equally, Hercules Hannay was a Captain in Myddelton's brigade, and from 1 June 1644 he commanded a dragoon company, until 12 December when it was converted to harquebusiers.[95] During their existence as dragoons, both Elliot's and Hannay's companies served alongside Sir Thomas' regiment of horse in the Midlands, Shropshire and Wales. On 2 November 1644

92 NA, C/QSM/1/13; CRO, DDX/428, ff 17v, 21r, 33r–33v, 84r; *BLB*, I, 32, 49, 99, 171.

93 TNA, SP28/138/18, unfol. ; SP28/346, unfol. ; NLW, Chirk Castle Ms 1/B3, f.93r.

94 BL, Ms Add 11332, ff.100r–102r. *BLB*, I, 186, 204, 435, 511; II, 869–70, 885.

95 TNA, SP28/41/4, ff.472r–473v, 476v, 480r, 482r.

Myddelton, with his cavalry and dragoons, numbering 'about 200', rendezvoused near Lampeter in Cardiganshire with an infantry force and ammunition sent by sea for his assistance. Driving northwards they defeated Royalist troops at a bridge near Machynlleth on 27 November, and less than a week later, assaulted the garrison of Abbeycwmhir in Radnorshire. Here they captured Colonel Barnard, the governor, several officers and men, plus quantities of arms and ammunition.[96] By January 1645 Captain William Leicester was serving as a Captain in command of a company of 23 dragoons serving with Sir Thomas Myddelton's brigade based in Montgomeryshire.[97] Furthermore, among the twelve soldiers belonging to the formation listed for exchange on 4 January 1646 were six dragoons – Robert Marsh, Peter Leonard, James Sparke, John Collins, Andrew Ashwell and Thomas Wright.[98]

In the Scots Covenanter Army, mounted regiments generally contained, or were reinforced by, dragoon elements. In 1644, Major-General David Leslie's regiment of horse consisted of ten troops, but from April 1645, when he received 40 muskets with bandoliers, the unit was boosted by Captain John Ferguson's command equipped as dragoons. This unit mustered one lieutenant, one cornet, a quartermaster and 42 dragoons on 19 January 1646.[99] On 7 June it received 100lbs of powder, 140lbs of match and 100lbs of musket bullets, and in September 1646 60 muskets were delivered to Ferguson's men, implying that they were armed with matchlock muskets.[100] Similarly, by May 1644 the Earl of Lanark's Horse had been established with six cavalry troops and two dragoon companies. Although the formation was for service in England, it served mostly in Scotland until its disbandment in 1647.[101]

One of the better known regiments of Covenanter dragoons was that of Colonel Hugh Fraser. James Somerville speaks of this unit 'as four complete companies, wherein they confided much, as they had good reason, these afterward being made up a regiment, being commanded by Colonel Frizall, and were known, with Lawer's regiment of foot, to be the stoutest regiment in the Scots army.'[102] The regiment was engaged at Marston Moor (where its firepower supported the left wing of the Parliamentarian horse), Carlisle, and Philiphaugh.

On 6 December 1645, it was ordered to return to England, and early in January 1646 was in Yorkshire. A troop was present at the muster at Newark on 17 January 1646 (32 rank and file and six officers). The men are described in the muster roll as 'lately dragoons and are not yet armed as troopers; more than that, there are some have pistols by their sides, nor have they horses

96 *CSPD 1644–5*, p.181; *Perfect Occurrences*, 20–27 December 1644.

97 NLW, Chirk Castle Ms 1/B3, f.93v.

98 BL, Ms Add 11333, f.95r; *BLB*, II, 1179.

99 Edward Furgol, *A Regimental History of the Covenanting Armies* (Edinburgh: John Donald, 2nd edn, 2021), pp.525, 587; Stuart Reid, *Scots Armies of the Seventeenth Century I: The Army of the Covenant 1639–51* (Leigh-on-Sea: Partizan Press, 1988), p.76.

100 C. S Terry, (ed & intro.), *Papers Relating to the Army of the Solemn League and Covenant 1643–1647* (Edinburgh: Scottish History Society, 1917), I, pp.136–7.

101 Furgol, *Covenanting Armies*, I, pp.139, 168; II, pp.311, 379, 535.

102 James Somerville, *Memorie of the Somervilles* (Edinburgh: James Ballantyne and Co., 1815), II, p.315.

fit for troopers.' The following commissioned officers of Fraser's regiment are listed by C. S Terry in his study of the Army of the Solemn League and Covenant:

Colonel Hugh Fraser, 1644
Lieutenant-Colonel William Crawford, 1644
Lieutenant-Colonel John Monro, 1646
Sergeant-Major John Monro, 1644
Captain Alexander Ferguson, 1644
Captain David Lumsden, 1644
Captain John Forrester, 1644
Captain Michael Bruce, 1644
Captain Andrew Munro, 1646
Lieutenant Alexander Hamilton, 1644
Lieutenant Andrew Beck, 1646
Cornet Andrew Kerr, 1644
Cornet William Elphinstone, 1644
Cornet William Borthwick, 1644
Cornet Edmund Borthwick, 1646
Quartermaster James Acheson, 1644
Quartermaster Malcolm Smith, 1644
Quartermaster David Simpson, 1644
Quartermaster Somerville, 1644
Quartermaster Alexander Fraser, 1644
Quartermaster Thomas Urquhart, 1644
Quartermaster William Gillespie, 1645
Quartermaster Tweedie, 1646

4

Pay and Quarter

During 1642 the Committee of Safety, the body appointed by Parliament to direct the war effort, expended various amounts via warrants issued to the Earl of Essex's army, in order get its regiments (especially those of the more expensive cavalry) into the field. On 28 July 'Allowances for raising of troops of horse' had been agreed upon, whilst Parliament's commitment to finance the complete expenses of the army meant that there was no requirement for officers to raise a troop, or company of dragoons or foot, from his own means or any other resource outside Parliament's dominion. Consequently, money was provided for equipment, provisions and ammunition, as well as 'coat, conduct, transportation, payment of dues, and wages.'[1] Seventeenth century soldiers used terms such as victuals, entertainment, proviant, and other less common terms to describe their food and drink.

Such payments were not intended to reimburse prior outlays, but to supply a ready sum of money for immediate expenses. Simultaneously it was agreed that captains of horse would receive £280 to provide mounts, equipment, 'and whatsoever [else] is necessary' for themselves and their officers. Money was also provided for outfitting non-commissioned officers, and troopers were to be mounted on horses donated under the Propositions and armed with weapons taken from Ordnance Office's magazines in the Tower of London. Beginning the war as a Captain of horse in Essex's army, Captain Hercules Langrish – later Captain in Colonel George Melve's and Colonel John Middleton's regiments of dragoons – was issued over £733 in August 1642, which provided his officers and non-commissioned officers with horses and equipment, and his troop with sixty scarves and one month's pay.[2] Likewise, Sir Samuel Luke received 64 horses and £538 to prepare his troop for service, although he supplemented this allowance with £58 15s 0d of his own money for buff coats.[3]

After men had been recruited into armies, and clothed and equipped, the main continuing outlay was their daily pay. During the British Civil Wars, this was irregular and often in arrears, thus encouraging an even higher

1 *CSPD 1641–3*, pp.362–3.
2 TNA, SP28/1A, ff.60v, 136r, 139r, 222v; SP28/5/205, f.206r; SP28/7/320, f.452v; SP28/9/216, f.9r.
3 TNA, SP28/127 ff.26r & 30r.

rate of desertion than would be the case normally and causing an erosion of military discipline. Both officers and men often went for long periods without pay, partly a reflection of the breakdown in army funding, and partly because of there being insufficient money to go round. At such times, the officers, if they were fortunate enough to be able to do so, dipped into their own pockets to pacify their men. Success in battle could lead to plunder, but for significant numbers of men, during some stages of their military service, it was their only way of obtaining food, clothing, and money. One cause of the desertion and sickness was undoubtedly the irregularity with which the soldiers received their pay. Accordingly, Parliament passed two ordinances, one of which provided for weekly assessments upon the counties, cities, and towns of England and Wales. The other Ordinance sequestrated the estates of delinquents and applied the revenues accruing therefrom to the maintenance of the army.[4] Yet even the prospects of punctual pay seem to have failed to bring in many recruits, as one Royalist newsbook mockingly reported, '[Colonel Richard] Browne, the woodmonger sets up tickets everywhere to signify that he will give 4s 6d per day to such as will bring horse and arms of their own to serve under him as dragoons.'[5]

In Royalist and Parliamentarian armies, the pay was theoretically standardised, but even within this structure the amount received in individual forces differed. The usual daily wage for a cavalry trooper was 2s 6d, while private sentinels of the foot were paid 8d. Documents dating to the mid or late summer of 1642 record the daily rates of pay of the northern Royalist forces, including dragoon officers:

Colonel £10s 0d
Major 15s 0d
Captain 10s 0d
Lieutenant 6s 0d
Cornet 5s 0d[6]

To what extent such rates were adhered to, and how often troops were paid amongst the Royalist field armies remains uncertain, given the occasionally haphazard nature of the King's finances, and a general lack of survivability of muster rolls and pay warrants. The accounts of some individual garrisons offer a glimpse of the payment of dragoons and other troops however, although these might to some extent reflect the local financial climate of the region and the availability of money. In January 1643, Sir William Russell, the governor of Worcester allowed to each trooper 17s 6d per week, to every mounted dragoon 10s 6d per week, and to those unmounted 6s 0d. For the same period Sir James Hamilton's company, consisting of 20 mounted and 50 unmounted dragoons, was paid the sum of £480, at £30 per week for 16 weeks. Moreover, on 12 February Captain Dennis's 60 dragoons – 15

4 *A&O*, I, pp.85–100, 106–17.
5 *Mercurius Aulicus*, 11–17 February 1643.
6 BL, Ms Harley 6804, f.194r.

mounted and 45 unmounted – received £279 3s 6d, for 13 weeks at the same rates.[7]

Such disbursements do not appear to have included the pay rates and quantities for commissioned and non-commissioned officers, which were presumably paid. In a similar fashion, captured dragoons belonging to the Skipton garrison, commanded by Captain Prideaux, received upon their exchange in April 1643 a month's pay of 18s 8d, with an additional 2s 6d for drink and travelling expenses.[8] By comparison, among the garrison of Great Chalfield, an outpost of the Parliamentarian stronghold of Malmesbury, the small dragoon company received five weekly payments in early 1645 at half pay and 'diet', presumably victuals for man and horse.[9] Such disbursements, of which the highest was £8 4s 0d and the lowest £7 12s 0d, indicates that at half the weekly rate of 5s 3d or daily rate of 9d each, the dragoon element comprised little more than 20 men besides officers

Despite the various discussions of standardised pay among modern researchers, the proscribed and actual pay of all troops in the Parliamentarian armies varied, depending on which forces they were part of and whatever resources were available to them at any given time. Very often in both Parliamentarian and Royalist formations pay remained at least one month in arrears, whilst officers and men were placed upon half pay. Sums owing to the commissioned and non-commissioned officers of a company of Sir Anthony Irby's Lincolnshire dragoons on 21 November 1642 amounted to £4 4s 0d for the captain for twelve weeks' service; to the lieutenant £1 15s 0d for five weeks; to the cornet £1 8s 0d for four weeks; to the quartermaster £1 1s 0d for three weeks; for the two corporals £1 8s 0d for four weeks (14s 0d each); and to the two drummers £1 8s 0d for four weeks (14s 0d each). By comparison, the outstanding arrears of pay for Irby's own troop of horse were £7 0s 0d for the captain for twelve weeks' service; for the lieutenant £2 2s 0d for five weeks; for the cornet £1 15s 0d for four weeks; to the quartermaster £1 4s 6d for three weeks; to the three corporals £3 8s 0d for four weeks (£1 2s 8d each); and for the three trumpeters £2 2s 0d for four weeks (14s 0d each). An additional sum of £45 10s 0d was remaining for the pay allotted towards the 52 horses for them.[10]

7 J. W. Willis Bund (ed.), *Diary of Henry Townshend of Elmley Lovett, 1640–1663*, 2 vols (London: Worcestershire Historical Society, 1920), p.156.

8 Newman, 'Royalist Army', II, p.38.

9 TNA, SP28/138/1, ff.29r–32r; Pafford (ed.), *Accounts*, pp.66, 68, 70.

10 TNA, SP28/313/2, unfol.

Table 1: Monthly cost of a regiment of dragoons in the Earl of Essex's Army, 1642, assuming six companies and 100 dragoons per company (TNA, SP28/140/17, fol. 400v.)

Regimental officers	£	s.	d.	x six coys	£	s.	d.
Colonel	1	10	0		1	10	0
Sergeant Major	0	9	0		0	9	0
Quartermaster	0	5	0		0	5	0
Preacher	0	4	0		0	4	0
Provost Marshall	0	5	0		0	5	0
Surgeon	0	4	0		0	4	0
Two surgeon's mates	0	5	0		0	5	0
Company Officers							
Captain	0	15	0		4	10	0
his five horses	0	5	0		1	10	0
Captain Lieutenant/Lieutenant	0	4	0		1	4	0
his three horses	0	3	0		0	18	0
Cornet	0	3	0		0	18	0
his two horses	0	2	0		0	12	0
Two sergeants	0	3	0		0	18	0
a horse for each	0	2	0		0	12	0
Three corporals	0	3	0		0	18	0
a horse for each	0	2	0		0	12	0
Two drummers	0	2	0		0	12	0
a horse for each	0	2	0		0	12	0
x 100 private dragoons	7	10	0		0	60	0
One Smith	0	1	0		0	6	0
his horse	0	1	0		0	6	0
Subtotals	8	5	0		43	19	6
Total per day	0	13	0		3	2	6
Total per month	18	4	0		87	10	0

These rates are analogous with those paid by the Suffolk Committee to Manchester's army in 1643.[11] Moreover, on 6 June 1645, the Committee was commanded by Parliament to raise soldiers for the New Model Army, and to 'allow both the several troops of dragoons and horse one week's pay.' The remuneration of each trooper was set at 14s 0d per week, and dragoons 10s 6d.[12]

Table 2: Total payments to the regiments of dragoons of Essex's army during the Reading Campaign, April-June 1643 (TNA, SP28/143/1, fols 17r.-20v.)

	£	s.	d.
Colonel John Browne's Regiment	3461	17	0
Colonel George Melve's Regiment	2370	5	0
Colonel John Middleton's Regiment	572	4	0
Sir John Norwich's Regiment	1207	0	0
Sir John Seton's Regiment	1725	17	0
Sir William Waller's Regiment	500	0	0
Colonel James Wardlaw's Regiment	3754	4	0
Independent/unidentified company level payments	1944	5	0
Total	15535	3	0

The individual disbursements for pay to officers and dragoons in the Earl of Essex's army between 1642 and 1644, are recorded in the accounts book of Francis Vernon, the deputy treasurer of the army.[13] In some cases these entries can be cross-checked with surviving pay warrants, but as Aaron Graham warns, the survival of such warrants is intermittent, and represents only a selection of payments made. This methodology is also limited because the records of the Treasurer, Sir Gilbert Gerrard, have not survived.[14] Moreover, although Essex, like other contemporary commanders, issued a set of ordinances in which false musters and fraudulent accounting were explicitly forbidden, these certainly occurred.[15]

11 Alan Everitt (ed.), *Suffolk and the Great Rebellion, 1640–1660* (Suffolk Records Society, 1960), p.41 – quoting from the 'Suffolk Committee Book, 1641–45'.

12 Abbott (ed.), *Writings and Speeches*, p.395.

13 TNA, SP28/143/1, ff.17r–80v.

14 Aaron Graham, 'The Earl of Essex and Parliament's Army at the Battle of Edgehill: A Reassessment', *WH*, 17 (2010), pp.276–93, (pp. 279–80).

15 Barbara Donagan, *War in England 1642–1649* (Oxford: Oxford University Press, 2008), pp.141–56.

Colonel John Browne's Regiment

Paid [unknown date] £518 3s 6d to Colonel John Browne for his dragoons for seven days

Paid 29 October 1642 the sum of £563 17s 0d to Colonel John Browne, Colonel of a regiment of dragoons for one half months' pay for the soldiers of his said regiment, being 537 soldiers, from 10 to 29 October.

Paid £801 1s 0d to Colonel John Browne for pay for himself, officers and dragoons of his regiment from 27 October to 15 November, being eighteen days

Paid the sum of £484 8s 10d to Colonel Browne, Colonel of a regiment of dragoons for himself and officers from 30 July last [1643].[16]

Colonel James Wardlaw's Regiment

Paid 29 October 1642 the sum of £979 19s 0d to Colonel James Wardlaw, Colonel of a regiment of dragoons for the officers and 600 dragoons of his said regiment, from 10 to 29 October.

Paid 29 October 1642 the sum of £200 0s 0d to Colonel Wardlaw for his regiment of dragoons, from 10 to 29 October.

Paid £680 19s 0d to Colonel Wardlaw for half a month's pay for his officers and regiment of dragoons to begin on 29 October.

Paid £70 0s 10d to Colonel James Wardlaw, Colonel of a regiment of dragoons, for his own pay as Colonel and Captain for a whole month beginning 10 October, including £2 10s upon account.

[1644?]

Paid £923 6s 0d to Colonel James Wardlaw Colonel of a regiment of dragoons in discharge of the regiment.

Payments of £50 1s 0d, £150, £200 0s 0d and £400 0s 0d to Captain Dundas, Captain of a company of dragoons late in Colonel Wardlaw's regiment.

Paid £100 1s 0d to Captain Dundas, Captain of 120 dragoons in the General's [Manchester's] regiment.[17]

Lord Brooke's Regiment

Paid £194 9s 0d to Lord Brooke, Colonel of a regiment of dragoons and for pay for 370 dragoons for seven days, to begin from 8 October 1642.

Paid £100 more to them upon account for the charges of raising and bringing horses to Windsor.

Paid £242 4s 0d more for half a month in pay of the officers of the officers of the said regiment.

Paid £150 0s 0d more on account for providing 300 saddles for dragoons.[18]

Colonel John Middleton's Regiment

Paid £18 1s 0d to Captain Ambrose Tyndall, for eighteen days' pay for him as captain of a company of dragoons from 15–23 [October 1642] present.

---

16 TNA, SP28/143/1, ff.17v, 26r, 34v, 43r; SP28/2B, f.459r.

17 TNA, SP28/143/1, ff.34v.–35r, 37v, 50r, 44v, 48v–49v, 52v, 53v.

18 TNA, SP28/143/1, ff.28v, 59v.

Paid £35 5s 0d to Captain Ambrose Tyndall, captain of a company of dragoons, for 15 days to 29 October 1642.

Paid £81 0s 0d to Captain Nicholas Devereux for the pay of 72 dragoons for fifteen days to end 28 October 1642.

Paid £35 5s 0d to Captain Nicholas Devereux, captain of a company of dragoons, for 15 days to 29 October 1642.

Paid £81 0s 0d to Captain Robert Turner for a company of dragoons for fifteen days to end 28 October 1642.

Paid £35 5s 0d to Captain Robert Turner, captain of a company of dragoons, for 15 days to 29 October 1642.

Paid £83 6s 0d to Captain Richard Turner for half a month's pay to begin on 29 October 1642 for himself, his officers and 48 dragoons[19]

Colonel Richard Browne's Regiment

October 1642 to February 1643

Paid £300 0s 0d to Colonel Richard Browne, Colonel of a regiment of dragoons, upon account.

Paid £200 0s 0d to Colonel Richard Browne, towards the payment of his regiment.

Paid £1,000 0s 0d to Colonel Richard Browne, towards the payment of his regiment.

Paid £70 0s 0d to Colonel Richard Browne, late Colonel of a regiment of dragoons

Paid on 8 May 1643 the sum of £97 13s 0d to Colonel Richard Browne's own company of 57 dragoons.[20]

Colonel John Seaton's/George Melve's Regiment

November 1642 to June 1643

Paid £198 4s 6d to Colonel Melve, Colonel of a regiment of dragoons and for 15 days' pay for the officers and soldiers of his own company.

Paid £60 0s 0d to Colonel George Melve as captain of a company of dragoons towards pay.

Paid £254 7s 0d to Colonel George Melve for the under-officers and 397 dragoons of his regiment for seven days

Paid £100 0s 0d to Colonel George Melve as Colonel of a regiment of dragoons towards his pay.

Paid £94 3s 0d to Colonel George Melve for fourteen days' pay for the officers and 57 dragoons of his company up to 23 June 1643.

Paid £97 13s 0d to Captain Thomas Melve for fourteen days' pay for the officers and 60 dragoons of his company up to 23 June 1643.

Paid £100 0s 0d to Captain Thomas Melve for half a month's pay for the officers and dragoons of his company.

Paid £89 12s 0d to Captain Thomas Melve for fourteen days' pay for his company of dragoons

19 TNA, SP28/143/1, ff.48v, 31v–33v, f.35v. Captains Tydall, Devereux and Turner are mistakenly assigned to Colonel Melve's regiment in the accounts, rather than Colonel John Middleton's

20 TNA, SP28/143/1, ff.43r, 48v, 50r, 60r, 62v.

Paid £72 0s 0d to Captain Thomas Melve for his company of dragoons
Paid £75 0s 0d to Captain Thomas Maynard for his company of dragoons
Paid £200 0s 0d to Captain Peter Hayward, captain of a company of dragoons in Colonel Melve's regiment towards pay of the same company.
Paid £57 12s 0d to Captain Hercules Langrish for his company of dragoons[21]

Additional disbursements to dragoon formations attached to Essex's army:

Sir John Norwich's Regiment

Paid £400 0s 0d to Sir John Norwich, Colonel of a regiment of dragoons, from 23 to 26 November 1642.
Paid £807 0s 0d to Norwich, his officers and dragoons during the Reading campaign, April-June 1643.[22]

Sir William Waller's Regiment

Paid £500 0s 0d to the regiment's officers and dragoons, April-June 1643.[23]

The Earl of Manchester's Regiment

Captain William Miller's company received the following monthly sums from Treasurer Vernon, amounting to £350 0s 0d:
6 September 1643 – £50 0s 0d
9 September 1643 – £50 0s 0d
7 October 1643 – £50 0s 0d
14 November 1643 – £150 0s 0d
3 January 1644 – £50 0s 0d

Captain St John Holcroft's company received the following monthly payments, amounting to £371 0s 0d:
6 September 1643 – £20 0s 0d
30 September 1643 – £50 0s 0d
6 October 1643 – £55 0s 0d
4 November 1643 – £120 0s 0d
4 December 1643 – £40 0s 0d
23 December 1643 – £60 0s 0d
26 January 1644 – £15 0s 0d
10 February 1644 – £5 0s 0d
An undated payment of £6 0s 0d for five of his soldiers sick and sent home.[24]

21 TNA, SP28/143/1, ff.35v, 52v, 53v, 60r, 62v, 68v, 74r, 76v–77r.
22 TNA, SP28/143/1, ff.18r, 39v.
23 TNA, SP28/143/1, ff.17v–18r.
24 TNA, SP28/143/1, ff.6v–7v.

Complete payments to the Earl of Manchester's Regiment, amounting to £2,398 3s 0d, made between 29 April 1644 and 1 March 1645.[25]

Paid to Lieutenant-Colonel Lilburne – £1,370 14s 0d
Paid to Sergeant-Major Ewer – £326 0s 0d
Paid to Captain Mercer – £494 15s 6d
Paid to Captain Abbott – £41 13s 0d
Paid to Captain Beaumont & Captain Langrish – £165 0s 6d

Disbursements to captains of Manchester's dragoons discharged, amounting to £518 19s 6d, same period[26]

Paid to Sergeant-Major Moore –£7 12s 0d
Paid to Captain Burket – £19 7s 6d
Paid to Captain Harbottle – £100 0s 0d
Paid to Captain Miller – £220 0s 0d
Paid to Captain Holcroft – £72 0s 0d

The below pay accounts made up for three companies of dragoons of the Eastern Association Army in spring 1644, a period of reorganisation and consolidation among Manchester's forces, are illustrative of actual practices. Those pertaining to Captain John Holcroft, from 1 January to 25 March 1644, record the following:

Due to Captain Holcroft for his half pay from 1 January to 25 March 1644 at 7s 6d per day [for] twelve weeks – £31 10s 0d
For his five horses at 5s 0d per day – £21 0s 0d
His lieutenant at 7s 0d per day – £29 8s 0d
His cornet at 5s 0d per day – £21 0s 0d
His muster-master two-thirds [pay] at £3 4s 0d per day – £14 0s 0d
One sergeant 12 weeks – £10 10s 0d
Two corporals at 4s 0d per day – £16 16s 0d
One drummer at 4s 0d per day – £8 8s 0d
11 dragoons three months with horses – £69 6s 0d
31 dragoons without horses for 12 weeks – £86 16s
Six men from 20 March to 25 March without horses – £1 0s 0d
Five men more, entered 1 March to 25 March without horses – £2 10s 0d

The overall sum owing to Holcroft and his men was £312 4s 0d. From this there was deducted £20 0s 0d already received by the company in money, £42 14s 9d for boots and shoes, and £20 0s 0d 'for all other expenses', bringing the remaining sum due to £299 9s 3d[27]

25 TNA, SP28/29/1, ff.82r–90v. Disbursements of Gregory Gawsell, Treasurer to Manchester's army, 29 April 1644 to 1 March 1645 – transcription by Godfrey Davies, in 'The Army of the Eastern Association, 1644–5', *EHR*, 46 (1931), pp.88–96.

26 TNA, SP28/29/2, ff.238v, 281v, 294r, 296v–297r.

27 TNA, SP28/25/2, f.296r.

The account for Captain Goddard from 20 January to 25 March 1644 comprises the following:

Due to Captain Goddard from 20 January to 25 March 1644 at 7s 6d one half pay for himself and 5s per day for five horses – £40 12s 6d
His lieutenant at 7s 0d per day – £22 15s 0d
His cornet at 5s 0d per day – £16 15s 0d
Three sergeants – £24 7s 6d
Three corporals at 6s 0d – £19 10s 0d
Two drummers at 6s 0d per day – £13 0s 0d
79 dragoons nine weeks and two days at 1s 6d per day – £385 2s 6d

The amount owing to Goddard's company totalled £521 12s 6d. Deducted from this was £190 0s 0d previously received at Bury St Edmunds and £70 0s 0d at Bedford, bringing the remaining sum due to £261 18s 6d[28]

The account for Captain Carter from 1 January to 25 March 1644 contains the following:
Due to Captain Carter for his half pay, and the five horses at 12s 0d per day – £52 02s 0d
His lieutenant and his horses – £29 8s 0d
His cornet and his horse – £21 0s 0d
His quartermaster and his horse – £21 0s 0d
Three sergeants – £31 10s 0d
Three corporals at 6s 0d – £25 4s 0d
Two drummers – £16 6s 0d
72 dragoons at 1s 6d per day – £453 12s 0d
16 dragoons wanting horses at 8d per day – £44 16s 0d

Thus, owing to the unit was £625 12s 0d, although it had already received £60 0s 0d, and the sum of £10 10s 0d was deducted for hats of an unspecified design for the soldiers and non-commissioned officers. The outstanding figure of £625 6s 0d was paid to the company on 12 April 1644.[29] In similar fashion, on 22 March 1644 William Fenn was paid £10 0s 0d for hats for Sergeant-Major Isaac Ewer's company of dragoons.[30]

Sir John Gell, the commander-in-chief of the Parliamentarian forces of Derbyshire, maintained roughly 100 dragoons in the county. These were commanded in 1642 by the Nottinghamshire officer, Captain Charles White (who later served as Sergeant-Major of dragoons and horse under Colonel John Hutchinson), but he was replaced by Captain Daniel Watson.[31] As elsewhere, pay was infrequent and often in substantial arrears, the Derbyshire troops often receiving less than their proscribed amounts. Thus, in April 1643, Lieutenant-Colonel Thomas Gell paid his foot company the

28 TNA, SP28/25/2, f.442r.
29 TNA, SP28/25/2, f.445r.
30 TNA, SP28/128/8, f.6v.
31 CRO, DDX/428, ff.26v, 95r; BLB, I, 79, 220; Lucy Hutchinson, Memoirs of the life of Colonel Hutchinson (London: H. G. Bohn, 1863), pp.103–4.

weekly rate of £1 10s 0d to the lieutenant; 13s 8d to the ensign; 10s 6d to the sergeants; 7s 0d to corporals, drummers and gentlemen of the arms; and 5s 4d (9d per day) to the common soldiers.[32] A weekly pay bill, possibly drawn up in early 1643 for the Derbyshire dragoon company includes the following:

Captain – £5 5s 0d
Lieutenant – £2 12s 6d
Cornet – £1 15s 0d
Quartermaster – £1 11s 6d[33]
2 sergeants – £1 15s 0d
3 corporals – £2 2s 0d
1 drummer – £1 3s 4d
100 dragoons – £52 10s 0d
Total £68 14s 4d[34]

Owing to the imperfect nature of the evidence and the varied sources of finance available to the Cheshire Army of Parliament, commanded by Sir William Brereton, understanding the patterns of pay made to its officers and soldiers is not simple. How applicable common pay rates were among each unit remains uncertain, mainly given the problems experienced in gathering the weekly or monthly contributions, restrictions placed on funds sent via the London treasurers, and the increasing stresses of the prolonged siege of Chester in 1645–6. Raised in London in November and December 1642 for service in Cheshire, Captain John Bramhall's company received various sums in its early stages. During the first recruitment period, between 21 November and 2 December, one captain, one lieutenant, one cornet, two sergeants, three corporals, one drummer, one clerk and 57 soldiers were mustered. On at least one occasion there was some grumbling over the availability of pay. Bramhall recorded how he sent, perhaps from his own pocket, £1 11s 0d by Sergeant Turner of his company to the soldiers 'to keep them in quiet.' The commissioned officers were paid £19 10s 0d in stages from 21 November to 15 December. Leaving London for the northwest, twenty of Bramhall's dragoons had £29 18s 6d between them at Abbots Langley on 2 December. Between 11 and 15 December the remaining 37 dragoons received £2 15s 6d at Watford.

Bramhall's detailed accounts record his initial outlay in pay for his officers and men to have been £53 15s 0d. Having marched to Northampton, his cornet and two sergeants had £1 4s 0d in pay, while 15s 8d was laid out for hay and corn for their horses. Captain Bramhall further claimed pay for 53 dragoons between 24 January and 31 March 1643, and 60 between 31 March and 20 May 1643. On that day one captain, one lieutenant, one cornet, one quartermaster, two sergeants, three corporals, two drummers, one clerk and 80 dragoons mustered for service.[35]

32 DRO, D258/30/9; D803/MZ9, f.57r.
33 TNA, SP28/226/3, f.40r.
34 TNA, SP28/226/3, f.40r.
35 BL, Ms Harley 2128, ff.20v–21r, 31v; 33r.

Warrants for the pay of other Cheshire dragoons in 1643 and 1644 record several amounts and also the frequency of their issue. For instance, payments made to Captain Gwilliam Goldegay's company on 15 April 1643 included sums to Lieutenant Monkes and Cornet John Marum, whilst Goldegay himself received various amounts on 19 August.[36] On 15 and 24 July 1643, the collector of revenues for Cheshire, Ralph Judson, made payments to 'Captain Kempton's soldiers'.[37] Evidence that this officer served as a captain of dragoons in the Cheshire forces comes from references to his clerk, John Urmston, who had been involved in paying dragoons at the beginning of 1643, and is listed as 'cornet to Captain Kempton' in warrants dated 15 July and December of the same year. Although Kempton is not implicitly stated to be a dragoon officer, Cornet Urmston served in Captain Godfrey Gimbert's company at the siege of Holt Castle in April 1646 and later with the Cheshire forces at Lichfield Close.[38]

On 18 December 1645, the companies under Captains Gimbert, Simon Finch and Joseph Holt benefitted from two major grants of money to the army. During the autumn of 1645, the Commons voted £10,000 'for such forces as are drawn together about Chester and North Wales.'[39] Out of this the Cheshire dragoons received £416 16s 0d, whilst on 12 January 1646 another company, commanded by Captain James Stockport, had £50 0s 0d.[40] A further grant of £12,000 was made by Parliament in September 1646, which was largely intended to settle the outstanding arrears of the Cheshire troops.[41] Captain Holt's company, which had recently been at the forefront of the assaults on Chester, received pay with the two other dragoon units, and following the city's fall he and his men received gratuities for their part in the siege. The total amount paid to 'Captain Joseph Holt, and his officers and soldiers' by Treasurer James Croxton from London sources was £811 5s 10d.[42] Holt's dragoons were still drawing pay on 26 November 1646 when Lieutenant John Reading signed a receipt for it as 'Lieutenant to Captain Joseph Holt.'[43] Undated warrants also exist for Sergeant/Cornet Thomas Canary and Sergeant Hugh Jordaine.[44] During the siege operations against Lichfield Close in 1646, companies of the Cheshire foot and dragoons under Sir William Brereton's command were badly in arrears of pay, including a bounty promised for their participation in the reduction of Chester. On 14 April Captains Finch and Gimbert received between them £102 18s 0d 'for pay for their companies that came upon service at Lichfield in discharge of the month's gratuity upon taking Chester.'[45]

36 TNA, SP28/225/3, ff.865v–866r; SP28/208, f.20v; SP28/196/1, ff.12v, 16v.

37 TNA, SP28/196/1, f.11v.

38 TNA, E121/5/7/351, ff.28v–29r; BCA, Ms 595611, pp.252–3.

39 *CJ*, IV, pp.293, 302; BL, Ms Add 11332, ff.2r, 99r–99v; 11333, f.32r; *BLB*, II, 667, 886–7, 1057.

40 BL, Ms Add 11333, ff.30v, 118r–118v; *BLB*, II, 1040, 1235.

41 TNA, SP28/128/13, ff.12r–13r; SP28/152/8 and 9, *passim*.

42 TNA, SP28/224, f.202v–202r; SP28/128/13, f.18r.

43 TNA, SP28/224/1, f.184v.

44 TNA, E121/5/7/351, ff.33r, 39r, 55v.

45 TNA, SP16/513/1, f.79v.

Further payments were made on 30 May, and 5 and 12 June to Finch's company, which had mustered one lieutenant, one cornet, two sergeants, one drummer, three corporals and 76 dragoons.[46] The figures for the company of dragoons and troop of horse commanded by John Bramhall are particularly striking. Between the end of 1642 and September 1645 his officers and men received £909 from the £6,880 to which they claimed to be allowed from central funds.[47] Since each of these claims were checked and certified by the Committee of Accounts there is no reason to suppose that they were significantly exaggerated. Arrears of pay were often severe amongst Brereton's dragoon officers themselves. Captain John Lea, who was discharged from the army after sustaining a serious wound, 'was in actual service from 7 November 1642 until 12 November 1643' being 370 days. Lea received £50 0s 0d in London, but an outstanding figure of £320 0s 0d, of the due £370 0s 0d, remained.[48] Although as a regional force, the main source of pay was London moneys, significant amounts of resources were drawn from local sources administered by Parliamentarian sequestration committees.

Various townships in Bucklow Hundred were responsible for finding pay, horses and rations for Captain Richard Littler's dragoon company. In late 1643 the constables of Mere laid out £2 9s 4d for 'a horse, men and arms under Captain Littler,' while their colleagues at Dutton provided pay for his men.[49] Similarly, two undated warrants relate to the supply of dragoon mounts and food. Littler ordered Thomas Woollett, one of the constables of Aston township (where the unit was permanently quartered) 'to provide Sergeant Hall [with] two horses, one of your own, the other from George Guest, for scout horses this night for our safeties and the safety of this township.' In addition, the constables of Bucklow Hundred charged those of Aston and Aston Grange with bringing each day two horse-loads of oats to Great Budworth, presumably for the dragoon horses. Similarly, a warrant issued by Colonel Henry Brooke on 2 September 1643 informed the same constables, 'I formerly sent out several leys to them for collecting of moneys for the dragoons and as you are, as appears, behind with your payment. These are henceforth to charge and command you that you are besides with and withal four weeks' pay more at 6s 6d per week, which you to supply at Norton before 7 [September] 1643 to my clerk.'[50]

In mid-1645 there emerged among the Cheshire army a system of pay known as the 'new model' or 'Cheshire model'. Not to be confused with the New Model Army, this was, according to the Cheshire army's historian, Nathaniel Lancaster, an attempt by Lieutenant-Colonel Michael Jones, Sergeant-Major James Lothian, and the deputy lieutenants to place the payment of the troops engaged at the siege of Chester on firmer ground after Brereton left for Westminster in June. He stated:

46 BCA, Ms 595611, pp.203, 252–3; TNA: SP16/513/1, ff.70r, 72r, 87v.
47 BL, Ms Harley 2128, ff.20r–33v.
48 TNA, SP28/252/1, f.184v; SP28/265/1, ff.68r–68v, 70r.
49 BL, Ms Harley 2128, ff.166r, 60v.
50 Aston, unlisted warrants, dated 20 November 1643 x 2 February 1644, 2 September 1643.

> These two soldiers laid the foundation to the work according to their own principles. First, they endeavoured to appease the soldiers who were desperately mutinous, and the horse on their march to leave the county for want of pay, and because of their deep arrears. This the gentlemen performed by fair language, a month's pay in hand (borrowed and out of their own purses) and by deep engagements for a constant monthly pay. Then they put in execution the new model, by which the soldiers were reduced to such order that they passed muster every night upon the parade, and all that came not daily upon duty lost their pay. The country [county] was as sensible of their own happiness, that they paid to none, but those that served, and that all free quarter to the foot was taken off.[51]

Under the terms of the 'new model', the monthly rates of pay for Brereton's army contained in army warrants of July to November 1645 include the following. For the horse – captains received £7 16s 0d; lieutenants £4; cornets £2, quartermasters £2, corporals, trumpeters, and clerks £1 12s 0d; and troopers 20s 0d. For the foot – captains had £4; lieutenants £2 16s 0d; ensigns £2; sergeants and clerks £1 8s 0d; corporals and drummers £1 4s 0d; common soldiers 10s 0d. For the dragoons – captains received £5; lieutenants £3; cornets £2 8s 0d; sergeants £1 12s 0d; clerks £1 10s 0d; corporals and drummers £1 8s 0d; dragoons 14s 0d.[52] Though significantly lower than the recommended pay for Essex's and Manchester's armies, the system promised consistent remuneration for troops operating in Cheshire and elsewhere from the limited funds received both centrally and locally, and areas where the financial demands of the Parliamentarian war effort were especially pressing.

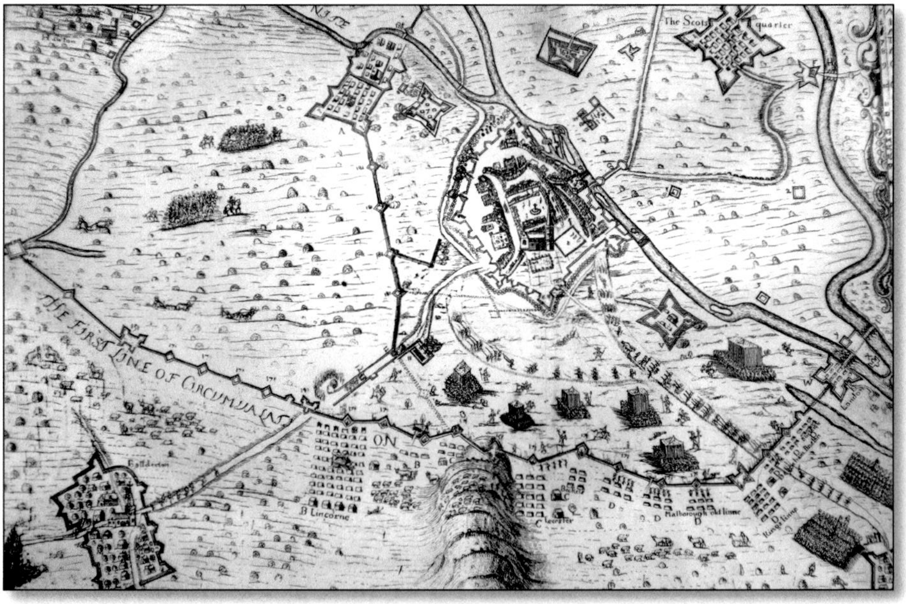

Plan of the Siege of Newark-on-Trent, 1646 (Open source)

51 Lewis (ed.), *Siege of Chester*, p.15.

52 TNA, SP28/224/1, ff.32r., 33r.-v., 43r., 47r., 49r.–50v., 62r., 85r.–86r., 88r., 193r.–94v.

When the Scots Covenanter Army under Alexander Leslie, 1st Earl of Leven, left the north of England in 1645 to undertake long marches through the Midlands, its difficulties increased daily. Before setting out from Appleby in May, Leven wrote to the Commissioners at York, to represent 'the great impediment we find through the want of draught and provisions.'[53] He was compelled to issue promissory tickets for the victuals he obtained, and the inhabitants were little disposed to furnish food with the indefinite prospect of repayment.[54] During the siege of Hereford, in August 1645, it was reported of the Covenanter Army that 'not seeing bread but one day, all the rest living upon beans, green corn, and fruit' for a period of ten days.[55] Similarly, in February 1646, before Newark, for two weeks the infantry had not received 18d worth of victuals weekly, and that there was not £10 worth of food in their magazines.[56] Leslie resorted to what his Parliamentarian allies condemned as 'free quarters and disorderly plunderings', taking upon credit the food and drink he was unable to pay for.[57] For the Scottish invasion of England in January 1644, the Committee of Both Kingdoms had proclaimed its desire 'to take the most orderly and reasonable way' for provisioning the army.[58] The districts through which it passed were ordered to furnish 'such provisions as shall be necessary' to the officers and men billeted upon them, the daily rates and allowances for all ranks (the maximum daily provisioning which could be demanded for them), or could be charged for their maintenance, being set out in a 'Schedule of Allowances' appended to the proclamation. For the campaign in England the daily rates of pay in Sterling were higher than that of the normal 'Scots Establishment'. Thus, officers of dragoons are to have entertainment at discretion, not exceeding the rates following:

> The lieutenant-colonel – 6s 0d
> The sergeant-major – 5s 0d
> The captain – 4s 0d
> The lieutenant – 3s 0d
> The cornet – 2s 6d
> The serjeant – 1s 4d
> The corporal and drummers 10d
> The dragoon is to have for himself 8d a day, and for his horse three penny-worth of straw or hay, and a groats worth [4d] of oats[59]

By comparison, the proposed monthly charge for the New Model Army, to consist of 14,000 foot in 12 regiments and 6,000 horse in 10 regiments, with 1,000 dragoons in single companies, according to the last establishment was:

53 *CSPD 1644–45*, p.537.

54 *Ibid.*, pp.556, 596.

55 David Buchanan, *Truth Its Manifest* (London: 1645), pp.46–7.

56 *LJ*, VIII, p.143.

57 *Ibid.*, p.34.

58 Rushworth, *Historical Collections*, V, pp.612–3.

59 *Ibid.*, p.603; The Scottish, or home service pay scale is outlined in the Act of 27 February 1645 (Anderson, Archibald, et al (eds), *The Acts of the Parliaments of Scotland, AD MCXXIV-AD MDCCVII* (Edinburgh: 1814–44), VI(I), p.351.

6 January 1645
Officers of a company of dragoons, £58 2s 0d
For 10 such companies, £581 0s 0d
For 1,000 dragoons, at 18d a day £2,100 0s 0d
Total for one month £2,681 0s 0d[60]

In December 1643, Lord Fairfax's Northern Army, outnumbered by at least four to one by Newcastle's Royalist forces, was in desperate need of pay and short of supplies, and losing considerable numbers of men through desertion. Fairfax had received no money from Parliament to pay his soldiers, and he warned that his army would disintegrate through desertion.[61] Thus, on 22 March he reported that the attached Lincolnshire dragoons of Sir Anthony Irby's regiment had deserted, and that without immediate supplies of money, all his remaining troops would abscond.[62] Clive Holmes observes that although the soldiers of the Earl of Manchester's army 'were better paid than any other [Parliamentarian] army on foot before the foundation of the New Model', their arrears were considerable and, as in other armies, military discipline suffered accordingly. The period up to mid–1644 was, according to him, 'marked by some confusion in the organization of the pay of the infantry', but after this a uniform system was adopted. Moreover, during 1644 and 1645, the foot was more frequently remunerated than their brothers in arms in the horse, although this is probably explained by the fact that the infantry and possibly the dragoons were generally less disciplined than the cavalry, and more ready to mutiny or desert if their arrears were not met.[63] Hence, on 28 May 1643, Colonel Oliver Cromwell requested from the borough of Colchester:

> some more strength to be speedily sent to us … [despite] the great defeat given by my Lord Fairfax to the Newcastle forces at Wakefield … should the force we have miscarry, expect nothing but a speedy march from the enemy up to you … [Newcastle] has about 3,000 foot and nine troops of horse, and we have about 24 troops of horse and dragoons. Reinforcements should be sent to Boston, but you must hasten to supply us, forget not money … I assure you the foot and dragoons are ready to mutiny; lay not too much upon the back of a poor gentleman, who desires without noise to lay down his life, and bleed the last drop to serve the cause and you.[64]

Yet the disbursement of revenue by army treasurers, the majority being for pay, remained extremely difficult, especially given the obduracy of the taxpayers within the eastern counties, and the resulting sluggishness with

---

60 *CSPD 1644–45*, p.232.

61 *A Second Letter from the Right Honourable the Lord Fairfax, of his late prosperous proceedings against the Earl of Newcastle and his Popish Army in Yorkshire* (London: 1643).

62 Andrew Hopper, *Black Tom: Sir Thomas Fairfax and the English Revolution* (Manchester: Manchester University Press, 2007), p.37.

63 Clive Holmes, *The Eastern Association in the English Civil War* (Cambridge: Cambridge University Press, 2008), pp.145–7.

64 ERO, D/Y 2/7/50.

which the local treasurers returned funds to the Cambridge Committee. The Treasurer of the Eastern Association, Gregory Gawsell, accompanied its army during the 1644 campaign and oversaw payments from moneys advanced to him by Treasurer William Leman at Cambridge. He informed Leman that his dearth of coinage prevented him from paying the soldiers, and that he was obliged to 'please them as well as I can with good words.' These were less welcome than cash, and on a further occasion, Gawsell wrote 'Sir, I am sick of the importunity and the unworthy use of the soldiers, and if you pay moneys at Cambridge … and leave me to be tormented with the soldiers I shall desire you to change places.'

Similarly, in September 1644 Gawsell was pressing 'that Parliament would do something for our army; to make us travel from south to north, and from north to south without taking care of us, I think … is strange.'[65] Such evidence that Manchester's army was poorly paid is corroborated by a report in the *Parliament Scout*, which in December 1644 commented that the regiments had received but six weeks' pay in six months, and, a fortnight later, that 'the soldiers of one regiment … as much bewailing the sufferings in the country, as the people them, were crying out, that they have but nine weeks' pay since Candlemas, and yet these soldiers are the subject of all other's wrath and hated by all sides.'[66]

In September 1644 the dragoons of Lieutenant-Colonel John Lilburne's regiment mutinied at Northampton, having obtained only half of the six weeks' pay promised, and they were only conciliated when Lilburne and his officers distributed to them the money they had received for themselves.[67] Lilburne later wrote, 'our soldiers being so poor for want of pay, that many times myself and other of my officers, were several times forced to lend them money to shoe their horses, and I am confident to this day, have fallen short of the payment of it again.'[68] In 1645, Lilburne remembered the privations suffered by his dragoons during the previous year as a result of the shortage of pay and victuals, and in his characteristically direct fashion questioned the reason for this:

> my Lord of Manchester's provision of money by Ordinance [of 22 January 1643], to pay his army was very large, and the countries made us believe they made very good payment, and yet if all the rest were like my particular, we received but a very small proportion of it, which makes me wonder what is become of the rest, surely it is either in those men's pockets that hath no right to it, or else it is sunk into the ground.[69]

The pay arrears of the dragoon company and the troop of horse commanded by Captain, then Sergeant-Major, John Bramhall of Sir William Brereton's army were severe. Between December 1642 and September 1645 his officers

---

65 TNA, SP28/22, f.281r; PRO/30/15/3, nos 528, 548; HMC, *Eighth Report, App. II*, pp.60–1.
66 *The Parliament Scout*, 12–19 December 1644, p.625; 24 December 1644–2 January 1645, p.638.
67 TNA, SP28/22, ff.338v–39r.
68 John Lilburne, *Innocency and Truth Justified* (London: 1646), pp.24.
69 *Ibid.*, pp.69–70; John Lilburne, *The Copy of a Letter from … a friend* (London: 1645), pp.11–12.

and men received only £909 from out of the £6,880 to which they claimed to be allowed from central sources.[70] During the final siege of Lichfield in 1646, the arrears of the companies of the Cheshire foot and dragoons were severe, and included an outstanding bounty promised for their part in the capture of Chester. On 14 April the dragoon captains, Simon Finch and Godfrey Gimbert received between them £102 18s 'for pay for their companies that came upon service at Lichfield in discharge of the month's gratuity upon taking Chester.'[71] As has been suggested:

> These were the only companies where this money came from Brereton, although payment was made to other individuals, and may indicate some competition between Brereton and the Cheshire Committee for the service of these elite troops who had spearheaded most of the operations against Chester. The rest of the Cheshire foot were paid their gratuity by the County Committee and sent on their way to Lichfield piecemeal as it secured the money.[72]

Sir William was in much need of the dragoons, who had served so effectively at various other sieges. On 1 April Lieutenant John Turner of Gimbert's company travelled from the siege-lines before Holt Castle to Lichfield Close 'on special service', and hence was reimbursed his expenses by Brereton. It is likely that Finch's and Gimbert's entire commands did not arrive until early May, however, as Captain Gimbert, six officers and ten of his dragoons were paid at Holt from Cheshire, while both captains received a month's wages there on 21 April from the same source.[73] On 13 May, Finch signed a letter with Gimbert and the 'Cheshire Commanders at Lichfield' to Sir William Brereton, complaining about lack of pay. Even so, his company was evidently much involved in the siege operations. On 25 May Brereton had reported a recent 'desperate sally' by the Royalist garrison upon the Parliamentarian earthworks, during which (among others) 'five or six of Captain Finch's firelocks [were] wounded.' Moreover, its junior officers were described on 12 June as 'being upon guard'.[74] Among the muster rolls of the Cheshire forces at the siege, drawn up ten days later, present under Captain Finch were one lieutenant, one cornet, two sergeants, one drummer, three corporals and 76 dragoons.[75]

Though every effort was made to remunerate the soldiers, the pay of officers was often substantially in arrears and they were sometimes obliged to procure money from their own pockets, often in the form of loans. Some of these may be gleaned from later petitions and certificates of service. A petition of Jane, widow of Ralph Castlon, to the Warwickshire Committee records that he served as Captain and Sergeant-Major of dragoons under Lord Brooke in Staffordshire from 27 January 1643 until 1 October 1644.

70 BL, Ms Harley 2128, ff.20r–33v.
71 TNA, SP16/513/1, f.79v.
72 Carr and Atherton (eds), *Civil War in Staffordshire*, p.59.
73 TNA, SP28/37/639–40, unfol.
74 BCA, Ms 595611, p.231; TNA: SP16/513/1, f.91r.
75 BCA, Ms 595611, p.203; TNA: SP16/513/1, ff.70r, 72r.

Ralph's pay arrears, at 15s per day and 5s for five horses per day, consisting of 224 days, amounted to £224, 'whereof, to be respited half pay [of] £112. He died in the service of King and Parliament on 15 March 1645 … his widow petitions for the outstanding sum.'[76] Likewise, Nicholas Devereux, Colonel of a regiment of foot in Gloucestershire, stated on 29 July 1646 that he had been Lieutenant-Colonel and Captain of dragoons by virtue of a commission from his relative, the Earl of Essex, dated 15 April 1643. He served under Colonel Arthur Forbes for five months and 14 days, with pay arrears (at £56 per month) amounting to £300.[77]

However, a warrant signed by Essex reveals that he had previously been a Captain in Colonel John Middleton's dragoon regiment during the Edgehill campaign, receiving pay for himself and his officers for their service between 14 and 26 October 1642, amounting to £35 5s 0d.[78] This is confirmed by entries in the account book of Francis Vernon, a treasurer to Essex's forces, in addition to other warrants recording disbursements to Lieutenant Thomas Lawrence and Cornet John Clayton, both of Nicholas Devereux's company.[79] The certificate of Captain John Lea of Brereton's forces testifies that he had 'been a very faithful servant to the Parliament, engaging not only on several engagements, freely endangering his life (being once shot through the body). And also we further certify that the aforesaid Captain John Lea was in actual service from 7 November 1642 until 12 November 1643.' It further records that his pay arrears 'for the above service, for 370 days due £370.' He received the sum of £50 in London, leaving £320 due to him.[80]

In the field, mounted troops were usually quartered in villages and hamlets, where civilians would be expected to accommodate several horses and men, in addition to feeding them. Preferably, this would be paid for by the soldiers out of their own pockets, but this was very rare in practice, mainly because pay was often far in arrears. More commonly, 'free quarter' – not free in the sense that no payment would be made but was so called because no immediate payment was necessary – was taken. In this case, tickets or vouchers were left with individual householders, noting the number of men and animals they had quartered, and the total charge incurred by them. Once endorsed by a commissioned officer, tickets were to be presented to the relevant army's treasury (if possible), where the figure would be reimbursed. Theoretically, regulations governed the requirements that troops could make of a householder, yet although bills for free quarter were sometimes honoured by the soldiers and officers themselves, they could be left unpaid, the intention being that the petitioner would claim them later.

The exception to this was the New Model Army. In April 1645, the Committee of Both Kingdoms formulated new procedures to govern the maintenance of the army on campaign. Hereafter, the Committee aimed to assuage the burden the army placed upon the localities while at the same

76 TNA, SP28/247, f.7r.

77 TNA, SP28/154, unfol.

78 TNA, SP28/2B, f.415r.

79 TNA, SP28/143, f.33r; SP28/2B, ff.305r–305v.

80 TNA, SP28/252/1, f.184v; SP28/265/1, ff.68r–68v, 70r.

time guaranteeing that quarter and provision would be readily available. It was able to ban officers from taking free quarter and provision, and when pay was delayed vouchers would be issued in return for quarter and rations.[81] In addition, the Committee ordered that no individual resident should be necessitated to provide services or products beyond their own means. This order protected the local administration from carrying the responsibility of assigning quarters and provision for the army, in addition to safeguarding the Committee from excessive individual claims for reparation. Each of these orders were accompanied by strict penalties, including cashiering of officers.[82] Throughout the Western Campaign of 1645–6, Sir Thomas Fairfax, the army's commander-in-chief maintained strict levels of discipline among the rank and file, and made every effort to refrain from free quarter because it alienated the local populace. However, by clearing the West Country the New Model extended the tax base from which it could be supported, but reducing the army's self-reliance and rendering the payment of troops more difficult. As the army reached Warminster on 27 September 1645, Joshua Sprigge sorrowfully reported, 'the soldiers being so out of money, that they were all enforced to take quarter, which they had not done till then.'[83] In May 1646, the Buckinghamshire township of Cuddington gave quarter for 240 horses and 60 dragoons of Captain Daniel Abbot's company belonging to Colonel Okey's regiment, for which the inhabitants were compensated.[84]

Overnight billets were sought out by troop, company and regimental quartermasters, who rode ahead of marching armies, and assigned accommodation to units and smaller quantities of soldiers. In the summer of 1643, when the Earl of Essex's army's headquarters was at Thame in Oxfordshire, 80 dragoons were billeted at the village of Aston Sandford for 25 days, leaving £1239s 8d owed to the inhabitants.[85] About the same time, Colonel John Meldrum's cavalry regiment, consisting of 300 men and horses, spent three weeks at Monks Risborough, for which the parishioners claimed £200 16s 0d.[86] On 6 March 1643 the Treasurer to the Earl of Denbigh disbursed the sum of £24 0s 0d to Quartermaster Thomas Roberts of his own cavalry troop towards the payment 'due for their abode in the county of Warwickshire.' Correspondingly, Benjamin Mason, Captain in Colonel John Fiennes's Parliamentarian regiment of horse was paid £50 0s 0d in London on 10 August 1644, 'to set forth his troop and to discharge his soldiers' quarters, [and] conveying arms and saddles to the regiment.' Hence, ten days later Mason distributed the sum of £27 1s 11d to several innkeepers in Warwick for discharging the quarters of the colonel's and his own troops.[87]

Surviving tickets from the inhabitants of Shrewsbury for quartering Royalist troops in 1643 contain one from Richard Falconer for various soldiers under Lord Capel, including three dragoons under Captain Allen

81 *CSPD 1644–45*, p.428.
82 Rushworth, *Historical Collections*, VII, 32–3, 838; *LJ*, VII, p.311.
83 Sprigge, *Anglia Rediviva*, p.127.
84 TNA, SP28/149/1, f.41v; SP28/149/4, unfol.
85 TNA, SP28/150/2, f.192r.
86 TNA, SP28/151, unfol.
87 TNA, SP28/136/4, f.9r; SP28/139/19, unfol.

for a week. Edward Forten of Woodcott in the parish of St Chad, presented a bill for the sum of £10 17s 6d for billeting troops 'since Lord Capel came to town [March 1643], including six dragoons under the command of Captain Edwards.' John Milford's claim for an unknown amount 'for quartering soldiers, including a bluecoat, two soldiers from Worcester, two dragoons and men under Capel,' and another for £13 0s 6d 'for quartering soldiers under the command of Sergeant-Major Trevor, Captain Edwards, Lord Capel and Captain Allen's dragoons.'[88] As the King was unable to properly pay his troops, he was compelled them to subsist on the country. The chief reason why dragoons and troopers were paid more than their brothers in arms in the foot, was that they were expected to take care of the quartering and feeding of their mounts. On 27 November 1642, as the Oxford Army was entering winter quarters, the King gave orders to Prince Rupert, authorising him to instruct the colonels of horse and dragoons:

> to quarter and billet their respective regiments in such places as we have assigned, and there to take up such necessary provision of diet, lodging, hay, oats, and straw, as shall be necessary for them. And if there shall not be sufficient for such their supply in their quarters, then they are to send out their warrants to the several hundreds and parishes adjacent, requiring the inhabitants to bring in all fitting provisions for their daily supply. For all which, as for that taken up in their quarters, they [are] to give their respective tickets, and not to presume, upon pain of Our high displeasure, to send for greater quantities than will suffice for their numbers of men and horses, and such as may be proportionable to half of each officer's pay by the day, for all manner of diet, lodging, and horsemeat, and half of every ordinary horseman's pay by day for diet only, their horsemeat being supplied by the counties adjacent to each quarter. In this manner we will that you proceed and continue until such time as the counties wherein they are quartered shall agree of and settle some other course for their constant and daily supply.[89]

Accordingly, a document entitled 'The Quarters of the Army thus settled the 7th of December 1642' lays out the locations of each of the Royalist regiments of foot, horse and dragoons:[90]

At Oxford

The headquarters to be, and there besides Colonel Charles Gerrard's Regiment
The Regiment of the Guard
The King's two troops of Horse
Sir William Pennyman's Regiment
Sir Ralph Dutton's Regiment

88 SA, 3365/2570/56; 3365/2570/168; 3365/2570/229; 3365/2570/317.
89 Warburton, *Memoirs*, II, pp.70–1.
90 BRO, R/Z10/2.

At Abingdon
Prince Rupert's Regiment of Horse
Lieutenant-General Wilmot's Regiment of Horse
Colonel Ussher's Regiment of Dragoons

At Woodstock
The Lord Lieutenant-General's Regiment
His troop of Horse for his guard at four villages adjacent to Oxford

At Reading
Colonel Fielding's Tertia:
Sir Arthur Aston's Regiment of Horse
Sir Thomas Aston's Regiment of Horse
Sir John Byron's Regiment of Horse
Two troops of dragoons
Colonel Fytton's Regiment of Foot
Colonel Lunsford's Regiment of Foot

At Wallingford
Colonel Blagge's Regiment of Foot
Colonel Belasyse's Regiment of Foot
Colonel Dive's Regiment of Foot

At Banbury
Earl of Northampton's Regiment
Prince's Regiment of Horse
Earl Rivers' Regiment of Foot

At Brill
Colonel Gilbert Gerrard's and Lord Molyneux's Regiments of Foot

At Marlborough
The Lord Grandison's Regiment of Horse
Colonel Grey's Regiment of Dragoons

At Islip
The Lord Andover's Troop of Horse

At Wantage
The Lord Digby's Regiment of Horse
Colonel Duncombe's Regiment of Dragoons

At Whitney
Prince Maurice's Regiment of Horse

The Earl of Caernarvon's Regiment of Horse to quarter beyond Oxford towards Banbury

Among the Royalist forces an agreement was sometimes made with the county in which troops were quartered to provide a fixed amount each month for their maintenance. In October 1643 Berkshire and Oxfordshire consented to pay £500 a week in money and £500 a week in victuals for the King's army.[91] As the Royalist Oxford Army advanced into the West Country in the summer of 1643, Charles I decided to settle the permanent weekly contributions of certain counties to maintain his regiments. On 17 August, at Oxford, such a settlement was created. It was decided that the Royal army should consist of 4,000 horse, with each trooper receiving 10s 6d a week, and 10,000 foot, with every common soldier paid 4s 0d a week. If counties such as Hampshire and Wiltshire could pay only a half or a third of their allotted contribution in cash, hay and oats would be taken as a fair substitute. By these means it was hoped to raise £7,600 weekly, and to add to this the undefined contributions from Somerset, Devon, and Dorset. In November 1643, the gentry and freeholders of Wiltshire agreed to pay £1,200 weekly, for one month, towards the maintenance of the Royalist forces. In return the King agreed to their proposals concerning the general conduct of his troops, who had been engaged in plundering the area. For their mounts, each soldier would pay 1s 6d for a bushel of oats, 2s 0d for a bushel of peas and beans, hay at 5d a ton, and grass at 2s 6d a week. Additionally, no officer was permitted to requisition horses without a Royal warrant. A similar agreement was made with the gentry of Hampshire in March 1644, whereby the soldiers would pay 6d per ton for hay, 1s 6d for a bushel of oats and 4s for a bushel of wheat.[92]

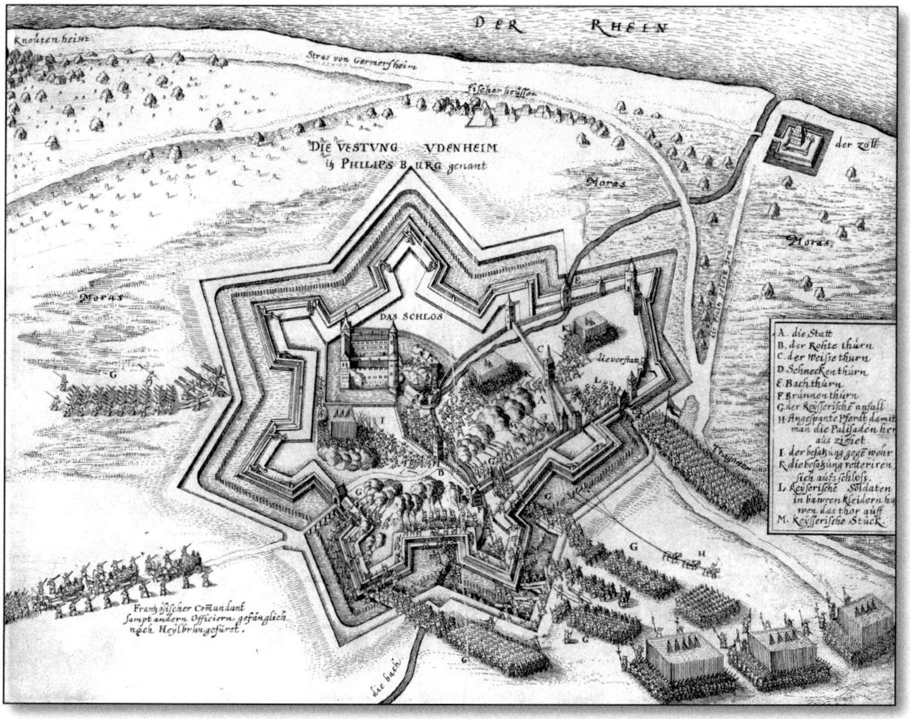

Company of Bavarian 'Tragoons', *Reconquest of the French-occupied fortress Philippsburg*, 1635 (Landesarchiv BW, GLAK H-BS P 39)

91 *Ibid.*, I, p.340.
92 BL, Ms Harley 6852, ff.175r–176v.

More often a single district was assigned to a particular regiment, brigade, or garrison for its upkeep. When Sir Thomas Aston's cavalry regiment arrived in Kidderminster in January 1643 (on its way to Cheshire, and after plundering much of the surrounding countryside), its officers and troopers accrued charges for free quartering, amounting to £28 8s 2d. The sum was ordered to be raised and paid according to a warrant issued by the King at Oxford:

> every of you that upon sight hereof you be aiding and assisting to him the said Sir Thomas Aston and to all persons commanding under him or employed by him for the quartering, billeting and providing necessaries for the lodging, diet and accommodation of all such forces both of horse and foot, as shall be by him raised or under his command in pursuance of the authority by us given, both in the raising of them, and in the conduct of them to Our army.[93]

While quartering in Evesham and the West during the winter of 1643–4 Aston's combined command of horse and dragoons was allotted contributions from the eight Hundreds of southwest Wiltshire. Although the county had initially actively supported the Parliamentarian cause, the Royalists made progress following the capture of Marlborough in 1642, while during the following year the Earl of Essex's forces were defeated at Aldbourne Chase, before Waller, failing to seize Devizes, was overpowered at nearby Roundway Down.

By way of contrast, the civil war Parish Loss Accounts of Warwickshire illustrate the extent to which various inhabitants were compelled to contribute to the upkeep of the county's Parliamentarian military units and garrisons via the weekly excise. In Priors Hardwick twelve householders each paid 13s 10d to the dragoon company, then cavalry troop of Captain Anthony Otway 'from 14th of July 1643 or thereabouts to 1st May 1646 after the rate of 30s 9d the week for the whole town[ship]'.[94] Lower Shuckburgh in the same parish furnished the sum of £1 14s 2d a week, amounting to £82 0s 0d from 23 February 1643 to 2 January 1644, and £99 2s 6d from 2 January 1644 to 1 May 1646. An entry belonging to the parish of Kingsbury records that Thomas Alsop provided one mare, carbine, saddle, and other furniture to Captain Otway's dragoons 'at the first raising thereof, valued at £7 0s 0d.' Similarly, Joseph Bennet of Bedworth Parish, south of Nuneaton gave 'for the service a musket, a saddle and bridle and delivered unto Captain Otway worth in value £1 6s 8d.[95]

Royalist organisation in Wiltshire functioned effectively from July 1643 to May 1644. Drawn up at York in June 1642, the Commission of Array was executed at Malmesbury in March 1643 and reissued from Oxford in March 1644. It provided the basis of an administration capable of collecting the

93 Bund (ed.), *Diary of Henry Townshend*, pp.102–3.

94 TNA, SP28/184/4, ff.3r, 6r.

95 TNA, SP28/201/2, f.7r; SP28/186/2, f.3v.

weekly contribution, and of dealing with sequestration and impressment.[96] From July to September 1643, the forces supporting the Royalist siege of Gloucester were quartered in most Wiltshire divisions. The King intended to build on the victories of Roundway and Bristol by storming this heavily defended city. His dealings with the local Commissioners of Array were thus chiefly dedicated to obtaining specific Hundreds as areas of temporary maintenance for his regiments. By such measures it was hoped to raise the weekly sum of £7,600, in addition to contributions from Devon, Somerset and Dorset, to enable a powerful, well-paid army to take the field for months at a time. Collecting such contributions, especially in areas where the demands of different regiments overlapped, proved more difficult than expected.

Thus, in January and February 1644 Colonel Apsley's regiment of foot was quartered on Hundreds from which the Royalist governor of Malmesbury, Colonel Thomas Howard, expected contribution for his garrison of 400 infantry and 200 cavalry. The King attempted to resolve the situation on 10 March by ordering all forces, other than Howard's regiments, to leave the county. He declared:

> For as much as the fortifying and defending that Our garrison of Malmesbury is of great importance to Our service and to the peace and security of that Our county and the parts adjacent. And whereas for want of the constant payment and collection of the rates agreed upon in the several divisions and hundreds, Our soldiers there have been much discouraged and the works there have not been made and perfected in that manner as is necessary.[97]

But one great hindrance to effective Royalist administration in Wiltshire was the presence of the King's commander-in-chief in the West, Sir Ralph Hopton with a substantial army operating in Hampshire and on the county border. In July 1643, he was summoned to Oxford, but in September Charles I ordered him to raise a new army to 'draw into the field for the clearing of Dorsetshire, Wiltshire and Hampshire, and so point forward as far as London as he could.'[98]

Royalist commanders like Sir Thomas Aston faced similar problems in drawing finance, sustenance, and clothing from their allotted areas in the West. As his troops marched into Wiltshire and Dorset the quartermaster of his cavalry regiment, John Cartwright, was continually assisted by the dragoons, who appear to have been constantly patrolling, obtaining supplies and contributions, and procuring quarters. In late 1643, Aston's horse and dragoons had been detached to the West as part of a brigade of the Oxford Army – which also included four cavalry troops and 400 foot commanded by Colonel Thomas Howard, and six troops of horse under Sir John Byron – to join Hopton's army. On 4 January 1644 Prince Rupert issued the following warrant to 'Sir Thomas Aston, baronet, Colonel of one regiment of horse and

96 George Anthony Harrison, 'Royalist Organisation in Wiltshire, 1642–1646', PhD thesis (University of London, 1963), p.293.

97 BL, Ms Harley 6852, f.175v.

98 Hopton, *Bellum Civile*, p.61.

one regiment of dragoons in his Majesty's army, or to one of the chief officers of his regiments present with the same':

> For as much as the contributions of the counties of Oxford and Berkshire are not sufficient for the maintenance of those his Majesty's troops, which are by special orders quartered therein I have thought fit hereby to authorize and command you immediately after sight hereof to quarter your whole regiments of horse and dragoons as conveniently as you may within any of the following Hundreds in his Majesty's county of Wiltshire, viz. Bradford Hundred, Melkesham, Whorwellsdown, Westbury, Dowarth and Mert, Branch and Dole, and Damerham South. But so succinctly that on all urgent occasions and orders you may call all your troops together upon three hours' warning. And for the accommodation and subsistence of your regiments you are from time to time to receive levy, take and fetch your maintenance for the same out of the aforesaid hundreds according to the number of your effective officers and soldiers, and his Majesty's allowance in the last establishment for the maintenance of his horse forces and dragoons. Which maintenance is to be allowed due and justly paid to your said regiments, from the present date hereof till such time as you shall receive orders contrary from his Majesty or myself. And in the interim, you must strictly command all your officers to by no means transgress or exceed your aforesaid directions or suffer any oppression to be enforced on any of the inhabitants of these towns, parishes, and places in the Hundreds aforesaid from which you shall receive your maintenance for your said regiments of horse and dragoons by any soldiers under your command. And if at any time any town, towns, parishes or places in these said hundreds, which by agreement shall be to allow you maintenance for your said regiments of horse and dragoons shall neglect the punctual payment or delivery for your due maintenance to such your troops as they shall be to maintain, immediately after the same shall become due it shall then become lawful for you from time to time to levy all and every their arrears by such parties of horse as you shall think fit. Always provided, that you exact not from the defaulters more than your dues, according to your directions aforesaid. And if you may with more facility perform these my commands, I do hereby strictly charge and command all his Majesty's officers and ministers of the said county and Hundreds whom it may concern, to be from time to time to be aiding and assisting to you in the effecting of his Majesty's service as much as in them lies. Hereof you, and they and every of them must in no ways fail as you will answer the contrary at your perils. And for your and theirs so doing there shall be to you and them, and every of them, sufficient warrant.

From Winchester, on 25 January 1644 Hopton complained to Sir Thomas Aston of the burdens placed upon local communities by the exactions of his troops:

> By the occasion of the quartering of two brigades of my horse of late in Wiltshire, I received many complaints of particular persons that have suffered in a disproportional manner to others in that service, especially innkeepers, my desire is that the burden being more extraordinary than I meant if I could have helped it be as equally set as may be of that reasonable satisfaction be given out of the

contribution of that county, which howsoever, I hear that other men call for (upon what order I know not) yet I know they belong by his Majesty's grant only to me, and I require they be paid to no other out of this I pray you to give reasonable consent to such as you find have such cause to complain of any inequality, upon whose care of that county and of the rights of this army from it.

Abraham Casembroot, *Kamp van Roma* (Rijkesmuseum, Amsterdam)

The following day Sir Thomas reported to Hopton the various problems encountered by himself and his officers in obtaining quarter and clothing, both in Wiltshire and elsewhere:

> I am importuned by divers [of] the inhabitants of the Hundred of Whorlesdown, to certify your lordship that by virtue of the King's express directions at a Council of War, and in pursuance thereof the Prince's warrant for quarter and maintenance of my men in this county. I have collected towards the present supply of my men to enable them to march, about six weeks' contribution out of that Hundred, without which they could not possibly have gone upon service, they are threatened to pay it again, which I hope your Lordship will forbid; certain I am, it was against my will and to the great loss of the regiment (being removed by the King's express direction out of Gloucestershire, where there was £1,200 in the quarters) to come hither, where we were again deprived of our quarters as soon as we came. The Hundreds of Whorlesdowne, Daworth and Mere, being it seems by his Majesty taken from us, in which we were promised means to cover the nakedness, with two summers' and almost two winters' perpetual service without rest or quarter worn out of the habit, and almost out of the souls of men, into despair ever to be clothed again or receive anything, I would to God things were so managed there were no such crossing of orders I am sure it is and will be the ruin of his regiments, and little comfort to the officer that spends his fortune in his service to be exposed to the inconvenience of such contradictions with others and to the clamour and daily mutiny of the soldiers for want of subsistence, but what

> inconvenience soever I feel, I know how to obey, since intimation of his Majesty's disposal of these quarters otherwise. I have forborne to demand anything but was due before, and must in all submit to his Majesty's pleasure, and for what is past being past redemption, I hope your Lord will give order the country shall not be oppressed by repayment, and both excuse this boldness and the unhappy trouble herein befallen so much to the prejudice of your Lordship's must humble servant, Thomas Aston.

Aston's methods and complaints, however, elicited the following rebuke from Hopton:

> It is very little satisfaction to me that having now these six weeks taken your pleasure in the quarters assigned by the King to this army even in our greatest necessity, should desire me not to oppress the country by repayment, I hope it shall appear the oppression was in your undue taking of which belonged to us instead, and not in my demand which was not assigned to me before I undertook this task, who I am sure have not had two months' ease of duty as you now have had since the war began, and now you have his Majesty's orders to remove into Dorsetshire, I shall strictly expect you to be totally removed accordingly, and that you demand not one penny of that country since that order, upon which pretence soever. Concerning the nakedness of your men, I cannot but take a little the more notice of it, because complaint is made to me of much cloth taken by you from honest men in the county whereof I expect an account. I must profess his Majesty's service under my command hath suffered by the wrong at hand had in Wiltshire than it hath, or could have done by Waller's force, any duty to his Majesty's service makes me insist upon, thus otherwise, I decline to continue.[99]

For the upkeep of Aston's, Howard's and Byron's troops the weekly sum of £1,000 was allotted from the county of Wiltshire by the King. An undated, though probably contemporaneous reckoning of these units and the amounts to be paid is reproduced below:

99 WRO, X3/119/AC/1; X3/119/AC/3; X3/119/AC/13–14.

Colonel Howard	The officers of 4 companies of foot 400 soldiers The officers of 5 troops of Horse 200 troopers	£ 33 12s 0d £ 80 00s 0d £113 12s 0d £ 99 15s 0d £120 00s 0d £219 15s 0d
Sir John Byron's Regiment:	Officers of 6 troops 280 troopers	£119 00s 0d £168 00s 0d £287 00s 0d
Sir Thomas Aston's Regiment	Officers of 7 troops 360 troopers	£139 13s 0d £180 00d 0d £319 00d 0d
Subtotal:		£940 14s 0d
The major of the brigade his allowance for 4 horses according to order: The general adjutant his allowance Total:	 [blank]	£ 3 10s 0d £944 04s 0d

By February 1645 Sir Thomas Aston's dragoons and cavalry had returned to the West Country, where they participated in Lord Goring's operations at Weymouth, then at Ilminster and Langport. According to a Parliamentarian source, Sir Thomas led an independent mounted command during this period, consisting of horse and dragoons, with a combined strength of 450–500 men.[100] An estimate of the cost of feeding three regiments of horse and three of dragoons for three months in Hopton's army, drawn up for the 1643 campaign, includes 'hay for the dragoons at 3s 0d per week for a horse', costing £165 0s 0d; the same proportion for oats, costing £238 16s 0d; and 'provisions of the dragoons and officers' horses', costing £477 12s 0d.[101]

100 *The Moderate Intelligencer*, 5–12 February 1644.
101 BL, Ms Harley 6804, f.303r.

5

Arms and Ammunition

In Continental armies, dragoons were originally formed from both pikemen and musketeers, but the pike was too unwieldy to carry on horseback, so was quickly dropped. Colonel George Monck's recommendation that 'all your dragoons ought to have swine-feathers' poses certain questions regarding both evidence and usage.[1] Turner, whose military manual was published in the 1670s, but describes earlier practices, described them thus:

> I think I may reckon in this place the Swedish feather, among the defensive arms, though it does participate in both defence and offence. It is a stake five or six foot long, and about four fingers thick, with a piece of sharp iron nailed to each end of it. By the one end it is made fast in the ground in such a manner that the other may lay out so it may meet the breast of a horse, whereby a body of musketeers is defended as with a palisade, against the rude charge of a squadron of horse, which in the meantime they gall and disorder with their shot. I have seen them made use of in Germany, and before I left that war saw them drop out of use. When the infantry of several regiments or brigades are drawn up in battle, and the pikes and those stakes are fixed in the ground, they make a delightful show representing a wood. The pikes resembling the tall trees and the stakes the shrubs.[2]

On 1 December 1642, Captain Thomas Moore's company of Waller's own regiment of dragoons was issued with hatchets, axes, and Swedish feathers.[3] Also known as 'swine feathers', these were essentially a musket rest, but with a pike head pointing towards the enemy to protect the firer from cavalry, although they could be used as a defensive palisade. Hence, they represented an early attempt to introduce a greater degree of flexibility and self-defence to the musketeer or dragoon. Without the need to be supported by slower moving divisions of pike, they could be used to form a defensive device of spear points if placed in the ground. Theoretically soldiers might retreat behind them and fire at their enemy in safety. Swedish feathers were used extensively on the Continent during the early seventeenth century, yet

1 Monck, *Observations*, p.27.
2 Turner, *Pallas Armata*, p.216.
3 TNA, WO 55/387, f.47r.

although some troops were issued with them during the British Civil Wars there is little evidence of their actual usage. In 1643, the Parliamentarian commander, the Earl of Denbigh, acquired 300 Swedish feathers in London and sent them to his forces in the Midlands, whilst in February 1644 he purchased 100 muskets with half pikes.[4] Similarly, in April 1643 the dragoon commander, Sir Anthony Irby paid the sum of £3 10s 0d for 'half pikes for the musketeers' – though he led a separate troop of cavalry, there is no evidence that he commanded any foot units, and hence this entry might have referred erroneously to his dragoons.[5] Additionally, when the Army of the Solemn League and Covenant Scots Covenanter Army marched into northern England in January 1644 it brought with it 6,269 muskets, 3,533 bandoliers and 10,600 Swedish feathers.[6] The eighteen 'Sweeds feathers with musket rests' in Denbigh's magazine at Stafford in February 1645 may have been the residue of his previously mentioned acquisition and this could indicate that some at least had been issued.[7] Other examples of their existence during the British Civil Wars are known. Richard Coe, who was among the Tower Hamlets Trained Bands at Cropredy Bridge, near Banbury on 29 June 1644 commented that:

> at 10 or 11 a clock at night a foolish fellow of our regiment, shot off his musket, (the watch being) which made an alarm in the enemy's quarters, they shot at our forlorn hope, which lay down by their works, and we shot at them, but we were there over-cunning for them, for our firelocks were placed under a hedge, and light[ed] match hung along on palisadoes a musket shot off.[8]

According to the military writer William Barriffe, 'palisadoes' was another name for swine feathers.[9]

When the wars began dragoons were predominantly issued with matchlock muskets, although some units were issued with flintlocks (known also as snaphaunce, firelock or dog-lock muskets), or replaced their matchlocks accordingly. On 18 November 1642 Colonel Richard Browne, the commander of a regiment of Parliamentarian dragoons raised in London, paid a carrier the sum of 6s 3d 'for bringing two loads of powder, and one load of bullets and match.' Similarly, in spring 1643 Sir Anthony Irby expended 6s 8d on 84 yards of match for his dragoons.[10] However, in August 1642 Colonel John Browne's regiment of the Earl of Essex's forces had 600 short muskets delivered to it.[11] Similarly, on 16 November a warrant was issued to supply Colonel Wardlaw's dragoons of the same army with

4 TNA, SP28/34/2, f.291v; TNA, SP28/143, f.12r.
5 TNA, SP28/313/4, unfol.
6 Terry, *Solemn League and Covenant*, I, pp.19–20.
7 TNA, SP28/28, f.367v.
8 *An Exact Diarie Or a brief Relation of the progress of Sir William Waller's Army since the joining of the London Auxilliaries with his forces* (London: 19 July 1644).
9 William Barriffe, *Military Discipline: or, the Young Artillery Man* (London: John Dawson, 3rd edn, 1643), p.356.
10 TNA, SP28/144/2, f.29r.; SP28/313/4, unfol.
11 TNA, WO55/1937, unfol. ; WO55/1754, unfol.

600 muskets, 600 bandoliers, 600 swords with belts, 2,000lbs of gunpowder and shot proportional from the Tower stores.[12] That no match was supplied infers that the firearms, which were received on 19 September and referred to as 'bastard muskets', were firelocks.[13] Sir William Brereton's dragoons in Cheshire were often referred to by him and his contemporaries as 'firelocks', owing to their association with these weapons, and it appears that from late 1642 all the soldiers were armed with them.[14] Despite having been provided with both matchlock and snaphaunce muskets on 21 November 1642, a year later Brereton petitioned Parliament to send by sea 100 pairs of pistols, 300 muskets and 200 or 300 firelocks, adding 'These are not to be procured upon any terms in this country [the county of Cheshire] wherein I could raise good store of men if I could arm them.'[15]

The Royalist dragoons at Edgehill certainly carried these weapons, as the papers of the King's Trayne refer to them transporting their match.[16] The Dutch writer, Johann von Nassau recommended Scottish snaphaunce muskets for dragoons, although matchlocks and wheel-lock carbines were also commonly used on the Continent.[17] But it was Vernon, who suggested in 1644:

> The dragoon's arming is only offensive, having a good fire and cock musket something, a wider bore, then ordinary hanging in a belt by a swivel at his side, with a good sword and ordinary horse, it being only to expedite his march, for he must perform his service on foot, the ordinary marching is usually ten abreast, and when they come in service, nine of them alight casting the bridle over the next sideman's horse's neck, and for one in ten serves to keep their horses, the rest perform the service; it is a good and special principle, to have our soldiers both horse and foot well chosen, well-armed, and well disciplined[18]

Likewise, Monck suggested that the offensive arms of the dragoon were:

> A musket, or a good snaphaunce to a musket barrel; the which I hold much better for dragoon service, being upon occasion they may be able to make use of their snaphaunces on horseback, and upon any service in the night they may go undiscovered He must have also a belt to hang his musket in, with a pair of bandoliers, and a good long tuck, with a belt. And all your dragoons ought to have swine-feathers[19]

Four hundred snaphaunce muskets for the Lord Lieutenant's Regiment arrived in Ireland in March 1642. A reference to such weapons in a letter from the Lords Justices in June 1642 indicates both their usefulness and that

12 TNA, WO55/1754, unfol.
13 TNA, WO55/1937, unfol.
14 BL, Ms Harley 2128, ff.25r, 34r.
15 HMC, *Thirteenth Report, App. I,* p.157.
16 TNA, SP28/2, f.668r.
17 Hahlweg, *Die Heeresreform*, p.315.
18 Vernon, *The Young Horse-man*, pp.8–9.
19 Monck, *Observations*, p.27.

they may have been shipped separately from the soldiers, 'that 1,000 firelock pieces fixed may be also sent us, which will be of singular use and advantage to us in the services here as we find by the experience we have of the 400 firelocks lately sent us, many of which are not fixed.'[20]

Snaphaunces had certain advantages over matchlocks in terms of safety, in that they reduced the danger of accidental powder explosions, and the weapon was also more economical in use, avoiding the need for large quantities of match. Due to the safety aspect, firelocks (infantry soldiers armed with the firearm, as opposed to dragoons carrying them) were frequently utilised to guard artillery trains. Thus, Richard Elton advised, 'Those who are ordained for their guard to be firelocks or to have snaphaunces for the avoiding of the danger that might happen by the coal of a match.'[21] Hence, Captain William Legge's company of firelocks acted independently at Edgehill in this role, as did the firelock companies of the Earl of Essex's forces, in addition to the two companies of tawny-coated soldiers guarding the train of artillery in the New Model Army at Naseby and later campaigns. Moreover, with the snaphaunce there was no damp match to consider during wet weather, while glowing matches were visible in the dark, and thus less preferable for night operations, although on occasion this was employed as a subterfuge. Turner contended, 'It is impossible to hide burning matches so well in the night time, especially if there is any wind, (though there be covers made of white iron, like extinguishers purposely for that end) but that some of them will be seen by a vigilant enemy, and thereby many secret enterprises are lost.'[22]

Military garrisons during the British Civil Wars habitually consumed large quantities of match, even if, at times, it was only issued to sentries. One specific problem, increasingly found in Royalist-held locations was obtaining raw materials. As Charles I pointed out to Colonel Francis Ottley, the governor of Shrewsbury and commander of the garrison's force of dragoons on 20 April 1643, 'our affairs here require a far greater proportion of match than all the tow, flax and hemp to be had in these parts.' Thus, Ottley was told to gain supplies from the surrounding neighbourhood.[23] On 30 May 1643 Sir William Savile, the Royalist governor of Sheffield advised his deputy, 'For the match you write for, I shall send you some, but I put you in mind once more to use your snaphaunce pieces to keep sentry with. They will save our match.'[24] One remedy for this was to issue a limited number of snaphaunces to each company for them to use on guard duty. In late 1643, the Parliamentarian garrison at Warwick procured from London gunsmiths 72 of these weapons.[25] However, the independent company commanded by Colonel John Needham at Kenilworth Castle – where he was governor – received 70 firelocks from the Tower stores in London, in addition to 30

20 *Calendar of the Manuscripts of the Marquess of Ormonde, K. P., preserved at Kilkenny Castle* (London: HMSO, 1902), II, pp.137, 142–3.

21 Elton, *Complete Body*, p.145.

22 Turner, *Pallas Armata*, p.176.

23 'Ottley Papers' (1895), p.316.

24 W. D Macray (ed.), *Beaumont Papers: Letters Relating to the Family of Beaumont of Whitley, Yorkshire* (London: Nichols, 1884), p.70.

25 TNA, SP28/136/4, f.281v.

matchlock muskets from Coventry. Given that this unit mustered between 60 and 70 common soldiers throughout 1643, and around 100 in early 1645 such figures would also suggest that it consisted entirely of musketeers.[26]

Every twenty musketeers were issued a snaphaunce musket at Stafford in December 1644, 'for want of muskets with firelocks upon the guards in this garrison there has been much match spent.' The governor, Colonel Simon Rugeley was still requesting these weapons two months later, 'in regard the garrison is short of match be pleased to lend the snaphaunces [from the Earl of Denbigh's magazine] to save the said match.'[27] During Waller's withdrawal from Lansdowne in July 1643 his musketeers left lighted match behind. The Royalist Richard Atkyns reported, 'we pelted at one another till half an hour before day, and then we heard not any noise, but saw light matches upon the wall, which our commanders observing, sent one to discover whether they had quit the field or not, who brought news that they were gone.'[28] Similarly, while preparing for a dawn assault on Chester's North Gate on 27 January 1645, Brereton's troops, 'approaching near the same unto their works, they perceived the walls by the light of their matches, well-guarded with soldiers.'[29] To save match musketeers and dragoons could extinguish their match, leaving just the file leader's match still lit, but this might lead to a frantic rush for the other soldiers to light theirs if they suddenly encountered the enemy.

But although flintlocks had certain advantages over matchlocks, they were also more expensive. In early 1645, matchlock muskets costing between 10s 0d and 11s 6d were paid for upon delivery to the Committee for the Army to be supplied to the New Model Army. In 1646, a contract was agreed between the Ordnance Office at the Tower of London and one supplier for 'English matchlock muskets and bandoliers', at 14s 0d apiece, for the forces in Ireland.[30] On 10 March 1645, the Commons resolved 'that 500 muskets, furnished now in the Magazine, which were of those which Mr Hill and Mr Pennoyer did furnish to the State, be delivered to Colonel White,' for the supply of Fairfax's new army.[31] A month later, two London gunsmiths, William Watson and Edward Burrows, provided the New Model with 200

26 TNA, SP28/136/1, ff.288r–289v; TNA, SP28/136/2, ff.211r–213v; TNA, SP28/136/4, f.282r.

27 D H. Pennington and I. A. Roots (eds and intro.), The Committee at Stafford, 1643–1645 (Manchester: Manchester University Press, 1957), pp.230, 256, 296.

28 Atkyns, *Vindication*, p.33.

29 James Hall (ed.), *Memorials of the Civil War in Cheshire and the adjacent counties by Thomas Malbon, of Nantwich, Gent., and Providence improved by Edward Burghall*, Lancashire and Cheshire Record Society, volume 19 (1889), p.159.

30 TNA, SP28/29/2, f.249r; ML, 46–78/709, ff.81r–81v, 87r.; Gerald I. Mungeam, 'Contracts of the Supply of Equipment to the 'New Model Army' in 1645, *JAAS*, 6 (1968–70), pp.53–114 (pp. 94, 100). Though an important resource, the composite volume of Ordnance Office records, assembled in the nineteenth century and edited by Mungeam, probably consist for the most part of Army Committee contracts for the supply of the New Model Army notified to the officers of the Ordnance between April 1645 and April 1646. The majority of these are also recorded in the minute book in The National Archives (WO47/1). Alternatively, the contents may have once formed part of another minute book which is now lost. Hence, ML, 46–78/709 should be used in conjunction with the Ordnance Office books covering the period 1645–6 at Kew (WO47/1, WO55/1660, WO55/1646–7, WO55/1662–4).

31 *CJ*, IV, p.74.

'snaphaunce muskets English full bore and proof' at 15s 6d each, while in October 1646, 17s 0d was paid for similar items.[32] On 22 December 1645 another consignment of snaphaunces 'full-bore and proof, and four foot long at 15s 4d apiece' was brought from the Tower. Similarly, 24 of them were purchased at the lower rate of 13s 4d apiece from the gunmaker Peter Gregor on 27 December 1645.[33] The accounts and warrants for 1645–6 record orders for 8,050 matchlock muskets and 3,300 snaphaunces, suggesting that in addition to the dragoons and firelock guard, although some may have been distributed to foot companies. On 10 January 1646, John Silke senior of Whitechapel was contracted to supply to the New Model 200 'snaphaunce dragoons full-bore and proof' at the same price, 'to be forthwith brought into the Tower of London.'[34] Except for the latter example, it seems likely, however, that most of the full-bore firelocks supplied to the army were not intended for Colonel Okey's dragoon regiment. Various contracts specified 'dragoon muskets', 'dragoon muskets with snaphaunce locks' and 'snaphaunce dragoons'.

In April 1645, during the arming of Sir Thomas Fairfax's nascent army, the sum of £77 was paid 'unto John Norcott in full of his contract for 100 dragoon muskets with snaphaunce locks at 15s 6d apiece.' Norcott also supplied a further 105 of the same firearms. Likewise, on 14 April, the London gunmakers John Watson, William Travis and George Day were paid for 100 snaphaunce muskets for dragoons at 15s 6d each. And, on 6 May 1645 Richard Jones, another London manufacturer was remunerated the sum of £287 14s 0d, 'in full of his contract', for delivering 300 matchlocks and 100 'dragoon muskets with snaphaunce locks.'[35] That these suppliers received their payments in full during this period indicates that such items had already been delivered to Fairfax's army. Moreover, a detailed survey of the primary equipment delivered to the New Model during 1645 demonstrates that the equipping of its regiments of horse and dragoons with saddles, pistols, carbines and snaphaunce muskets was a critical function of the Ordnance Office's magazine. Issues of these items were at their highest level during the late spring and summer months of 1645. They included supplies to recruits and this high level endured until the following year.[36]

Perhaps, like some of those purchased for the Earl of Essex's forces and possibly units of the Royalist army in 1642, snaphaunces issued to the New Model Army's dragoons were shorter (36-inch, rather than 48-inch barrels) and lighter models that those supplied to the foot and the firelock guard of the New Model's train of artillery. Evidence in support of this derives from contractor's warrants. One, dated 1 August 1645, to pay Daniel Judd, plumber and shot caster the sum of £119 0s 0d 'for 7 tons of bastard musket shot at £17 0s 0d per ton.' On 22 October Judd also received a contract for

32 *CJ*, IV, p.698; ML, 46–78/709, ff.98r, 110r, 114r; Mungeam, 'Contracts', pp.106, 112, 114.

33 ML, 46–78/709, ff.78r–79r; Mungeam, 'Contracts', pp.92–3.

34 ML, 46–78/709, f.73r; Mungeam, 'Contracts', p.90.

35 TNA, SP28/29/1, ff.198r., 218r.–219r.; SP28/29/2, f.249r.; SP28/30/4, f.338r.

36 TNA, WO47/1, passim; WO55/1646, passim; SP28/29/1, ff.166r, 204r, 218r–219r, 258r; SP28/29/2, ff.249r, 258r; SP28/31/3, f.378r.

10 tons of bastard musket shot and 1 ton of pistol shot at £17 0s 0d each ton weight, to be delivered into the stores in the Tower of London before 1 January next for the use of Sir Thomas Fairfax's army.'[37] Alternatively, the casting of such bullets could be carried out in the field. In April 1645 Captain John Phipps, a commissary officer in the New Model Army ordered 2cwt of lead for ordnance, three iron pots to melt lead in, 12 great melting ladles and 24 small dipping ladles. He also obtained 60 bastard musket moulds.[38]

Writing in 1672, Venn recommended that dragoons' muskets 'are to be somewhat wider in the bore than the field musket, and about two foot and nine inches in length.'[39] William Watson had previously supplied Essex's forces with firearms. On 18 November 1643, he was paid £193 6s 8d for 200 muskets, and 200 pairs of bandoliers at 1s 10d each. Richard Hinton also delivered 100 bandoliers for 1s 6d.[40]

According to Francis Markham:

> About their bodies baldrickwise from the left shoulder under the right arm, he shall carry bandoliers of broad leather ... and to this bandolier shall be fastened by long double strings (at least a quarter of a yard in length a piece, that they may with more ease be brought to the mouth of the musket) one large priming charge ... and at least twelve other charges of wood, all made of some tough light wood or else of horn, and covered with leather.[41]

Similarly, Turner recommended in his *Pallas Armata*:

> To a musketeer belongs also a bandolier of leather, at which he should have hanging eleven or twelve shot of powder, and bag for his ball, a primer, and a cleanser. But it is 30 years ago since I saw these laid aside in some German armies; for it is impossible for soldiers, especially wanting cloaks (and more want cloaks than have any) to keep these flasks (though well and strongly made) from snow and rain, which soon spoils them, and so makes the powder altogether useless. Besides, the noise of them betray those who carry them in all surprisals, onslaughts, and sudden enterprises. Instead of those let patrons [cartridges] be made, such as horsemen use, whereof each musketeer should be provided of a dozen; these should be kept in a bag of strong leather, or the skin of some beast well sowed, that it be proof against rain, this bag he may carry about his neck in a bandolier, or if the weather be extremely rainy, in one of his pockets, and in the other a horn with priming powder, and his cleanser tied to it. By this a musketeer hath these advantages, he shall be sure to charge with dry powder, and that is no small advantage; next, it is a more ready way to charge than the other, for he hath no more to do but to bite off a little of the paper of his patron and put his charge of powder and ball in at once, and then ram both home.[42]

---

37 TNA, SP28/31/4, f.441r; SP30/37, f.13r.

38 TNA, SP28/34/1, f.62r; SP28/30/3, f.240r.

39 Venn, *Military and Maritine [sic] Discipline*, pp.8–9.

40 TNA, SP/28/227/1, unfol.

41 Markham, *Five Decades of Epistles of Warre*, p.34.

42 Turner, *Pallas Armata*, p.176.

Musketeers and some dragoons were commonly issued with the smoothbore, muzzle-loading matchlock musket (though various dragoon units possessed snaphaunces), bandolier and sword. Instructions issued in 1636 for arming the English and Welsh militia declared that muskets were meant to be of one standard bore (of twelve bullets to the pound) and that each musketeer 'shall be furnished with a sufficient whole musket, the barrel thereof shall be four feet in length and no more,' the total length of the weapon being five feet two inches.[43] Besides, 'every such person appointed to serve with a full musket shall be further furnished and armed with a good bandolier, and with fifteen good and serviceable charges of turned wood, covered with leather and fastened there unto. Also with a good primer, worm and scourer, and a bullet bag annexed unto it, with a mould to cast such bullets as aforesaid.' A list for 'provision of arms and other necessaries for his Majesty's store [in Ireland]', dated 20 September 1642, mentions 'Boxes according to fifteen to the pound for decayed bandoliers for musketeers, 90,000; and primers for every fifteen boxes of that number, 6,000; and girdles to supply decayed bandoliers, 6,000.'[44]

On 16 September 1642, it was ordered that the newly formed Parliamentarian dragoon regiment commanded by Colonel James Wardlaw in Essex's army to be supplied with 600 muskets, bandoliers, and swords from the Tower stores.[45] Likewise, at Romford on 16 August 1643 the Parliamentarian Committee for Essex issued a warrant for the payment of £30 0s 0d to Thomas Jupe in full 'for 360 bandoliers at 20d a pair delivered to Captain Holcroft, Captain Harbottle and Captain Miller.' Similarly, the sum of £342 0s 0d was paid to John Watson, a London gunsmith for '360 muskets with ringnails, belts and swivels.' These firearms, which were 'furnished for dragoons', were to be delivered to the same captains. On a like occasion, the Committee ordered Lieutenant-Colonel Edward Birkhead, an officer in the Essex Trained Bands and agent for the procurement of arms to the Eastern Association Army, 'to deliver and direct you to pay unto Captain Holcroft, Captain Harbottle [and] Captain Miller, or any one of them, the sum of £9 0s 0d, for and towards three colours and six drums for their several companies of dragoons under the

Reproduction collar of bandoliers, with pewter bottle tops (courtesy of Graham Webb)

43 Wrye, State Papers Relating to Musters, p.89.

44 James Hogan (ed.), *Letters and Papers Relating to the Irish Rebellion Between 1642–46* (Dublin: The Stationery Office, 1936), p.134; *CJ*, II, pp.576, 793, 807.

45 TNA, WO55/1754, unfol.

command of the Earl of Manchester.' On 13 September 1642, Birkhead had been instructed to pay the sum of £73 6s 8d to Watson for 800 bandoliers at 22d per pair, while eight days later he was to authorise the manufacturer 'to provide forthwith 200 muskets, full-bore with rests, at the rate of 17s 6d the musket and rest, and so many bandoliers at 22d the pair.'[46]

The reason why the bandoliers issued to Manchester's dragoons the month previously were fractionally cheaper is unclear, although prices were known to fluctuate among army suppliers depending on availability. In February 1644, 1,500 bandoliers were purchased from London suppliers for Sir William Brereton's army in Cheshire.[47] It seems likely that some of these were supplied to the dragoons as no mention is made in sources of these troops being issued powder bags. Captain John Kynaston's company of foot in Sir William Myddelton's regiment of Sir Thomas Myddelton's brigade, received 60 swords and belts, 60 collars of bandoliers and 24 muskets on 2 September 1644.[48] Similarly, Sir Thomas purchased 300 sets at 1s 2d each in October 1644.[49] The price of these bandoliers compares with those supplied to Fairfax's army in early 1645, which were got for between 12d and 20d each (mostly the latter).[50]

One contract with the bandolier makers John Gace of East Cheap and Richard Newbury of Aldgate, London, dated 17 March 1646 for the supply of 2,000 items (1,000 each) for the New Model, stipulated, that they were 'to be of wood with whole bottoms to be turned within and not bored, the heads to be of wood and to be laid in oil, viz: three times on, and to be coloured blue, with blue and white strings, with strong thread twist, and with good belts at 20d apiece.'[51] Two further agreements – one dated 29 April 1645, another 7 January 1646 – ordered the same design and tint, but how common this was among the various batches of bandoliers supplied to Fairfax's forces remains unclear, given that other contracts specify no colour. It must therefore be implied that they were left plain and oiled by the manufacturer prior to delivery.[52] Either way, by June 1645 at least 7,000 collars of bandoliers, produced by five different manufacturers, had been delivered to the Committee for the Army.[53]

Like other military items large quantities of bandoliers were captured by both sides. Following the Parliamentarian victory at Marston Moor in July 1644 the Eastern Association Army's stores were augmented by 4,550 muskets, 800 pikes and 40 barrels of powder, also ordnance, shot, swords and bandoliers, while the garrisons that surrendered to these forces in the weeks following the battle, delivered up lesser amounts of weapons and ammunition.[54] Some examples survive of a different design of bandolier,

46 TNA, SP28/227/1, ff.4r, 6r–7r, 9r.
47 *CSPD 1644*, p.26; *LJ*, VI, p.446; JRL, TW/287.
48 TNA, SP28/45/1, f.130v; SP28/346, f.283r.
49 TNA, SP28/346/2, unfol.
50 TNA, WO47/1, f.211r; ML, 46–78/709, ff.72r, 89r; Mungeam, 'Contracts', pp.90, 102.
51 TNA, WO55/1662, ff.6v, 31v; ML, 46–78/709, f.69r; Mungeam, 'Contracts', pp.87–8.
52 ML, 46–78/709, ff.67r, 72r, 69r, 89r; Mungeam, 'Contracts', pp.90, 102.
53 TNA, SP28/29/1, ff.193r, 196r, 202r–203r, 223r.
54 Lilburne, *Innocency and truth*, pp.25, 70.

considered rare by historians – although, it seems, on little or no evidence – which may have been issued to civil war soldiers. Fragments of two items in Barnstable Museum and a complete set at Haddon Hall, Derbyshire, dated to the seventeenth century, contain a leather flap to protect the bottles from rain, and a system to retract the bottles within the flap. This could also protect them from tangling or spilling powder when not in use or on horseback.

The Haddon example has twelve wooden charges with wooden caps and appears to be complete. An archaeological survey of the area of the Cheriton battlefield, known today as Dark Copse Field, undertaken in 2007 revealed the presence of 47 pewter powder-bottle caps belonging to bandoliers and tops from powder flasks.[55] Although in April 1645 Colonel John Okey's New Model regiment of dragoons was issued with snaphaunces, archaeological finds include similar items around the Sulby Hedges on the Naseby battlefield, well away from infantry positions, indicating that this was still the method of carrying ammunition.[56] A contract with the London manufacturers Thomas Jupe (who also furnished Essex's forces), Thomas Roche and Nathaniel Humphries, dated 7 January 1646, was for the supply of 4,000 bandoliers, 'the boxes of strong double plate, the heads of the same with whipcord strings, and with good belts according to the pattern at 20d apiece.'[57] Likewise, among the list of substantial quantities of arms and equipment ordered by the Committee of the Army for the re-equipping of Sir Thomas Fairfax's troops in December 1645 were '8,000 bandoliers of tin covered.'[58]

Whether some or any of the blue-painted, plate or pewter-topped, bandolier bottles were intended for Colonel Okey's regiment is impossible to know, given that it was formed out of Lieutenant-Colonel John Lilburne's dragoons of Manchester's and other pre-existing units, who may have brought their bandoliers with them. However, the disbandment of some armies to merge into the New Model Army led to the return of some clothing and equipment to London. In November 1646, the chief collector for Cambridgeshire received £21 19s 6d expended on conveying coats, breeches, knapsacks and shirts to the Tower stores.[59] Nonetheless, although some archaeological finds associated with bandoliers have been discovered around the positions held by Okey's dragoons at Naseby, no direct references for their issue have come to light. This is perhaps unsurprising as clothing and equipment supplied by contractors were habitually sent to the army's magazine at Reading during this period, and hence distributed to military units as required.

Contrary to the idea of the use of bandoliers by Okey's men is a warrant of 18 April 1645, which records the disbursement of £20 16s 8d to the London contractor Nathaniel Humphries 'in full for his contract for 500 cartouches

55 James Bonsall, 'The Study of Small Finds at the 1644 Battle of Cheriton', *JCA*, 3 (2007), pp.29–52, (pp. 34–5); Kevin M. Claxton, 'The Battle of Cheriton: The analysis of artefacts from an English Civil War Battlefield', *JCA*, 13 (2018), pp.80–96, (p. 85).

56 Foard, *Naseby*, pp.59–64.

57 ML, 46–78/709, f.72r; Mungeam, 'Contracts', p.90.

58 *CJ*, IV, p.388.

59 TNA, SP28/41, f.376r.

[cartridge boxes] for dragoon muskets at 10d apiece.'[60] These had been contracted for on 9 April and were received into the Tower Stores seven days later. A similar consignment of 500 more cartridge boxes for the dragoons from Richard Bradley (indented for on the same day as Humphries) was delivered on the 23rd. Moreover, 1,200 cartouches ordered from Nathaniel Humphries and Thomas Roach 'for the supply of Sir Thomas Fairfax his Army' came into the Stores on 7 February 1646. The fact these items were included in an order with 1,500 bandoliers indicates that the boxes were intended for the use of musketry, rather than for cavalry operations, and thus some of them could have been earmarked for Colonel Okey's regiment and perhaps the army's firelock guard. Either way, it appears that at least during the first year of their existence, the New Model dragoons were equipped with both snaphaunce muskets and cartridge boxes.

For evidence of the production and issues of bandoliers among the Royalist armies we must largely turn to the Ordnance Papers, which due to their nature, concentrate on the Oxford Army and some of the garrisons in the West Country. On 29 January 1644, before his transfer to Bristol, where he supervised the procurement of powder and arms to Royalist troops, Richard March, the Keeper of the Stores in the Ordnance Office, informed the commander of the King's Artillery Train, 'The 25th of this month I provided 200 muskets (all of them held the proof) and brought into his Majesty's store this day. There will be ready to provide within one week 200 more … Likewise received into the stores 200 bandoliers, and 200 more will be ready the latter end of this week.' As March reported, on 3 February the Bristol gunsmiths were contracted to produce 200 muskets per month, in accordance with a warrant for the issuing of 500 muskets and bandoliers 'for the several regiments within the garrison.'[61] Hence, on 19 March 1644, 102 muskets, with the like number of bandoliers and 50 pikes were issued from Oxford 'for the arming of the new-raised men of the Queen's Lifeguard.'[62] Military hardware continued to be manufactured in, and supplied from, the city until its surrender to the New Model Army in May 1646. On 28 May 1644 there was received into New College 495 muskets, 497 collars of bandoliers, 4 barrels of powder and 1cwt 11lbs of powder, 'sent from Bristol and designed for Malmesbury, which garrison being taken by the enemy.'[63]

The provision of firearms for the Royalist army during the early months of the civil wars was a matter of immediate concern, and from 1643 onwards the King's forces had only limited access to London's manufacturing industries, including gunsmiths, armourers, cutlers, and the city's Livery and Saddlers' Companies. On 14 December 1642, the Council of War at Oxford ordered Sir John Heydon, Lieutenant-General of the Ordnance, to find 'workmen and speedily employ them in the making of muskets for dragoons,' which were to be three feet long, although it is unclear if these were ever produced

60 TNA, SP28/29/1, f.233r.

61 Bod Lib., Ms Rawlinson D395, ff.102v–103r, 145r–146v.; *ROP*, II, p.388.

62 TNA, WO55/459, f.66r; *ROP*, II, p.338.

63 TNA, WO55/1661, f.2r; *ROP*, I, p.136.

and issued.[64] According to Sir Ralph Hopton's memoirs, at the beginning of hostilities in the West Country in 1642 he 'levied a troop of dragoons to the number of 40, armed with good fowling pieces.'[65] These long-barrelled weapons, usually associated with gamekeepers, but sometimes used by marksmen or snipers, could have been of a more practical length for use on horseback. Captain John Strachan at Weymouth, writing to Charles on 9 March 1644, described the poor quality of arms and ammunition shipped from France to ports in the West, which included 'some little fowling pieces.'[66]

Significant quantities of arms and ammunition were imported into Britain from abroad by both sides during the civil wars. Control of northern ports like Newcastle and Scarborough provided the Royalist army with a means of bringing in consignments. When Queen Henrietta Maria arrived from Holland in early 1643, she brought with her substantial amounts of weapons, whilst supplies were still reaching Scarborough in May 1644.[67] However, deliveries could not only be intermittent, but vary greatly in quality. In March 1644, Captain John Strachan, the King's agent at Weymouth, reported the poor condition of arms and ammunition shipped from France to ports in the West for the army at Oxford and elsewhere:

> Now is Mr Naper and Mr Villa Nova the French merchant both come down, and we have viewed their powder, which is nothing else but old cannon powder that has lain in some magazine these four or five years, it will never do good service till it be refined, and the muskets, there are about 1,000 of them, I am assured they are of three or four score sundry bores, some pistol bores, some carbine bores, some little fowling pieces, and all the old trash that could be rapt together; I must say that the pistols are good, and the swords are reasonable (but come to the price) shall I eat Queen Maria's bread, and see a company of cheating merchants to deceive openly (hang me, draw me, quarter me, or beggar me let it be what it will I will speak the truth), I have suffered these five years for being an honest man, I hope to God for never being a knave, but to give them £7 for 112lbs of powder; 16s for a musket; 10s and 6s 8d for the best swords, and bad swords; 30s for a dozen of bandoliers which have one charge as big again as another.[68]

This example, along with early issues of match and ammunition by the Ordnance Office to Royalist units, indicate that some were in possession of a mixture of firearms. In November 1642, the newly appointed governor of Reading and Colonel-General of dragoons to the Oxford Army, Sir Arthur Aston, ordered Sir Edward Grey's regiment to be furnished with twelve bundles of match, four barrels of powder, two barrels of musket bullets and two of carbine shot.[69] On 24 November Colonel James Ussher's dragoons (after he was killed at Lichfield in April 1643, Sir Henry Washington's

64 TNA, WO55/547, f.28v.
65 Hopton, *Bellum Civile*, p.11.
66 TNA, WO55/423, ff.211r–211v; *ROP*, I, p.167.
67 *CSPD 1644*, pp.120 & 157.
68 Bod Lib., Ms Rawlinson D395, ff.118r–118v.; *ROP*, II, p.413.
69 TNA, WO55/423, ff.211r–211v; *ROP*, I, pp.166–7.

regiment, but also known as Prince Maurice's) received out of his Majesty's stores 4cwt (448lbs) of powder, 12 bundles of match, 2cwt of musket shot and 2cwt of carbine shot.[70] However, by the following month, only musket bullets were being issued to the unit. Munitions for 500 dragoons were delivered to Ussher's dragoons on 19 December 1642 from Thomas Martin, one of the Conductors of Ammunition in his Majesty's Train of Artillery. These consisted of 4 barrels of powder, 4cwt of match and 4cwt of musket shot. A supplement of 4cwt of powder, 4cwt of match and 4cwt of musket bullets was also issued to the regiment.[71] The consistent appearance of match implies that the formation by this point was armed with matchlock muskets alone.

The records of the Ordnance Office pertaining to the King's Oxford Army suggest that most of its dragoon units were issued with matchlocks. This assumption is largely based on the incidences of the issue of match among other ammunition. However, this has its limitations in that it merely offers a snapshot of examples, because it may be assumed (as with other Royalist documents) that a large number have not survived. Besides, issues of arms and ammunition to Royalist forces at a distance from Oxford and Reading are more difficult to determine. On 23 April 1643, it was reported by a Royalist source that supplies of powder and ammunition had recently arrived safely in Reading:

> It was advertised this day, that the rebels lying before Reading, having notice (as they have very good intelligence) of certain provisions of powder and ammunition, which were sent from Oxford by his Majesty to be conveyed into the town, had so filled up the ways with their troops of horse, and lined the hedges on both sides (where they were to pass) with their musketeers, that his Majesty's forces sent along for the convoy of it, had almost fallen into the danger ere they were aware: that they possibly might have received some notable loss, but that the most noble and valiant Earl of Carnarvon with some troops of horse faced a whole regiment of the rebels, and made a stand until his Majesty's foot with the ammunition, were got off in safety.[72]

On 14 May, another convoy reached Oxford. According to *Certaine Informations*,

> News is lately come hither out of Northamptonshire, that the Earl of Newcastle has sent 1,500 horse and foot from Newark-upon-Trent, to convey above 20 wagons laden with powder, match, and arms to Oxford, which provisions were seen at [Market] Harborough in that county, from whence they went to Daventry, and were expected at Oxford the last night, and that Prince Maurice met them with many horse to guard them safe into Oxford.[73]

70 TNA, WO55/423, f.157r.
71 TNA, WO55/423, ff.175r–175v.
72 *Mercurius Aulicus*, 23 April 1643.
73 *Certaine Informations*, 14 May 1643.

Another newsbook reported:

> This day came in the ammunition, which came to Woodstock the last Saturday, as was told you then; there being 40 loads in all, besides the ordnance: 300 barrels of powder, 1,500 muskets, as many bandoliers, a proportionable quantity of match, and some store of corslets, helmets, and other arms. Concerning which it is advertised from London, that when the news came first that it was brought in safety as far as Banbury, and was within the protection of his Majesty's quarters. It did so much deject the leaders of the faction there, and utterly disanimate the greatest part of their followers, that the Earl of Essex, coming to the Parliament House was fain to put himself to an apology, as well to give them satisfaction, as for to justify himself.[74]

Colonel Edward Grey's regiment of dragoons fought at Edgehill and was involved in the storm of Marlborough on 5–6 December 1642. Prior to this, it had received 21 bundles of match, 4 barrels of powder, 'and ball proportional' at Oxford.[75] This delivery seems to have been part of a universal supply of the Oxford Army dragoons by Sir Arthur Aston, their Colonel-General. On the same date Colonel James Ussher's regiment, which had been in service since August 1642, had four barrels of powder. The following December and January, Ussher's, Colonel Duncombe's and Sir Robert Howard's dragoons were supplied in all with 8½cwt of powder, together with match and shot proportional. On 24 February 1643, Prince Rupert authorised the delivery of 100cwt of powder, match and bullet proportionable to Ussher's regiment. Howard's men received 2cwt of powder with match and bullet proportional from the Oxford magazine on 20 June 1643.[76] Similarly, in November 1642, Colonel John Innes' regiment was issued as much carbine shot as musket shot, but by December, only musket shot was being issued. On 14 May, the unit received a dozen halberds, in addition to 'forty muskets that are fixed and fit for service with bandoliers, and the same to deliver to this bearer for the supply of Prince Rupert's regiment of dragoons, commanded by Colonel Innes.' The next day a dozen muskets, powder bags with belts, and hangers with belts were received by the regiment.

On 6 June 1643, it was issued 1cwt of powder, match, and musket shot.[77] Such issues imply that the regiment was armed with a mixture of carbines and muskets initially, but quickly transitioned to matchlock muskets alone. Moreover, a further 36 repaired muskets, with the like quantity of powder bags and hangers, were issued to Innes' dragoons on 16 June.[78] In a similar fashion, on 21 February 1643, Captain Erasmus Sachaverall's company of dragoons, belonging to Colonel Gerard Croker's cavalry regiment (which served with the Oxford army in 1644 and with Goring in the West in 1645)

74 *Mercurius Aulicus*, 14 May 1643.

75 *ROP*, I, pp.166–7.

76 TNA, WO55/423, ff.74r, 76r, 143r, 216v, 238v–239r; WO55/475/60, f.32r; W. D Macray (ed.), *Ruthven Correspondence: Letters and Papers of Patrick Ruthven, Earl of Forth and Brentford* (London: Nichols, 1868), p.78.

77 TNA, WO 55/215, f.2r; WO 55/459, f.215v.

78 TNA, WO55/1661, f.216r; WO/55/459, ff.249r, 256v; *ROP*, II, pp.246–7.

benefitted from '½ barrel of powder, with a proportion of bullet and match.'[79] Ussher's, later Washington's, regiment of dragoons was issued 1 barrel of powder, 1cwt of match and 1cwt of bullets on 11 May 1643, whilst the same quantities were received on 7 September. The regiment participated in the siege of Gloucester by the Royalists, and while quartered at Burford on 10 December 1643 it received 5 barrels of powder, 5cwt of musket shot and 8cwt of match.[80] A note appended to the germane warrant, addressed to 'Ralph Killinghall, one of the conductors of his Majesty's Trayne of Artillery', instructed him to:

> repair to the town of Burford in the county of Oxford with two covered wagons laden with five barrels of powder, 5cwt of musket shot and 8cwt of match, the which powder, shot and match you are there to deliver to Colonel Washington, or to such as he shall appoint, taking his receipt thereof for your discharge, which receipt you are to return to the officers of his Majesty's magazine here at Oxford, thereof fail you not at your peril.

Evidence shows, however, that some Royalist dragoons, were armed with snaphaunces. On 5 November 1644, Charles I issued a warrant to Sir John Heydon, his Lieutenant-General of the Ordnance, stating,

> Our will and pleasure is that you forthwith deliver out of Our Magazine in New College to Our trusty and welbeloved Sir Thomas Hooper, Knight, or to such person as he shall appoint to receive them, 30 muskets with snaphaunces towards the arming of the regiment of dragoons of Our dear nephew Prince Rupert.'[81]

It is a possibility that thus armed, Hooper's soldiers were among the bodies of commanded shot serving with Rupert's cavalry at Naseby on 14 June 1645. Another unit, Sir Thomas Aston's regiment of dragoons, received the sum of 2s 1d on 6 October 1643 from the Hundred of Highworth in Wiltshire, for the purchase of 1cwt of musket shot.[82] There is evidence that Aston's four companies were armed with both matchlocks and snaphaunces – he purchased locks of the 'new fashion' suitable for dragoons in late 1641.[83]

---

79 TNA, WO55/423, f.139r.

80 TNA, WO 55/458/65, f.4v; WO 55/1661, f.12v; WO 55/459, ff.735v–737r; *ROP*, II, pp.231, 286.

81 TNA, WO55/423, f.313r; *ROP*, II, p.355.

82 WSHC, X3/119/AC/4.

83 Thanks to Gary Ashby for this information.

6

Standards, Equipment and Clothing

Military standards, known by contemporaries as cornets for troops of horse, ensigns for companies of foot soldiers and guidons for dragoons, were carried while on the march and on the battlefield, but they were also used for rallying men during or after the chaos of battle. Standards were constructed from lengths of silk (taffeta or the less expensive sarsenet) and made up by tailors –hence the appearance of cloth and trimmings in tailor's bills. Distinguishing marks in the form of emblematic images and mottos on cornets of horse, but also on dragoon standards, were then applied by specialist painters. During the British Civil Wars, standards were observed and recorded for the purpose of estimating the strengths of opposing forces. Soldiers were obligated to 'follow their colours', whereas 'to depart from the colours' (desertion), whether on the march or in battle, elicited the death penalty. Moreover, 'articles of war' produced by both sides insisted that it was 'a disgrace worse than death' to abandon or lose the colours. Standards and colours captured from an enemy were also prized trophies of war.

Cornets belonging to cavalry troops measured approximately two feet square, and usually showed devices and religious mottos that exemplified spiritual motivation for war. Surviving evidence for the design and hue of guidons for dragoon units during the British Civil Wars – carried, like those in the horse, by cornets, the junior commissioned officers in each company – is comparatively slight, but some illustrations and descriptions do appear in contemporary documents. Though the actual methods employed in the use of standards by dragoons are absent in contemporary manuals, some clues might be gleaned from those referring to the practices of cavalry units. Writing in the 1620s, Gervase Markham stated:

> The cornet shall be armed and horsed in all points both defensive and offensive, like the lieutenant, only instead of the truncheon, he shall carry charged on his right thigh, his captain's cornet, which (being a private captain) should be compounded of colour and metal impaled, that is, the one half colour, the other metal. The substance of the cornet should be of damask [patterned textile], and the form must be almost square (only a little longer from the staff then on the

> staff) and fringed about suitably. The staff shall be small like a foot ensign, and not so long as an ordinary lance; it must be headed with steel, and either guilt or silvered; with fair tassels suitable to the cornet. If the cornet belongs to a greater officer, it shall then be of one entire colour, of less quantity and full square. And in this cornet, the captain may carry device and word, or else none, at his own pleasure.

To this he added:

> The captain of dragoons shall be armed like the lieutenant of the harquebusiers; the lieutenant of dragoons like the cornet of harquebusiers (the cornet and pistols excepted for he shall carry the weapons of his own troop) and the guidon (for these shall not be led with a cornet) of the dragoons shall be armed like a private gentleman of harquebusiers. And here is to be noted, that the difference betwixt the cornet and the guidon is much; for the guidon is the first colours that any commander of horse can let fly in the field. This guidon is of damask fringed, and may be charged either with the crest of him that is the owner thereof, or with other devise at his pleasure. It is in proportion three foot at the least deep in the top next the staff, and upon the staff and so extended down narrower and narrower to the bottom where the end is sharp, but with a slit divided into two peaks a foot deep; the whole guidon is six foot long, and should be carried upon a lance staff. If the captain (owner of this guidon) shall do a good day's service, or produce from his virtue something worthy [of] advancement, so that he is called to a better command, as to lead harquebusiers, or cuirassiers, then the general or officer in chief, shall with a knife cut away the two peaks, and then it is made a cornet which is longer one way than another.[1]

Much in the same vein, his brother Francis (who habitually equated the rank of cornet with the term guidon) instructed that:

> The cornet or guidon is the same that the ensign on foot is, and he ought ever to have two or three faithful and valiant friends in his range, which in all charges will have an extraordinary care of his colours, which is the captain's honour, and the company's safety. Now to speak a little of the guidon or colours themselves, howsoever in our latter times either by pride or ignorance they have been infinitely abused (every man taking upon him to carry what he pleases, and in what form he pleases) yet it is most certain that no man under the degree of a banneret may carry them square, but they must be of damask, either with device or without, three foot deep at the top, and so narrower to the nether end, which must be with two corners or peaks, which whensoever he is made a baron, or knight banneret, those corners are cut away, and the guidon is made square. These colours are carried upon a lance, and are in length full two yards or better. This gentleman which carries this cornet hath all the privileges which an ensign of foot has, and in his captain and lieutenant's absence commands the company, and by either of their deaths ought in right to be advanced into their places In the quarter he is

1 Markham, *Soldier's Accidence*, pp.45–6.

> lodged as well as his captain, and in all marches has the leading of the middle file and follows next after his captain.[2]

The treatment of the 'two corners or peaks' of the standard was confirmed by Thomas Venn in the 1670s, who recounted, 'And then the light horsemen [harquebusiers] had their guidon which was somewhat long and sharp at the end but with a slit which made it double pointed much like to our late dragoons.'[3] Thus, probably the same size as cavalry cornets and fringed, civil war guidons were distinctive because of their rounded swallow-tail shape. Guidons seemed to have adhered to the system of differencing used by foot regiments for their ensigns, usually to identify individual troop or companies and to denote the order of dignity of seniority of captains within those units. An indication of the importance of the latter is contained in a letter written by Edward Wolf, a Captain in one of the Essex Trained Band regiments of foot, to the County Committee of Essex at Chelmsford on 1 August 1643. On the 'differences between the officers' of his regiment, he declared:

> Yesterday the major would have delivered a pair of new colours, which had three spots in them, to Captain Ewers, and Major Halford was to have his, which he has marched withal since Colonel Skipworth went off; but he [Ewers] would not receive them, but would have mine or hold them he had still, and said he scorned to march below me, and did upbraid me concerning my profession, being a tradesman. I told him, though I were a tradesman, I was a gentleman, and I can show my coat [of arms]. The major said it should be disputed before a commander of note, but Ewers would not, and resolved to appeal to Sir John Barrington [the leading member of the Essex Committee].

Captain Wolf subsequently appealed to Barrington, 'who gave me my colours', declaring that he yielded precedence to Sergeant-Major Halford and so lost one degree, but hoped that he 'shall not lose two.'[4] Exactly which regiment these colours belonged to is unclear – Wolf's comment that Sir John bestowed them upon him could mean that the unit referred to was that commanded by Colonel Barrington, although Laurence Spring asserts that the standards received at the time belonged to the Earl of Warwick's Trained Band foot, 'which had spots as devices'.[5]

On 26 September 1643, Sir William Waller's regiment of dragoons was observed by Richard Symonds when it mustered alongside the London Trained Band and Auxiliary regiments in the Artillery Yard at Finsbury Fields. He described its colours as yellow and differenced by one to five black plates (or gunstones).[6]

An inventory and the accounts for 'Arms bought by the sub-committee sitting in Salters' Hall and employed for arming the Auxiliaries raised anno:

---

2 Markham, *Five Decades*, pp.83–4.
3 Venn, *Military and Maritine [sic] Discipline*, p.179.
4 BL, Ms Egerton 2647, f.139v; HMC, *Seventh Report*, p.557.
5 Spring, *Eastern Association*, p.74.
6 BL, Ms Harley 986, ff.111r–112v.

1643' enumerates various quantities of muskets, rests, bandoliers, pikes, helmets and swords, in addition to several 'trophies' or standards which had been purchased and distributed to the Auxiliary regiments of London in 1643. It includes the entry, 'received from … Colonel Gower [of the Orange Auxiliaries] 20 snaphaunces and five colours for dragoons'. Similarly, a note on the reverse of the document, reads: 'arms delivered by the Committee at Salters' Hall to the several commanders of the Auxiliary forces: To Lieutenant-Colonel Gower six drums, 20 snaphances, five colours for dragoons.'[7]

The possibility remains that these are the five yellow guidons belonging to Waller's regiment, which were seen by Symonds in 1643. That the receipt was endorsed on 2 May 1644 would tend to suggest that they were not the standards of Colonel Richard Browne's regiment, which was raised and supplied in the capital in autumn 1642. Hence, the yellow guidon possessing one plate is known to have belonged to Sergeant-Major Archibald Strachan's company of Waller's dragoon regiment; two to Captain John Clerke's; three to Captain Nicholas Moore's; four to Captain John Bennett's; and five to Captain William Turpin's. Waller's own company conceivably possessed a plain yellow standard. The background hue of such dragoon standards corresponds with the yellow of Sir William's cavalry cornet, which according to Thomas Blount, 'figured a tree full of fruit and a coat of arms hanging on it, the motto *Fructus Virtutis*.'[8]

Colonel John Browne's regiment of the Earl of Essex's army received £40 0s 0d for its colours and drums on 19 August 1642.[9] On 8 October the regiment originally raised in London and Southwark for service in Kent under Sir John Seaton, partly from veterans from the Netherlands where he had previously served, received 'nine dragoon colours with staves, belts, boots and swivels, and nine pairs of tassels and strings at 35s 0d per foot', costing £15 15s 0d.[10] A corresponding pay warrant from the Committee of Safety to the army treasurer Sir Gilbert Gerrard for these guidons and sixteen drums, dated 10 January 1643 – though the document survives with considerable damage and foxing – states,

> These are to will [and] require you forthwith out of the treasure remaining in your hands to pay unto Hugh Croxton for nine dragoon's colours with appurtenances at 35s 0d per piece, £15 15s 0d and for sixteen drums at 30s 0d each amounting to £24 0s 0d. In total £39 15s 0d being delivered to Sir John Seton as by two several notes [herein] subscribed [and] appended.'[11]

Likewise, on 16 August 1643, the Essex County Committee paid to 'Captain Holcroft, Captain Harbottle [and] Captain Miller, or any one of them, the

7 TNA, SP28/198, unfol.
8 J. T. Blount, *The Art of Making Devises* (London: 2nd edn, 1655), p.78.
9 TNA, SP28/1A, f.164v.
10 TNA, SP28/2B, f.674r.
11 TNA, SP28/263, ff.75r., 120r.

sum of £9 0s 0d for and towards three colours and six drums for their several companies of dragoons under the command of the Earl of Manchester.'[12]

The five known guidons of Colonel James Wardlaw's regiment of Essex's army were uniformly *azure* (blue), and fringed in blue and white, with a canton containing a St George's cross. That of the colonel's own company, led by Lieutenant-Colonel George Dundas, bore the Latin motto, in gold lettering: *Deo Dvce Vincimus*; the guidon of Captain Alexander Nerne: *Bella Beatorum Bella*; Captain John Barne: *Iusta Triumphat Causa*; Captain James Stenchion: *Vincmus Auspice Christo*; Captain George Forbes: *In Monte Videbitur Deus*; and perhaps Captain Archibald Hambleton: *Pro Rege Religione et Parliamentio*.[13]

The only confirmed Royalist examples of dragoon standards are two recorded by Jonathan Turmile as 'Dragooners collours taken by the Earl of Essex', during his army's relief of Gloucester in September 1643.[14] Both are drawn as if damaged; one has an *argent* (silver or white) field, with a St George cross in the upper left corner of the cloth, with a black and white fringe. The second is white with no fringe but contains five red crescents in the manner of differencing. They could be of the same regiment. Colonel Henry Washington's dragoons participated in the Royalist breakthrough at Bristol in support of Colonel Henry Wentworth's brigade near Brandon Hill, which precipitated the capture of the city's defences by Prince Rupert on 26 July 1643. They were also present at the siege of Gloucester. It remains uncertain whether Washington's men fought at Marston Moor, although they had formed part of Rupert's army earlier in the campaign. Captured at the battle, however, was a dragoon standard, described in *A Full Relation of the Late Victory* as 'A white cornet of dragoons with a blue and white fringe in the midst of whereof is painted a Roundhead face, and on its top the letter P. (which is conceived to signify a Puritan) with a sword in a hand reaching from a cloud, with this motto, *Fiat Iustitia* ('Let Justice be Done')'.[15] However, none of these items can be definitively assigned to Washington's regiment.

In terms of identifying devices, coloured scarves or sashes were for the most part limited to officers and cavalrymen, although there is some evidence for their use by sergeants and drummers of foot and dragoon regiments. In his practical manual of drilling or training soldiers, *The Art of War, and Englands Traynings*, published in 1619, William Davies (who described himself as a gentleman and alluded to his long years of military service in the Spanish Army) stated:

> During the wars (or else not) he [the common soldier] ought to wear in some convenient place of his garments, that is most apparent to the view of the band, a token, red cross, or scarf, whereby in skirmishes and other attempts he is to be known of what part he is (the Imperials use a red scarf, Englishmen St George's

12 TNA, SP28/227/1, f.4r.

13 DWL, Modern Ms Folio 7, f.103r; Young, *Emblematic Flag Devices*, III, p.102.

14 DWL, Modern Ms Folio 7, f.134v.

15 *A Full Relation of the Late Victory obtained (through Gods providence) by the forces under the command of Generall Lesley, the Lord Fairfax, and the Earl of Manchester* (London: 11 July 1644).

> cross, the French the white cross) or such a sign as the general of the field shall make choice of, which he ought to do willingly, thereby to remove suspicion out of the mind of his captain and chieftains, that they need not to stand in doubt of him: and for divers other worthy respects, since that by these and like manifest means, the soldier shows inward faith and loyalty to the officers and captains which govern. But if otherwise they carry the said token and mark loose at their neck, breast, arms, or any other place, it gives matter and occasion of doubt touching their fidelity, specially being but newly entertained, since that being not made fast, they may easily cast away or hide the same in time of peril or doubtful fight. Which suspicion ought diligently to be removed by him which carried an entire desire and full intent to deal truly and loyally.[16]

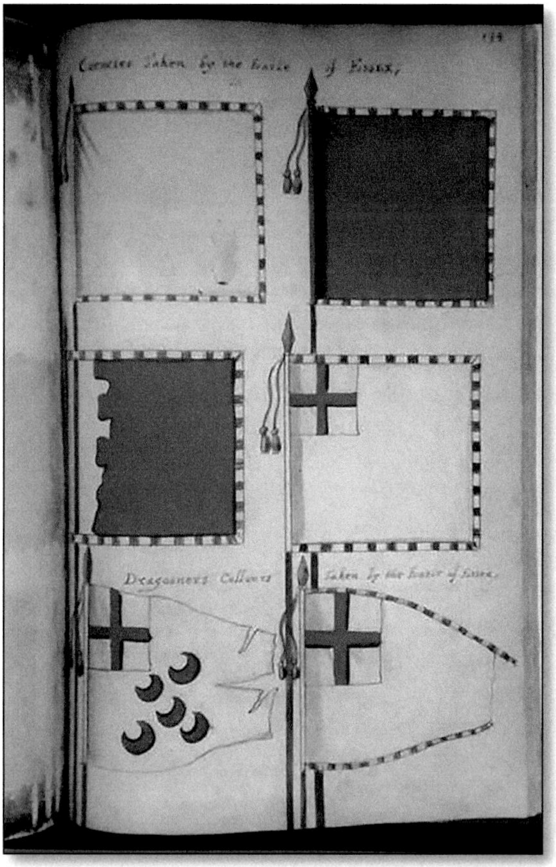

'Dragooners collours taken by the Earl of Essex' Doctor Williams Library, Modern Ms Folio 7, f.134v (courtesy of the Dr Williams Library)

Scarves were an essential purchase for captains of troops of horse alongside the clothing and equipment of trumpeters. In August 1642, most individual captains of cavalry troops raised for service in Essex's army received a special warrant authorising a payment of £30 to provide a troop of 60 harquebusiers with orange-tawny scarves, although some, including Captain Richard Grenville of Colonel Arthur Goodwin's regiment of horse, received this money out of a larger payment for equipment.[17] In similar fashion, the Earl of Denbigh laid out the sum of £22 12s 10d in July and August 1643 on scarves and ribbon for his troops in the Midlands.[18] Such items were vital for battlefield identification and the fostering of unit identity, even though it is possible that within individual armies there were variations between regiments and even sub-units, depending on the taste of their commanding officers. Although it is unclear how common such items were in dragoons units, their purpose among mounted troops was emphasised by Vernon, who stated,

> Every horseman must wear a scarf of his general's colours, and not leave it off neither in his quarters nor out of his quarters, it being an ornament unto him, besides it will cause him to forbear many unfitting actions, as being thereby distinguished from the vulgar or common soldier, it is likewise a good and visible mark in time of battle to know one another.'[19]

16 Edward Davies, *The Art of War, and Englands Traynings; plainely demonstrating the dutie of a priuate souldier* (London: 1619), pp.26–7.
17 TNA, SP28/1A, ff.74r–79v, 170r, 192v, 194r.
18 TNA, SP28/149, f.149r; SP28/34, ff.237r, 250r, 265r, 274v.
19 Vernon, *The Young horse-man*, p.8.

Clarendon observed that in an attempt to deceive their enemy in 1642, Royalist troops 'had marched, from the time they left Oxford with orange-tawny scarves and ribbons, that they might be taken for the Parliament side.'[20] One of the items in the possession of Captain Simon Finch, who had served in the English army in Ireland under Ormond, before his capture at Nantwich in 1644 and subsequent change of sides to become a dragoon officer under Sir William Brereton, was a 'red scarf'.[21]

According to Peter Young, writing in the 1960s, 'Earlier in the war a Parliamentarian officer would not have worn a crimson scarf. In 1642 the orange-tawny colours of the Earl of Essex were universally adopted by the Roundheads, and crimson scarves were the mark of a Royalist.'[22] This notion has become rather an outdated cliché, however, and it is known that Royalists wore red, pink and blue scarves, whilst among the Parliamentarian armies other colours were worn. The officers of the New Model Army possibly wore blue scarves in 1645. A contemporary newsbook described that 'Sir Thomas Fairfax's colours are blue,' although this could equally well refer to Fairfax's regiment of horse. This colour was also associated with Fairfax during the First Civil War.[23] In other Parliamentarian armies, where their leader retained an independent commission, that is, where he did not, or did not consider himself to be, under the direct command of the Earl of Essex, scarves of different hues were also worn. The Cheshire commander Sir William Brereton purchased a crimson scarf silk at 2s 0d the ell in July 1643 for his own cavalry troop. How universal this colour was among the rest of the Cheshire horse and even his army is unclear.[24]Among the items of equipment promised on 22 March 1644 by Sir Thomas Myddelton for the newly raised infantry regiment of his cousin, Sir William was 'scarfs for the sergeants and drummers', besides '6d apiece for ribbons for the said regiment of foot.'[25]

Ribbons, also known as 'favours' were lengths of tape or ribbon given by some captains to soldiers of regiments and sub-regimental units, to be sewn onto their coats or caps, and consequently distinguish them from others. However, they may have caused some damage to soldiers' coats if removed. In March 1639, the Marquess of Montrose instituted the distinctive blue bonnet ribbons and cavalry scarf among the Covenanter Army. As Stuart Reid argues, 'Although attributed to Montrose, the adoption of blue scarves may have been not unconnected with the fact that this was the colour of the Swedish Army from whence came the professional officers serving in the army.'[26] The practice of wearing bunches of ribbon in their bonnets seems to have lasted longer than the short-lived 'Montrose's whimsy' as the blue

20 W. D Macray (ed.), Edward Hyde, Earl of Clarendon, *The History of the Rebellion and Civil Wars in England* (Oxford: Clarendon Press, 1888), VI, p.71.

21 BL, Ms Harley 2135, f.71r.

22 Young, *Edgehill*, pp.27–8.

23 *Perfect Passages*, 2–9 April 1645.

24 TNA, SP28/8, f.15r.

25 *CSPD 1644*, p.65.

26 Stuart Reid, *Scots Armies of the Seventeenth Century I: The Army of the Covenant 1639–51* (Leigh-on-Sea: Partizan Press, 1988), p.44.

ribbons were described. On 8 January 1644, the Scottish soldier, Sir Thomas Hope, noted in his diary that the men of Colonel Lindsay's foot regiment were issued their 'colours' of blue and yellow silk ribbons that they wore in their bonnets, to match their regiment's colours.[27] In the summer of 1642, members of the Worcestershire trained bands were provided with sixteen yards of broad ribbon, at a cost of 8s 0d, with which to make 'colours', presumably to either decorate their company's colours, or to attach to their hats or clothing.[28] Sir Thomas Aston's Royalist dragoons wore yellow and white favours, which possibly corresponded with their company guidons – in October 1643 they (and maybe also Aston's horse) received £1 10s 0d for ribbons.[29]

The regimental accounts of Sir Anthony Irby's dragoons of the Eastern Association include a payment of £45 6s 2d for cloth to one Jepson, a Boston tailor, with £8 9s 4d for 'ribbons and colours for the soldiers.'[30] Similarly, on 22 June 1643 Brereton spent £3 12s 0d on 'ribbon for colours for soldiers' of the Cheshire Parliamentarian forces.[31] Such devices often indicated an allegiance to a particular commander. When Sergeant-Major Thomas Sanders returned with his Derbyshire horse in July 1645 from a period of attached service under Sir Thomas Fairfax, he reported 'my soldiers wear his Excellency's colours and for that are called rogues and threatened to pull them out of their hats; [Sir John] Gell's soldiers wear his colours and brave it to our faces.'[32] Distinguishing marks or field signs, such as a scrap of paper or sprig of greenery tucked in the hat, or a white rag tied around the arm, were also worn by armies or particular regiments, although mistakes were frequently made, sometimes with fatal consequences. According to Simeon Ashe, a chaplain with the Earl of Manchester's army, at Marston Moor 'our signal was a white paper, or handkerchief in our hats' and while following the fleeing of his cavalry Sir Thomas Fairfax removed his white emblem and rode around the Royalist positions where he joined the victorious Eastern Association horse and foot.[33] In similar fashion, it was reported by John Rushworth, Fairfax's secretary in the New Model Army that at Naseby on 14 June 1645, 'They [the Royalists] had beanstalks in their hats, we nothing; some of ours of their own accord had white linen or paper in their hats.'[34]

27 David Lang, (ed.), *A Diary of the Public Correspondence of Sir Thomas Hope of Craighall, 1633–1645* (Edinburgh: Bannatyne Club, 1843), p.201.

28 Atkin, *Worcestershire under Arms*, p.17.

29 WSHC, X3/119/AC/4.

30 TNA, SP28/313/4, unfol.

31 TNA, SP28/196/3, f.7r; *CSPD 1644*, p.65.

32 DRO, D1232/0/40; Ron Slack, 'Colonel Gell and Major Sanders: Internal feuding among the Parliamentary forces in Derbyshire during the Civil Wars of 1642–1646', *DM*, 16 (2) (2001), pp, 34–48.

33 *A Continuation of true intelligence from the English and Scottish forces in the north in the services of King and Parliament, 13 July 1644* (London: 1644), p6. TT, E2 [14]; Bodl. Lib., Ms Fairfax, ff.15v–16r.

34 *An Ordinance of the Lords and Commons ... with two exact Relations of the said Victory Obtained against the Kings forces, nere Knasby in Northampton-shire the fourteenth of this instant Iune* (London: Edward Husband, 17 June 1645).TT, E288 [26].

As in foot formations, drummers of dragoon companies transmitted commands by the beat of the drum, in addition to undertaking special roles, such as acting as messengers. In 1619, Davies recommended that:

> Drums and fifes must be chosen of able qualities and personage, secret and ingenious, skillful in the sound and using of their instruments, which must warn as the mouth of a man to all intents of service, diligent in times convenient to instruct soldiers in the same, that none by ignorance neglect their duties. These be oftentimes sent on messages, importing charge, which of necessity require languages, sometimes to summon or command the enemies to render, sometimes carry ransoms, or redeem, or conduct prisoners[35]

Similarly, the English military writer, William Barriffe, stated in 1635, 'the drum is the voice of the commander, the spur of the valiant and the heart of the coward, and by it they must receive their directions, when the roaring cannon, the clashing of arms, the neighing of horses, and other confused noise causes than neither captain, nor other officer can be heard.'[36] Soldiers during the civil wars were recruited by the 'beat of the drum'. Hence, for the raising of forces for Ireland on 30 May 1642, Parliament authorised various captains to 'have liberty to beat up drums in all places within the Kingdom of England, and Dominion of Wales; and thereby, or otherwise, to raise and levy so many soldiers volunteers, as shall suffice to make up unto every of the said captains, one complete company of 100 foot, besides officers, to be employed in the aforesaid service.'[37] Similarly, it was reported on 13 December that Sir Richard Hopton, who had been commissioned by the Earl of Essex to raise troops from the trained bands and volunteers of Herefordshire 'had promised the Earl of Stamford that he had 1,000 dragoons at four days' warning to be ready for his service, came into Ledbury and brought with him his colours and his drum, and there in a commanding manner called all the countrymen, in order to bring in their dragoons.'[38]

In regiments of foot and dragoons drum majors were on the strength of the colonel's company and were responsible for the training of drummers and upkeep of instruments. They were also charged with the taking into custody of any captured enemy drummers. Hence, they were paid and treated as senior non-commissioned officers. Abraham Butterworth acted in this role in Colonel Robert Duckenfield's Parliamentarian regiment of foot in Cheshire during the First Civil War.[39] As for the supply of drums and drumming equipment; in January 1643 Duckenfield paid the sum of 13s 0d for a drum from Thomas Bostock, presumably a local maker, while the sum of 12s 4d was spent on drumheads. Likewise, the Parliamentarian governor of Leek, Colonel John Bowyer, regularly employed his drum-major

35 Davies, *Art of War*, p.69.

36 William Barriffe, Military Discipline: or, The young artillery man (London, 1635), pp.11–12.

37 *CJ*, II, p.594.

38 *CSPD 1643–45*, p.378; HMC, *Fifth Report, App.*, p.142; Peachey and Turton, *Fall of the West*, VI, p.631.

39 TNA, SP28/128/10, ff.4v, 5v.

in the maintenance of his regimental drums, on one occasion sending him to Stafford to purchase parts and make repairs.[40] Colonel John Browne's regiment of dragoons of the Earl of Essex's army received £40 0s 0d for its colours and drums on 19 August 1642.[41] In August 1644 Sir William Waller, Parliament's commander in the West, asked the Committee of Both Kingdoms for 50 guidons (ten to a regiment), 100 dragoon drums, 5,000 belts for muskets and 2,000 swords.[42] This represented enough equipment for five regiments.

Sir William Brereton paid £4 10s 0d in July 1643 for the painting of his coat of arms on 20 drums (enough to fit out his entire regiment at two drums per company, as well as his dragoon units), while sixteen drums were shipped as part of a consignment of arms, equipment and powder from London to Liverpool for the Cheshire forces in March 1645.[43] Similarly, in April 1644 Giles Smart, a London-based supplier, was contracted for 20 drums for Sir Thomas Myddelton's foot.[44] In addition to serving as Colonel of a regiment and Captain of a troop of harquebusiers, and Colonel of a regiment and Captain of a company of foot, between 30 August 1644 and 15 June 1645 (when his commissions under the terms of the Self-Denying Ordinance were suspended), Myddelton also drew pay as Colonel of a regiment of dragoons and Captain of a company of dragoons.[45] The list of arms and equipment purchased for the London Auxiliaries in 1643 includes an extra six drums listed together with dragoon colours and snaphaunce muskets.[46] The possibility remains that these were intended to be delivered jointly to the dragoons. Purchases made for Sir Thomas Aston's Royalist dragoons include one for a drum, costing the remarkably modest sum of 5s 0d.[47]

As might be expected, substantial quantities of new drums were supplied to the New Model Army upon its formation in 1645. Edward Tench provided 60 drums at 24s 0d apiece, which were delivered in early April.[48] Nonetheless, Treasury warrants of April and May record the delivery of 135 drums to the New Model regiments of foot. Colonel Okey's dragoons were not left out, however. Christopher Mercer, one of his captains, secured ten drums to be supplied to the emerging regiment.[49] At 24s 10d such instruments were more expensive than a consignment of military equipment dispatched to Ireland on 24 October 1649, which encompassed 15 drums at 20s 0d each and 100 halberds costing 5s 0d apiece.[50]

When riding, the dragoon probably secured his musket by a leather belt or sling, as depicted in Wallhausen's *Kriegskunst*. The exact mechanics of

40 TNA, SP28/134/5, ff.75v, 79r.
41 TNA, SP28/261, f.42v.
42 *CSPD 1644*, p.460.
43 TNA, SP28/225/1, f.3r; CRO, DDX/428, f.80r; *BLB*, I, 139.
44 TNA, SP28/346/1, unfol. ; SP28/346/2, unfol.
45 TNA, SP28/138/18, unfol.
46 TNA SP28/198, unfol.
47 Aston, accounts, unfol.
48 TNA, WO47/1, f.210r; SP28/29/1, f.170r.
49 TNA, SP28/29/1, ff.174r, 176r, 180r, 196r; SP28/29/2, f.259r; SP28/30/3, f.339r, 353r; SP28/31/5, f.532r;SP/31/5, f.532r; SP28/36/1, f.658v.
50 *CSPD 1649*, pp.575, 580.

this remain unclear, though it is possible that the item followed the same principle of the crupper – a piece of harness looped around a horse's tail to keep the equipment placed on its back from slipping forward – in that a loop was secured around the barrel and the other end of the device attached further down the weapon's stock. According to Wallhausen, in arming the dragoon:

> The musket has attached to the stock, top and bottom a sling of leather with which, when mounted, the dragoon hangs the musket on his back with the sling on his neck. When mounted, he holds the burning match and reins in his left hand with the lighted end of the match between his fingers.[51]

Similarly, Gervase Markham described:

> for offensive arms, they have a fair dragon fitted with an iron work, to be carried in a belt of leather, which is buckled over the right shoulder, and under the left arm, having a turnell of iron with a ring through which the piece runs up and down; and these dragons are short pieces of 16 inches, the barrel, and full musket bore, with firelocks or snaphaunces.[52]

Some documentary references to the issue of musket belts and slings exist for the British Civil Wars. Sir Thomas Aston's newly raised dragoons were issued cartridge boxes, 'French belts for dragoons' and 'dragoon belts' in February 1643 at Chester. How the last two are to be interpreted remains uncertain, but although they may have been girdles or waist belts, they could also have been musket slings. More certain, however, was the request by the Parliamentarian commander, Sir William Waller at Farnham on 28 August 1644 for (among other items) the supply of '5,000 belts for their muskets' for the conversion of his foot into dragoon regiments.[53] Also, upon the formation of Colonel Richard Browne's London-raised and equipped dragoon regiment in November 1642 the sum of £30 0s 0d was paid to 'Mr Leighton and his partners in full for belts', and £88 19s 0d 'to Mr Coward for slings and belts', whilst a carrier received 10d for the delivery of such items.[54] In spring 1643 the sum of £14 15s 8d was paid for swords, belts and other items for Sir Anthony Irby's Lincolnshire dragoons.[55] The use of musket slings would, even in part, necessitate the fitting of metal swivels on muskets. Warrants for the supply of arms and equipment to the Commonwealth army in Ireland in August 1649 included one for the payment of £2,988 1s 8d to Roger Carlisle and three other gunsmiths for 2,000 matchlocks, 474 snaphaunce muskets and '1,000 dragoons' arms with swivels'.[56]

51 Wallhausen, *Kriegskunst*, pp.16–17

52 Markham, *Soldier's Accidence*, p.42.

53 *CSPD 1644*, p.460.

54 TNA, SP28/144/2, ff.30r–31r.

55 TNA, SP28/313/4, unfol.

56 *CSPD 1649*, p.586.

Cartridge boxes and powder bags, worn about the waist, were an alternative to the bandolier, especially it seems, where these were in short supply. On 12 October 1643, the Parliamentarian deputy lieutenants of Lancashire ordered that, '100 snaphance muskets and the 200 grey coats, and the portmanteaus [leather shoulder bags], knapsacks, and other small things shall be delivered to Colonel Rigby, he paying for the carriage of them.'[57] As Alexander Rigby senior (as opposed to his son, Lieutenant-Colonel Alexander Rigby junior) is not known to have commanded any dragoons, it would seem that these items were for his infantry regiment, which operated with the Northern Association in Lancashire and its adjacent counties. The issue of powder bags to musketeers and dragoons may have been more prevalent among Royalist forces, though the evidence for this is far from certain. The officers of foot regiments belonging to the Oxford Army mustering at Culham Camp, near Abingdon, in May 1643 protested at the shortages of bandoliers for their soldiers. A supply of 250 of these was included in one delivery of arms on 22 May, and five days later a council of war ordered as many powder bags as were complete to be directed to the army.[58]

The Royalists cultivated facilities for fabricating leather accoutrements for weapons and military equipment, especially belts and slings for bandoliers, swords, muskets, and carbines. The unpublished dispersed accounts relating to Sir Thomas Aston's regiments of horse and dragoons seem to show that the latter were issued both cartridge boxes and bandoliers in Chester upon their raising in February 1643, although some of the boxes might have been for cavalry troopers as well. The city's leatherworkers were fashioning these for around 1s each. There are also several entries for purchases of 'paper for cartridges', but what proportion and types of cartridges were made from this is uncertain. Various glovers in Oxford and the surrounding areas produced powder boxes or bags, as well as girdles and hangers. On 6 June 1643, the King's stores in New College took possession of 401 powder bags from them, and 200 girdles, hangers and bags from Thomas Jones, a leading manufacturer.[59] In June and July, he sent in 2,000 girdles and hangars, a prodigious figure.[60] Among the smaller consignments delivered into the magazine at Reading from Oxford on 24 October 1644 were '60 muskets, 60 powder bags with girdles and hangers, [and] 200 long pikes'.[61]

The exact design of the powder bags or boxes remains uncertain since none are known to have survived. However, in January 1646 a contract was agreed with the manufacturer Nathaniel Humphries of the parish of St Michael, Crooked Lane to supply the New Model Army with 1,200 cartridge boxes of 'strong plate covered with black leather, 700 of them half-round and the other 500 double at 10s 0d a piece.'[62] Such a substantial quantity may have been intended for some of the horse, and more specifically for the army's

57 HMC, *Tenth Report, App. IV*, p.67.
58 BL, Ms Harley 6804, ff.92v–93r.; *ROP*, I, p.54; II, note 160.
59 TNA, WO55/1661, f.5r; *ROP*, I, p.103.
60 TNA, WO55/1661, ff.91r, 96r, 99v, 109v, 111r; BL, Ms Add 34352, f.49r; *ROP*, I, p.103.
61 TNA, WO55/1661, f.54; *ROP*, I, p.116.
62 ML, 46–78/709, f.73r; Mungeam, 'Contracts', p.90.

Roeland Savery, *Harquebusiers or dragoons* (Rijkesmusem, Amsterdam)

firelock guard (although there remains no direct evidence for the latter). A Royalist warrant of 7 June 1643 records that '200 powder bags for musketeers with girdles and hangars for swords, and 40 bandoliers to be delivered to the officers [of] Lord Grandison or Colonel Wentworth's.' This suggests that they were fixed to a belt around the waist. Another warrant refers to them as 'leather bags to carry powder'.[63]

Though 'musketeers' are mentioned in this document, the recipients were clearly Wentworth's dragoons, who participated in the major battles of the Oxford Army in 1643 and 1644. On 14 June 1643 a further warrant, signed by Jacob Astley, Major-General of the King's foot, ordered that '100 leather bags for the musketeers' be dispatched to the tercio commanded by Lord Viscount Grandison.[64] Similarly, Sir Lewis Dyve's regiment of foot received '80 powder bags with girdles and hangers' from the Oxford magazines, while two days later, just prior to its departure for Chalgrove, Captain Henry Colthorpe's company of Ussher's/Washington's dragoons benefitted from an issue of 136 powder bags, with belts and hangars, in addition to quantities of powder, match and musket shot.[65]

At the same juncture, 'Prince Rupert's regiment of dragoons commanded by Colonel Innes' received 40 muskets 'that are fixed and fit for service, with bandoliers', in exchange for delivering into the Oxford magazine 40 unserviceable muskets. On 15 June, the same unit took possession of 12

63 TNA, WO55/459, ff.217v–219r; Bod Lib., Ms Rawlinson D395, f.31r; *ROP*, II, pp.244–5.

64 TNA, WO55/459, f.252r; *ROP*, II, p.247.

65 TNA, WO55/459, ff. 244v–245r, 248r, 252r, 256r; *ROP*, II, p.247.

reconditioned muskets, powder bags with belts, and hangers for them.[66] Furthermore, in October 1643 dragoons attached to Sir Charles Lucas' regiment of horse (also serving in the Oxford Army) received 80 collars of bandoliers, whilst the cavalry troopers were supplied with arms consisting of 'three score pair of pistols with holsters and spanners, and 40 carbines with belts and swivels.'[67] Correspondingly, on 7 August 1643 Andrew Byrd and Ralph Killinghall, conductors of his Majesty's Trayne of Artillery, were instructed to 'repair to the rendezvous at Randcombe and North Cerney in the county of Gloucester, near Cirencester with four carts laden with 173 muskets, and the like number of powder bags for musketeers, with girdles and hangars, and 227 pikes.'[68] A month later, at Oxford, Captain Price of Colonel Gerard's regiment of foot received eighteen long pikes, one partisan, 32 musket rests and 32 powder bags (presumably for his own company) in exchange for broken pikes.[69] Similarly, another conductor of the Train, Robert Horne, received orders on 23 October to convey 60 muskets, powder bags with girdles and hangars for them, with 200 long pikes into the magazine at Reading.[70]

The powder in these bags may have been carried in cartridges (a sealed paper tube, containing a measure of black powder and a bullet at one end). Writing in 1616 Wallhausen maintained that harquebusiers should either use powder flasks and bullets from a bag or, alternatively, cartridges.[71] Likewise, Cruso, writing in 1632, and Vernon in 1644, agreed that only paper cartridges were used as ammunition for both cuirassiers and harquebusiers.[72] The latter wrote in his popular manual:

> if you use cartridges, you shall find in your cartridge case a turned wooden pin which you must take, having cut lengths of white paper something broader than the pin is in length, and roll the paper on the pin, then twist one end of the paper, and fill it almost full of powder, then put the bullet on top of the powder, twisting that end also, then put it into your cartridge case, now when you come to load your carbine or pistol with these cartridges, you must bite off that end of the paper where the powder is, pouring it into your carbine or pistol, then put in that bullet, and some of that paper will serve as a wad after it, and ram home, but always observe that your bullet be not too big, but that it may roll home to the powder, for if there be any distance between the bullet and powder, it is like to break the barrel of your carbine or pistol. But if you use a flask, which in my judgement is far better than cartridge, because that many times the trotting of your horse in long march, shakes out all the powder of your cartridges and thereby causes you to be unprovided for the sudden charge of the enemy, you must gauge your flask and so lade your carbine and pistol with powder and bullet as before, but never prime

66 TNA, WO55/459, f.249v; *ROP*, II, pp.246–7.
67 TNA, WO55/459, f.514r; *ROP*, II, p.298.
68 TNA, WO55/459, f.389r; *ROP*, II, p.266.
69 TNA, WO55/1661, f.410r.
70 TNA, WO55/459, f.540r; *ROP*, II, p.300.
71 Wallhausen, *Kriegskunst, p.35.*
72 Cruso, *Militarie Instructions*, pp.37–42; Vernon, *Young Horse-man*, p.8.

> before you have spanned. Now the quantity of the powder usually required for the loading of either carbine or pistol is half the weight of the bullet.[73]

In similar fashion, Monck suggested that musketeers marching at the vanguard of an army 'ought to have two pairs of bandoliers furnished with powder and bullet, and in case you have no bandoliers, let there be provided for each musketeer … twelve cartridges, which they ought to carry in their right-hand pocket, and twelve bullets apiece in their pockets besides.'[74] As to the practicality of bandoliers and cartridge boxes among dragoons, Orrery observed:

> I am also on long experience an enemy to the use of bandoliers, but a great approver of boxes of cartridges; for then, but by biting off the bottom of the cartridge, you charge your musket for service with one ramming. I would have these cartridge boxes of tin, as the carbines use them, because they are not so apt to break as the wooden ones are, and do not in wet weather, or lying in the tents, relax.[75]

How common the use of powder bags and cartridges were among civil war dragoons is unclear, but bandoliers seem to have been preferred in European armies at least up to the reign of James II (1685–88). In 1683 Turner, who served in the Swedish army during the Thirty Years' War, claimed, 'it is thirty years ago since I saw these (bandoliers) laid aside in some German armies', although he probably related an occasion when some musketeers were using cartridges and cartridge boxes.[76] Since there is no reason to distrust his account, there are no other historical sources stating that musketeers used cartridges in this conflict, and it is unclear whether he was referring to that or a later time. The scarcity of extant examples, albeit the dating of which is very broad, makes it hard to be certain what these might have looked like in practice.

The type of sword commonly issued to infantrymen and dragoons during the British Civil Wars was the tuck (from the French *estoc*), a munition quality thrusting sword – a cheaper and lighter version of the cavalry weapon – although such soldiers also utilised the butts of their muskets in close-quarter combat. After 1600, English levies in Ireland were furnished with basket hilted swords, Francis Markham recommended the use of 'a basket hilt of a nimble and round proportion after the Irish, strong scabbards of lacquered or well-rosend leather, chapes of iron, and girdles and hangers suitable to the same.'[77] However, instructions issued to the English and Welsh trained bands in 1626 referred to 'a good strong and serviceable sword, the blade thereof not to be above three foot in length, in a good scabbard with belt or girdle and hangers fitted thereunto.' Similarly, in 1635 they were to

73 Vernon, *Young Horse-man*, p.10.
74 Monck, *Observations*, p.150.
75 Orrery, *Treatise*, p.31.
76 Turner, *Pallas Armata*, p.176.
77 Markham, *Five Decades*, p.34.

be issued with 'a good sword of three foot long, cutting, stiff-pointed, with girdle and hangers.'[78] Monck recommended for musketeers, pikemen and dragoons 'a good long tuck, with a belt', whilst the Royalist Richard Atkyns described his sword at Roundway Down in 1643 as a tuck, and a colleague as wearing a hanger, although he himself was an officer in Prince Maurice's regiment of horse.[79]

In September 1642, Colonel Wardlaw's Parliamentarian dragoons received 600 swords with belts.[80] When Colonel Richard Browne's regiment was formed two months later the sum of £265 7s 0d was paid to five London manufacturers (Richard Jones, Sampson Robinson, Mr Hill, Mr Tissier and Lawrence Bromfield) for swords. Bromfield, a member of the London Cutlers' Company and a Captain in the Red Regiment of the London Trained Bands, also provided Browne's regiment with quantities of 'swords and belts' at a cost of £253 0s 0d. He also sold nearly 3,000 swords to the Committee of Safety in the first eighteen months of the war.[81] Although the numbers of swords are not provided in the accounts, based upon the purchase of a single weapon from Tissier for 7s 0d, it is possible to calculate that the first disbursement of £265 7s 0d equated to upwards of 760 items if no discounts for bulk orders were applied. Given the likelihood that at least ten companies of 100 dragoons, besides commissioned and non-commissioned officers could have been raised by Browne (or at least intended to be so), this and the additional sum of £253 0s 0d for 'swords and belts' would appear to be a reasonable one.

This corresponds exactly with an agreement made with Bromfield on 21 September 1643 to supply 300 swords for dragoons (possibly those in the Eastern Association Army), for which he was paid £105 0s 0d, or 7s 0d apiece.[82] In like fashion, on 6 May 1644 '200 swords and belts at 7s 0d each' were procured by the Earl of Denbigh's commissary, Nathaniel Cholmley from an unknown supplier, though his troop of horse had previously been equipped with arms and armour produced in London by Thomas Stevens.[83] Sir William Savile's northern Royalist dragoon regiment received 100 swords at York on 14 November 1643, while five days later he requested that the magazine in the city issued twelve swords, 'and as much powder and shot as Captain Henry Attey would ask for'.[84]

Parliament contracts for the supply of the New Model Army in 1645 included '400 swords and belts, Dutch blades at 4s 6d each' from Daniel Judd; 2,000 of the same items from Thomas Freeman, Warden of the Cutlers of London, at the same price; a further 9,000 swords and belts at 4s 8d apiece were contracted with five suppliers. These were certainly procured for the

78 W. Wrye, W. (ed.), *State Papers Relating to Musters, Beacons, Ship-money, &c. in Norfolk from 1626 chiefly to the beginning of the Civil War* (Norwich, 1907), pp.90, 200.
79 Monck, *Observations*, pp.26–7; Young and Tucker (eds), *Military Memoirs*, p.51.
80 TNA, WO55/1754.
81 TNA, SP28/144/2, ff.29r–34r; Peter Edwards, *Dealing in Death: The Arms Trade and the British Civil Wars, 1638–52* (Stroud: Sutton, 2000), p.72.
82 TNA, SP/28/227/1, unfol.
83 WA, CR2017/C9/91; CR 2017/C10/68.
84 WYA, WYL100/PO/2/A/I/20; WYL100/PO/2/A/I/26.

foot and dragoons, because Freeman separately delivered 200 'horsemen's swords, plus belts at 5s 0d each'.[85]

Following the outbreak of war in 1642, the King's Office of the Armoury was relocated from the Tower of London to Oxford, where a new establishment was overseen by William Legge, the Master of the Armouries. This Office would supply swords to the Royalist Oxford Army throughout the First Civil War. These weapons were stored at Gloucester Hall in Oxford, before being issued. On 20 November 1643, Legge was given £100 'to be employed in building a mill at Wolvercote near Oxford, for grinding of swords and for building forges, providing tools and other necessaries for sword-blade makers to be employed to make swords for Our service.'[86] Similarly, a sum 'not exceeding £2,000', was ordered to be paid to Legge on 26 February 1644 'for providing swords and belts in the office of armouries, the same to be made at the usual price and according to the patterns by us appointed: also to provide tools and other necessaries for sword-blade makers employed by the said Master of the Armouries.' Such weapons were to cost '7s 6d for every sword and 2s 0d for each belt.'[87]

Various contemporary accounts include references to dragoons and musketeers engaging in close quarter fighting with the butt-end of their muskets, often immediately following musketry volleys and the expenditure of ammunition. As Turner recommended with the delivery of the *salvee*, 'Next, firing by three ranks at a time, should not be practised, but when either the business seems to be desperate, or that the bodies are so near, that the pikemen are almost come to push of pike, and then no other use can be made of the musket but of the butt-end of it.'[88] During the first Royalist assault on Bolton on 16 February 1643 by eleven companies of foot and two of dragoons supported by horse and light cannon, an eyewitness recounted 'there was such sharp service for a great while together as I think hath seldom been heard.' Some Parliamentarian soldiers were cut off as the Bradshaw Gate and three earthen sconces were cleared, though there was some fierce hand-to-hand fighting. The defending musketeers subsequently poured into them 'such storms of bullets ... as powdered them to purpose, and after Royalist soldiers entered one house, they were initially repelled by musket butts.' It was later reported, 'A second house, similarly occupied, had also to be dealt with where there was such a threshing as never was heard of before, for besides the hand blows that past, the enemy was so desperate that three times they came to the ends of their muskets, and caught hold of them as they went off.'[89] At Hopton Heath on 19 March 1643, three companies of Cheshire dragoons were reported by Sir William Brereton as fighting 'so long, and so

85 TNA, WO47/1, ff.208r–209v, 299r.; WO55/1662, f.17v; ML, 46–78/709, ff.98r, 114r; Mungeam, 'Contracts', pp.106–7, 114–15.

86 *CSPD 1641–3*, p.501.

87 *ROP*, I, p.176.

88 *Ibid.*, p.237.

89 *First Assault on Bolton-le-Moors by Lord Derby's Wigan Forces*, from *Speciall Passages*, 20 February 1643.

fiercely, until all their powder and bullet was spent. Afterwards they joined, and fell to it pell mell, one upon another, with the stocks of their muskets.'[90]

On 15 October 1644, Sir William Waller received orders to march east and effect a rendezvous with Essex's and Manchester's forces, although due to inclement weather and enemy activity he stalled at Andover and Basingstoke. Five days later, he reported to the Committee of Both Kingdoms that elements of the Parliamentarian forces were close at hand, but added:

> 800 suits of clothes will serve us for the present. If his Excellency [Essex] has any to spare we fain would borrow them; it would be very seasonable and comfortable to the poor creatures, who are so pitiful an object that the like is not to be seen in England … It is no little grief to us that our poor dragoons go naked in this weather. Oh! That they may be thought upon for clothes[91]

Waller's entire regiment of foot had been converted to dragoons on 13 July 1644, but how many soldiers he succeeded in changing is not clear, as horses were in very short supply; however he had no foot with him by early October 1644 and he had 1,500 dragoons as opposed to 150 in early September.[92] Nevertheless, on 21 October the Commons ordered 'That 800 suits of clothes, etc. [be] provided for my Lord General's army, be sent down to clothe Sir William Waller's dragoons (my Lord General's foot being first supplied). And the Committee formerly appointed to provide these clothes is to take care herein.'[93]

Following the Royalist victory at Lostwithiel in 1644 Charles I marched his forces towards London, but they were blocked by the combined Parliamentarian armies of Waller, the Eastern Association and Essex, which had rendezvoused at Basingstoke on 20 October. That day, Waller wrote to the Committee of Both Kingdoms, speaking of:

> our orderly retreat, bringing a brave body of horse safe to Basing, but we are not well armed. Last night the King with his Trayne went to Winchester ... We hope there will be a battle shortly. To our understanding, it cannot be avoided. We desire the prayers of all our friends. We trust more in that than in our army.'[94]

The following day, the Commons directed the Earl of Essex to supply the much-needed clothing to Waller's threadbare and starving dragoons.[95]

There are far less direct references to the clothing of dragoons during the British Civil Wars than those for regiments of foot, although it might be inferred that the former benefitted from some of the more general issues of cloth and garments to various armies. Items of clothing issued to civil war armies are sometimes referred to as 'suits' or 'uniforms', which could include

---

90 *History and Antiquities of Staffordshire*, I, p.59.
91 *CSPD 1644*, p.60.
92 *CSPD 1644*, pp.485, 495, 521, 523.
93 *CJ*, III, p.671.
94 *CSPD 1644–45*, p.60.
95 *CJ*, III, p.671.

coats and breeches, and perhaps other items such as caps. Outer clothing, such as coats and breeches, were usually made by tailors in their own workshops, such those in London supplying Essex's and Manchester's forces, and at Oxford, where garments were produced for the King's army. Entries in the accounts of John Bramhall, a dragoon Captain in Sir William Brereton's forces, as well as those in the accounts of the army's treasurer, disclose that he – possibly having been a Nantwich mercer before the war – engaged in the supply and production of garments with his mother in the town. From January 1643, they outfitted his dragoons with quantities of cloth and made-up clothing, including coats, breeches and shirts – the costs of which were deducted from the soldiers' pay.[96]

On 20 May 1643 Bramhall disbursed £1 4s 3d 'for cloth to make my drummer a suit of clothes' and a further 3s to a tailor for making it up. He also paid the sum of 11s 1d to Thomas Mottershaw for made-up uniforms, 5s 4d to Henry Meeke for trimming a suit, with a further 9d for buttons. The Cheshire Parliamentarian Colonel, Robert Duckenfield paid £85 0s 0d to John Gaskell, a Manchester draper on 5 April 1645 'for new uniforms for my regiment'. At a rate of 18s 0d per set, this works out to over 90 sets of coats and breeches. Additionally, in April 1644, Duckenfield disbursed the sum of £1 0s 0d to Roger Ridgeway, a local tailor for making up soldiers' coats.[97] Warrants for the Earl of Essex's army issued in October 1642 include one to Lord Rochford, 'for the completing of his said regiment 200 coats, 200 shirts, 200 pairs of shoes and 200 knapsacks.' An initial delivery of 400 coats, 'blue lined white', had already been made. Colonel John Holmstead's regiment of foot was to receive 1,000 coats, 1,000 shirts, 1,000 pairs of shoes and 1,000 knapsacks, whereas 800 of each item were supplied to Colonel Henry Bulstrode's soldiers.[98] In October 1646, 'soldiers' suits according to the pattern of cloths shrunk, as they are delivered for Sir *Thomas Fairfax's* soldiers, at 18s 0d apiece' were contracted for troops going to Ireland.[99]

Sufficient evidence exists for supplies of cloth and complete suits of clothing to the King's Oxford Army in 1643 – referred to by modern writers as the 'Oxford refit'. The Royalists quickly moved to make the city a centre for the manufacture of clothing. On 23 January the Oxford schoolboy, Anthony Wood recorded in his diary:

> so the magazine for cloth for soldiers' apparel and coats was in the Music School, and in the Astronomy School adjoining to it. That day also were a great many tailors, as well foreigners as townsmen, set on work to cut out these coats, to the number 4,000 or 5,000 (as I was told), which presently afterwards put forth to the tailors here inhabitants, and to strangers within ten miles who were called into Oxford, to be made up and finished[100]

96 BL, Ms Harley 2128, ff.23v–26v, 28v, 31r; TNA, SP28/31/4, ff.433r–434v.

97 BL, Ms Harley 2130, f.91v.; TNA, SP28/128/10, f.5r.

98 TNA, SP28/1A, ff.38r, 248v; SP28/3B/1, ff.299r, 482r, 504r–505r.

99 *CJ*, IV, p.698.

100 Anthony Wood, *The Life and Times of Anthony Wood, antiquary, of Oxford, 1632–1695, described by Himself* (Oxford: Oxford Historical Society, 1891–2), I, pp.83–4.

Oxford lay on the fringe of the West Country clothmaking industry and as the war progressed, the King's forces procured much of their materials from clothiers in the region. On 1 February 1643, Charles I wrote to Rupert:

> Most trusty and entirely beloved Nephew, We greet you well whereas we are credibly informed that at Cirencester, Stroud, Minchinhampton, Tetbury, Dursley, Wotton-under-Edge and Chipping Sudbury great quantities of cloth canvas and lockram are to be had for supplying the great necessities of Our soldiers [to] have of suits. We have thought good to advise you thereof and do hereby pray you to send a competent party of horse under the command of some able person to visit those several places which lie not far asunder, and to bring from thence all such cloth canvass and lockram as they shall find there to Cirencester. Giving a ticket to the owners for all the parcels they shall take up and keeping a perfect account thereof, and from what persons the same was taken with this intimation that every one of them shall upon his repair to Oxford receive such security for his commodity as he shall have no cause to except against. For the better ordering and managing of this service. We shall expressly send Mr Nevill, Mr Bradburne and Mr Ball, men of experience, to take order for receiving and putting of the cloth whereof We intend the best shall be reserved for the service of our troopers, and the rest for the dragoons and foot of our army. In this we pray you to use you wonted diligence.[101]

In March 1643, the Bristol manufacturer and contractor Thomas Bushell undertook to fit out the foot regiments (and possibly the dragoons) of the Oxford Army, comprising caps, cassocks, breeches and stockings 'at reasonable rates to be delivered at Oxford, and at the delivery to receive ready money, or a bill of exchange to be paid at London, the choice to be left to them who provided the clothes.' A testimony to Bushell's service, dated 12 June, in addition to a later petition from him, mention 'your clothing our Life Guard and three regiments more, with suits, stockings, shoes, and monteros which we were ready in the field.'[102] By 15 July, Wood could record, 'upon the next, viz. Saturday all the common soldiers then at Oxford were new appareled, some all in red, coats, breeches, and monteroes, and some all in blue, whilst shortly afterwards a Parliamentarian spy reported to Sir Samuel Luke, 'they have clothed all their foot soldiers in red and blue, having all of them monteroes, coats and breeches.'[103] The montero cap was a design commonly issued to soldiers and was conceivably a pattern unique to the military as 'the fashion of the Montero [is] much differing from other men's hats', and was often worn by European soldiers.[104]

---

101 Quoted in Kenneth, G. Ponting, *The Woollen Industry of South-West England* (Bath: Adams & Dart, 1971), p.143 – citing a letter 'in possession of Messrs Strachans of Stroud'.

102 TNA, SP16/494, f.16v; SP28/251, f.209r.

103 Wood, *Life and Times*,p.103; Luke, *Letter Books*, p.119.

104 F. Strada and R. Stapylton, *De Bello Belgico: The History of the Low-Countrey Warres* (London: 1650), p.56.

Musketeer fighting with butt of musket Wallhausen, *Kriegskunst zu Pferd* (Open source)

On 13 November, while at Oxford, Prince Rupert wrote to the Sheriff of Merionethshire about the arrival of troops from Ireland and the need to supply them with clothing:

> Many of the soldiers there being English Protestants are coming over to and are daily expected to land in some of the counties of North Wales. Rebellious subjects were the promoters of the rebellion in Ireland, and now they untruly charge the King on the occasion of the coming over of the soldiers, with bringing over the Irish rebels. Since the rebels have lately forced their passage over Holt Bridge and obstructed all the ways to Chester, orders have been given to the soldiers from Ireland to repair to those parts (of North Wales) for succour. The county of Merioneth having been freed of many burdens which other counties have sustained in the paying and free billeting of soldiers, the King's will and command is that there be provided, at the charge of the county, cloaks, shoes, stockings, and apparel sufficient for 500 men, and likewise victuals for 4,000 men for fifteen days, or money sufficient for the same use to be brought forthwith to Conwy where a magazine has been provided.[105]

According to one Parliamentarian newsbook, when Colonel Richard Bolle's forces belonging to the Oxford Army surrendered to Waller at Alton on 13 December 1643:

> the whole regiment consisted mainly of Welsh (and which is very strange) they were very well habited which put our soldiers presently upon exchange of hats,

105 NLW, Clenennau Letters and Papers, p.539.

> cloaks, doublets, etc., which the enemy (by reason of the present danger they were in) told our men they would exchange with all their hearts[106]

Sir Thomas Dallison, in command of Prince Rupert's infantry regiment at Welshpool in August 1644 informed him:

> I have had 113 coats and caps for foot soldiers in the house of my Lord Powys, one hundred of which are blue, which will serve very well for your Highness's regiment of foot. The rest are green, which may be for Colonel Tillier's regiment. There are also three or four hundred yards of cloth, which may serve to make coats for your Highness's regiment of horse.[107]

Both sides made use of Welsh cloth. A consignment captured by Parliamentarian troops at Oswestry in June 1644, intended for Rupert's army, instead clothed the Shropshire forces and the Earl of Denbigh's regiment of foot.[108] Similarly, a batch of cloth seized in North Wales by Sir William Brereton's troopers in April 1645 consisted of 12 yards of gladen (Welsh flannel – *gwlanen*), 4 yards of coarse gladen, 4¼ yards of red cloth, 4 yards of green cloth, 1¼ yards of green cloth and 3 more yards of white gladen in 2 pieces.[109] Although it is not known how this fabric was subsequently used, it is possible that some of it went on riding coats for the horse or dragoons.

In addition to Bushell, the King's armies were supplied by clothiers from the West Country and the Thames Valley area. The narrative of John Ashe, the West Country clothier and Parliamentarian Deputy Lieutenant for Somerset, was reprinted in pamphlet form from a letter he wrote to the Speaker. In March 1643, the Royalist newsbook, *Mercurius Aulicus*, reported the governor of Reading's seizure of Ashe's supplies for London:

> Certain news also came this day, that Sir Arthur Aston had seized on seven cartloads, one wain-load and 24 horse-loads of broad fine cloth, amounting in the whole to 380 cloths, and that in many of the packs were found some belts and bandoleers, and great store of match, and a considerable sum of money. All of which were sent towards London from one Mr Ashe, the greatest clothier in the kingdom, as it is conceived, but of so turbulent a spirit and so pernicious a practitioner in the maintaining and fomenting of this rebellion, that he stands excepted by his Majesty amongst some others, out of his Majesty's general pardon for the county of Somerset.[110]

Soon afterwards, the 'clothing tradesmen' of Reading petitioned Charles I, 'requesting that the cloths seized by Sir Arthur Aston may be kept in safe custody until they and the inhabitants of Somerset, Devon, Wiltshire

106 *Weekly Account*, 18–25 December 1643.

107 *The True Informer*, 17 August 1644.

108 *The Perfect Occurrences of Parliament and Chief Collections of Letters*, 28 June–5 July 1644; *CSPD, 1644*, p.429.

109 CRO, DDX/428, f.85v.; *BLB*, I, 199–200.

110 *Mercurius Aulicus*, 1–7 March 1643.

and Gloucestershire have procured safe conduct from Parliament for the transport of their goods to London.' The appeal included the claim that Reading 'is an ancient clothing town solely consisting of the traffic and trade with London, which your petitioners did enjoy until your Majesty made the town of Reading a garrison town.'[111] Reading, which had been garrisoned for the King in late October 1642, had been a clothing town since the Middle Ages, although its declining economic prosperity was not assisted by Charles I's refusal to allow manufacturers to sell their goods in London. Although the writer of *A Catalogue of the Taverns in ten Shires about London* (1636) stated 'Reading is the prime and principal town in this county of Berkshire, for fair buildings, large streets for clothing and other blessings,' and the governing charter of the borough was granted by Charles I on 17 December 1638, the decline in the prosperity of the town followed this event with astonishing swiftness.[112] This was partly caused by a rapid deterioration in the fortunes of the local cloth trade, which faced increased competition from northern and West Country manufacturers, but also the self-serving members of the corporation. A 'petition from the mayor and burgesses to James I's commissioners for grievances, relating to the unemployment due to the decline of clothmaking in Reading,' dated c.1623 foreshadowed the situation:

> Due to a sudden decay of clothing in our town many poor families, men, women and children who had their means and livelihood from the work of the clothier, to which only they have been trained, are now for want of work exposed to great misery, and have in woeful manner complained to your petitioners expostulating with them why they did not now as in former times furnish the poor people of the town with work. Their answer is they cannot because they have not that sale for their cloth as heretofore, they have had which causes them to make a less quantity of cloth; and so by consequence theirs is a necessity of the failing of work to the poor.[113]

Hence, the clothiers attributed the inability to sell cloth to 'the small number of merchants to whom they are limited to sell their clothes', and their inability to transport their cloth as cheaply as northern merchants, who have also recently altered the size of their cloths from twelve yards to the same length as Reading cloth and sell it under the name of Reading cloth. They might be restored to their former position and supply the poor with work if merchants of white cloth were required to purchase at least one coloured cloth for every ten white ones, as the manufacture of one coloured cloth requires as much labour, and yields as much profit to the King, as six white ones. This would relieve 'many hundreds of poor people distressed for want of work [who are] ready to perish, and relief of whom will be insupportable for the town.'

Payments made during the Royalist occupation of Reading in October 1642, include those for bread and cheese to be sent to Charles I at Henley-

111 BRO, R/Z3/36.

112 John Taylor, *A Catalogue of the Taverns in ten Shires about London* (London: Henry Gosson, 1636), unpag.

113 BRO, R/Z3/24.

on-Thames and Bagshot, for making soldiers' uniforms, wood and lights for the court of guard, the sum of £2,000 loaned to the King for the maintenance of the army, fortifying the town, as well as victuals for horses and soldiers provided by the inhabitants of the town and not paid for.[114] On 4 November, from Oxford, Charles I instructed the mayor and aldermen of his permission to the clothiers of Reading to continue in their trade and vowed to take no more garments from them without payment, provided that they send none to London. An earlier order to the inhabitants 'to bring to the town hall all their arms and armour' for the use of Royalist troops appears to have resulted in limited success, however, as they needed to be reminded that unless it was adhered to by 1pm on 7 November, 'any house in which such weapons are discovered thereafter shall be immediately given unto the soldiers to plunder.'[115]

It is evident, nevertheless, that significant quantities of clothing continued to be produced in the town for the King's army. On 8 November, sixteen days after the Battle of Edgehill, Charles I issued a warrant to the mayor to impress all the tailors within a six-mile radius of the town to employ them in making clothing for the soldiers of the Oxford Army. The following day the King ordered the tailors and merchants of Reading to supply 1,000 suits of clothes for soldiers, the town of Abingdon having sent the mayor 137 cloths (sufficient to make 1,644 suits). The sum of £1,500, being the cost of 'dying, drying and making cloth into suits for the King's soldiers, the cloth (valued at £1,000) having been freely given by the borough' was levied on the population. However, as this erroneous figure was found to be impossible to raise, the entire county of Berkshire petitioned Charles I to be permitted to shoulder the burden.[116] In addition to this, on 12 November a further warrant was issued to the mayor and aldermen authorised them to 'take up [requisition] such carts, boats or barges as shall be most convenient' to deliver the clothes and victuals to be provided by the town for the King's army throughout the county of Berkshire.[117]

When Sir Thomas Aston's cavalry troopers and dragoons rode into the West under the command of Sir Ralph Hopton in early 1644, they were probably clothed in the grey-green hue previously suggested by their commander's kinsman, Sir Arthur Aston. The veteran soldier had also suggested that the hue of such garments should suit early morning attacks, 'or else the colour of your men's coats will give away the advantage gained.'[118] Money was provided from Oxford for cloth and clothing for the Royalist forces in the region. On 6 January, Charles I wrote from his headquarters to 'the clothiers and mercers of the townships of Trowbridge, Bradford and Westbury in Our county of Wiltshire, and of Frome Elwood in Our county of Somerset':

114 BRO, R/Z3/28.

115 BRO, R/Z/6/1/5; R/Z/6/1/19.

116 BRO, R/Z3/27/1–7; R/Z3/29; R/Z3/38/1.

117 BRO, R/Z/6/1/3.

118 Aston, Dispursed Accounts

> Whereas we for Our present service were constrained to cut off certain arrears amounting to a considerable sum, due to the regiment of Sir Thomas Aston, Baronet, in Our county of Gloucester, which by Our letters we did promise to supply some other way. Now for that there is an urgent necessity for clothing of the soldiers under his command, which by reason of Our urgent occasions we cannot presently supply in ready moneys, these are therefore to desire you forthwith upon sight hereafter to deliver unto the said Sir Thomas Aston or such as he shall appoint to receive the same such a proportion of cloth as will amount unto the sum of £300 for the use above mentioned. And we do hereby promise you and every, or any of you that shall furnish the same that we shall truly repay the same within three months next after the delivery thereof upon ticket, to be given by the said Sir Thomas Aston under his hand, acknowledging his receipt thereof. And in the meantime, we shall give order for passing Our letters of Privy Seal for payment of the same out of Our Exchequer at the time prefixed by us And we shall take it for a good and acceptable service, and it a testimony of your good affection to us and to Our service.[119]

On 26 February Aston, his men now in threadbare uniforms, wrote to Hopton regarding the procurement of quarter and clothing:

> I am importuned by divers [of] the inhabitants of the Hundred of Whorlesdown, to certify your Lordship that by virtue of the King's express directions at a council of war, and in pursuance thereof the Prince's warrant for quarter and maintenance of my men in this county. I have collected towards the present supply of my men to enable them to march, about six weeks' contribution out of that hundred, without which they could not possibly have gone upon service, they are threatened to pay it again, which I hope your Lordship will forbid; certain I am, it was against my will and to the great loss of the regiment (being removed by the King's express direction out of Gloucestershire, where there was £1,200 in the quarters) to come hither, where we were again deprived of our quarters as soon as we came. The Hundreds of Whorlesdowne, Daworth and Mere, being it seems by his Majesty taken from us, in which we were promised means to cover the nakedness, with two summers' and almost two winters' perpetual service without rest or quarter worn out of the habit, and almost out of the souls of men, into despair ever to be clothed again or receive anything, I would to God things were so managed there were no such crossing of orders I am sure it is and will be the ruin of his regiments, and little comfort to the officer that spends his fortune in his service to be exposed to the inconvenience of such contradictions with others and to the clamour and daily mutiny of the soldiers for want of subsistence, but what inconvenience soever I feel, I know how to obey, since intimation of his Majesty's disposal of these quarters otherwise. I have forborne to demand anything but was due before, and must in all submit to his Majesty's pleasure, and for what is past being past redemption, I hope your Lord will give order the country shall not be oppressed by repayment, and both excuse this boldness and the unhappy trouble

119 WRO, X3/119/AC/2.

> herein befallen so much to the prejudice of your Lordship's must humble servant, Thomas Aston.

The following day Sir Ralph replied:

> It is very little satisfaction to me that having now these six weeks taken your pleasure in the quarters assigned by the King to this army even in our greatest necessity, should desire me not to oppress the country by repayment, I hope it shall appear the oppression was in your undue taking of which belonged to us instead, and not in my demand which was not assigned to me before I undertook this task, who I am sure have not had two months' ease of duty as you now have had since the war began, and now you have his Majesty's orders to remove into Dorsetshire, I shall strictly expect you to be totally removed accordingly, and that you demand not one penny of that country since that order, upon which pretence soever. Concerning the nakedness of your men, I cannot but take a little the more notice of it, because complaint is made to me of much cloth taken by you from honest men in the county whereof, I expect an account. I must profess his Majesty's service under my command hath suffered by the wrong at hand had in Wiltshire than it hath, or could have done by Waller's force, any duty to his Majesty's service makes me insist upon, thus otherwise, I decline to continue.[120]

Subsequently, contracts were agreed with various Wiltshire manufacturers to supply and dye quantities of broad cloth for the clothing of Aston's troops.

On 29 February 1644, Westbury parish consented to 'furnishing the soldiers of Sir Thomas Aston's regiment with some cloth for their present supply … to the sum of £125 0s 0d', while the inhabitants of Bradford Hundred responded to a Royal warrant to purchase £150 worth of cloth 'to supply that portion fourteen days from the date hereof, we shall cause to be dyed and dressed at our charges fit for wear, eighteen whole cloths of our white cloths of 28 yards the pure white, of the usual rate of £7 0s 0d a yard, white and not under, of such colours as the said Sir Thomas Aston shall appoint.' Another agreement for the supply of cloth from the Hundred of Frome, Somerset, to the value of £100 detailed that a 'piece' of broad cloth woven in Westbury (Wiltshire) and Ilminster (Somerset), was between 24 yards and 26 yards, the colour being 'Ilminster grey' (an off-white shade, also known as 'West Country whites'), and 'to be dyed into such colours as Sir Thomas Aston shall appoint.'[121] The cloth industry of West Wiltshire rivalled that of Salisbury and other locations by the end of the fifteenth century. Bradford-on-Avon became an important town, and other centres of production were established at Trowbridge, Steeple Ashton, Warminster, Devizes and Westbury. At this period fine white broadcloths produced in Wiltshire (especially at Bradford-on-Avon) were in great demand abroad and this stimulated the production of wool locally.[122] By April 1644, Sir Thomas Aston's horse and dragoons

120 WRO, X3/119/AC/13–14.

121 WRO, X3/119/AC/unnumbered.

122 Peter J. Bowden, *The Wool Trade in Tudor and Stuart England* (London: Palgrave Macmillan, 1962), pp.47–8.

had been issued blue soldiers' coats and riding coats of 'double-dyed woad', a colour particular to Wiltshire, although the cultivation of woad was also linked to the dying industry in Warwickshire, where batches of cloth were appropriated by both Royalist and Parliamentarian armies.[123]

Among West Country producers, woad was the chief dye to produce blues. In the late sixteenth century woad was grown on more than 300 acres in Wiltshire by major landowners, perhaps reflecting a strong local demand.[124] Dyeing with woad to produce various shades of blue could be done in-the-wool as it did not necessitate a fixative, as wood ash or potash were only added to make the woad soluble in water.[125] It is reasonable to think that the other Royalist units quartered in Wiltshire – Sir John Byron's cavalry, and Colonel Howard's regiments of horse and foot were similarly clothed. Following the Royalist surrender of Arundel Castle on 4 January 1644, Hopton described how he 'Presently dispatched his orders with several officers into Wiltshire, and other West Counties, for recruits of foot and horse, and to Salisbury and other towns within his quarters he sent upon his own credit to take up cloth and other necessaries to clothe those he had, which orders being dispatched in season took their reasonable effect in due time.' Soon afterwards, he remarked, 'recruits begin daily to come up to him, so as he had gotten to the number of 2,000 foot well-clad and 2,000 horse.'[126]

From his base in Huntingdon on 1 August 1643 Colonel Oliver Cromwell wrote to the deputy lieutenants of the county of Essex that he had been compelled to borrow the sum of £100 from the mayor of Nottingham 'for the payment of the three companies belonging to your counties [the Eastern Association], besides shoes, stockings, shirts, and billet money, which I promised shall be repaid I, receiving no money out of your counties wherewithal to do it, I can but refer it to your considerations, for I think it is not expected that I should pay your soldiers out of my own purse.' Moreover, the Cambridge Committee wrote to Sir Thomas Barrington (head of the Essex Committee) on 5 September, 'There is such a want of arms we know not what to do ... There is a great stir among the soldiers for coats, and shoes and money. Sir William Roe has persuaded me to let them have coats and some shoes, and he has bespoken 200 coats, which will cost 12d each ... I never saw worse tattered soldiers for the general [the Earl of Manchester].'[127]

Specifically issued to foot soldiers and dragoons, soldier's coats – worn over a fitted doublet and breeches – formed the basic item of clothing. Any notion of actual uniformity in the style and shade of clothing issued to civil war troops is a modern idea, however. There appears to have been no one set pattern for coats, nor construction method, while linings could be entirely arbitrary. Coat colours might also fluctuate, depending upon

123 TNA, SP28/185, ff.438r–478r; SP28/136, unfol.

124 J. H. Bettey, *Wiltshire Farming in the Seventeenth Century* (Trowbridge: Wiltshire Record Society, 2005), p.280; John Gailsford, 'Capital in the Countryside: social change in West Wiltshire, 1530–1680', PhD thesis (Birkbeck, 2015), pp.91, 150.

125 John Oldland, *The English Woollen Industry, c.1200-c.1560* (Abingdon: Routledge, 2019), pp.28–29, 53.

126 Hopton, *Bellum Civile*, pp.76–77.

127 BL, Ms Egerton 2647, f.138r; HMC, *Seventh Report*, p.557.

the availability of batches of cloth and dye stuffs. Moreover, some civil war regiments received coats of a particular colour at different times, and once a campaign was underway coats were not always replaced in the same hue. On 2 October 1643 Commissary William Harlackenden informed Sir Thomas Barrington, the leading deputy lieutenant for Essex, 'I received even more [letters] from Major Moore, I should speedily sent to [you] for coats for his regiment, being 2,100 odd men, that they may be speedily sent, my Lord Manchester bids me write and that the coats be green cloth lined with red, there is already 200 odd coats made in Cambridge.' The garments were to be made by William Gray, and it could have been this order to which he referred when he wrote to Barrington on 14 October, 'I have bought 400 or 500 which I hope to be ready for Saturday next, though I find this material so hard to get that the bargain will be very hard to meet if I can find anything, it will be as much as I expect for that sort of cloth is not to be had for money at the present, but I hope in a little time to perfect the 1,000 coats.'[128] Being unable to clothe his foot regiment entirely in green the Earl of Manchester was compelled to accept red coats, therefore during autumn 1642 some companies were issued green coats lined with red and others red coats lined in green.

On 26 April 1644, Lieutenant-Colonel Clifton's company was provided with 141 red coats, costing £77 10s 0d, whilst a batch of clothing issued to Manchester's regiment on 16 September included 698 green soldiers' coats lined in red at 10s 0d each.[129] Red was becoming the standard issue for coats in the Eastern Association Army by 1644. Thus, Samuel Moody of Bury St Edmunds received £2,488 0s 0d for 5,240 coats that were to be distributed between the foot regiments of Colonels Hobart, Palgrave, Pickering, Walton and Russell. On 13 December, Moody had a further £250 0s 0d for supplying 500 red coats to Colonel Francis Russell's regiment, whereas Colonel Edward Montague's were issued with red coats faced white.[130] Red soldiers' coats were similarly not uncommon in other Parliamentarian forces. On 29 November 1642, an order was given for 'the delivery unto Colonel Herbert Morley for the service of the County of Sussex 60 red coats, sixty caps, shoes and shirts, and other necessities which are for the clothing and furnishing of that recruited regiment which was commanded by Colonel Holles.'[131] The latter regiment had served with the Earl of Essex's army in 1642 until it was destroyed at Brentford. During 1644 and 1645 coats of this hue were purchased for the Kentish foot regiments of Colonel Ralph Weldon and Sir William Springate.[132] Likewise, upon the regiment's formation in November 1642 Colonel Richard Browne's dragoons were referred to as 'redcoats', although the reformed unit was wearing grey by 1645.[133]

128 BL, Ms Egerton 2647, ff.140r, 148r–148v.; HMC, *Seventh Report*, pp.562, 565–7.
129 TNA, SP28/18, f.88r; SP28/25, f.345r.
130 TNA, SP28/128/8, ff.9v–10r; SP28/24, f.388r; SP28/25, ff.426r–428v; SP28/26, f.117r.
131 TNA, SP28/262, f.374v.
132 TNA, SP28/130/3, ff.62r., 67v.
133 TNA, 144/2, f.30r.; BL, Ms Add 18982, f.409v.

Stefano della Bella, *Twee trommelaarstepaard* (Rijkesmusem, Amsterdam)

On 1 May 1645, one Royalist newsbook described the New Model Army as it proceeded out of Windsor, 'with Major General Skippon marched in the van of the foot and leadeth the General's own regiment, Sir Thomas Fairfax's colours are blue; the men are redcoats all, the whole army, only are distinguished by several facings of their coats, the firelocks (only) some of them are tawny coats.'[134] Although the term 'facings' has been generally interpreted as 'linings', as with British armies of later periods, there remains no evidence to corroborate this assumption. Men conscripted as recruits from Essex sent to Fairfax's army by the county's Committee in March 1645 were to be issued 'as has formerly been the practice, with 1,000 red coats faced with blue.'[135] On 10 March, the Commons declared that 'money, arms, and clothes be in readiness and ordered to be presently given out, as soon as the several recruits come to their several regiments,' adding eleven days later that each common soldier conscripted should be furnished with a coat, breeches, a shirt, one pair of stockings and shoes, and knapsack, by several county committees 'so as the charge do not exceed 24s 0d for each, besides the conduct-money.'[136] The extent to which the recruits received such clothing before they were conducted to the army, however, is uncertain, given the huge demands made upon county committees and suppliers,

On 3 April 1645, Sir Thomas Fairfax travelled from London to Windsor, where he appointed a general rendezvous of the forces that remained of the armies of the Earl of Essex, the Earl of Manchester and Sir William Waller. Five regiments Essex's foot were quartered at Reading, and on 6 April they were mustered for the purpose of reduction. Major-General Skippon addressed the officers and soldiers of his old army, promising:

134 *Perfect Passages*, 30 April–7 May 1645.
135 *CSPD 1644–5*, pp.358–9.
136 *CJ*, IV, pp.74, 85.

> There is (at present) a fortnight's pay to be paid to such officers as shall go off, which they shall presently have upon their muster. And as for the officers and soldiers that are continued (as soon as they shall be mustered and listed) they also shall have a fortnight's pay; and there are clothes come down for the soldiers already in part, and I assure you, that upon my life and honour there are more providing, and you shall be all furnished with coats, breeches, stockings, shoes, and such arms as you shall stand in need of, with all good usage and constant pay.[137]

The Committee of Both Kingdoms informed Lieutenant-General Cromwell and Major-General Browne on 14 May:

> We have received yours of the eleventh, and are very much affected with the wants of your soldiers, which we have endeavoured to have supplied. Clothes have been provided, only some of these have been distributed to the recruits from the country, so that they are at present deficient, but will be supplied as fast as they can be made ready, which we think will be within a week.[138]

The earliest surviving warrant authorising payment for the delivery of such items is dated 17 April 1645.[139]

Although contracts for the supply of coats and breeches were agreed with contractors in April and May 1645, Treasury warrants authorising payments to them, either in full or part of their contracts (in other words following the delivery of goods to the Committee of the Army upon the fulfilment of them), demonstrate that by early June 1645 upwards of 9,000 soldiers' coats, with similar quantities of breeches, stockings and shoes had actually been received. These were presumably placed in the magazine at Reading to be issued to the New Model Army.[140] On 24 August freight was paid for the transportation, by river from Windsor to London and from there by sea to Lyme Regis, for 938 coats, 800 pairs of breeches, 270 shirts, 190 pairs of shoes and 118 pairs of stockings for Sir Thomas Fairfax's army in the West.[141] The earliest known delivery of clothing from the Ordnance Office is that of 5,770 coats; 5,700 breeches; 6,500 pairs of shoes; 5,000 pairs of stockings; and 6,000 shirts on 27 September 1645.[142] A list of clothing in the army's magazine at Reading, dated 20 October 1645, includes 3,210 coats, 3,260 pairs of breeches, 3,510 shirts and 3,820 pairs of shoes.[143]

Surviving contracts for the manufacture of uniforms for the New Model indicate that, like the magazine clothing supplied to the Protestant army in Ireland from the Tower stores in 1642-3, they were expected to conform to specific requirements. On 14 February 1646, an agreement was made between the Committee of the Army and the City merchant Richard Downes for the

137 Rushworth, *Historical Collections*, VI, p.20.
138 *CSPD 1644–5*, p.487.
139 TNA, SP28/29/1, f.189r.
140 TNA, SP28/29/1, fols193r–200r, 210r; SP28/29/2, ff.252r, 255r; SP28/30/4, ff.355r, 369r.
141 TNA, SP28/147/2, f.352r.
142 WSL, Ms Salt 463, unfol.
143 TNA, SP28/31/4, f.341r.

provision of 2,000 coats, breeches and pairs of stockings, which stipulated that:

> The coats to be of a red colour and of Suffolk, Coventry or Gloucester cloth, and to be made three-quarters and a nail long, faced with baize or cotton, with tape-strings according to a pattern delivered to the said Committee. The breeches to be gray or some other good colour and made of Reading cloth or other cloth, in length three-quarters one eighth, well-lined and trimmed suitable to the patterns presented, the said cloth both of the coats and of the breeches to be first shrunken in cold water. The stockings to be of good Welsh cotton.[144]

Moreover, contracts drawn up on 1 April 1645 had specified that 4,000 coats were to be supplied with white, blue, green and yellow tapes, whilst another 1,100 were with 'orange ribbon.'[145] It is notable that neither the 1642–3 Irish coats nor those contracted for the New Model Army in 1645–6 and 1649 include any cloth for facings (presumably of cuffs and perhaps the inside of collars).[146] As the latter specifies the use of tape rather than facing the New Model coats with fabric, it is possible that facings were not subsequently used on their coats, or only among the first batches in spring 1645. There is also no provision for the lining of these garments. As Stuart Peachey suggests:

> In [the 1642] coats the tape was specifically for binding the coat, which could imply binding the edges as an alternative to hemming, which would make the cloth go a little further. This would be particularly important in an unlined coat, as the edges would be exposed on the inside unless turned in a second time. In the New Model and Irish issue coats, the tape is tape strings, which like knee strings might imply a dangling tape that can be tied in a bow. The 1649 New Model specification was 'faced with baize or cotton, with tape strings, or round about with tape in lieu of the cotton', implying that at least the cuffs and front edge of the tape might be used as binding.[147]

Though significant numbers of coats were contracted for and supplied to the New Model Army during the early months of its being, the extent to which red coats were universal amongst its foot regiments remains uncertain, although county communities were meant to issue such items to conscripts before they were sent to enroll in its ranks. Initially, moreover, contingents from various weak regiments were reduced into Fairfax's infantry, thus, the Parliamentarian newsbook *The Moderate Intelligencer* reported that on 22 July 1645 during the Fairfax's Western campaign 'the grey coats of Colonel Morley's, and Colonel Leyton's are put in Colonel Pickering's and Colonel Waller's Regiments'.[148] Given that some dragoons were issued soldiers' coats

---

144 TNA,WO47/1, ff.209r – 210v; ML, 46–78/709, ff. 27v–28r; Mungeam, 'Contracts', p.69.

145 ML, 46–78/709, f.114v; Mungeam, 'Contracts', p.115.

146 TNA, SP28/139/9, ff.103r-104v; SP28/33/4, f.443r; *CJ*, IV, p.698.

147 Stuart Peachey, *The Soldier's Life in the English Civil War: Organisation, Food, Clothing, Weapons, and Combat* (Bristol: Stuart Press, 2016), pp.24–5.

148 *The Moderate Intelligencer*, 17-24 July 1645. TT, E293 [23].

in other armies, it might be assumed that at some point Colonel John Okey's men received New Model red coats akin to their comrades in the foot, although no evidence for this has so far emerged.

Formerly the commander of dragoons in Manchester's army, Lieutenant-Colonel John Lilburne, was described as provocatively 'drawing a paper-book from under his short red coat' at one meeting of the Levellers in 1648, although it seems unlikely that he was wearing soldiers' apparel.[149] On 16 September 1644 the contractor Thomas Buckley was paid £258 6s 0d for 500 doublets at 10s 4d each, possibly for the Earl of Manchester's foot and dragoons, and a further £415 3s 0d for '1,167 pairs of cloth breeches delivered by order with making and linings at 7s 2d each.'[150] Similarly, on 9 March 1645 a payment of £5 0s 0d was made to John Wetherby a tailor for making 150 canvas waistcoats, whilst on 7 May, among a consignment for 1,000 shirts, 200 ells of canvas costing £11 0s 0d were delivered to the New Model Army.[151]

In early 1643, Captain Bramhall of Sir William Brereton's Cheshire forces received 52 coats for his dragoon company 'which were accordingly disposed of'.[152] Four Nantwich tailors made 344 infantry coats and 55 troopers' coats during the winter of 1643–4 and delivered them to the army's commissaries on 22 February 1644.[153] They were paid 1s 2d per soldiers' coat and 1s 8d per trooper's coat for their construction and carriage. On 24 December 1644, Brereton paid £100 'to William Barratt of Ridgeway in Cheshire to buy cloth for soldiers' coats in Cheshire, which was accordingly bought and disposed of for the soldiers' coats.'[154] Some consignments of soldier's coats for the Cheshire army specify their colour.

Between October 1642 and October 1643 the constables of Mere in Northwich Hundred paid the sum of £2 14s 10d for grey coats sent to Knutsford garrison, most probably for soldiers under Colonel John Leigh.[155] Similarly, in April 1645, the Staffordshire Committee disbursed £30 12s 11d for grey coats for Captain Monke's company, belonging to Brereton's own regiment.[156] Three months earlier, the same Committee had laid out £9 6s 0d for the making up soldier's coats, which could have been an earlier batch.[157] In this light, it is possible to suggest that a proportion, if not most of the Cheshire dragoons and foot were clothed in grey coats. Similarly, in October 1644, Sir Thomas Myddelton, who commanded small units of infantry and dragoons in Wales, received from London manufacturers 36 red soldiers' coats, along with white cloth to make drawers and waistcoats.[158]

---

149 *A Declaration of Some Proceedings of Lieutenant Colonel John Lilburne* (London: 1648), p.17; Austin Woolrych, *Britain in Revolution: 1625–1660* (Oxford: Oxford University Press, 2002), p.410.

150 TNA, SP28/18, f.226r.

151 TNA, SP28/26, f.19r; SP28/30/4, f.340r.

152 BL, Ms Harley, 2128, f.34v.

153 TNA, SP28/49/1, f.100v.

154 TNA, SP28/152/7, f.16r.

155 BL, Ms Harley 2128, f.60r.

156 TNA, SP28/134/12, f.395r; LCL, Ms Lichfield 24, f.83r.

157 TNA, SP28/134/12, f.391v.

158 TNA, SP28/211, ff.130v–141r; SP28/300/1, f.93v; SP28/346/1, unfol.

In addition to their more general clothing, there is evidence to show that cavalry troopers and dragoons were supplied with riding coats (sometimes referred to in sources as long coats or smock coats) for cold and winter wear. During the siege of Chester Sir William Brereton's horse and dragoons were quartered in open terrain to the Welsh side of the city, and constantly engaged in patrolling and picket duty. On 8 November 1645, Sir William reported to the Speaker that in establishing such *perdues* (outposts) his soldiers had been hampered 'by extreme foul weather which is violent that our men cannot endure out of doors.' Similarly, the following month, Sir Richard Lloyd, the Royalist governor of Holt remarked, 'the river [Dee] is frozen, and can be passed over with horse and foot under this castle,' while Brereton recounted on 9 January 1646 that 'Our duty is very hard; the weather extreme and piercing.'[159] On 22 February 1644, tailors in Nantwich produced 344 infantry coats costing 1s 2d each and 55 troopers' coats costing 1s 6s 0d.[160] In instructions given in a tailor's bill of 2 October 1643 one of Brereton's officials, stated: 'we desire you to let Captain Stukeley and his cornet have so much frieze as will make 40 suits and smock coats, and we will see you satisfied for the same.'[161] Another Parliamentarian commander in Cheshire, Colonel Robert Duckenfield, paid the sum of £41 8s 0d for '60 and odd new coats' for his cavalry troop in either November 1644 or April 1645 when it was at Beeston.[162] The 'smock coats' (riding coats) for Stukeley's troop were to be made of frieze, while another bill for 'fabric and trimmings' supplied to the same unit, dated 3 October 1643, included a further 'sixteen yards of frieze at 4s 0d per yard', costing £3 4s 0d, although it is likely that this went into cassocks or other clothing for his trumpeters.[163]

According to Eric Kerridge, 'Friezes had a hard, rough feel. They were best suited to winter gowns and rough overcoating but were also used for doublets and jerkins.'[164] In 1549 William Baldwin remarked, 'The coarsest frieze best pleaseth the finest of them in winter,' whereas William Stafford in 1581 reflected on serving men being content to go in 'a Kendal coat in the summer, and a frieze coat in winter.'[165] Moreover, Welsh frieze was described by Thomas Fuller in the 1660s as 'a coarse kind of cloth, than which none warmer to be worn in winter.'[166] Cottons in the seventeenth century were cheap woollen fabrics, mainly produced in Wales and the northwest of England. They appear to have been regularly used for riding coats, even among the elite. Conversely, baize – a coarse woollen cloth, similar in texture to felt –was produced largely in the West Country, although it is possible

159 BL, Ms Add 11332, f.59v; 11333, ff.36r, 107r; *BLB*, II, 840, 1007, 1220.

160 TNA, SP28/49/1, f.100v.

161 TNA, SP28/8, f.17r.

162 TNA, SP28/128/10, f.8r.

163 TNA, SP28/8, f.16r.

164 Eric Kerridge, *Textile Manufacturers in Early Modern England (Manchester:* Manchester University Press, 1985), p.19.

165 *The Canticles or Ballads of Salomon, phrase like declared in English Metres, by William Baldwin* (London, 1549), p.4; F.J. Furnival (ed.), *William Stafford's Compendious or Brief Examination of Certain Ordinary Complaints of Divers of Our Country Menin these our days* (London, 1876), p.64.

166 Thomas Fuller, *The History of the Worthies of England* (London, 1840), III, p.485.

that much of the cloth supplied to Sir William Brereton's forces derived from Lancashire merchants, as they were supplied with quantities of so-called 'Manchester baize'. The antiquarian and topographer William Camden, writing in 1610, spoke highly of the clothing industry in Manchester, saying it has, 'the best trade of any in these Northern parts … Manchester surpasses the towns hereabouts in woolen manufacture … woolen cloths called Manchester cottons.'[167]

In 1643, Sir Thomas Aston's regiments of horse and dragoons were kitted out with 'long' or 'large' coats (riding coats) ordered from local tailors. These garments were unlined, presumably because they were to be worn over doublets and jump coats (a short, buttoned type of soldier's coat), and in some cases were constructed from 2½ to 3 yards of broadcloth, silk, buttons (including a long button) and other items such as loop-lace.[168] Writing in early 1642, the Earl of Bedford, in his role of Lord Lieutenant of Devon had recommended that the county troopers 'be handsomely furnished [in] comely apparel with coat of buff with long skirts [and a] coat of cloth to keep both himself and furniture from the violence of the weather.'[169] In 1643 or 1644 Sergeant-Major George Purefoy of the Warwick garrison paid £15 3s 4d 'to Mr Jarman of Warwick for cloth which made coats for the troop.'[170] Moreover, on 3 April 1644 the sum of £245 12s 0d was paid for coats and boots for the Earl of Manchester's regiment of horse.[171]

A major concern of all civil war armies was the supply of footwear. Riding boots, issued to the horse, and in some instances to dragoons, were necessarily more expensive than shoes. A batch of 1,000 pairs of cavalry boots was delivered to the Eastern Association's agents at St Albans in September 1644 by the London shoemakers Richard Crofts and Edward Poole. Likewise, the army's treasurer employed various men to acquire boots and shoes in bulk – including 1,312 pairs of shoes at 3s 6d per pair – which he issued to captains, 'deducting the costs from the sums owed to their companies for pay.'[172] Whilst returning from London to Cheshire in June 1644, Sir William Brereton – who had been raising new troops in the city – purchased quantities of cavalry boots from Thomas Pendleton at Northampton 'where boots are cheap', at a cost of 10s a pair. He paid a further £5 'for carrying the above mentioned boots from Northampton to Coventry, where they were distributed to the troopers.'[173] Boots were purchased for 14s 0d and 15s 0d a pair in 1644 for Captain Vincent Potter's cavalry troop in Warwickshire.[174] Moreover, in November 1649, the London cordwainers James Graves, Theodore Reynolds, Jenkin Ellis and Francis Marriot were engaged by the Council of State to manufacture 2,000 pairs of boots for troopers in Ireland:

167 E. Gibson (ed.), William Camden, *Britannia* (London, 1695), II, p.963.
168 https://the1642tailor.com/?s=long+coat. Thanks to Gary Ashby for sharing information on these coats
169 TNA, SP16/492, f.49v.
170 TNA, SP28/136/37, f.6v.
171 TNA, SP28/25, f.570r.
172 TNA, SP28/25, ff.143r–144v, 163v; Holmes, *Eastern Association*, p.152.
173 TNA, SP28/152/7, f.6v.
174 TNA, SP28/136/27, f.2r.

> of good neats-leather, well-tanned and waxed, viz., 600 pair of fourteens, 700 pair of thirteens, and 700 pair of twelves, at 14s 10d per pair, and deliver them into the stores at Botolph's Wharf, free of charge, within three weeks; all the boots to be approved by the master and warden of the Cordwainers' Company, and those not approved to be returned £500 0s 0d to be paid in advance to buy leather, and a warrant to be issued to the treasurers-at-war to pay it out of the 14 days' pay to be received by them out of the assignations for the Irish army; the residue to be paid upon certificate of receipt of the boots.[175]

Shoes worn during the British Civil Wars were generally low and straight sided. Among the contracts for shoes sent to Ireland, one of June 1642 specified that the 10,000 pairs were to be of well-seasoned leather in five sizes (nine to thirteen).[176] A similar contract with Jenkin Ellis for the supply of the New Model Army on 5 January 1646 stipulated:

> 4,500 pairs of shoes with good neats-leather with good soles of the several sizes of tens, elevens, twelves and thirteens of each size, a like number of all of them to be punched, and each pair tacked together and marked on the soles with the several marks hereafter mentioned at 2s 3d a pair, to be brought into the Tower of London.'[177]

Thirteen shoemakers entered into contracts on 24 February 1646 to deliver 8,000 pairs of shoes of 'good neats-leather'. They evidently completed and delivered these to the army, since four weeks later they were issued warrants for payment 'in full of their contract'.[178]

The sizes of the thousands of shoes indented for by the New Model Army in particular, equate roughly to modern British sizes between seven and ten, therefore indicating that to some extent civil war examples were meant to be both comfortable and practical. Shoes contracted for the Parliamentarian army in Ireland in October 1646 cost 2s 10d the pair.[179] During autumn 1643, significant quantities of shoes and stockings were produced by suppliers at Chester for Ormond's returning soldiers from Ireland. John Hilton supplied 494 pairs of shoes at approximately 2s 8d per pair, 136 pairs of stockings and 100 pairs of hose, whilst the city's Shoemaker's Company provided 320 pairs of shoes. Likewise, various individuals supplied small batches of footwear, whereas Samuel Ince, Widow Hilton and others delivered produced what amounted to hundreds of pairs of stockings.[180]

On 1 December 1644, 74 pairs of shoes were purchased at Nantwich by Lieutenant Thomas Hunt for Captain John Sadler's company of Sir William Brereton's own regiment.[181] On 29 September 1645, the Nantwich

---

175 TNA, SP28/300, ff.700v–2r; *CSPD 1649–50*, pp.412, 594.

176 V. F. Snow and A. S Young (eds), *The Private Journals of the Long Parliament: 2 June to 17 September 1642* (New Haven and London: Yale University Press, 1992), II, p.388.

177 ML, 46–78/709 f.71r; TNA, WO55/1663 f.66v; *CSPD 1649–50*, pp.369, 594, 598.

178 TNA, SP28/37/3, ff.355r–357r.

179 *CJ*, IV, p.698.

180 TNA, SP28/128/12, unfol.; SP28/152/12, ff.1r–5v.

181 TNA, SP28/225/4, f.723r.

sequestrators paid John Tench, shoemaker, £3 3s 6d 'for boots and shoes for the soldiers.' The accounts of the officials of the upper division of Wirral Hundred reveal that in November 1645 they disbursed £1 10s 0d for three pairs of cavalry boots, as well as 5s 6d for leather for the making of shoes for the garrison at Hooton.[182] The sum of 3s was paid to John Price, a local cordwainer on 12 August 1643, 'for one pair of shoes for Samuel Elliot', a dragoon in Captain Bramhall's company in Cheshire. Similarly, in November 1644 £9 9s was disbursed by Brereton 'for stockings and shoes for soldiers who came out of Liverpool when it was besieged, took the Covenant and have done very good service for the Parliament under whom they formerly served in Ireland.'[183] These men, 50 in number, brought with them their arms and were formed into a new dragoon unit under Lieutenant-Colonel Michael Jones. Hence, another payment of £5 14s was made on 11 December 'to Lieutenant Colonel Jones to pay for shoes bought for some of his company of firelocks, 40 pair [at 2s 8d each].'

Similarly, on 6 February 1645 £2 10s was paid 'for shoes for some soldiers lately entertained [impressed] who wanted necessaries.'[184] At the end of October 1645, outstanding vouchers for the army included '£9 9s for soldiers' stockings and shoes', while Treasurer Croxton disbursed 8s to John Harper of Stafford on 20 November 1645 for cavalry boots 'for soldiers employed at the Leaguer before Chester.'[185] A direct comparison with prices paid by the Eastern Association for shoes implies that those issued to the Cheshire soldiers were of a better quality. During 1644 two London cordwainers, Richard Crofts and Edward Poole charged 2s 6d, 2s 7d or 3s 0d for the shoes they delivered, including transport costs, whilst the Hertfordshire merchant William Gardiner asked for 2s 8d and 3s 4d a pair.[186] This range of prices reflects differences in quality and the added price for waxing shoes. They may also have been hobnailed.

Although evidence is limited, the footwear issued to Brereton's dragoons may have included both shoes and boots. Some contemporaries felt that the most commodious footwear for dragoons were shoes rather than boots and spurs, which might snag in the stirrup when mounting and dismounting, although such comments may reflect little more than their personal preferences. No widespread issue of boots to dragoons during the British Civil Wars is known, although this might be due to documents listing them being lost. So far, no issues to nor purchases of boots for Royalist dragoons is known – Sir Thomas Aston's seem only to have been given shoes, for example. Though undated, a list of moneys 'lent to the dragoons' includes the sum of 2s 6d for shoes for Captain Thomas Newland, Sergeants Corke and East, as well as dragoons Robert Gay, Richard Phillips, Thomas Webb, William Jenkin, Abraham Hickman, John Edwards, John Phipps, William Twyford, George Cowley and Richard Hume. The sums of 4s 6d and 3s 10d

182 BL, Ms Harley 1999, ff.69r, 17r.; 2166, f.132v.

183 TNA, SP28/152/7, f.25r.

184 Ibid., ff.26v, 32v; *CSPD 1644–45*, p.80.

185 BL, Ms Add 11332, ff.38r, 99r.; *BLB*, II, 796, 887.

186 TNA, SP28/25, ff.136v, 143v–144r, 163v, 167r.

were furnished for shoes and stockings for dragoons to Richard Stakier and Richard Pretley respectively. Likewise, shirts costing 3s 10d apiece were provided to Sergeant Norris, and dragoons John Smith, Richard Hume, Edward Wately and Thomas Webb.[187]

However, in November 1642, Colonel Richard Browne's Parliamentarian regiment benefitted from the disbursement of 9s 6d to 'Mr Wells for boots'; another 10s 0d was given to a carrier for transporting boots and spurs, whereas Bartholomew Grantham received the sum of £1 8s 6d 'for watering the horses for 7 days and delivering our boots.'[188] In Cheshire on 2 March 1643, the sum of 9s 0d was distributed 'to a soldier of Captain Lea for boots', while the clothing and accoutrements provided for a dragoon by the constables of Hollingworth included boots and spurs.[189] On 22 March 1644, the Bedford cordwainers John Crofts and John Symes were paid £25 0s 0d between them for supplying boots and shoes to Captain John Holcroft's company of dragoons from the Earl of Manchester's army, whereas Symes also received £10 8s 7d for shirts and stockings for the same unit.[190] Soon afterwards, these same dragoons had the sum of £42 14s 9d deducted from their pay for boots and shoes.[191] Wallhausen, writing in 1616, advocated that dragoons 'shall wear, if they so wish, cassocks and *gamaches* [gaiters] instead of boots, for greater ease in walking when necessary.'[192] A mounted dragoon is illustrated in the *Kriegskunst zu Pferd* wearing these with fastenings or buttons, worn over shoes. Such items – leather or canvas gaiters, known as 'cockers' – were designed to protect shoes and hose from damage, but they were also a cheap alternative to riding boots. No issues of boots are known for Sir Thomas Aston's dragoon regiment, which was raised in February 1643, though its soldiers received shoes and 'leather leg pieces', which may have been cockers.[193] Even so, without further evidence, the question of whether shoes, possibly worn with gaiters, were more regularly issued to civil war dragoons must remain an open one.

Knapsacks or snapsacks, sausage-shaped bags worn over the shoulder and made of leather, were important pieces of equipment carried by civil war infantrymen and dragoons. They were supplied for 'the carriage of small provisions of victuals for their better accommodation in their journey.'[194] An English volunteer in the Bohemian Army in 1620 recalled:

> Our general gave command to draw out part of every company to be of the forlorn hope to give the onset, whereof my self was one of the number, and Dr Burgess our minister, did encourage us to fight valiantly, and did assure us we shall find our reward in heaven; whereupon we feasted ourselves with such victuals we had

187 BL, Ms Add 36913, ff.118r–119v; Aston, accounts, unfol.
188 TNA, SP28/144/2, ff.31r–32r.
189 TNA, SP28/196/3, f.14v.; BL, Ms Harley 2128, ff.29r, 8r.
190 TNA, SP28/128/8, f.51r.
191 TNA, SP28/25/2, f.296r.
192 Wallhausen, *Kriegskunst, pp.16–17.*
193 BL, Ms Add 36913, f.118r.
194 Owen (ed.), *Calendar of the Cecil Papers*, XXII, p.299.

> and threw away our knapsacks, with all our provisions, both linen and woolen because it would be troublesome to us.[195]

In 1627, the Ordnance Office paid 15d apiece for leather knapsacks, although their dimensions are unknown.[196] Many thousands of these items were issued during the British Civil Wars. In November 1642 the London manufacturer, Mr Langham was paid £51 0s 0d for supplying an unspecified number of knapsacks for Colonel Richard Browne's regiment of Parliamentarian dragoons. This seems a considerable sum of money, but his regiment was recently raised with seven companies of 100 men each, besides non-commissioned officers, although Browne's accounts drawn up on the raising of the unit list at least ten captains.[197] Going by the 8d and 9d paid to London manufacturers in 1645, the money paid to Langham would equate to over 1,330 knapsacks.

The Parliamentarian commander Sir Thomas Myddelton purchased 2,000 such items on 6 June 1643 and another 300 in 1644 from a leading London-based supplier.[198] Nevertheless, he never raised more than 2–300 foot, but the endorsement at the bottom of the first bill mentions 'the several forces abovementioned'. This could be taken to mean that the Parliamentarian troops of North Wales, Cheshire and Shropshire, including Myddelton's and Brereton's dragoons, which were 'brigaded' together during the operations in Shropshire and the Welsh borders during these periods, benefitted from such batches. On 13 March 1644, a convoy of ammunition bound for the Parliamentarian garrison of Gloucester was reported 'not as yet further than Warwick'; ten days later when the desperation of the garrison was further emphasised, 1,000 horse and dragoons were still mentioned as being around Stratford-upon-Avon, waiting 'to carry in their knapsacks and on spare horses powder and provisions into Gloucester.'[199] When the Red Regiment of the London Trained Bands entered the Wiltshire village of Chiseldon in September 1643, its soldiers reportedly 'could get no accommodation either for meat or drink but what we brought with us in our knapsacks.'[200] Considerable quantities of these items were ordered for the New Model Army from London suppliers between March 1645 and December 1646. Thus, Raphe Fairbank of Cheapside was contracted to supply 3,000, 'large and of good leather' at 8s 0d per dozen [8d each]; Michael Rayner of Friday Street supplied 1,000 knapsacks at 9d apiece, and 8,000 more 'at the same price and goodness according to the former contract'; a further 2,000 were supplied by John Browne of Paternoster Row, and 1,000 by Joshua Primate of Fleet Street under same conditions. By the end of 1646, 17,600 knapsacks

195 A. M., *A Relation of the Passage of our English Companies from time to time, since their first departure from England to the parts of Germanie, and the United Provinces* (London: 1621), p.4.
196 TNA, WO49/55, f.174r.
197 TNA, SP28/144/2, ff.1r–7r.
198 TNA, SP28/346/1, unfol. ; SP28/346/2, unfol.
199 WSL, Ms Salt 518/2; *CSPD, 1644*, p.67.
200 *Certain Informations*, 11–18 September 1643.

had been received into the Ordnance Office land stores, whilst 18,245 had been issued to Sir Thomas Fairfax's troops.[201]

201 TNA, WO47/1, passim;WO55/1660 f.8r; WO55/1662, f.55r; WO55/1664, passim; ML, 46–78/709, ff.9r, 64v, 87v, 88r; Mungeam, 'Contracts', pp.86, 100–1.

7

Horses, Equine Care, Saddlery and Fodder

Dragoons during the British Civil Wars were generally supplied with inferior horses and were issued equipment akin to infantrymen. Hence, they were cheaper to recruit and maintain than the expensive regiments of harquebusiers. On 25 March 1642, it was ordered that the King's Commissioners appointed to treat with the Scots, 'shall prepare an order to enable the Scots to take up baggage-horses in Ireland for the service of their baggage and their dragoons.'[1] According to Cruso, a dragoon's horse was to be the 'least price, the use thereof being but to expedite his march, alighting to do his service.'[2] The supply and retention of suitable cavalry, dragoon and draught horses represented a major task for seventeenth century armies. The Parliamentarians procured many of their mounts on the open market. London, especially Smithfield, met the heavy demands imposed on it, and a cavalry horse could sell for £10 0s 0d or £12 0s 0d, a nag for under £1 0s 0d, although prices of between £2 10s 0d and £5 0s 0d were typical for dragoon mounts. In October 1642, Colonel Richard Browne of the Earl of Essex's army was paid £3,000 to mount the 600 dragoons in his regiment. This equates to £5 0s 0d per horse.[3] By comparison, purchases made for the New Model in the spring of 1645 included various quantities of dragoon horses at £4 0s 0d apiece.[4] The Parliamentarian Propositions (voluntary loans) of June 1642 called for the contribution of horses, arms, and horsemen, in addition to plate and cash.[5] This was widely applied and allowed significant numbers of mounted units to be raised and equipped.

The Parliamentary Ordinance of 10 May 1643, 'to redress the abuses in taking horses for the supply of the army', authorised the deputy lieutenants and the Propositions Committees in every county to regulate the acquisition of mounts, while an amendment of 29 May approved the levying of horses

1 *CJ*, II, p.498.

2 Cruso, *Militarie Instructions*, p.31.

3 TNA, SP28/1A, f.164v; SP16/503/62, f.62r.

4 TNA, SP28/29/1, ff.166r–166v, 204r; SP28/29/2, f.258r.

5 *LJ*, V, pp.121–2.

by county quota.[6] Hence, on 3 December 1642 Parliament had ordered that the Cheshire commander, Sir William Brereton should 'have liberty to raise 300 horses in the several counties where they shall be brought in voluntarily, upon propositions.'[7] According to Peter Edwards, saddle horses for the cavalry 'ideally had to be fifteen hands high, nimble and capable of charging at pace.'[8] Various warrants and levies were directed for the procurement of dragoon mounts for the Parliamentarian forces. Sir William Waller's army contained roughly seven dragoon regiments of differing strengths and dispositions, including his own regiment of foot, which was converted to dragoons during the summer of 1644. On 7 January 1645 Parliament ordered that '1,000 dragoons be added to the horse appointed for service in the West; [and] a subcommittee be appointed to consider where the horses may be had for these 1,000 dragoons, and to report to this Committee.'

Thus, the Committee of Both Kingdoms was to write to the Associated counties of Sussex, Surrey, and Kent 'to provide speedily 500 horses for mounting 500 dragoons of Sir William Waller.' Subsequently, the same body informed the Parliamentarian Committee of Sussex:

> The forces of the enemy growing strong in the West, if they meet not with a speedy check are like to endanger the port towns, and so wholly subject that country as to be able to draw levies and supplies from thence to infest your borders lying next them, and also lengthen out the war. We have designed a great party of horse and dragoons immediately to march thither for their removal, and therefore desire that 500 dragoons' horses may be had out of counties Kent, Sussex, and Surrey. You are to make ready your proportion with all expedition, that a service of so great importance, and in which yourselves are specially interested may not be retarded or overthrown through any want of diligence in furnishing those supplies[9]

The forces of the Eastern Association were originally commanded by William, Lord Grey of Wark, who had been an officer of horse in Essex's army. Some dragoons were raised in Norfolk in December 1642 to defend its own county, whilst in the spring and summer of 1643 a combined brigade of horse, foot and dragoons under Grey served with Essex's army, including during the siege of Reading.[10] On 9 August 1643, the Earl of Manchester was appointed Sergeant-Major-General of the Eastern Association in succession to Grey.[11] However, under the conditions of this Parliamentary Ordinance, mounts obtained from certain Eastern counties were to be transferred to the Earl of Essex or to Sir William Waller as and when required. Nevertheless, the order made it possible to raise new cavalry and dragoon regiments in

6 *LJ*, VI, pp.39–40, 68–9.

7 *CJ*, II, p.874.

8 Peter Edwards, 'Turning Ploughshares into Swords: The Arms and Military Equipment Industries in Staffordshire in the First Civil War, 1642–1646', MH, 27 (2002), pp.52–79, (p.68); 'The Supply of Horses to the Parliamentarian and Royalist Armies in the English Civil War', HR, 68 (1995), pp.49–66.

9 *CSPD 1644–45*, pp.233–4.

10 Holmes, *Eastern Association*, p.59.

11 *CJ*, III, pp.198–200; *LJ*, V, p.145.

the Eastern Association as well as remounting and expanding existing units. In addition to 500 horse, the county of Essex was required to raise 1,000 dragoons. This levy was imposed by a further Ordinance of Parliament of 12August, which specified that £13,500 was to be assessed on the county to raise the 1,000 dragoons and 500 cavalry.[12] This assessment was divided between the Hundreds of the county, the lowest proportion being £195 17s 0d for Clavering Hundred, and the highest, £926 1s 0d for Bastable Hundred.[13]

Some horses were bought for as little as £1 0s 0d or £2 0s 0d each, but these were almost certainly dragoon horses. The mounts obtained at Bedford in April 1644 had an average value of around £3 0s 0d, suggesting that these were also dragoon mounts.[14] Most of the horses purchased by the Eastern Association in 1644 were cavalry troop horses, and relatively few dragoon mounts were bought, partly because there were fewer dragoons in the establishment of the army. The general impression, then, is that dragoon horses were less likely to be acquired and were probably supplied by other means.[15] By September 1644, when Manchester's army was quartered at Reading, the levies were forced by the Cambridge Committee, as there is no record in the proceedings of Parliament of any others being imposed on the Eastern Association counties at this time. In the same month, the Norfolk Committee sent 100 dragoon horses to Huntingdon to assist in the recruitment of the Eastern Association forces.[16]

In contrast to the horse, the Earl of Essex's treasurers were resolute in purchasing mounts for soldiers who enlisted in the first two of his army's dragoon regiments. Hence, they were obliged to expend an astonishing sum of money towards the creation of these units. Two warrants authorised the payment of £7,488 to provide the two dragoon colonels, John Browne and James Wardlaw, with the means to completely mount the two full regiments of 600 dragoons each, plus commissioned and non-commissioned officers.[17] Colonel Browne was paid £3,792 in full on 20 August, while Wardlaw's portion was delivered on 1 September. Additionally, both colonels also received further funds, amounting to £2,536 10s 0d, for the arming of their regiments, and for wagons and other equipment.[18] During April and May 1645, the Smithfield dealers, John Stiles, Harvey Conway, Richard Clough and Peter Everard also provided 300 dragoon horses at £4 0s 0d each to the New Model Army.[19] Delivery of these amounts must have been prompt because Treasury payments began to be disbursed to suppliers in the July.[20] There were no significant changes in the prices paid by the Army Committee for the horses supplied by the dealers. Although the price for cavalry horses

12 *A&O*, I, p.245.
13 TNA, SP28/227 unfol.
14 TNA, SP28/24/2, ff.178v, 188v; SP28/24/3, f.292r.
15 Gavin Robinson, 'Horse Supply in the English Civil War 1642–1646', PhD thesis (University of Reading, 2001), p.105.
16 BL, Ms Add 22619, f.206r.
17 TNA, SP28/1A, ff.164r; SP28/143, ff.17r–17v.
18 TNA, SP28/2A, ff.54r, 105r; SP28/261, ff.43r, 73r, 139r, 191v.
19 TNA, SP28/29/1, ff.166r–166v, 204r; SP28/29/2, f.258v; SP28/140/7, f.276v.
20 TNA, SP28/31/5, f.542r.

could fluctuate slightly, dragoon horses were consistently supplied at £4 0s 0d each. Towards the end of 1645, the London Militia Committee sold 200 dragoon horses to the Army Committee for the use of Fairfax's army. This was an unusual arrangement, which was authorised by Parliament on 23 December.[21] Cavalry troopers (and possibly dragoons) who came from the armies of Essex, Manchester and Waller tended to bring their horses with them when transferring into the New Model. Besides, during the first ten months of the army's existence several thousand horses were taken from the enemy, especially at Naseby, where 2,000 mounts were captured, and upon the capitulation of Hopton's forces in Cornwall, when a further 2,500 more were taken.[22]

On 10 January 1646, the Army Committee issued a warrant for £410 10s 0d to Edward Cludd, muster-master of the New Model 'for the use of the Militia of London for 200 dragoon horses', and this amount was paid by the Treasury two days later. The deal must have been done straight away, since on the 13 January, the Army Committee authorised the payment of £102 0s 0d to the commissary, Thomas Richardson, 'to pay the quarters of 200 dragoon horses at Brentford and Hounslow bought by this Committee of the Militia of London.' These horses were then conducted to the army by Captain Christopher Mercer of Okey's regiment, with the assistance of 20 dragoons.[23] Given that there was only one regiment of dragoons in the New Model Army, there can be no doubt about which unit received these mounts. As Gavin Robinson found in his analysis of the supply of mounts to the army, there are no dragoon horses unaccounted for in the army commissaries' account, so the statistics for Okey's regiment are far more precise than those for the cavalry. Consequently, they had 667 horses from the commissaries, amounting to 67 percent of the establishment of 1,000 dragoons. Having received 200 new horses in July 1645, Okey's soldiers did not receive any more from the commissaries until November. Between June 1645 and June 1646, the regiment was supplied with 572 horses, representing 57 percent of the establishment. Robinson further estimates that a replacement rate of 78 percent per year was maintained, an appreciably higher rate than for the New Model horse. Going by the same figures, the attrition rate for dragoon horses was 78 percent compared to 63 percent for New Model's cavalry. A total of 630 saddle mounts, equating to about 10 percent of the cavalry establishment, were issued in July 1645, though numbers increased during the winter of 1645–6.[24]

The procurement of cavalry, dragoon and draught horses was a considerable task for Parliamentarian armies, whilst combat, prolonged campaigning, theft and desertion were responsible for the sizeable losses. The detailed financial accounts of Captain, then Sergeant-Major, John Bramhall, who commanded one of the Parliamentarian dragoon companies sent fully mounted to Cheshire in late 1642, provide a useful picture of the number

21 *CJ*, IV, p.383.
22 *CSPD, 1644–5*, p.594.
23 TNA, SP28/36/6, ff.659r, 646r, 707v.
24 Robinson, 'Horse Supply', pp.138–9.

of horses 'lost upon service'. Of the 128 mounts lost, 34 were at Hopton Heath; 8 at Hanmer (where some dragoons and cavalrymen of Brereton's forces were captured); 6 at Tern Hill; 27 at Loppington (when Bramhall, with a number of his officers and men were taken prisoner); four at Leigh Bridge; 24 at Longford; 12 at Kelsall; 9 'to mount Scottish officers that came under Sir William Brereton's command'; in addition to these, 4 mounts were confiscated to be used as draught horses.[25]

An 'account of what horses for dragoons have been sent into the castle of Windsor' between 28 October 1642 and 3 June 1644 provides evidence of the origin, description and price of various animals procured from the locality as well as others in the Thames Valley area. These include the following: 'from Mr Child of Wraysbury, one sad bay mare £3 0s 0d; from Humphrey Hedges of Egham, one roan gelding £3 0s 0d; from Andrew Durdant of Staines, one black mare £2 10s 0d; from Mr Harrison of High Harefield, one gray gelding £3 0s 0d; [and] from Mr Symerson of Binfield, one sorrel nag £2 10s 0d.'[26] Similarly, another list of mounts maintained by the Windsor garrison between August 1643 and June 1644 records that from 29 August to 13 September 1643 there were 20; between 13 September and 30 October 1643 there were 36; between 30 October and 17 December 1643 there were 54; from 17 December 1643 to 12 January 1644 54 were mustered; from 12 January to 30 March 1644 there were 48; between 30 March and 14 April 1644 34 were present; whilst from 14 April to 2 June 1644 the garrison accounted for 20 horses. According to a note by Commissary Benjamin Blundell, however, 'all sent out with the party to Greenland House and not yet returned.'

The reference to 'Greenland House' must refer to the military operations following the fruitless attempts by the Earl of Essex and Sir William Waller in June 1644 to capture Oxford and the King. Consequently, Sergeant-Major General John Browne was given command of the Parliamentarian forces in the area, with instructions to reduce Oxford, Banbury, Wallingford, and the Fort of Greenland House. Furthermore, the following month Lieutenant-Colonel John Bradley led 300 foot from the Windsor garrison at the siege of Greenland. Under the heading 'Dragoon horses dead' it was reported that, on 6 October 1643 1 grey nag had died; on 14 January 1644 1 horse; on 20 January 1 horse; on 30 January 1 horse; on 13 February 2 horses; on 17 February 1 white nag; on 26 February 1 flea-bitten mare; on 1 March a bay nag; on 15 March a roan nag; and on 20 April a bay gelding, one white mare and a sorrel nag were deceased. '17 several' additional horses were stated 'lost and stolen'; one white mare had been pilfered by Sergeant Sawyer; another brown nag was lost, sent by Lieutenant Cole to Farnham (possibly the Captain Cole in Colonel Richard Norton's regiment of dragoons, whose company attempted to seize Basing House in July 1643); one grey nag was 'taken away by Sir William Waller's coming from Basing', whereas a brown gelding was sent and never returned. In total, 13 mounts were reported dead,

25 BL, Ms Harley 2128, ff.34r–34v.
26 TNA, SP28/126/1, f.28r.

18 lost or stolen, and a further three horses were provided to support other Parliamentarian operations and did not come back.[27]

Deserters during the British Civil Wars frequently took their horses and arms with them, usually to sell them. In most cases, the main reason for this was lack of pay. Hence, on 25 November 1642, Parliament was informed that several dragoons of Colonel Richard Browne's regiment had deserted and sold their horses and arms.[28] Colonel William Hughes, a Royalist officer serving in the Midlands, reported to Captain Robert Davies at Flinton 16 June 1644, that the condition of his cavalry unit was so poor, owing to the lack of pay, that his men 'sell their horses from under them and say they lost them.'[29]

Upon the impending breakup of the Earl of Denbigh's regiment of horse in the Midlands Association in July 1644, he received a petition from Sergeant-Major Thomas Fraser, commanding the unit, which informed him, 'we your lordship's poor officers, knowing what prejudice it would be to the Parliament that such a regiment should be disbanded, have engaged our horses and clothes for money to give your soldiers some satisfaction for the present (everyone according to his ability), so that thereby we hope to keep together.'[30] The problem was so acute in some armies that the Committee of the Eastern Association issued an order in April 1643 forbidding civilians to buy or pawn any horses or arms from soldiers.[31] On 26 March 1644, the Commons ordered that any person who did so would forfeit them, fined treble the value and be imprisoned for 28 days without bail.[32]

Charles I (Rijkesmuseum, Amsterdam)

Dragoon mounts might also be procured from remounts – available stocks within existing or disbanding mounted units. On 14 November 1642 Richard Grenville, Captain of one of the first troops of harquebusiers in Colonel Arthur Goodwin's regiment of horse of the Earl of Essex's Army, was:

27 Ibid., f.34r.

28 *CJ*, II, p.868.

29 WA, CR 2017/C9/126; HMC, *Fourth Report, App.*, p.267.

30 WA, CR 2017/C10/20; HMC, *Fourth Report, App.*, p.269.

31 BL, Ms Egerton2651, f.140r.

32 *A&O*, I, p.404.

> commanded by His Excellency the Lord General to take the horses which were of Captain Francis Ingoldsby's troop (he having given them over) and to deliver them at Moorfields for dragoons' horses, I paid upon the receipt of them at the Bell, Whitehorse, etc., in Holborne where they had stood for seven or eight days and nights, the sum of £13 1s 4d and from there carried them to Moorfields, and delivered them to Commissary Richardson, as appears by his acquittances for them. They were in number 64 horses, nags and mares[33]

Given the comparatively modest amount of surviving documentary material pertaining to Charles I's armies, knowledge of the sources, cost and methods for the procurement of horses in Royalist cavalry and dragoon regiments remains far less than for their Parliamentarian adversaries. Following the Battle of Edgehill, on 15 December 1642 the King issued a proclamation at Oxford requesting his subjects to provide horses, saddles, bridles, and other stores for dragoons:

> A proclamation is divulged in the King's name, but not attested by him, nor any printer, wherein these imputations are cast upon the Lord General's soldiers, (but falsely) that they seize the horses of his loving subjects without their consents, and to which they are authorized by a late pretended Ordinance, that they pillage and plunder his good subjects with unheard of rapine, insolence and inhumanity, whilst his horse for want of assistance of dragoons, in respect of the lanes and deep narrow ways, cannot prevent those outrages, though he hopes never to be forced to follow the example of those ill men who having received such vast sums of money from his subjects, and seized all his, can yet have no cause of such impositions, but their love of rapine. Under colour of which untruths he declares, that it will be an acceptable service to him for any to send him in at this time, horses, geldings, mares or nags to be used as dragoon horses for his service, and the defence of Oxfordshire, not doubting but that every man will send in such horses with saddles and bridles, and whosoever can send in men armed with muskets upon those horses, shall much add to this service, and those horses are to be sent in to the sign of the Katharine Wheel in Oxford, and to be delivered to Walter Grant his wagon-master general. Behold herein a subtle trick of the cavaliers, to defraud people of their horse and arms[34]

During the war's early months, the King permitted the officers of his field armies the right of compulsory purchase of horses. So many mounts were drafted from Stafford during the King's stay there in September 1642 that the town corporation pleaded with him to stop more being taken.[35] When Charles ordered Aston to Cheshire in January 1643, he authorised him to conscript horses in the county to mount a new dragoon regiment. Such was the need for saddles that agents for Aston set about buying up all available items from the saddle makers of Chester and surrounding areas. These

33 TNA, SP28/149, f.146v; Wilson, *Buckinghamshire Contributions*, p.112.

34 *England's Memorable Accidents*, 15 December 1642.

35 WSL, Ms Salt 402, f.204r.

ranged from 'war saddles' for cavalry troopers to the less expensive pad-saddles for the fledgling dragoons.[36]

However, despite various efforts to secure a supply of horses, there were shortages, although these appear to have been more common for the Royalists (who generally kept considerable mounted forces in the field) than for the main Parliamentarian armies of Essex and Manchester, who could rely heavily on the financial contributions from London and its horse markets, including Smithfield. Describing the Royalist cavalry on the eve of Edgehill, the Earl of Clarendon (chief adviser to Charles I) perhaps only slightly exaggerated when he wrote, 'amongst the horse, the officers had their full desire if they were able to procure old backs and breasts and pots, with pistols and carbines for their two or three first ranks, and swords for the rest.'[37] By the winter of 1642, the defensive equipment worn by Royalist cavalrymen was becoming more consistent. On 23 December, Sir Arthur Aston received 60 backs and breasts, and 53 headpieces from the King's stores at Oxford.[38] By comparison, Parliament's control of weapon manufacture meant that most of its cavalry at least carried pistols during the opening campaigns, even so, in November 1642 Colonel Robert Duckenfield equipped his Cheshire troop with 63 pairs of pistols, 25 carbines and '63 body armours for so many troopers', purchased in London.[39] In the King's army, the clothing and equipping of soldiers, as well as the procurement of horses, was, to a great extent, the responsibility of individual colonels or troop captains. In September 1642, Sir Thomas Aston, having accompanied Charles I into Chester, ordered the seizure of arms and horses from those who had mustered for Parliament's militia in the county, which was well-equipped.[40]

The accounts of Sir Thomas Aston's regiments of horse and dragoons – containing notes for all of the troops for 1644 and for part of 1645, and a troop-by-troop listing of 'monies dispersed by troop' – indicate that he purchased mounts for his soldiers from his own pocket. Moreover, in 1644, if not in other years, individual troopers were rewarded for the capture of good quality horses. Though the record is associated with a now lost regimental 'great book' of accounts, the impression given is that at least during their service in the Southwest in 1644 Aston's soldiers were well mounted, clothed, armed, and equipped. The petition document, entitled 'A brief of the whole' by Aston to the King in May 1645 details the cost he had incurred in equipping his regiments of horse and dragoons, with the exact numbers, by troop and company, that he had recruited and 'brought in' to serve under his colours. In total, Aston spent the sum of £5,353 12s 3d in the raising, mounting, arming, and maintenance of his regiments of horse and dragoons between 1642 and 1644. In common with other Royalist officers, he received nothing from the King in return for his service.[41]

36 BL, Ms Add 36913, f.112r.
37 Clarendon, *History*, VI, p.73.
38 TNA, WO 55/423, ff.120r, 155r.
39 TNA, SP28/128/10, ff.1r.–2r.; SP28/262, f.395v.
40 Malbon, *Memorials*, pp.25–6.
41 Aston Papers, uncalendared petition of Sir Thomas Aston.

By 1644, if not earlier, the supply of mounts to Royalist armies seems to have been generally uncertain, yet this does not seem to have prevented Charles I from deploying large bodies of horse in the field. Some mounted units, however, were hampered by a lack of horses. The pay accounts of the Royalist governor of Worcester, record that among the 310 dragoons of the garrison in January and February 1643, 130 were unmounted, although Captain Blunt's 100 men all possessed horses.[42] Similarly, in March 1644, Prince Rupert, then at Shrewsbury, requested that Henry Hastings, the Royalist commander in the Midlands, supply him with dragoon horses, upon which to mount musketeers, otherwise he could not march.[43] The following month Colonel Nicholas Mynne, who had recently garrisoned Newent in Gloucestershire, urgently petitioned Rupert for saddles and bridles for the mounting of dragoons. These items were urgently required because of an imminent Parliamentarian counter-attack.[44]

Among the Parliamentarian forces, funds to purchase dragoon mounts for the Warwick garrison in September 1642, including Captain Anthony Otway's company, were levied on various south Warwickshire parishes, including Sherbourne, Southam, Pillerton Priors, Brailes and Tysoe.[45] The 'Warwickshire Loss Accounts' are littered with references to 'the raising of dragoon horses', initially for Lord Brooke, and soon after for the Earl of Denbigh as well. Thus, the inhabitants of various parishes advanced significant sums from the summer of 1642.[46] According to Francis Smith, Lord Brooke 'received the horses, bridles and saddles himself,' whilst he had 'a new musket and sword delivered at Warwick Castle unto Mr Brian.' In some instances, Parliamentarian commanders issued warrants for the supply of horses complete with saddles and equipment. Milverton Parish sent 'One dragoon horse with saddle and bridle from the said town[ship] by warrant from the late Lord Brooke in or about October 1642.'[47]

Some time after March 1643, Bourton on Dunsmore claimed:

> By command from the honourable the Lord Brooke (since deceased) our parish was charged with a dragoon horse and furniture, thereunto belonging; whereupon a bay gelding, which then cost £3 10s 0d, and saddle and bridle worth other 10s 0d was accordingly by our constable delivered to the officers of the said Lord Brooke at the castle in Warwick.

In a similar way, the constables of Dunchurch, near Rugby, maintained:

> By warrant from the honourable the Lord Brooke (Dunchurch being charged with a dragoon horse and furniture thereunto belonging). Upon receipt of the said warrant a white gelding, valued to be worth £5 0s 0d And a saddle, bridle,

42 Bund (ed.), *Diary of Henry Townshend*, pp.149–50, 156.
43 HMC, *Hastings*, II, p.125.
44 BL, Ms Add 18981, f.141v.
45 TNA, SP28/136/10, unfol.
46 TNA, SP28/182/2, ff.1v, 26v, 28r; SP28/182/3, f.1r; SP28/183/29, f.1r.
47 TNA SP28/183/35, ff.1r–5v.

> sword, musket and other furniture valued at £3 0s 0d were presently provided by the inhabitants thereof and delivered for the public service unto the officers under the command of the said Lord Brooke within the castle in Warwick.[48]

Another example, this time concerning the parish of Bishops Itchington elucidates how contributions were made by thirteen inhabitants (including the vicar) for raising a dragoon's horse and furniture for Brooke's troops. Under the heading, 'Whereof accounted unto us by and paid by' is shown that the Reverend Hunt, Widow Avery, Widow Beale, Robert King, Thomas Tomkins and John Tomkins gave 10s 0d each; Thomas Smith 7s 0d; William Poole and John Hickson 5s 0d each; Thomas Analey 4s 0d; Richard Bolton and Henry Nichols 2s 6d each; whilst Richard Worrall paid 1s 0d, thus bringing the total sum to £4 7s 0d.[49]

When cavalry and dragoon mounts were in short supply in the Eastern Association in January 1644, there were only 18 horses for the 38 soldiers in Captain Miller's dragoon company, while Captain Holcroft's command mustered 41 men, of which 31 were in need of mounts.[50]

The indiscriminate requisitioning of horses – in some cases, simply thieving – upon which the Royalists relied was exceedingly unpopular with civilians, especially those who had often been the victims of previous plundering. The universal impression is that the King's armies were more likely to take horses from outside their 'home region', as well as in counties under Royalist control, yet civilians in disputed areas may have suffered more. On route to Cheshire in January 1643, Sir Thomas Aston and his troopers passed through Worcestershire, a county mostly loyal to the King and regarded as 'the vital centrepiece of the Cavalier corridor between Oxford and Wales.'[51] Although large sums of money were obtained by voluntary donations, the city of Worcester bore most of the expense of maintaining and quartering large numbers of Royalist troops.

Even allowing for the understandable tendency of victims to overstate losses and the frequently propagandist intent of reporting, during early 1643 Royalist cavalry stripped much of Shropshire and northern Worcestershire of produce, to the extent that many towns were unable to pay their tax assessments.[52] The general problem had been somewhat exacerbated by Aston's admission that during prior operations in Cheshire he had not always been able to prevent his troops from plundering (sanctioned and indiscriminate looting).[53] However, the Royalist commander of Chester, Orlando Bridgeman, overruled an arrangement between Aston and the Commissioners of Array for the supply of his cavalry and newly formed dragoon regiment, and thus his soldiers were compelled to pillage in order to

48 TNA, SP28/182/3, f.1v; SP28/183/4, f.2v.

49 TNA, SP28/186/2, f.2v.

50 TNA, SP28/25, ff.212v, 305r.

51 Ronald Hutton, *The Royalist War Effort 1642–1646* (Harlow: Longman, 1982), p.76; Malcolm Atkin, *Worcestershire Under Arms: An English County During the Civil Wars* (Barnsley: Pen and Sword, 2004), pp.52–3.

52 Malbon, *Memorials*, pp.46–60; HMC, *Twelfth Report, App. IX*, pp.39–40

53 BL, Ms Harley 6804, ff.139v.–40r.

subsist. In December Anglo-Irish soldiers arriving in Chester 'faint, weary, and out of clothing', became a burden on the city, and there was thievery and disorder.[54] Other sources of dissent included rivalries between the Royalist officers in the city and the Commissioners of Array, and between the military commanders and the mayor.

In June 1643, Sir Thomas Aston's men reportedly committed further 'plundering and abuses' in northeast Worcestershire and south Warwickshire. The inhabitants of Anscote and Blackwell in the parish of Tredington petitioned the King that Aston's troops had stolen 140 of their horses, beaten up and robbed the owners, and his cavalry had ridden through their field of beans and peas to spoil the crop. They had even gone to Oxfordshire where Aston's regiments were quartered, to reclaim the horses, but to no avail.[55] Though such examples fostered discontent among the civilian population, they were chiefly caused by military instability, and the heavy passage of troops through areas, often in peripheral areas distant from the protection of major garrisons, and where irregular taxes were levied by both sides.

As early as December 1642, Charles I had been anxious that want of pay among his troops would result in 'some violence upon the country' in Worcestershire and its borders. In February 1644, Rupert (who possessed a reputation for plundering) went to great pains to alleviate the situation, temporarily increasing the monthly assessments and banning free quarter, but complaints about soldiers' behaviour continued. The constable of Elmley Lovett received a demand for the parish's arrears, 'at your perils of pillaging and your houses fired and your persons imprisoned.'[56]

Nevertheless, the King issued various proclamations warning the officers and soldiers of his army against plundering his subjects, and wrongdoers were punished. Symonds records that in July 1644, during the Oxford Army's campaign in the West, one soldier was hanged for plundering and his regiment was marched under the gallows.[57] As already noted, surviving warrants issued by Royalist commanders for the supplying of horses are not abundant.

However, on 24 February 1644 Sir Thomas Aston, commanding a composite force of horse and dragoons issued a warrant to Captain Thomas Prestwich at Dorchester for the requisitioning of horses from the village and parish of Steeple Aston, ten miles south of Banbury, an area that had been previously allotted for the maintenance of his regiments:

> These horses are accounted to be taken from the quarters:
>
> Jones the trumpeter – a horse of Christopher Geatleyes
> Quartermaster Clarke – a horse of Anthony Marks

54 Thomas Carte, *The Life of James, Duke of Ormond* (Oxford: Oxford University Press, 1851), V, pp.529–30; John Barratt, *'The King's Irish': The Royalist Anglo-Irish Foot of the English Civil War* (Solihull: Helion & Co., 2019), pp.48–9.

55 BL, Ms Harley 6804, f.140r.

56 BL, Ms Harley 6804, ff.139v–40r; Bund (ed.), *Diary of Henry Townshend*, II, pp.238–9.

57 Symonds, *Diary*, p.41.

Robert Stansby – a horse of John Longs
A horse pressed from Moore Jennings

> I desire order to be taken for restitution of these horses, to the bearer or bearers thereof. And that some of the adjacent villages to the quarters you now are in to be ordered by warrant to bring in able horses in their places, upon a rate to be agreed on by a ticket signed for the same by yourself or the major, I pray fail not to see this performed.[58]

Frontispiece from *Markham's Masterpiece* (1644) (Open source)

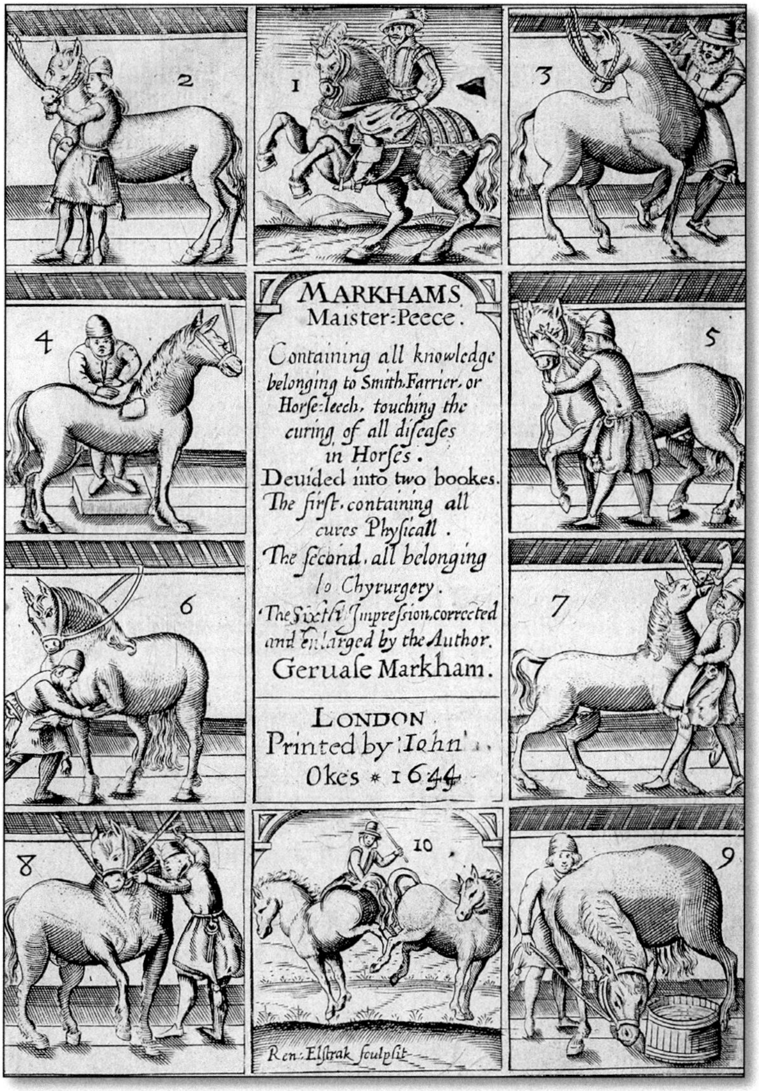

In mid-1644, the Oxford Parliament authorised a series of rapid reinforcements of the King's forces, including the formation of a new army in the Welsh Marches under Prince Rupert. Thus, the addition of 1,000 horses for the mounted units required an immediate response. On 24 May, the King ordered Henry, Lord Wilmot, Lieutenant-General of the Horse, to collect 600 mounts immediately from Oxfordshire and the five adjoining counties. The collection and dispatch of these horses was the sheriffs' responsibility. Wilmot's agents were to make lists of the horses taken, the prices of these and names of their owners, and deliver them to the sheriff. He paid the owners for their forfeiture out of the weekly contribution of the county, but if such officials neglected this, the Treasurer at War reimbursed them.[59]

Like their Royalist counterparts, various methods were employed by Parliamentarian committees and military officers away from the main field armies of Essex, Manchester and Waller to procure horses and military equipment for dragoons.

58 WRO, X3/119/AC/12.

59 BL, Ms Harley 6852, f.192r.

In Derbyshire, Sir John Gell, the local commander, ordered all the constables of the county to bring in all the horses they could obtain, together with harnesses, for military use. Additionally, he commandeered what he required from the Derby market and horse fair. In September 1642, Gell raised 140 foot and dragoons in Wirksworth, although these may have been motivated to enlist as much by their dislike of the recent plunder of their town by Royalist cavalry as by any especial attachment to the Parliament's politics.[60] On 3 December 1642, the Cheshire commander, Sir William Brereton was authorised 'to have liberty to raise 300 horses in the several counties where they shall be brought in voluntarily, upon Propositions.'[61] James Chudleigh was commissioned Colonel of a regiment of dragoons, which originated in London, and after recruiting in the West Country was intended for Ireland. On 6 January 1643, Parliament commanded, '£1,000 be advanced to the officers, upon account; and likewise, ready money, to provide arms, and 1,000 saddles. And that the said £1,000, and money for arms and saddles, shall be repaid out of plate raised in the counties of Devon and Cornwall, upon the Propositions.'[62]

Similar orders were sent to various counties (some of which had already provided quantities of men and equipment for the Parliamentarian forces) for the procurement of dragoons and horses during the early months of fighting. In November 1642, the collectors of Gloucestershire were instructed to draw up lists of 'men who are able serve as dragoons and of the horses and arms to be loaned, and the money given for the troops' maintenance.'[63] Correspondingly, on 2 November 1642 the constables of Suffolk were to attract subscriptions of 'every man who is willing to contribute either nags or mares and all such as are willing to serve in the dragoons.'[64] In Yorkshire, the Lords and Commons advertised in September 1642 that any persons advancing money to raise £1,600 for the recruiting of 1,000 dragoons 'shall have the public faith for the repayment of the advances with 8 percent interest.'[65] Particularly overstretched was the Hertfordshire Committee, who on 19 September 1643 petitioned Parliament that 'having been ordered, at their own expense, to raise 120 horses for dragoons to be sent to Manchester's army, the county is devoid of mounts due to having previously been commanded to raise a troop of harquebusiers and other regiments, and the county had furnished 1,000 or 1,200 horses [already]'.[66] In September 1644, contributions were made from the tithes of Blagdon in Somerset towards, among other things, the raising of dragoon horses and saddles for Sir William Waller (for Parliament), Sir Lewis Dives and Colonel Coker (for the King) in the West Country.[67]

60 DRO, D267/269c.
61 *CJ*, II, p.874.
62 TNA, SP28/262, f.215r; *CJ*, II, p.878.
63 GA, D7115/2/47; D2510/26.
64 Suffolk RO, FB/130/I/1/8.
65 WYA, WYW1352/1/1/12/23/127; WYW1352/1/1/12/23/130.
66 HMC, *Thirteenth Report, App. I*, p.131.
67 G. Dyfnallt Owen (ed.), *Calendar of the Cecil Papers in Hatfield House* (London: HMSO, 1971), XXII, p.381.

In a new preface (2016) to his 2008 article, 'Horse Supply and the Development of the New Model Army, 1642–1646', Gavin Robinson revised his contention that frontier areas were 'bled dry' of mounts and shows that horses were not simply seized from the countryside (as pressed horses).[68] This was liable to cause substantial problems for the Parliamentarian armies with claims of theft and payment of compensation. Occasionally, however, direct methods of acquisition were authorised by Parliament, especially where expediency was essential, such as forfeit by people who had either not paid sufficient taxes to support the raising of forces, or who may have supported the Royalist cause in some fashion. On 23 August 1644, the Committee of Both Kingdoms authorised Sir William Waller 'to seize horses to mount his musketeers in such places about Abingdon or Oxford as are under the King's power.' Whilst in January 1645, as part of the operations to counter Royalist threats in the West, the same Committee ordered the Associated counties of Sussex, Surrey, and Kent to 'provide speedily 500 horse for mounting 500 dragoons of Sir William Waller's.'[69] The detailed financial accounts of the Cheshire dragoon Captain, John Bramhall, provide a useful picture of the quantities of horses employed by the unit during the first year of the war. Bramhall received 88 mounts: 60 in London; 14 'on arrival in Cheshire'; and 14 'from Sir George Booth' (a deputy lieutenant of the county).[70]

Surviving accounts of some of the constables and of the Parliamentarian sequestration committees in Cheshire contain details of the supply of horses, equipment and pay of Brereton's dragoons. During the winter of 1643–4 the constables of Aston were ordered to provide two 'scout horses' for Captain Littler's company, while around April 1644 the constables of Mere laid out £2 9s 4d for 'a horse, men and arms' for the same unit.[71] Similarly, the constables of Nether Whitley expended £8 16s 0d on 1 October 1643 'for one horse, and horse furniture and apparel for a dragoon by warrant of Sir William Brereton,' and a further £4 0s 0d 'for riding the horse.' Additionally, between 1 October 1643 and 1 October 1644 the same officials paid 18s 0d 'for maintaining a man, horse and arms for three weeks at the first voyage into Wales under command of Captain Goldegay.' In late 1642 or early 1643 the same officer received two mounts with furniture and arms from the constables of Mere at a cost of £6 0s 0d, while in 1644 the collectors at nearby Lymm paid the sum of £11 3s 0d for three dragoon horses and three soldiers in his company.[72]

When in regular service, horses required metal shoes to protect their hooves from wear and tear. However, shod hooves would still grow, regardless of terrain and the shoes needed to be refitted to avoid lameness, consequently, armies needed to keep their horses shod and re-shod. On 23 November 1643,

68 www.core.ac.uk/download/pdf/147827902.pdf?fbclid=IwAR2Po9PnF7KAJ32wr27I_YZPGlwNltFesxLpf4h 7I1_00ZAvllKaCcvRJY; Gavin Robinson, 'Horse Supply and the Development of the New Model Army, 1642–1646', *War in History*, 15 (2008), pp.121–40.

69 *CSPD 1644*, p.459; *CSPD 1644–45*, pp.233–4.

70 BL, Ms Harley 2128, ff.34r–34v.

71 Aston, unlisted warrant, dated 20 November 1643 x 2 February 1644; BL, Ms Harley 2128, ff.166r, 60v.

72 BL, Ms Harley 2128, f.41v.

it was reported of Sir William Waller's army in Hampshire, which included seven companies of dragoons, that 'many of them cannot stir for want of money to shoe their horses.'[73] Civil war financial accounts often include charges for shoeing, but the records are nowhere near comprehensive, possibly because it was considered such an everyday activity. Each cavalry troop was supposed to have its own farrier, although evidence of their existence in dragoon units remains unclear. In 1645 John Springer, the farrier of Captain Francis Hanson's company of London dragoons received 2s per day, the same as the corporals and drummers.[74] Shoeing horses was the main task carried out by farriers in the early modern period, although many of them were skilled medical practitioners as well. Their work with horseshoes and metal also associated them with blacksmiths. The Parliamentarian commander, Sir William Brereton paid the sum of £2 16s 4d in June 1644 'to Richard Stelfox [one of his officials] at Northampton in my march from London to Cheshire in discharge of the smith's bill for shoeing troop horses and the saddler for repairing saddles for troopers.'[75]

In November 1642, Colonel Richard Browne's newly formed Parliamentarian dragoon regiment paid £6 14s 3d to 'the farrier for shoeing horses', 5s 6d to a farrier for two days, £7 8d 0d 'to Garfield Wilman and others for shoeing dragoons' horses,' and a further payment of £1 7s 9d for shoeing mounts. The regiment also paid out £1 7s 9d for 6 dozen horseshoes and 5s 7d for 750 horseshoe nails.[76] Similarly, £1 5s 6d was paid 'for shoeing dragoons' horses' for Sir Anthony Irby's regiment in early 1643.[77] In May 1644, Sergeant-Major Bramhall of Brereton's army made various payments to the farrier Abraham Lindop for shoeing dragoon and cavalry mounts, while on 1 February 1645, the sum of £15 11s 10d was disbursed to Randle Walton for shoeing his entire command's mounts, formerly dragoons who had converted to a troop of horse.[78] Contracts made with suppliers to the New Model Army include those made on 1 February 1646 for 3,000 horseshoes costing 4d each and 30,000 horseshoe nails at 9d the pound.[79]

Many farriers' bills during the civil wars include charges for 'curing horses' and other treatments. For example, Captain Richard Grenville in April 1643 paid £2 10s 0d to Mr Webb of Uxbridge 'for keeping and curing a lame troop horse, which I left with him, for thirteen or fourteen weeks', and a further £1 9s 4d to a Mr Hussey of Henley for the same thing, the horse being left in his care for about five weeks.[80] On 8 August 1644, Corporal George Day of Colonel Purefoy's Parliamentarian regiment of horse in Warwickshire paid the 2s 4d to a farrier 'for bleeding, dressing and shoeing' a troop horse, whilst further disbursements were made for dressing mounts.[81]

73 HMC, *Thirteenth Report*, App. I, p.159.
74 TNA, SP28/131/8, f.1r.
75 TNA, SP28/152/7, f.8r.
76 TNA, SP28/144/2, ff.29r.–34r.
77 TNA, SP28/313/4, unfol.
78 BL, Ms Harley 2128, ff.25r–29v.
79 ML, 46–78/709, f.25r; Mungeam, 'Contracts', pp.67–8.
80 TNA, SP28/149, f.159v; Wilson, *Buckinghamshire Contributions*, p.125.
81 TNA, SP28/136/26, ff.1r, 7r–8r.

The accounts of materials and equipment purchased for the Earl of Essex's artillery train in September 1642 include items purchased for the use of its farrier, such as turmeric, liquorice, aniseed and white mercury.[82] Similarly, the financial accounts of the Parliamentarian garrison of Windsor give an idea of the welfare of its horses and the supplies purchased to keep them healthy. William Wright and other farriers were employed to shoe mounts, whilst between August 1643 and July 1644 the garrison had up to five grooms who were paid 2s 4d a week. The accounts also contain payments for items such as curry combs, cantles, girths, bridles and halters, in addition to supplies 'for medicines at several times for horse baths' and 'medicines for horse backs', among other treatments.[83]

In 1610, Gervase Markham wrote the first book exclusively concerned with farriery and equine medicine. Aimed at horsemen, his treatise on horse care was considered authoritative and thus came out in dozens of editions. Markham followed the prevailing philosophy about health and illness in this period for both humans and other large animals: the humoural theory of disease and wellness, whereby the four humours of the body (blood, phlegm, bile, and black bile) needed to be kept in balance, and illness was a result of a lack of balance between them.[84] Thus, each of the work's images depicts the horseman caring for the horse in various ways; ranging from internal problems that require potions to protecting mounts from sickness. The civil war diary of Richard Symonds, includes some farriers' recipes for cures. If a horse had worms, he recommended:

> two spoonfuls of honey in a good quantity of milk, given in a home. This is sweet, and draws the worms out of the maw, and fill their bellies, and draws them on a heap. Then a while after give him the like quantity of sweet ale or beer, and in it a handful of salt, and that will kill them all.

For stomach-ache, Symonds advised 'brimstone beaten to powder, black soap to make it into a paste, and give him the quantity of a hen egg.'[85] One of the troopers of Sergeant-Major John Desborough's troop of the Eastern Association Army paid 10s for curing his horse of farcy in February 1644.[86] Farcy was described by Markham as a highly infectious and fatal disease, characterised by ulcers or pustules along the horse's veins.[87]

In describing the arms and equipment of dragoons, Monck observed that they 'ought to have a good ordinary horse, saddle, snaffle, reins, stirrups, and stirrup-leathers, a halter, and two girts.'[88] Dragoon saddles were both much lighter and cost far less than cavalry saddles. As dragoons used their horses simply for transport and did not usually fight mounted, they required

82 TNA, SP28/131/2, ff.9r–12v.

83 TNA, SP28/126/1, ff.28v–29r, 40r.

84 Gervase Markham, *Markham's Maister Peece, Containing all Knowledge Belonging to Smith, Farrier, or horse-Leech, Touching on Curing All Diseases in Horses* (London: 1610), preface.

85 Symonds, *Diary*, pp.225–6.

86 TNA, SP28/28/4, f.358v.

87 Markham, *Markham's Maister Peece*, pp.457–8.

88 Monck, *Observations*, p.28.

much less support from their saddles. As compared to great saddles and troop saddles, issued to the cavalry, some dragoons were issued with a pad saddle, an item derived from the oldest form of saddle, which was merely a pad on a horse's back. However, the design had become more complex by the seventeenth century, with separate pads on either side of the horse's back, akin to a modem riding saddle. Pad-saddles were fashioned without a tree for easier mounting and dismounting, but they were supplied with a crupper and martingale to restrict the saddle's movement, and two thick side panels padded underneath.[89]

Various warrants refer to purchases of saddles and pad-saddles for Parliamentarian dragoons. In November 1642, Colonel Richard Browne's regiment, absorbing the dragoon units in London, received over 800 saddles, purchased from eleven different saddlers in the capital. Priced between 5s 0d and 7s 0d the sum of £288 7s 0d was spent exclusively on saddles, while additional amounts of £4 13s 0d were paid to 'Mr Deacon for saddles and furniture', £142 10s 0d to 'Mr Burton for saddles and bridles', 8s 0d for 6 new bridles, and 2s 0d to a carrier for the delivery of 48 saddles; another £3 10s 0d was laid out to 'Mr Potter for mending saddles.'[90]

In December 1642, Lord Brooke was given £100 towards purchasing horses and £150 for 300 saddles for his dragoon regiment, at a rather inflated cost of 10s each.[91] Similarly, Sir Anthony Irby's accounts record the payment of £11 8s 6d for 'saddles for dragoons.'[92] At a posited cost of 6s or 7s each, this would equate to roughly 35 pieces of equipment. Although many of the descriptions given in the contracts for equipping the New Model Army seem ambiguous to the modern reader, one from April 1645 describes the saddles as 'pad saddles with good iron plates and stran bits with good furniture complete' at 17s 0d each, whereas another contract from later in the month was for 'pad saddles with two loops behind and no great buckles for the crupper' at 18s 0d.[93] Although

Parts of the horse Vernon, *The Young Horseman* (Open source)

89 G. Tylden, *Horses and Saddlery: An Account of the Animals Used by the British and Commonwealth Armies from the Seventeenth Century to the Present Day* (London: J. A. Allen, 1965), pp.112–13.

90 TNA, SP28/144/2, ff.29r–34r.

91 TNA, SP28/2A, ff.328r, 339r.

92 TNA, SP28/313/4, unfol.

93 ML, 46–78/709, f.110r; Mungeam, 'Contracts', pp.112–13.

references to purchases of cavalry saddles – early in the war 'great saddles' and later, 'troop saddles' – are plentiful among the State and Ordnance Office papers for the main Parliamentarian armies, those procured for dragoons are simply mentioned as 'dragoon saddles'. On this basis of this evidence, such items for Essex's army in 1642 appear scarce, though it must be assumed that the dragoon regiments that bought horses must have acquired saddles for them. One warrant from February 1643 for dragoon saddles for the army lists them at 7s 0d each, while dragoon saddles purchased in Hertfordshire for the Eastern Association forces in 1644 cost 6s 6d each.[94]

Various contracts were placed for the New Model Army with Elizabeth Betts – a major producer of troop and dragoon saddles, and saddle furniture in London. In May and June 1645, the Committee for the Army engaged with her to supply 100 and 140 'new dragoon saddles with furniture at 7s 6d per saddle.'[95] The first batch was delivered on 23 June, though only 100 of the remaining 140 came into the Stores on 11 August. Another contract recorded at the Ordnance Office on 4 April 1645 had required George Langley and Nathaniel Rawlinson to provide 300 saddles for dragoons, 100 by the following day and the remainder a week later. The order was fulfilled, although the saddles were not new.[96] Nicholas Rechford was engaged on 14 July to supply 50 dragoon saddles for the army at 7s 10d each saddle with furniture, to be delivered into the Tower stores the following day.[97] Clearly, Rechford's stocks were sufficient to be able to fulfil the contract so quickly.

Although the contract books record that issues of saddles to the New Model Army started at the end of March 1645, warrants for their purchase begin the following month.[98] Between April 1645 and April 1646, the Ordnance Office took delivery of an estimated 9,370 saddles, of which 759 were for dragoons.[99] Additionally, 500 unserviceable dragoon saddles were repaired at 5s 6d apiece by the London saddlers George Langley and Nathaniel Rawlinson. These were paid for and returned to the Ordnance Office within a remarkably short space of time, and issued to Fairfax's army.[100] In total, 9,379 saddles were supplied to the New Model Army in the space of twelve months, and of these, 1,230 were dragoon saddles. Such items were somewhat cheaper than cavalry saddles, which were procured for between 16s 0d and 18s 0d each.[101] The large volume of saddlery manufactured during this period reflects the significant expansion of the army, and its mounted capability especially.

In most Parliamentarian forces, saddles were procured both in London and locally, where they could sometimes cost less. However, the provincial saddlers probably ran smaller operations and were unable to fulfil the large contracts in the way that their London counterparts were. In November

94 TNA, SP28/5, f.271r; SP28/231, unfol.

95 TNA, WO47/1, ff.136v, 140r; ML, 46–78/709, f.21r; Mungeam, 'Contracts', p.66.

96 TNA, WO47/1, f.211r; WO55/1662, f.18v.

97 ML, 46–78/709, f.45r; Mungeam, 'Contracts', p.78.

98 TNA, WO55/1646; WO55/1662, f.54r; WO55/1663, unfol.; WO55/1664, f.24r.

99 Robinson, 'Horse Supply', p.284.

100 TNA, WO47/1 f.109r; WO55/1663 f.40r; SP28/29/1, ff.212r, 240r; SP28/140/3, unfol.

101 ML, 46–78/709, ff.91v, 109r–112v; Mungeam, 'Contracts', pp.66, 80–1, 103–5, 111–13.

1642, Colonel Herbert Morley's regiment of horse and dragoons serving in Waller's Southern Association received money to equip the unit with 100 saddles, and William Jones of St Albans supplied six dragoon saddles at 16s 6d each in October 1644, which were sent to the Earl of Manchester's army at Reading.[102] Manchester's army also had smaller contracts with several saddlers in Cambridge and elsewhere in the Eastern Association. By comparison, however, the Southern Association was never given the power to set up its own treasury, and so the Association Committee was never able to purchase mounts for Waller's army in the way that the Cambridge Committee did for Manchester's army. The records of the Cambridge Treasury are not complete, but they suggest that purchases of horses declined in the autumn of 1644, despite the need to replace losses from the year's campaigns. This was perhaps a symptom of a general financial crisis in the Association.[103] The Cambridge Committee supplemented its purchases by setting quotas on the Associated counties in 1644. In September, dragoon horses were sent to Huntingdon for employment in Manchester's army, including 100 from Norfolk and 30 from Hertfordshire.[104] London saddlers also supplied many items to Waller, Manchester, and other regional commanders.

Both the Parliamentarian commanders, Sir William Brereton and Sir Thomas Myddelton, purchased saddlery in the capital for their forces during their stay there. When Brereton's three dragoon companies, which had been recruited in London, marched to Cheshire in late 1642, they were completely equipped with horses, firearms and presumably, saddles. The detailed accounts of Captain John Bramhall, whose soldiers participated in the action at Turnham Green in the November, make no account of saddlery and furniture, thus leading to an assumption that they had been supplied by London contractors, possibly with money provided by Parliament of the dragoon officer themselves.[105] Brereton testified to the Committee of Accounts on 3 November 1645 that 'I raised and took down with me in December [1642] these companies of dragoons: Captain Bramhall, Captain Goldegay and Captain Lea which, together with my horse and all the force with me, were put upon service by the way and the first night after we came into Cheshire.'[106] The Manchester saddle trade was, unsurprisingly, utilised by the Parliamentarian forces in the northwest of England. In 1643, the Cheshire commander, Colonel Robert Duckenfield, paid out various amounts to the saddlers William Walker and Peter Cork, for saddles and furniture for his cavalry troop.[107] Similarly, other Lancashire and Cheshire officers made payments for the repair of saddlery.[108] Saddles, canvas and shoes were also procured from Warrington, which had been in Parliamentarian hands since May 1643.[109]

---

102 TNA, SP28/262, f.268v; SP28/231, unfol.
103 Holmes, *Eastern Association*, pp.160–61.
104 TNA, SP 28/231, unfol.; BL, Ms Add 22619, f.206r.
105 BL, Ms Harley 2128, ff.20r–35v.
106 BL, Ms Add 11332, f.43v; *BLB*, II, 809.
107 TNA, SP28/128/10, ff.4v, 5r–5v; 6r–6v.
108 TNA, SP28/196/1, ff.14v–16v.
109 TNA, SP28/299, f.1102r; SP 28/300, ff.1071r,1076v.

Probably in November 1642, the constables of Wraggoe Hundred on the Lincolnshire Wolds sent forth for service in Sir Anthony Irby's regiment, 'one dragoon, with bridle and saddle, and musket and sword, and bandoliers, which was delivered unto Colonel Cole at Hainton' at a cost of £4 10s 0d.[110] In a similar fashion, in early 1644 the constables of Hollingworth in Cheshire completely equipped a dragoon of Brereton's army, except for his musket. The soldier was provided with a horse, costing £5, with a 'saddle, bridal, stirrups, boots, spurs, sword, girdle and other furniture for a rider to the said horse', at a total cost of £4. Items of equipment purchased for Bramhall's company on 1 February 1644 include a bridle costing 4s and six girths at a cost of 2s, while 3s was paid for the mending of spurs and bridles.[111] Also, during the build-up of Sir Thomas Myddelton's second brigade in 1644, significant quantities of items for horses were purchased, including the payment of £65 10s 0d to William Platt, saddler, for 70 pad-saddles, bridles, and other harness, while Ellis Parry (judging by his name, a local maker) was contracted twice 'for 39 pad saddles with their furniture at 20s a piece.'[112]

In the absence of evidence, it remains unclear how the King's forces, and the Scots and Irish for that matter, procured their saddlery, but various quantities were imported from abroad and some produced by local manufacturers. There is some evidence that the Royalists brought saddles in greater numbers than the Parliamentarians. Charles I had already imported many saddles during the Bishops' Wars, but these almost certainly fell into the hands of Parliament in 1642.[113] During that summer, the Queen, Henrietta Maria, sent a shipment of arms from the Netherlands, which included 3,000 saddles.[114] This is far in excess of any shipments of such items known to have been received by Parliament and indicates that the domestic supplies available to the King were wholly inadequate. When Sir Thomas Aston went to Cheshire in January 1643, he had Royal authority given to him to conscript horses in the county to mount a new dragoon regiment. Such was the need for saddles that agents for Aston set about buying up all available items from the saddle makers of Chester and surrounding areas. These ranged from 'war saddles' for cavalry troopers to the less expensive pad-saddles for the fledgling dragoons.[115]

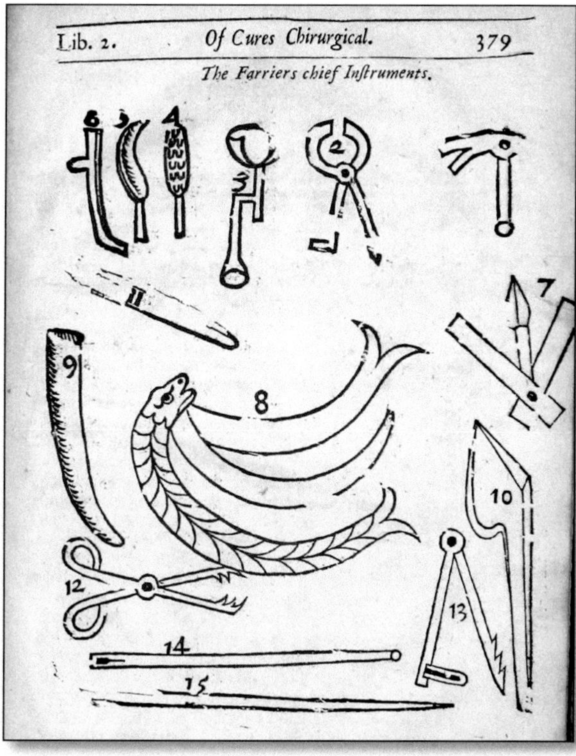

The principal tools of the farrier *Markham's Masterpiece* (Open source)

110 TNA, SP28/313, f.3r.

111 BL, Ms Harley 2128, ff.8r, 25r, 27v, 29r, 42r, 48v, 60r.

112 TNA, SP28/346/1, unfol.; SP28/346/2, unfol.

113 Edwards, *Dealing in Death*, p.185.

114 Ibid., p.159.

115 BL, Ms Add 36913, f.112r.

The imperfect records of the Ordnance Office at Oxford reveal few examples of issues of equipment to the mounted formations in Charles I's army, although on 2 May 1644 60 case of pistols with holsters, 40 carbines and 'the same proportion of saddles and bits or as many as you have for the arming of a troop of 100 cuirassiers' were distributed to Colonel Thomas Blagge's newly raised cavalry troop.[116] It is likely that, like their Parliamentarian opponents, Royalist officers received cash to buy saddles for their troopers and dragoons if supplies were not readily available. The governor of Lichfield, Richard Bagot, expended £900 0s 0d on saddles, pistols and carbines for the four troops of horse he raised in 1643.[117]

While English production was dominated by London saddlers, and thus largely beyond access by the King's supporters, there were some hubs of manufacture in Royalist areas. York was an important centre of saddle making in the north, while various Worcestershire towns produced saddlery and horse tack.[118] The absence of records, though, makes it difficult to establish how important these towns were in supplying the Royalist forces.

Similarly, horses advanced on the voluntary Engagement in 1642 came with saddles, since the Lords undertook to provide horses and riders, although no exact details have survived. Some of the mounts stopped by order of Parliament on the way to York are mentioned as having great saddles with them, which suggests that those who voluntarily provided horses for the King also provided saddles for them. This idea is supported by some of the warrants issued by Charles and his military officers. Wiltshire's contribution of 150 mounts to the Oxford Army in May 1644 included 'bridles, saddles, and furniture'.[119] A possibly contemporary warrant ordered the Sheriff of Wiltshire to 'send all the trained horses contributed in the county to Reading for the use of Sir Thomas Aston's regiment', duly warning the recipient that 'any persons standing charged with horse dare not at present so furnished as may be fit for our service, that then you compound with such persons for such of money as may supply us with a serviceable horse, arms and furniture.'[120]

Reproduction dragoon saddle. Made by Tomáš Filip-Leatherwork (courtesy of Graham Webb)

In the seventeenth century, military horses were usually

116 TNA, WO55/423, f.305r–305v; *ROP*, II, pp.348–9.

117 LCL, Ms Lichfield 24, f.78v.

118 *CJ*, II, p.853; HMC, *Thirteenth Report*, App. 1, pp.70–1; Edwards, *Dealing in Death*, p.172.

119 BL, Ms Harley 6852, f.192r.

120 WRO, X3/119/AC/24.

fed hay and oats on campaign, but this diet was sometimes supplemented with peas and barley. The standard daily ration for cavalry mounts in the British Civil Wars seems to have been one peck of oats (usually about two gallons or eight quarts). However, measures were not fixed with the same exactness as today, and they inclined to fluctuate from location to location. As Robinson asserts, 'It also possible that measures which apparently had the same name were actually different for different commodities, and that in some places words had completely different meanings, so that under certain circumstances, bushels were called pecks and pecks were called bushels.'[121] In October 1644, Symonds noted that at Blandford there were six quarts to a peck and 24 quarts to the bushel.[122] That he found this extraordinary enough to record demonstrates the broad variations in practice. Documents relating to the financing and supply of Sir William Brereton's Parliamentarian forces the Cheshire include various payments for horse provisions. In 1643, the constables of Bucklow Hundred instructed the townships of Aston and Aston Grange to bringing two horse-loads of oats to Great Budworth each day, presumably for the dragoon horses, along with firewood and hay, with teams of oxen to transport it from Rocksavage.[123]

Likewise, in March 1644 Commissary John Miller received quantities of provisions from the Bucklow sequestrators, including 12cwt of cheese and 240 measures of oats 'for the use of the army'.[124] A few months later, Miller received 240 measures of oats at 11d per measure from the sequestered estate of Peter Leycester of Tabley, while, probably in late 1645, the Bucklow Hundred contributed '120 measures of barley, ground into maize and carried to the Leaguer at Chester', valued at £13, with further delivery of provisions to the value of £54.[125] Although the source is unknown, on 18 September 1643 51 stone (714lb) of oats was supplied to Colonel Robert Duckenfield's cavalry troop at 8s 8d per stone, to a total cost of £20 8s 1d.[126] However, some of Brereton's cavalry officers took measures into their own hands when faced by shortages of provisions and concentrated feed. Whilst quartering in the Wirral in mid–1645, the Parliamentary officials at Hooton complained when Captain William Shepley's troopers commandeered land and harvested – among other commodities – 50 measures of oats 'without order' at 12d per measure, and a further '46 measures of oats not paid for to the state.'[127] Equally, the sequestration accounts of Macclesfield Hundred record that sometime in late 1644 three measures of oats worth 3s 4d were issued to Brereton's dragoons to be fed to their horses.[128]

When the Parliamentarian garrison arrived at Windsor in October 1642, there was only a fraction of the amount of fodder required to feed its

121 Robinson, 'horse Supply', p.209.

122 Symonds, *Diary*, p.127.

123 Aston, unlisted warrants, dated 28 November 1643, 2 December 1643, 16 February 1644, 30 May 1644, 19 July 1644, 5 September 1644, 7 September 1644.

124 Ms Harley 2166, f.130r; 1943, ff.7r–7v, 8v; 2137, ff.105v, 152v; TNA, SP28/224, f.25r.

125 BL, Ms Harley 2137, ff.55v, 95v, 105v, 199r, 152v–153r, 203r, 204r.

126 TNA, SP28/128/10, f.6r.

127 BL, Ms Harley 1999, ff.17r, 69r, 71v.

128 BL, Ms Harley 2130, f.209v.

horses. As Robinson observed, by the end of the following year, the whole of Berkshire was drained of hay and oats, and was unable to support the Parliamentarian forces, which also included the armies of the Earl of Essex and Sir William Waller.[129] The extensive accounts of the garrison's treasurer confirm that because of the shortage in the Windsor area in particular, fodder had to be procured from surrounding counties. During the harvest period of September to October 1643, 60 cartloads of hay (including ten from Eaton College Meadow), 13 quarts of oats, 1,210 bushels of grain, two quarts of beans, one of barley and 'malt for the mash' from unnamed localities are recorded as having been purchased by the Windsor Castle garrison and supplied to the dragoons for their horses.[130]

One estimate of equine nutrition suggests that horses performing a moderate day's work require roughly 25,000 calories per day and 45 litres of water. Therefore, a 500-strong regiment of dragoons or horse needed 3,400–4,500kg of fodder and 5,000 gallons of water every 24 hours. All of this had to be purchased or requisitioned and then distributed to mounted units by commissaries.[131] Cruso recommended in 1632, that 'to lodge or encamp the cavalry, a special care must be had of the commodity of water, and where they may be under shelter: for one cold or rainy night might ruin the cavalry, nothing hurting a horse sooner than cold or wet.'[132] Thus, when on 4 August 1641 Sir John Conyers, Lieutenant-General of the horse ordered Captain John Mennes of Commissary-General Henry Wilmot's regiment to rendezvous with the King near Doncaster, he added:

> It will be requisite, when they do march, that every trooper carry behind him in his oat sack three or four baits of oats or bread for his horse, and provision for himself, for some of them will be more than 24 hours from their quarters; and in the meantime let them feed their horses as well as they can, and put their equipage in good order that they may not be ashamed to be seen. And when they march let them have ammunition delivered to them.[133]

Consequently, any dearth of foodstuffs for the feeding of cavalry and dragoon horses could seriously limit the effectiveness of mounted formations, as well as the general condition of animals. On 27 November 1643, the newly appointed Royalist Governor of Oxford, Sir Arthur Aston, appraised Prince Rupert of the military situation in Northamptonshire and Oxfordshire. While reporting that 'the fortifications at Towcester will be complete enough next week to be defensible against a surprise,' he added that Royalist purveyors had arrived to thresh corn recently seized from Parliamentarian sources to supply Towcester and Oxford. With only three cavalry troops remaining at Northampton, Aston advised Rupert that the majority of the Royalist Horse

129 Robinson, 'Horse Supply', p.228.
130 TNA SP28/126/1, ff.20v, 28v.
131 Robin Higham, 'Some Thoughts on the Thirty Years War', *Bellum Tricannale* (Prague, 1997), p.340.
132 Cruso, *Militarie Instructions for the Cavalrie*, pp.66–7.
133 *CSPD 1641–43*, p.72.

in the area 'must withdraw to avoid ruin because of their bad losses already.' In a further dispatch, Sir Arthur objected to the Prince's orders to use parties of horse to obtain provisions for a magazine at Towcester, which Rupert had made strong by constructing water filled ditches and using the remains of the Roman walls. He left a powerful mounted force in the town before returning to Oxford. Aston warned Rupert that covering the threshing and carrying in of corn was too dangerous and time-consuming, and thus refused to undertake it. His advice was that it was easier to remove the main cavalry force, 'preventing its ruin and removing the worst burden.'[134]

134 WSL, Ms Salt 477/11–2.

8

The Oxford Army

In 1642, there was no standing army in England, and so Charles I's forces needed to be new raised. The general custom was to issue Colonel's commissions to the King's supporters to raise '500 Horse volunteers', or other specified units. In turn, such colonels and other Royalist commanders might grant commissions in the King's name to their subordinates. Sir Arthur Aston issued a commission to Sir Walter Pye on 20 November 1642 to be Lieutenant-Colonel of his cavalry regiment.[1] Similarly, Charles I's nephew, Prince Rupert, commissioned John Warcup as Lieutenant-Colonel in Sir Thomas Aston's Regiment of dragoons on 5 January 1644.[2] Although Aston formally received his commission from the King on 3 October 1642, he had begun recruiting his regiment of Horse the previous month, if not even earlier. Evidence for the actual commission dates of many Royalist officers is slight, nonetheless, this kind of gap appears to have been commonplace. The King's Lifeguard of Foot was among the first regiments of foot raised for Charles I, with recruiting starting in June 1642, while the King was still at York. By 27 June, there was reportedly 1,000 foot, although men continued to be recruited up to the Edgehill campaign three or four months later.[3] Even so, the Lifeguard's Colonel, Lord Willoughby d'Eresby, only received his commission on 22 August.[4] Henry Hastings, the driving force behind the Royalists in Staffordshire, received a commission by virtue of a warrant from the King in August 1642 to raise 400 cavalry, and by the middle of the month had at least two troops under his command.[5]

From the outset of the fighting in England in September 1642, dragoons represented a considerable proportion of the mounted arm of both sides and were often classified as part of the cavalry. The King's Oxford Army was his main 'marching' army of the First Civil War, based at Oxford, which was the location of the court and the centre of Royalist government and

1 BL, Ms Add18980, f.8v.
2 SofA, Ms 138, f.130r.
3 SRO, D868/2/33.
4 NAM, 1993-10-112-1. For his commissions as Colonel of a regiment of horse, dated 5 August 1642, see Lincolnshire Archives, ANC XII/A/5-6.
5 HMC, *Twelfth Report*, II, p.373.

administration from autumn 1642 until June 1646. As such, the army formed the backbone of the Royalist war effort. Prince Rupert and Sir Arthur Aston junior, together with other European and British veterans and mercenaries with Continental experience, introduced innovation and experimentation into the armies, including more combined arms cooperation between mobile mounted formations of horse and dragoons, as well as between horse and foot.[6] Some officers from the British Isles had specifically commanded dragoon regiments during the Thirty Years' War.

The Scottish Roman Catholic, Sir John Henderson, may have begun his military service in the army of Denmark between 1625 and 1629. He led four companies of dragoons at the Battle of Lützen on 16 November 1632, though because of a paucity of horses for them his soldiers had to operate as musketeers. During the British Civil Wars Henderson's experience aided his appointment as the Royalist governor of Newark, but he was defeated by Parliamentarian forces under Sir Thomas Fairfax at Winceby on 11–12 October 1643.[7]

When the Royalist Army rested at Stafford on 17 September 1642, en route to the Welsh borders, where the King intended to raise recruits, reports arrived of the Earl of Essex's intention to seize Worcester. In response, Rupert was ordered to take eight troops of cavalry and ten of dragoons to the city.[8] The following day, Charles I instructed his nephew 'immediately to order eight troops of Horse and five troops of dragoons, under commander of his choice, to march towards Nantwich, to quarter nearby on Tuesday night, and remain there until they receive further orders from Charles, Lord Strange, one of the Commissioners of Array for Cheshire.'[9] Soon afterwards the Prince set up headquarters at Bridgnorth, where further orders were received to move towards Worcester to guard Sir John Byron, with a convoy of college plate and money he was conveying from Oxford, in addition to the King's authorisation to engage the enemy as he saw fit. On 23 September, as Rupert and Byron edged around the south of the city near Powick Bridge on the River Severn, with part of Rupert's mounted force aiming to cover the latter's retreat to the north, they encountered Essex's 500–1,000 horse and dragoons under the overall command of Colonel John Browne.[10]

The action began when the leading Parliamentarian cavalry, funnelled into a narrow lane, was fired upon from the hedgerows by Rupert's dragoons. The Prince's Horse subsequently charged the remaining enemy cavalry, drawn up in open order in an adjacent field, routing them, although the Parliamentarian

6 Michał Paradowski, 'Aston, Butler and Murray – British Officers in the Service of Polish Vasa Kings 1621–1634', in Serena Jones (ed.), *'Britain Turned Germany': The Thirty Years' War and its Impact on the British Isles 1638–1660: Proceedings of the 2018 Helion and Company 'Century of the Soldier' Conference* (Solihull: Helion & Co., 2019), pp.53–68.

7 David Worthington, *Scots in Habsburg Service, 1618–1648* (Leiden: Brill, 2004), p.159; University of St Andrews, Institute of Historical Research, HENDERSON, JOHN [SSNE 53] (www.st andrewsac.uk/history/ssne/item.php?id=53).

8 Warburton, *Memoirs*, I, p.396.

9 WSL, Ms Salt 496.

10 C. H. Firth (ed.), *The Memoirs of Edmund Ludlow, Lieutenant General of the Horse in the Army of the Commonwealth of England, 1625–1672* (Oxford: Clarendon Press, 1894), I, p.41; *CSPD 1641–43*, p.393.

dragoons fought a rearguard action to protect the retreat. During September and October 1642, scarcely a day passed without the London newsbooks reporting the composition and strength of the Royalist army. These alleged that their accounts were trustworthy because they quoted from information contained in letters that the Earl of Essex had conveyed to Parliament. On 10 October, it was reported that the King's main army numbered 12,000 foot and 4,000 horse, whereas the following day 9,000 foot, 2,500 horse and 1,500 dragoons were said to be in the field.[11] Such discrepancies, however, reflected the Parliamentarian uncertainty about the actual strength of the Royalist army. Whatever his strength actually was, on 15 October, the King, lacking the resources of London, requested the assistance of 500 dragoons from the Marquess of Newcastle, since he did not have enough with him in the Midlands.[12]

Some of the Royalist sources for Edgehill are contradictory, while modern assessments of the deployment of the King's dragoons vary. However, it seems that it is possible to discern their general deployment as well as the position of Sir Arthur Aston during the battle. Aston had been appointed Sergeant-Major-General of dragoons three days previously. Clarendon located him on the left flank, while the Duke of York mentioned him as being on the right, however, as Serena Jones suggests, 'it is perfectly possible that Aston as Sergeant-Major-General responsible for troops on both wings, made his way back and forth across the battlefield as his command required.'[13] At least two dragoon formations were deployed on the Royalist left flank; Colonel John Innes' Regiment, with a party in reserve commanded by Colonel Edward Grey, consisting of his own regiment plus perhaps some additional units. On the other wing was the dragoon regiment of the Anglo-Irish veteran Colonel James Ussher – recruited in the south Midland counties of Warwickshire, Worcestershire, and Leicestershire – and possibly Colonel Edward Duncombe's regiment.

Their Parliamentarian counterparts, the regiments of Colonels John Browne (who had been at the defeat at Powick Bridge) and possibly that of James Wardlaw, were deployed on the Earl of Essex's right flank among a series of undergrowth and ditches.[14] The two Royalist brigades of dragoons cleared the hedges and ditches on both flanks of the King's army 'with great courage and dexterity'. On the Royalists' right wing Ussher's dragoons, led by Lieutenant-Colonel Henry Washington (who seems to have had some Continental military experience prior to 1640, at which time he was a Captain in the Earl of Northumberland's regiment on the Scottish border) engaged a body of 400 commanded musketeers from Colonel Denzil Holles' regiment of foot, deployed in divisions in the spaces between the troops of

11 *England's Memorable Accidents*, 10–17 October 1642; *A Perfect Diurnal of the Passages in Parliament*, 10–17 October 1642.

12 BL, Ms Harley 6988, f.74r.

13 Serena Jones, *No Armour But Courage: Colonel Sir George Lisle, 1615–1648* (Solihull: Helion & Co., 2016), p.65, note 10.

14 Young, *Edgehill*, pp.99–100, 246–8; Christopher L. Scott, Alan Turton, and Eric Gruber von Arni, *Edgehill: The Battle Reinterpreted* (Barnsley: Pen & Sword, 2004), pp.84–5.

cavalry, and an additional 300 of Colonel Thomas Ballard's regiment in an intense firefight amongst 'enclosures and briars'.[15]

The Royalist, Richard Bulstrode described how 'Colonel George Lisle, with Lieutenant-Colonel Innis were in the left wing, with a regiment of dragoons, to defend the briars on that side.'[16] Lisle, who had gained his military education in the Low Countries and entered Charles I's service early in the conflict, was at the forefront of the Royalist attack at Chalgrove and 'bravely led up the forlorn hope' at the First Battle of Newbury on 20 September 1643, where he was wounded. Although contemporary sources tended not to assign a specific command to Lisle during the Edgehill campaign, he appears to have been involved in similar activities. In her biography of Lisle, Jones describes him in 1643 as 'an ad hoc forlorn hope of dragoon officer with Continental and Edgehill experience to his credit.'[17] The Royalist dragoons on the right flank initially fought along a right-angled hedge line, from which they poured enfilading fire into Ballard's men, before clearing the position by way of a frontal assault.[18] It seems that it was the resolve, experience (especially among most of the company commanders, who held previous military service) and tactical flexibility of Ussher's dragoons that enabled them to overcome their opponents, 'which they very well performed.'[19]

In accordance with the drill manuals of the time, their opponents were trained to operate as standard divisions of shot, capable of delivering single-rank musket fire or salvos. Besides, Nehemiah Wharton's account of the progress of Colonel Holles' regiment from August to October 1642 suggests that the soldiers – recruited predominantly from London apprentices – possessed a reputation for ill-discipline and had received barely limited training.[20] The Royalist success was not without loss, however. Captain (later Sergeant-Major) Gawdy, one of the officers in Ussher's regiment, who had considerable Continental military experience, 'was shot at Kineton with two shots in the thigh, that he gave up his command three months since.'[21] Significantly, once the Royalist dragoons had cleared the musketeers on the Parliamentarian left, Prince Rupert found himself in a position to lead his mounted right wing forward. Perhaps simultaneously, on the Royalist army's left flank a combined mounted attack was commenced by Commissary-General Henry Wilmot's brigade of fifteen cavalry troops and the six companies of dragoons led by the King's Colonel-General of dragoons, Sir Arthur Aston. Wilmot, like Aston was an experienced veteran of the wars

15 *Relation of the Battel*. TT, E126 [24]; *An Exact and True Relation of the Dangerous and Bloody Fight Between His Majesties Army, and the Parliaments Forces, neere Kyneton in the County of Warwick, the 23., of this instant October. Sent in a Letter to John Pym Esquire* (London: 28 October 1642). TT, E124 [26].

16 Bulstrode, *Memoirs*, p.81.

17 Jones, *No Armour But Courage*, p.74.

18 *A Most True Relation*; Bulstrode, *Memoirs*, p.77.

19 *A Relation of the Battel*. TT, E126 [24].

20 Stuart Peachey, *The Edgehill Campaign and the Letters of Nehemiah Wharton* (Leigh-on-Sea: Partisan Press, 1997), p.15.

21 Luke, *Letter Books*, p.10.

on the Continent, having begun his military career as a captain of horse in Dutch service and having been wounded at Breda in 1637.[22]

According to James, Duke of York, at Edgehill

> Each wing [of the Royalist army] had a second line or reserve, the one composed of the Lord Digby's and Sir Thomas Aston's regiment, with whom were some dragoons under the command of Colonel Edward Grey, the other of the Lord Byron's regiment, they themselves being at the head of them; and on the right-hand of the right wing were likewise some dragoons commanded by Sir Arthur Aston.[23]

An entry in Prince Rupert's 'Diary', penned some years later, recounts, 'Lord Wilmot fell upon the dragoons, and they ran away.'[24] After Rupert's Horse had broken and routed the Parliamentarian left flank, the development of the dragoon action on the opposite wing began with the deployment by the Earl of Essex of his available regiments, including that commanded by Colonel John Browne and possibly that of Colonel James Wardlaw. These were located with an estimated eighteen troops of cavalry under the command of the experienced professional, Sir William Balfour.

Positioned among a series of natural obstacles, including ditches, scrubland trees and brushwood, which would have provided cover and a place to tether their horses, they provided a formidable line of defence. Somewhat outnumbering his opponents, however, Sir Arthur Aston did not find extricating these dragoons to be the relatively straightforward undertaking which Ussher's men had experienced on the Royalist right flank. The Parliamentarian commander, Edmund Ludlow, who served as one of the 100 gentlemen forming Essex's Lifeguard during the campaign, reported, 'By this time the foot began to engage, and a party of the enemy sent to line some hedges on our right wing, thereby to beat us from our ground, were repulsed by our dragoons without any loss on our side.'[25] However, Aston's dragoons worked in combination with their own cavalry, firing into the Parliamentarian dragoons from the front and side. It was enough to enable the troopers to outmanoeuvre their opponents, who rather than remounting and reforming, fled to the rear.

Of the role played by the Royalist dragoons in this action, Clarendon wrote a tad flamboyantly, 'Sir Arthur Aston, with great courage and dexterity, beat off those musketeers with his dragoons; and then the right wing of their horse was as easily routed and dispersed as their left, and those followed the chase as furiously as the other.'[26] Yet the overall course and outcome of the hard-fought and bloody battle fought between Radway and Kineton in October 1642 – the first full-scale military encounter between the forces that would

---

22 Clarendon, *History*, I, p.206; II, p.288; Bulstrode Whitelocke, *Memorials of the English Affairs* (London: Nathaniel Ponder, 1682), pp.102–3.

23 T. S Clarke (ed.), *The Life of James the Second, King of England* (London: Longman, 1816), I, p.11.

24 WHSC, 413/444/A, unfol.

25 Ludlow, *Memoirs*, II, p.261.

26 Clarendon, *History*, IV, p.82.

prosecute the King's and Parliament's causes during the British Civil Wars – was inconclusive. Even so, it had far-reaching implications. The armies spent the night within shot of each other, and during the following day both sides withdrew from the field; Essex and the Parliamentarian army retreated on Warwick, whereas the King considered a march on London with the Royal army. A month after Edgehill, perhaps in consideration of the respectable performance by his hitherto largely inexperienced dragoons during the campaign, and even to replace battlefield losses, Charles I complained to the Earl of Newcastle, 'I want dragoons, which is the rebels' strength, their foot not liking winter marches.'[27] In January 1643, due to shortages and perhaps a further lack of recruits, he was again compelled to request Newcastle to send him 1,000 dragoons 'that I be not oppressed for want of them.'[28]

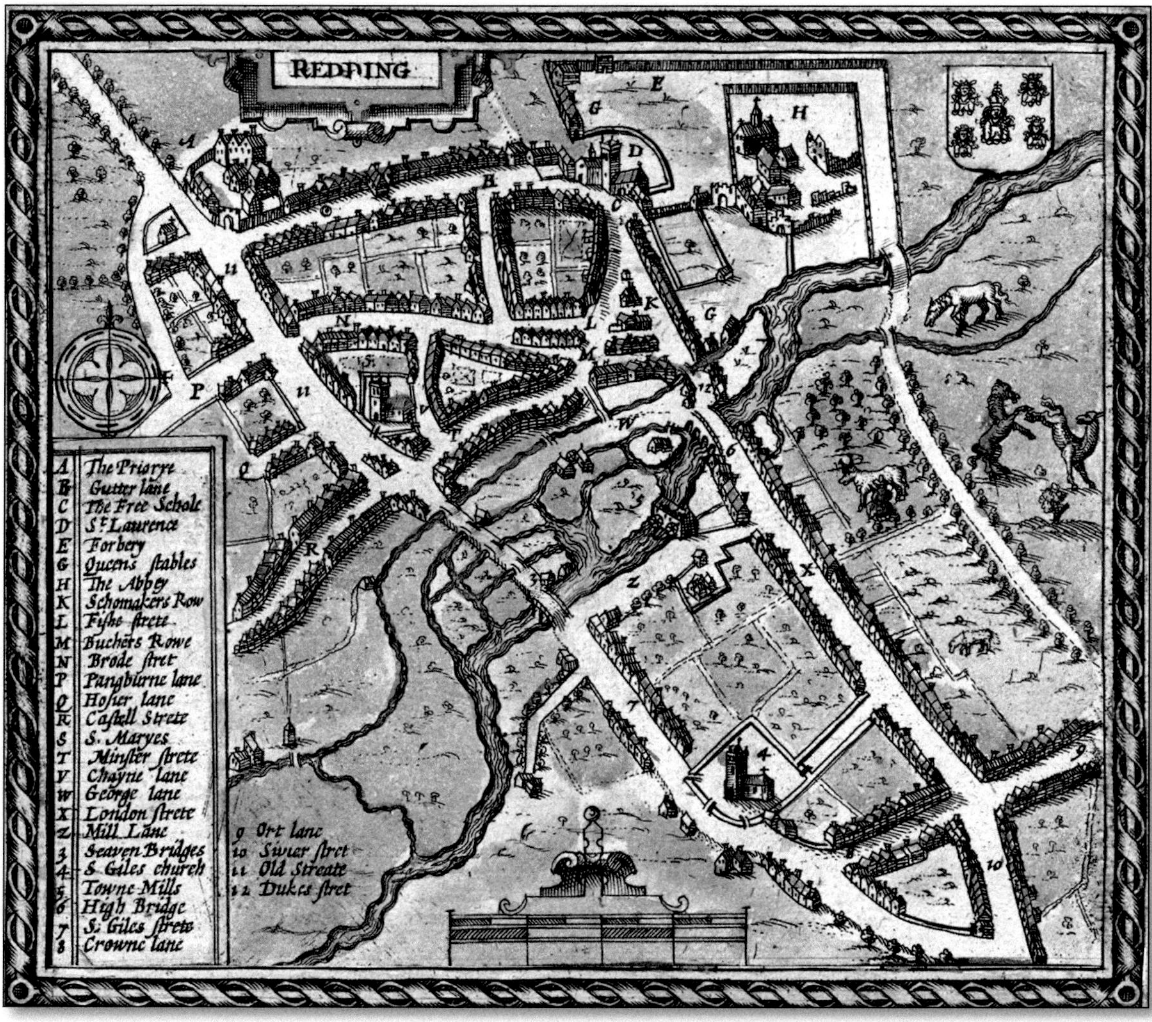

Map of Reading John Speed (1611) (Open source)

27 Warburton, *Memoirs*, II, p.79.
28 BL, Ms Harley 6988, f.76r.

References to 'his Majesty's horse forces' during the British Civil Wars in contemporary sources commonly infer mounted troops, often consisting of a combination of mutually dependent units of cavalry and dragoons. Faced by a Parliamentarian army of 24,000 under the Earl of Essex, Charles I's advance on London on 13 November 1642 stalled. After a day's skirmishing and a stand off at Turnham Green, the Royalist Army withdrew to Oxford, where it went into winter quarters. Prince Rupert subsequently ordered a supply of ammunition for the mounted units, which were located to the east of the city. On 5 December, he issued the following warrant to Sir John Heydon, Lieutenant-General of his Majesty's Ordnance:

> These are to desire, and straightly require you forthwith, upon sight hereof to deliver to this bearer, for the present use of his Majesty's horse forces, six barrels of your best powder, twelve bundles of the best match, 2 cwt of musket ball, 2 cwt of carbine ball, and 2 cwt of pistol shot. All which you are forthwith to send to Tame, the quarter of my dear brother Prince Maurice … hereof you must not fail, and for your doing so this shall be your warrant.[29]

At the end of October 1642, the town of Reading – located across the Great West Road and dominating the route to the West Country, and the Thames, a vital artery for the transport of military equipment and material from London to Parliament's forces – was delivered up to the King. The Royalists immediately occupied it, and Charles I was there in person on 3 November, where messengers from the Parliament found him. The King determined to keep Reading garrisoned and remained there until a line was drawn around the town and the new fortifications were well advanced. On 22 November 1642 Sir Arthur Aston, the unpopular Catholic officer, although with considerable military experience, was appointed governor. His commission stated:

> Charles, by the grace of God King of England, Scotland, France and Ireland, Defender of the Faith, etc. To Our trusted and welbeloved Sir Arthur Aston, Knight, Sergeant Major General of the horse of Our army Greeting. Whereas We have thought fit for the defence and security of Our good town of Reading in Our county of Berkshire, to settle and appoint therein a governor with such number of soldiers as may on all occasions be of force to defend Our said town and the inhabitants thereof, and likewise other of Our good subjects of Our said county of Berkshire against any attempts that be made against them, by the traitorous proceedings of the Earl of Essex and his adherents, constitute and appoint you governor of Our said town of Reading, and of all such forces, both of foot and horse, as shall either be left in garrison of Our said town or shall be sent or commanded thither for your assistance, and better defence of the same, hereby willing and requiring you immediately to take into your charge and command, the government of Our said town, and of all both officers and soldiers in garrison there, and to dispose and govern them therein, as you shall find best for your service the security and defence of that Our town, streightly commanding and

29 TNA, WO55/423, ff.228v–229r; *ROP*, I, p.175.

> charging all colonels, lieutenant colonels, sergeant majors, captains of both foot and horse, and all other inferior officers and soldiers of the said garrison, you to obey and serve as governor.[30]

Charles I borrowed £2,000 from the mayor and burgesses of Reading 'for the maintenance of the King's garrison', which was composed of 2,000 foot and a regiment of horse.[31] From this, the town was also compelled to provide cloth and victuals for the army, and to find labourers to work on the fortifications. To compound the situation, all trade with London was prohibited, which was particularly onerous, given Reading's dependency on the clothing trade, and the enduring economic impoverishment of the town due to competition from northern manufacturers.[32] On 3 January 1643, Aston demanded an additional £2,000 for the King.[33] With characteristic harshness, he supplied the corporation, at Charles I's command, with a list of men who had refused to pay the first loan and hence were to be taxed double for the new one.

On 17 March Aston received a commission from Prince Rupert as Captain of an independent company of dragoons by his authority as 'general under his Majesty of all his Majesty's forces of horse, as well as all troops of horse, cuirassiers, dragoons and carabiniers of all and all manner of horse forces.' Aston was duly appointed:

> captain of a free company of dragoons, consisting of 100 men to remain and constantly with your regiment of horse as an auxiliary company to the same, which company you are presently to raise and levy in many parts of his Majesty's Kingdom of England and the dominion of Wales of such as will willingly and voluntarily serve for his Majesty's pay, for the defence of the true Protestant Religion, his Majesty's person, the two Houses of Parliament and their instant privileges, and the proprieties of his subjects … And yourself likewise diligently to observe and expedite such orders and directions as you shall, from time to time, receive from myself and all other superior officers of his Majesty's army to whom of right you are, or may be, subordinate, according to the Discipline of War.[34]

Sir Arthur Aston's dragoon formation may have counted amongst its ranks officers and soldiers of foreign birth who possessed considerable military experience.

Rupert's own dragoons were evidently part of, or attached to, Sir Arthur Aston's regiment of horse in January 1643. However, during a raid on Henley-on-Thames on 22 January, in the confusion one of the dragoons shot and killed Sergeant-Major Holby of Aston's horse, triggering the failure of the enterprise. Sir Arthur was so disgusted by the conduct of the dragoons that

30 BRO, R/Z10/11.
31 Clarendon, *History*, VI, p.155.
32 BRO, R/Z3/35; R/Z3/36; R/Z3/39; R/Z3/42.
33 BRO, R/Z3/31; R/Z3/33.
34 BRO, R/Z10/12.

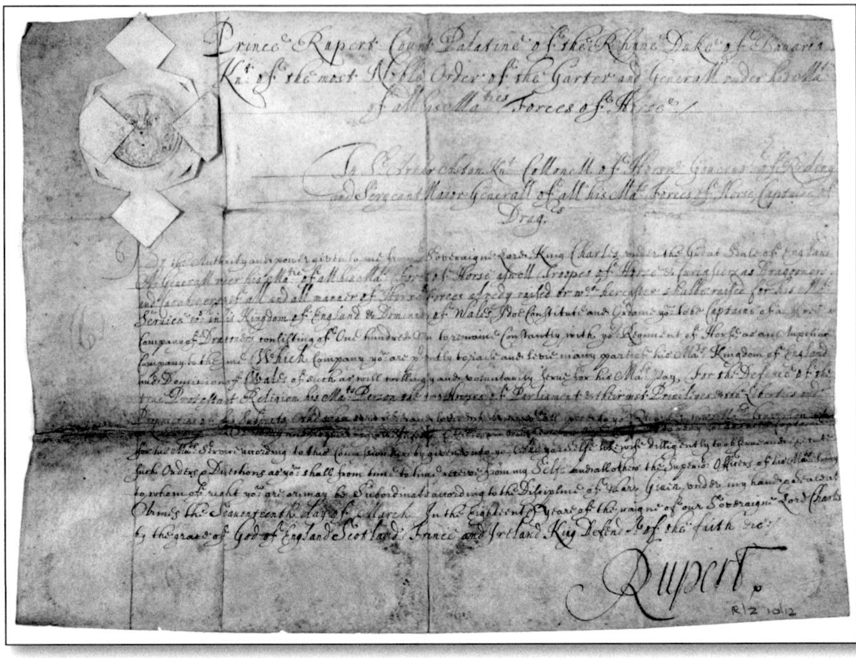

Prince Rupert Count Palatine of the Rhine Duke of Bavaria Kn^t of the most Noble Order of the Garter and Generall under his Matie of all his Maties Forces of Horse

Rupert

Commission of Sir Arthur Aston as captain of an independent company of dragoons, Berkshire Record Office R-Z10-12 (courtesy of the Berkshire Archives)

he sent them back to the Prince at Reading, as he wanted rid of them.[35] Aston duly wrote to Rupert:

> With all the expedition possibly I could I have sent these dragoons after you, I beseech God send your Highness better success than I had with them, for they and my horsemen did most shamefully lose the bravest design at Henley that ever was undertaken since my coming to this army, and lost it not but gave the victory away when they had already possession of all that they went for, and with it I lost as brave an officer as I ever hope to command in this kingdom. May it please your Highness I am so extremely dejected at this business that I do wish with all my heart that either I had some German soldiers to command, or that I could infuse some German courage into them, for your English common soldiers are so poor and base that I could never have a greater affliction light upon me than to be put to command any of them I beseech your Highness to present my humble services unto Lieutenant-General Wilmot, I am loath to repeat my disasters too often or else I would have written also unto him, whom I know will suffer in this thought with me.[36]

This was echoed on 24 January 1643 by Sir Edward Nicholas, one of the King's wisest and most loyal advisers, who reported from Oxford:

> I would not suffer this bearer to pass without this tender of my respects and duty. Sir Arthur Aston understanding of some forces come into Henley, sent thither a party Friday night under the command of the Sergeant-Major of his Horse,

35 *Mercurius Aulicus*, 22–28 January 1643.

36 William Ansell Day (ed.), *The Pythouse Papers: Correspondence Concerning the Civil War* (London: Bickers and Sons, 1879), pp.12–13.

> Mr Holby, they entered the town and possessed themselves of the ordnance in the market place, but, by an unfortunate shot out of a window Sergeant Major Holby being slain, the dragoons [of Rupert's regiment, commanded by Captain Sir Thomas Hooper] ran away and the Horse did little better, notwithstanding the earnest[ness] of their officers and so they lost the effect of their own pains and hazard. The rebels do approach towards Aylesbury.[37]

However, on 2 February 1643, Thomas, Lord Wentworth succeeded Aston as Sergeant-Major-General of the Oxford Army's dragoons.

Another dragoon regiment in the Oxford Army in 1642–3 was that commanded by Colonel Edward Grey of Ulgham Grange, Northumberland. Grey served as Colonel of dragoons from 1642 until the surrender of Newark in 1646, and although he subscribed to the Covenant and was compounded, he took up arms for the King in the Second Civil War of 1648. Like Sir Edmund Duncombe's regiment, Grey's dragoons were raised in Northern England early in the war, although their period of service was relatively short. In September 1642, Grey's soldiers plundered Great Houghton, the home of the High Sheriff of Yorkshire, Sir Edward Rodes, before retiring to Mansfield. Of the event, one Parliamentarian newsbook reported:

> Now the fair pretences of the cavaliers appears, that t'was fire and sword they meant, they have lately plundered Sir Edward Rodes his house, burnt al his out houses and taken away £600 worth of goods, slain one of his servants, and violently used others, it was done by Captain Grey's regiment, a Northumberland gentleman, who hath the command of 500 dragoons, most of them consisting of Papists and popish commanders, though to this worthy knight it was a sad accident, yet it hath put courage into our West Riding, for on a sudden 1,500 men were in arms to take these cavaliers, and being on their march, the cavaliers got notice, and by a still march in the night, escaped to Mansfield in Nottinghamshire.[38]

Colonel Edward Grey's dragoons fought at Edgehill and were involved in the storm of Marlborough on 5–6 December 1642. Prior to this, at Oxford it had received 21 bundles of match, 4 barrels of powder, and ball proportional.[39] The regiment, numbering 200 dragoons, was quartered at Faringdon with Colonel Duncombe's dragoons and Prince Maurice's horse in December 1642 after the storm of Marlborough, but most of its officers and other ranks were captured whilst defending Winchester on 12 December.[40] Charles I's secretary, Sir Edward Walker, wrote to the Earl of Lindsey at Warwick Castle:

> I know not how by my actions and less by my thanks to answers those noble expressions of your lordship's favors to me. For the state of things here, I can say little, we being in our winter quarters, the security of which I doubt not of, notwithstanding the late unfortunate surprisal of my Lord Grandison at

37 BL, Ms Add 18980 f.16r.

38 *Speciall Passages*, 13–20 September 1642.

39 *ROP*, I, pp.166–7.

40 BL, Ms Harley 6851, f.120r; *CJ*, II, p.892.

> Winchester (by the flying army of dragoons of the Parliament) and his regiment of horse and Colonel Grey's regiment of Dragoons, consisting of about 500, who were enforced to yeald upon the terms of the officers departing on horseback and the troopers on foot, but conditions were not kept they say, the rude multitude over-swaying their officers, so that our officers being detained were enforced to make escapes … Those flying dragoons made since for Chichester, but as yet have not been able to attempt anything against it.[41]

Some impression of the composition of the mounted forces belonging to the Oxford Army during this period is provided by 'A List of such Regiments, Troops and Companies of horse, Dragooners and Commanded Men as are now Quartered by Order from his Highness Prince Rupert,' an undated document but probably produced in February 1643:[42]

> Horse
>
> Sir John Byron in the Earl of Caernarvon's quarter at Ensem
> Sir William Pennyman at Cirencester
> Sir Richard Willis at Malmesbury
> Colonel Gerrard at Abingdon
> Colonel Croaker at Stratford-upon-Avon
> Threescore commanded men of his Highness the Prince of Wales, his regiment at Stratford-upon-Avon for six days from the twenty-third day of this present
> Captain Robert Cousins at Malmesbury
>
> Dragoons
>
> Sir Robert Howard at Reading
> Colonel Innes at Cirencester
> Colonel Kirke there
> Colonel Wagstaffe at Stratford-upon-Avon
> Lieutenant-General Lunsford at Malmesbury

Another Royalist Colonel of horse and dragoons was Sir Thomas Aston, Baronet, of Aston-by-Sutton, near Runcorn. His family had been present in Cheshire since the twelfth century, but his elevation to the rank of baronet in 1628 raised it to the status of major gentry in the County. Sir Thomas, kinsman of his fellow Royalist, Sir Arthur Aston, was educated at Macclesfield Grammar School, Brasenose College, Oxford, and probably at Lincoln's Inn. By 1635, he was Gentleman Extraordinary of the Privy Chamber. Aston's prominence in the county community was enhanced by his resistance to the payment of ship-money, and his election in early 1640 – alongside Sir William Brereton of Handforth – as MP in 'the Short Parliament'. However, in the elections to 'the Long Parliament', which followed, Sir Thomas Aston

41 LA, 8ANC8/47; HMC, *Report on the Manuscripts of the Earl of Ancaster, preserved at Grimsthorpe* (Dublin: HMSO, 1907), p.411.
42 BRO, R/Z/10/4.

lost his seat, whereas the puritan Brereton, his main ideological opponent in Cheshire, retained his. Following this, Aston became a leading lay defender of the Book of Common Prayer and of the Episcopal government of the Church of England. During 1641 and 1642, he was engaged in petitioning, writing, and publishing in support of the Established Church, and he conducted a pamphlet war with Brereton.[43]

When the defence of episcopy broadened into support for Charles I against his Parliamentarian opponents, Aston and his supporters were reconciled to the King and developed their association with the Royal court. Sir Thomas by this time had won a significant portion of the Cheshire gentry to the cause of the King. These men included Robert, Viscount Cholmondeley; William Lord Brereton; Robert Needham, Viscount Kilmorrey; Sir Edward Fytton of Gawsworth: and John Savage, Earl Rivers. Notably, only the latter, a Catholic, did not openly support Aston's religious stance. Sir Thomas Aston attended the King at York in June 1642 and was present at Nottingham on 22 August when he raised the Royal standard, thus effectively declaring war on Parliament. At this point Charles regarded Aston as his chief supporter in Cheshire, and when in the company of Rivers, he returned from York, he had with him a Commission of Array (an obsolete system that bypassed Parliament's authority, and 'empowered the recipients to raise the armed men of their county for the King and imprison his opponents').[44] While, in July and early August 1642, the middle group of the Cheshire gentry was gathering subscriptions to the Cheshire Remonstrance – a petition calling on the King and Parliament to settle their differences and avoid war – Aston and Rivers were promoting a declaration of loyalty in the form of an 'Attestation of the Commissioners of Array.'[45]

Hence, Commissioners, protected by bodies of cavalry, held local musters in Cheshire, and detained ministers who refused to read Royalist propaganda in their churches. Moreover, constables and others who had executed Parliament's Militia Ordinance (which claimed the right to appoint military commanders without the King's approval), suffered harassment. On 6 September 1642, the county's moderates met in what they termed 'an association at Knutsford', complaining that 'the country is put in fear, not only by several meetings of the commissioners of array for this county … some of them have given out threatenings and desperate language, that they would plunder, batter down, burn the houses and disarm the persons of all such as comply not with them.'[46] During the next few months, Earl Rivers intimidated and plundered the family and tenants of Henry Brooke of Norton (his and Aston's neighbour), the Parliamentarian Deputy Lieutenant, and later Colonel and Sheriff, from his base at Halton Castle. Henry's brother Richard, later an officer in Sir William Brereton's army in Cheshire, admitted

43 John Morrill, *Cheshire 1630–1660: County Government and Society during the 'English Revolution'* (Oxford: Oxford University Press, 1974), pp.45–6; Judith Maltby, *Prayer Book and People in Elizabethan and Early Stuart England* (Cambridge: Cambridge University Press, 1998), pp.156–78.

44 Hutton, *Royalist War Effort*, p.86.

45 Morrill, *Cheshire*, pp.58–9.

46 BL, Ms Harley 2095, f.245r; Ms Harley 2135, f.100r.

that he was one of the earliest gentlemen to declare for Parliament in the northwest of the shire, others having not done so because of Rivers' influence in the locality.[47]

Whether Sir Thomas Aston possessed any military experience prior to 1642 is unknown. His brother John substituted for him during the First Bishops' War in 1639.[48] Sir Thomas's relative, Sir Arthur Aston, was a Catholic professional soldier of considerable experience, who had fought for the Polish-Lithuanian Commonwealth until the Truce of Altmarck in 1629. In 1639, he returned home and was commissioned Sergeant-Major-General to Viscount Conway in the Second Bishops War.[49] Despite his religious persuasion, Sir Arthur led a brigade of Royalist dragoons at Edgehill; he raised a regiment of horse which served as part of the Oxford Army and the garrison of Oxford; was appointed governor of Reading on 22 November 1642, and commissioned by Prince Rupert on 17 March 1643 'as captain of a free company of dragoons to act as auxiliary to your regiment of horse, and to be raised from volunteers in any part of the Kingdom of England and dominion of Wales.'[50]

Commission of Sir Thomas Aston as Colonel of a regiment of Horse USM 009 (courtesy of Scottish Rite Masonic Museum & Library, Lexington Massachusetts)

47 CRO, DCH/X/15/14; Hall (ed.), *Memorials*, pp.38–9.

48 J. C. Hodgson (ed.), John Aston, 'Iter Boreale, Anno Salutis 1639 et Dissidae Inter Anglos at Scotos Inchoatus 1 Aprilis finitum 29 Junii', *Six North Country Diaries*, Surtees Society, 118 (1910), 124 (1915).

49 TNA, SP95/3, f.105r; Paradowski, 'Aston, Butler and Murray', pp.53–68.

50 BL, Ms Add 18980, f.8v; BRO, R/Z10, 11–13.

Sir Thomas Aston's commission as Colonel of a regiment of horse was issued by Charles I at Shrewsbury on 3 October 1642.[51] He was duly authorised:

> for the defence of our Royal person, the two Houses of Parliament, the Protestant religion, the laws of the land, the liberty and property of the subjects, and privileges of Parliament, who have present occasion to have in readiness 500 horse and horsemen, well-armed and furnished with all things necessary for such our suit, to be employed for those purposes in such sort as we under our Royal hand and seals shall set in due form of law. We, trusting to your fidelity, diligence, and duties in such affairs, so as intending to employ you for such our duty, according to such directions as we shall give unto you, we by this present, will and require you, and do give [damaged – *sic.* us] full power and authority for [damaged – *sic.* unto you] and in our name and for our order as aforesaid to impress, raise, enroll, and retain one regiment of 500 horse [damaged – *sic.* and] horsemen so furnished and armed as aforesaid (officers therein comprised), wheresoby you shall be able with this our Kingdom of England or Dominion of Wales who will willingly and voluntarily serve as aforesaid for such wages and contentment by the month, week, or day, or for a longer or shorter time as you on our behalf shall agree.

Additionally, Sir Thomas was granted:

> full power and authority as Colonel over them to command, arm, discipline, train, and order in warlike manner, and with all possible expedition to conduct unto our Royal standard. Willing and commanding all officers and soldiers which by witness hereof you shall retain, you to obey and readily to receive and accomplish your directions, commandment and summons in all things hereto appertaining or necessary to be done, as also all mayors, sheriffs, justices of peace, commissioners of array, and all other our officers and loving subjects to be aiding and assisting herein both unto you, and to all such officers or other persons whom you shall appoint under your hand and seals, for the furthering and advancement of this our especial service, for which these shall be to you and to them, and obey of them a sufficient warrant.

Aston had clearly established his regiment some time before this date. When at Oxford on 19 November Prince Rupert, the King's nephew, and commander of the cavalry in the main Royalist field army (the Oxford Army) referred to the issuing of commissions to colonels of regiments:

> Many commissions are given out, but no money, to raise the regiments of horse. Sir Arthur Aston, the governor of Reading, has one; Sir William Pye has a commission to be his lieutenant-Colonel for raising a troop upon his own charge. Sir Thomas Aston raises a regiment, and some others to ten or twelve new regiments[52]

51 SRMML, USM 009.

52 Warburton, *Memoirs*, II, p.69.

Sir Thomas Aston initially raised two cavalry troops from his estate in Cheshire, and various townships in the locality. Those troops commanded by Sir William Radcliffe and Captain Prestwich (described by Sir Thomas as 'not raised by me but brought in') were recruited in Lancashire, possibly from their holdings in Ordsall and Salford, which supported the King, in contrast to Manchester just across the River Irwell. By the time his regiment fought at Edgehill on 23 October 1642, it numbered 150 troopers, besides commissioned and non-commissioned officers, and in October 1643, whilst quartered in Wiltshire it consisted of 300 men, exclusive of officers, in seven troops, although this is likely to have included dragoons.[53] Fundamental to the recruitment and composition of the regiment was Aston's support of Anglicanism.

On 13 April 1643, the Earl of Essex's army marched from Windsor and quickly established itself around the south and west of Reading, where the town's defensive works were weakest. Six days later the governor, Sir Arthur Aston wrote to Prince Rupert, warning him that the Parliamentarian forces were preparing a major assault on the town. He reported that the garrison possessed far fewer soldiers than the officers had claimed in the musters and bade the Prince to persuade the King to 'forward me 1,000 more foot, or result will be disastrous.' Sir Arthur further requested 'the removal of useless, troublesome unarmed men from this garrison,' and suggested the sending out of Sir John Byron's regiment of horse to forage for provisions.[54]

Parliamentarian reports of the siege of the town, undertaken between 14 and 26 April 1643, spoke of the presence of Royalist dragoons – probably Sir Arthur Aston's own and those of Sir Thomas Aston – but although the former's cavalry regiment formed part of the garrison, Sir Thomas Aston's Horse had left the area by that time.[55] Sir Robert Howard's small regiment, possibly the 'two troops of dragoons' listed as being part of the garrison of Reading in December 1642 and again in February 1643, had been sent to the Welsh borders the following month.[56]

Sir Arthur Aston, however, relinquished command of the Reading garrison after being struck on the head by a roof tile dislodged by cannon-fire while he was inspecting one of the courts of guard in the line of fortifications.[57] Another (Parliamentarian) newsbook, however, reported, 'the governor, Colonel Aston was so ill and bruised in the head and neck from the falling of bricks on chimney above him, which were shot down by a cannon bullet from our army, that he was unable to speak.'[58] Similarly, in a letter of 20 April 1643 the King's secretary, Sir Edward Nicholas, informed that 'Sir Arthur Aston is incapacitated by a chimney-brick which struck his

53 WSHC, X3/119, unfol.

54 WSL, Ms Salt 477/4.

55 *Victory Proclaymed, in an exact relation of the proceedings of the Parliament Forces in their Siege before Reading, 15 to 27 April* (London, 15 April [1643]). TT, E.100[4]; *The third Intelligence From Reading. Dated from His Excellency His Quarters Before Reading, April 26. at night* (London: 28 April 1643). TT, E.99 [29]; *A Perfect Diurnall*, 3–10 June 1643.

56 BRO, R/Z/10/2; R/Z/10/4; SA, LB7/1994.

57 *Mercurius Aulicus*, 16–22 April 1643.

58 *Kingdomes Weekly Intelligencer*, 25–27 May 1643, p.130.

head, and delirious until trepanned last night. This has encouraged rebels to besiege them more closely.'[59] The governorship of Reading devolved on Colonel Richard Fielding, who sent word to the King that unless he was relieved within a week the town must be surrendered. His position was made more difficult by the approach of a Parliamentarian force under Lord Grey, which captured the northern and eastern sides of the town, although these regiments seem to have been composed primarily of raw recruits.

Warrant of Charles I to the clothiers and mercers of Wiltshire to provide clothing for Sir Thomas Aston's Regiment WA, X3119AC3 (courtesy of the Wiltshire Archives)

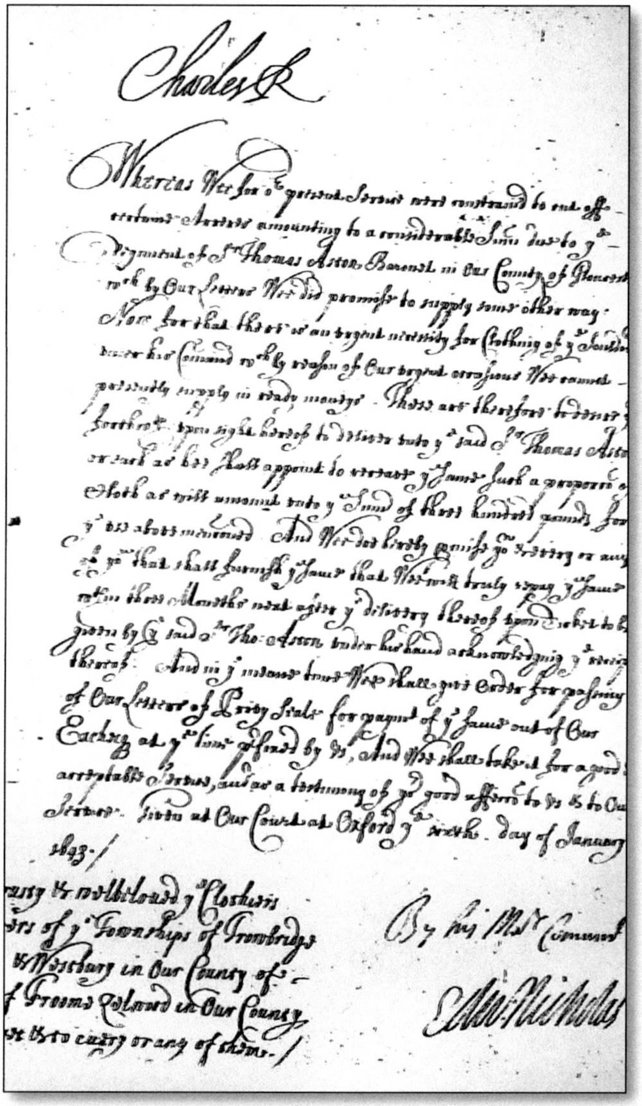

Despite the arrival of Prince Rupert and the Earl of Forth at Caversham with a relief force, Reading fell to the Earl of Essex on 26 April 1643. It was agreed that the Royalist garrison might march out, and the former governor, Sir Arthur Aston, was carried out first. According to one report, 'in a horse litter covered with red and lined with white, after him both coaches and wagons, and then horse and foot beat a march and so departed with their colours flying towards Oxford.'[60] Even so, barely two regiments of the garrison had left the town when the Parliamentarian soldiers began to plunder the baggage wagons and the town itself, despite Essex reportedly offering each man 12s to desist.[61]

As the Earl of Essex's army began its march back to London from Gloucester in September 1643, Charles I's forces set off in pursuit. Essex's intention was to reach Reading. Once there his foot could resist attacks by the Royalists against the rear of the army.

On 18 September, however, Prince Rupert's mounted troops, advancing ahead of the main body of the Oxford Army, encountered Essex's formations on the Marlborough Downs at Aldbourne Chase.[62] One Parliamentarian observer related, 'My Lord General fell on with his foot, and gave them a gallant charge, which accompanied with a volley of our dragoons rattled for the

59 WSL, Ms Salt 564.

60 *The Last Intelligence from his Excellency his Quarters at Reading, since the surrendering of the town* (London: 27 April 1643). TT, E100 [5]

61 *Mercurius Aulicus*, 20–27 April 1643.

62 Warburton, *Memoirs*, II, pp.289–90; *A True and Impartiall relation of the battaile betwixt, His Majesties Army, and that of the rebells neare Newbery in Berkshire, Sept. 20, 1643* (Oxford: L. Lichfield 1643). TT, E69 [10].

space of an hour without any cessation.'[63] Robert Codrington's biography of the Earl of Essex, published directly after his death in 1646, and consisting largely a gathering of pamphlet accounts of the battle, mentions 'In the meantime, the dragoons on both sides gave fire in full bodies one another on the side of the hill.'[64] It was also reported that 1,000 commanded musketeers under the command of Colonel Lisle accompanied Rupert's Horse, but it seems likely that dragoon units were among the Royalist cavalry, including those led by Sir John Byron. The regiments of horse and dragoons raised and commanded by Sir Thomas Aston (a kinsman of Sir Arthur) certainly operated in a combined regimental-sized formation, in which both elements were mutually dependent.

During the subsequent First Battle of Newbury on 20 September 1643, Aston's Regiments were brigaded together on the Royalist's right flank in the second line, in the vicinity of Round Hill, and with those of Sir Robert Howard's Shropshire dragoons, Sir John Byron's Horse, and other small regiments, including Sir William Pennyman and Colonel Gerard Croker's cavalry. Sir Thomas' combined command had numbered almost 450 men in August 1643.[65] Four troops of his dragoons, advancing in support of Colonel George Lisle's body of commanded shot, initially cleared their objective of two lines of hedgerows. 'Commanded men' were soldiers commanded out of their companies for service away from their regiment. These contingents were typically musketeers and were detached to fight in bodies of about 50 men alongside the horse, or to operate in broken or wooded ground, or amongst hedges. Upon the formation of Sir Thomas Aston's regiment of dragoons in early 1643, Aston's soldiers had been issued with hedging bills and buckets, perhaps intended for use among such obstacles. However, they received a severe mauling from the Parliamentarian dragoons opposing them from the cover of their embanked hedges or were shot by musketeers from the Earl of Essex's foot during the intense fighting around the enclosed area known as Bottom Dark Lane.[66]

As *A True Relation of the Late Expedition*, regarded as the 'official' Parliamentarian version of the First Battle of Newbury related:

> two pieces which belonged to the major general's regiment, and one drake of Sir William Brooke's were by his Excellency's regiment under the command of Major Boteler, with the assistance of two hundred musketeers recovered; and the enemy drew away from their pikes (which with their colours kept standing, with many great bodies of horse to guard them) five or six hundred musketeers, besides dragoons, to encompass our men on the right hand among the hedges; just at which time his Excellency sent to have two hundred of the three hundred musketeers of the forlorn-hope to go to the relief of Colonel Barclay and Colonel

63 *A True Relation of the Late Battell Neere Newbury* (London: 26 September 1643). TT, E69 [2].

64 Robert Codrington, *The Life and Death of the Illustrious Robert, Earle of Essex* (London: 1646), p.31.

65 BL, Ms Add 36913, ff.135r–139v.

66 Symonds, *Diary*, pp.64–6; Walter Money, *The First and Second Battles of Newbury and the Siege of Donnington Castle during the Civil War, 1643–6* (London: Simpkin, Marshall & Co., 1881), pp.33–4.

> Holborn's soldiers. But then the enemy falling on upon our right hand diverted them, who with other of our musketeers thereabouts beat the enemy off, who else had done us great mischief; this was about four a clock in the afternoon, when all our whole army of foot was engaged in the fight.[67]

Sir John Bryon's cavalry, including his own troop and Aston's regiment of horse, hastening towards the Parliamentarian positions, made little headway, and were forced to wheel about. According to Byron's own narrative, penned four years after the event:

> my brigade of horse was to have the van, and about fine in the morning I had orders to march towards a little hill full of enclosures, which the enemy (through the negligence before mentioned) had possessed himself of and had brought up two small field pieces and was bringing up more, whereby, they would both have secured their march on Reading (the highway was lying hard by) and withal so annoyed our army which was drawn up in the bottom, where the King himself was, that it would have been impossible for us to have kept the ground. The hill, as I mentioned, was full of enclosures and extremely difficult for horse service, so that my orders were, only with my own and Sir Thomas Aston's regiment to draw behind the commanded foot led by Lord Wentworth and Colonel George Lisle, and to be ready to second them, in case the enemy's horse should advance towards them; the rest of my brigade was by Prince Rupert commanded to the heath, where most of the other horse and foot were drawn.

Sir John, who lost his horse in the action, continued:

> The passage being then made somewhat wide, and I not having another horse, drew in my own troop first, giving orders for the rest to follow and charged the enemy, who entertained us with a great salvo of musket shot, and discharged their two drakes upon us laden with case shot, which killed some and hurt many of my men, so that we were forced to wheel off and could not meet them at that charge. I rallied my men together again, but not so soon but that the enemy had got away their field-pieces for fear of the worst, seeing us resolved not to give over, so I charged them a second time, Sir Thomas Aston being then come up with his regiment, we then beat them to the end of the close, where they faced us again, having the advantage of a hedge at their backs and poured in another volley of shot upon us, when Sir Thomas Aston's horse was killed under him, and withal kept us off so with their pikes we could not break them, but were forced to wheel off again, they in the meantime retreating into another little close and making haste to recover a lane which was very near unto it, finding then they could not keep the ground, which before they could do, I rallied the horse again, and charged them a third time, and then utterly routed them, and had not left a man of them unkilled, but that the hedges were so high the horse could not

67 *A True relation of the Late Expedition of His Excellency, Robert Earle of Essex, for the relief of Gloucester with the description of the fight at Newbury* (London: 1643), pp.18–19.

> pursue them, and besides, a great body of their own foot advanced toward the lane to relieve them.[68]

Similarly, the Royalist newsbook *Mercurius Aulicus* reported:

> A fresh supply of near 200 musketeers advancing up a lane to have surprised our pikes and colours, by that gallant resolute charge made by Sir Thomas Aston with his own troop (through a double quick-set hedge) those poachers were dislodged, their fresh supply routed, and fled before him in such haste, that though his horse was shot in the entrance of the lane, and drew him by the led amongst them, they had not the civility to help him up, but let him walk away on foot.[69]

But despite Aston's counter-attack, the advantage was lost as the Parliamentarians heavily reinforced their left wing with 1,440 horse under Colonel John Middleton. The casualties suffered by Sir Thomas Aston's dragoons and horse during the bitter fighting at Newbury were particularly heavy. The dragoons were reduced from a strength of 220 men to 120 – so, two troops' strength of dragoons were lost. Captain Thomas Salway left the regiment to join Sir Lewis Dyve's foot regiment, and during the following year, the commands of Captain Thomas Newland and Sergeant-Major Michael Mason were amalgamated. Similarly, at least five of Aston's cavalry troops were severely mauled. In early November 1643 Sir Thomas Aston's horse and dragoons were ordered into the West Country, where they joined Sir Ralph Hopton's and Lord Goring's commands, and by January 1644 they were quartered in the Evesham area.[70]

Such was the danger of attacking infantry in defensive enclosures with mounted units, that during the Second Civil War that at Preston in August 1648, Captain John Hodgson fighting among the Parliamentarian cavalry remembered 'ordering the men to follow me, and there drew out a small party; and we came up to the hedge end, and the enemy, many of them, threw down their arms and run to their party, where was their stand of pikes, and a great body of colours.'[71] Similarly, when Colonel Robert Lilburne's troopers were attacked by the Earl of Derby's Royalists at Wigan Lane on 25 August 1651, the Cheshire foot companies accompanying him stood fast, 'our horse not being able to do any service but in lanes.'[72]

The continuing development in the tactical role of mounted troops was a distinct feature among the Royalist armies operating in the West Country – especially those commanded by Sir Ralph Hopton and Prince Rupert – where

68 Quoted in Money, *First and Second Battles of Newbury*, pp.28, 30, 35–6, 39.

69 *Mercurius Aulicus*, 14 October 1643.

70 Bodl. Lib., Ms Firth C6, f.279v; WRO, X3/119/AC/1–2, 14.

71 Sir Henry Slingsby and Walter Scott, *Original memoirs, written during the great Civil War: being the life of Sir Henry Slingsby, and memoirs of Capt. Hodgson* (Edinburgh: J. Ballantyne, 1806), p.116.

72 *A Great Victory by the Blessing of God obtained by the Parliament's forces against the Scots forces, commanded by the Earl of Derby, on the 25 of August 1651, near Wiggon in Lancashire, certified by a letter from Col. Lilburne and two letters from Chester, also a letter from Col. Birche to Mr Speaker* (London: 29 August 1651). TT, E640 [27].

the mobile nature of dragoon warfare provided cavalry formations with essential fire support as well as other services. Rupert's extensive utilisation of the mobility of Royalist dragoons during raids across the South and Midlands in the winter and spring of 1642–3, culminated in the destruction of Parliament's Western Association army at Roundway Down, in addition to the storming of Cirencester and the capture of Bristol on 26 July 1643.

At the latter, Colonel Henry Washington's dragoon regiment, consisting of seven companies – commanded by Colonel Washington, Lieutenant-Colonel Henry Huddleston, Sergeant-Major Nathaniel Grey and Captains Henry Colthorpe, Francis Morrison, William Tuke and Henry Norwood – formed part of Colonel Henry Wentworth's brigade for the actual assault on the city's defences. Washington's, formerly commanded by Colonel James Ussher, was a seasoned regiment, and fought well at Edgehill, the capture of Marlborough in December 1642, the first storming of Birmingham, at Lichfield (where the dragoons spearheaded the assault, though Ussher was killed), and the raid led by Rupert which resulted in the action at Chalgrove in June 1643. The last major achievement of the Oxford Army dragoons was the storming of Bristol on 26 July 1643, where Rupert's regiment was probably present, along with five companies of Washington's and two belonging to Colonel Robert Howard's. Nevertheless, the Royalist losses were heavy, and the dragoons doubtless suffered accordingly. In mid–1644 Colonel Washington's dragoon regiment marched with Prince Rupert's army into the Welsh borders, before leaving for Yorkshire and the north with Rupert's own dragoons, now led by Sir Thomas Hooper.[73]

According to *Mercurius Aulicus,* Washington's men drove the Parliamentarian foot from the hedges outside Stockport when Rupert stormed the town, although evidence of their participation at Marston Moor is lacking.[74] Probably due to a lack of horses, the regiment, except for one mounted company, converted to a foot regiment either in late 1644 or in early 1645 during Colonel Washington's temporary governorship of Evesham. It then formed part of the garrison of Worcester when he was appointed governor of the city.[75]

73 Bulstrode, *Memoirs*, p.100.

74 *Mercurius Aulicus*, 1–8 June 1644.

75 WA, 1714/899/192, ff.686r–752r; BL, Ms Add 11332, ff.13v–14r, 21r, 27r, 52v, 68v,78r; *BLB*, II, 687, 717, 726, 749, 770, 802, 857.

9

The Earl of Essex's Army

On 15 July 1642 the Lords and Commons appointed Robert Devereux, 3rd Earl of Essex, the most senior nobleman to support Parliament, Captain General of the Parliamentarian armies. His commission of 15 July authorised him to raise and levy both horse and foot, to issue commissions to officers, and to appoint a provost marshal for the execution of his commands. In a wider, more national sense, it also gave him absolute authority over the direction of all Parliamentarian forces, while the officers of the army were bound into obedience through an oath to 'defend, maintain and obey' both Parliament and the Lord General.[1] Essex was also one of the few English nobles with any military experience. Between 1620 and 1624, he had served in Protestant armies in Germany and the Low Countries. Essex joined Sir Horace Vere's expedition to defend the Palatinate in 1620 and served with Prince Maurice of Nassau from 1621. In 1624, he led a regiment in the unsuccessful campaign to relieve the siege of Breda. The following year, Essex was appointed Vice Admiral in Sir Edward Cecil's expedition against Cadiz, which ended in defeat for the English forces. Despite his experience, as Captain General of the Parliament's armies during the First Civil War Essex's military performance and record was somewhat mixed – while he was meticulous in planning his campaigns, he was often over-cautious, tended to move slowly and was accused of lacking initiative.

The Earl of Essex's army was principally raised and funded in the Capital and in the County of Essex, though it was augmented during some campaigns by the London Trained Bands and City of London Auxiliaries.[2] In

1 *A&O*, I, pp.14–16; *CJ*, II, pp.672, 696, 699.

2 For more in depth studies of the recruitment, funding, conduct and campaigns of the Earl of Essex's army, see Thomas Crawshaw, 'Military Finance and the Earl of Essex's Regular Army: 1642–1644', PhD thesis (York University, Toronto, 2013); Aaron Graham, 'Finance, Localism and Military Representation in the army of the Earl of Essex (June-November 1642)', *HJ*, 52 (2009), pp.879–98; 'The Earl of Essex and Parliament's Army at the Battle of Edgehill: A Reassessment', *WH*, 17 (2010), pp.276–93; Christopher L. Scott, and Alan Turton, *Hey for Old Robin!: The Campaigns And Armies Of The Earl Of Essex During The First Civil War, 1642–44* (Solihull: Helion & Co., 2017); Scott, Turton and Eric Gruber von Arni, *Edgehill: The Battle Reinterpreted* (Barnsley: Pen & Sword, 2004); Turton, *The Chief Strength of the Army: Essex's horse (1642–1645)* (Leigh-on-Sea: Partizan Press, 1992); Young, *Edgehill 1642*.

late 1642 Essex appointed Philip Skippon to be Sergeant-Major-General of the foot, in which capacity he served at the siege of Reading in spring 1643, in the relief of Gloucester, and the other battles and campaigns of the army. Skippon was a professional soldier of Continental experience, who had been chosen as commander of the London Trained Bands in January 1642, and at Turnham Green his 'brave boys' halted the King's advance on London. Equally, the nominal commander of Essex's horse, William Russell, Earl of Bedford, had been an officer in the Scots brigade in the Dutch army, although he was replaced in August 1643 by the Yorkshire soldier Sir Philip Stapleton.[3] Stapleton had been commissioned Captain in the Earl of Essex's Lifeguard troop of cuirassiers at the beginning of hostilities and Colonel of Essex's own regiment of horse, in which role he and his troopers helped stabilise the Parliamentarian infantry at Edgehill.

On 23 October 1642, Essex's army fought the first major battle of the conflict against the King at Edgehill. Contemporary newsbooks and other accounts proffer wildly different estimates of the relative strength of both forces. The report sent by several of Essex's senior officers to Parliament after the encounter recorded that the army had deployed with 42 troops of horse, 11 regiments of foot and near 700 dragoons.[4] However, as Graham suggests, in over-reckoning the size of the King's army 'they may have deliberately underestimated the size of their army in order to excuse their failure to win the decisive victory that Parliament required.'[5] Crucially, however, Essex's troops blocked the Royalist advance on London at Turnham Green three weeks later. In 1643 and 1644, the Lord General's army largely operated in and around the Thames Valley. On 26 April 1643 it captured and occupied Reading following a 10-day siege, but the army was severely understrength by this stage, as campaign casualties, sickness and a shortage of horses reduced its effectiveness. Numbers were reduced further when the attached brigade of 5,000 horse and foot commanded by Lord Grey of Wark returned to the Eastern Association.

The first dragoon regiment in Essex's army to be raised was that of Colonel John Browne's. On 19 August 1642 Browne, who, like other dragoon officers may have been a Scots professional, received £3,792 to pay and equip his projected regiment of 600 men in six companies, besides officers. A week later, he received 600 short muskets with which to arm them.[6] The regiment also obtained £40 for its colours and drums on the same day.[7] A series of pay warrants among the Commonwealth Exchequer Papers issued by Essex's treasurers between 25 and 30 August 1642 afford information on the commissioned officers and the muster strength of each of Colonel Browne's companies. By 15 September:

3 *CJ*, II, pp.850–1;*CSPD 1642*, pp.366–7.

4 Young, *Edgehill*, p.291.

5 Graham, 'Earl of Essex and Parliament's Army', p.277.

6 TNA, SP28/1A, ff.164r, 288r.; SP28/261, f.43v.

7 TNA, SP28/1A, f.164v.

94 dragoons had enlisted in the Colonel's company under Captain-Lieutenant John Carrs
96 in Sergeant-Major Nathaniel Gordon's company
100 in Captain Sir John Browne's company
81 in Captain Robert Mewer's company, officered by Lieutenant Thomas Mewer and Cornet Nicholas Mewer
91 under Captain William Buchan's command
75 in Captain Robert Marine's company, seconded by Lieutenant Francis Bradbury. Quartermaster John Blackman and Provost Marshall Daniel Lyon were also listed in the regiment.[8] Browne's regiment therefore contained almost 90 percent its proposed strength, mustering 537 dragoons, excluding commissioned and non-commissioned officers, all of whom received their first month's pay in advance less than a week after they enrolled.[9]

Browne's officers, like many in the harquebusier and cuirassier units, began service much earlier than their soldiers. Their first pay period commenced on 30 July, and unlike their men, who were not expected to enlist before receiving advance pay, were treated much like their cavalry officers in that they had to wait for their pay, which they eventually received in full.[10]

In September 1642, Colonel John Browne, leading a mounted force of about 1,000 horse and dragoons, was sent by the Earl of Essex to intercept Prince Rupert and Sir John Byron, who were approaching Worcester. On 23 September, Browne's dragoons deployed to provide cover for Colonel Edwin Sandys' regiment of horse at Powick Bridge on the River Teme. Sandys' troopers came under fire from Royalist dragoons in the hedges, however, which resulted in a disordered dash across the bridge and a brief, if violent, mêlée against the Royalist cavalry. Fortunately, Browne's positioning of his own dragoons prevented the complete destruction of Sandys' regiment – although Sandys was mortally wounded and died the following month – and their fire halted Rupert's pursuit.[11] Despite this broader Parliamentarian setback, the Colonel John Browne's dragoons served at Edgehill, but the regiment was disbanded by the following spring. On 29 October 1642 the sum of £563 17s 0d was paid to Colonel Browne, 'Colonel of a regiment of dragoons for one half months' pay for the soldiers of his said regiment, being 537 soldiers, from 10 to 29 October.'[12]

The regiment still contained almost 90 percent its establishment strength, and although this figure was roughly the same as it had been in mid-September the unit must have sustained some casualties at Edgehill, where it was engaged against Lord Wilmot's mounted attack on the Parliamentarian right flank. If the report of the battle by the Parliamentarian officer Captain

---

8 TNA, SP28/1A, f.288r; SP28/2B, ff.43r, 45r, 48r–50r, 66r; *A List of the Army raised under the command of his Excellency, Robert Earle of Essex* (London: 1642). TT, E117 [30].

9 TNA, SP28/1A, ff.167r–177r, 188r–189v, 312r; SP28/143, f.17v.

10 TNA, SP28/2A, ff.43v, 268r.

11 Ludlow, *Memoirs*, I, p.41; Stuart Peachey, *The Edgehill Campaign and the Letters of Nehemiah Wharton* (Leigh-on-Sea: Partisan Press, 1997), pp.17–18.

12 TNA, SP28/2B, f.459r.

Edward Kightley is to be believed, they also participated in the pillaging of the army's baggage train as they passed to the rear.[13]

Attached to Colonel John Browne's dragoons for the Edgehill campaign was a small regiment under the command of Sir Anthony Irby. On 10 August 1642 Irby of Whaplode, Lincolnshire, a local gentleman and MP for Boston, received a commission from Robert, Earl of Essex 'to raise a troop of 100 dragoons in county Lincoln, and to be captain of the said troop.' A further commission to Thomas Welby, 'appointing him Provost-Marshal of the regiment of dragoons of which Sir Anthony Irby is colonel' was issued on the same date.[14] Irby claimed pay as Captain of a company of dragoons and Colonel of a regiment of dragoons from 10 August 1642 to 2 May 1643.[15] Although Irby's men served at the Battle of Powick Bridge and the Edgehill campaign attached to Browne's regiment of Essex's army, they were intended as a separate entity. Muster rolls pertaining to Irby's dragoons, dated 2 November 1642, 8 November 1642, 8 December 1642, and 1 March 1643 list 172, 172, 134 and 100 men respectively, as always, excluding commissioned, and non-commissioned officers.[16] It appears that although the unit was referred to as a regiment of dragoons, it was more akin to a single, if strong, company. The dispersed 'Account of moneys paid to the officers and soldiers belonging to Colonel Sir Anthony Irby', begun in spring 1643, records various payments to the formation.[17]

Following his service in Irby's dragoons, Lieutenant William Patrick took a commission as Captain in Colonel Oliver Cromwell's regiment of horse in the Eastern Association Army from August to September 1643, and he might be the same officer who later served in Sergeant-Major-General Laurence Crawford's regiment of foot.[18] Atkins had replaced Richard Le Hunt, the original cornet, by mid–1643.[19] The latter later served as a Captain in the Eastern Association cavalry regiments of Colonel Francis Russell and Colonel Bartholomew Vermuyden and, from March 1644, under Colonel Charles Fleetwood, before serving in the New Model during the Naseby campaign, and subsequently in Wales and Ireland.[20] On 8 December 1642, Irby's men were ordered to Hull in support of Lord Fairfax's army in Yorkshire. As the Fairfaxes consolidated their grip on the clothing districts, they also undertook offensive operations against various Royalist-held towns. Though Lord Fairfax had expected to be reinforced by 500 Lincolnshire dragoons and other troops, he instead found himself lamenting that 'only 120 dragoons of Sir Anthony Irby's regiment are come hither, which I sent to Bradford with my

13 *A Full and True Relation of the Battle between the King's Army and the Earle of Essex, in a letter from Captain Edward Kightley* (London: 1642). TT, E126 [24].

14 *CSPD 1641–43*, p.369.

15 TNA, SP28/31, ff.575r–575v.

16 TNA, SP28/120, ff.1245r–1245v.

17 TNA, SP28/313/4, unfol.

18 Spring, *Eastern Association*, I, pp.22, 45.

19 *A List of the Army raised under the command of his Excellency, Robert Earle of Essex* (London: 1642). TT, E117 [30].

20 *Ibid.*, pp.34, 45; Wanklyn, *Reconstructing*, I, pp.51, 61–2, 72.

Robert Devereux, 3rd Earl of Essex (Open source)

son.'[21] These dragoons may have been present at the storming of Leeds on 23 January 1643 as part of the force led by Sir Thomas Fairfax.

During a heavy snowstorm, Fairfax detached a company of dismounted dragoons and five companies of foot from his main force, who worked southwards along a trench towards the River Aire and attacked the Royalist positions near Briggate. Here they engaged in a firefight with the defenders, and some of the dragoons poured so much musket fire on one defensive sconce that the Royalists were obliged to abandon it.[22] Sir Anthony Irby's men were still in Yorkshire on 22 March when Lord Fairfax, whose army at Selby was unpaid and short of supplies, reported to Parliament that the Lincolnshire dragoons had deserted, and that without instant supplies of money, all his remaining troops would follow them.[23] However, an undated payment for £157 13s 0d was made during this period to Quartermaster Rooksby of Irby's regiment 'for equipping dragoons in Yorkshire.'[24]

Irby's dragoons were also part of the composite force of different local detachments engaged in the reduction of the Royalist garrison of Crowland in Lincolnshire on 25 April 1643. The site of an eighth-century abbey, at the time of the civil wars it was still largely surrounded by fens, giving the impression that it was an island. The fighting conditions, however, were particularly onerous as the final assault was preceded by two days' heavy rain and strong winds, during which the Parliamentarians fired on and harassed

21 *Perfect Diurnall*, 20–27 February 1643; [Multiple], *The Parliamentary or Constitutional History of England*, XII (London, 1753), p.113.

22 *A True and Plenary Relation of the Great Defeat given by my Lord Fairfax forces unto my Lord Newcastles forces in Yorkshire, by Thomas Crompton* (London: 23 January 1643). TT, E88 [19]; *A Relation of the taking of Leeds and Wakefield by Sir Thomas Fairfax* (London: 23–24 January 1643). TT, E88 [23].

23 BL, Ms Add 31116, f.53v.

24 TNA, SP28/313/4, unfol.

the defending troops.[25] Though Cromwell, who was present at the siege, received most of the credit for the victory, he possessed no formal authority in Lincolnshire, and was socially outranked by the local commanders, Sir Miles Hobart and Irby himself. Following the culmination of Irby's commission on 2 May 1643 his dragoon regiment, then of a single company strength, came under the command of Captain Thomas Atkins, who had been the unit's second cornet.[26]

Colonel James Wardlaw of Pitreavie Castle, Fife, was given command of the second regiment of dragoons in Essex's army. Wardlaw had previously been in Swedish service, though in 1632 he was a Sergeant-Major in Colonel Alexander Leslie's regiment, which departed to Russia during the Smolensk campaign. In April 1640, as a Lieutenant-Colonel, Wardlaw returned to Scotland to enlist the Army of the Covenant, but the vessel he was in was driven into Newcastle where he remained for a month before being imprisoned in York Castle. He applied for compensation from the Scottish Parliament on 17 August 1641, but by the following year found himself in the service of the Earl of Essex.[27] By 1 September 1642, Wardlaw had been commissioned Colonel of a dragoon regiment, consisting of six companies.[28] The companies were commanded by Captain-Lieutenant George Dundas (in charge of the Colonel's company), Captain Archibald Hamilton, Captain Alexander Nerne, Captain John Barne, Captain James Stenchion and Captain Forbes, the regimental surgeon was James Heithley.[29] As the names of some of these captains suggests, Wardlaw's regiment was almost entirely officered by Scots, who are likely to have had previous military experience on the Continent. On 16 September 1642, a warrant was issued to supply the regiment from the Tower stores with 600 muskets, 600 swords with belts, 600 bandoliers, 2,000lb of powder and shot proportional.[30] That no match was issued implies that the firearms that were issued to Captain Nerne on 19 September and referred to as 'bastard muskets' were essentially snaphaunces or firelocks.[31] Wardlaw's dragoons were administered differently to that of Colonel John Browne's regiment in October 1642, in that disbursements of pay to himself, his officers, and his soldiers was authorised by 'blended warrant' rather than by individual documents.[32]

One such warrant, dated 28 October 1642, ordered the payment of money to:

---

25 *Speciall Passages and Certain Informations*,18–25 April 1643; and 2–9 May 1643; *Certain Informations*,1–8 May 1643; Peter Gaunt, 'Learning the Ropes in 'His Own Fields': Cromwell's Early Sieges in the East Midlands', *Cromwelliana* (2003), pp.27–39.

26 TNA, SP28/298, f.326r.

27 *CSPD*, 1639–40, p.64; Robert Frost, 'Scottish soldiers, Poland-Lithuania and the Thirty Years' War', Steve Murdoch (ed.), *Scotland and the Thirty Years' War, 1618–1648* (Leiden: Brill, 2001), pp.191–213.

28 TNA, SP28/2B, f.318r; TNA, SP28/146, ff.400r–406v

29 *List of the Army*. TT, E117 [30].

30 TNA, WO/55/1754.

31 TNA, WO/55/1937.

32 TNA, SP28/2A, f.318r.

> Colonel James Wardlaw, Colonel of a regiment of dragoons, as well as pay for the officers of the said regiment for 14 days from the 15th day of this instant October inclusive, to the 29th day of the same month, exercising £187 19s 0d; as also for the pay of 600 dragoons for 14 days from the fifteenth day of this instant October inclusive, to the 29th day of the same month, £720; and for the pay of 12 sergeants, 23 corporals and 12 drummers for the same time £72; in all the sum of £940 19s 0d.[33]

However, by early December 1642, Wardlaw's regiment mustered six captains, six lieutenants, six cornets, 12 sergeants, 18 corporals and 5 drummers, but only 210 dragoons.[34] This clear decline in the unit's strength – which might have been partly caused by losses when the regiment, or at least two companies belonging to the regiment, saw action at Brentford on 12 November – could be the main reason why its pay continued to authorised by blended warrant. In the following year, the strength of the unit was reduced to a single company of 120 soldiers under Captain George Dundas, which was attached to the Earl of Essex's regiment of Horse.[35] In July 1644, a single company of nine officers and 65 men was mentioned by the Royalist soldier and antiquary, Richard Symonds in his diary.[36] The reason for such an apparently significant decrease in the unit's strength is unclear, but Wardlaw may have taken most of his regiment with him when he left Essex's army to become Governor of Plymouth.

In January 1644 Wardlaw was replaced by Sir William Gould. However, Wardlaw's petition to Parliament, dated 4 September 1644, resulted in a payment of £200 to be deducted 'out of the arrears due unto him for his service in the Lord General's army as a Colonel of a regiment and Captain of a company of dragoons.'[37] Wardlaw's regiment was present during the Edgehill campaign, although its role remains unclear. During the fighting at Brentford, a strategic river crossing on the Thames, on 12 November 1642 Prince Rupert's cavalry and dragoons advanced to the outskirts of the town under a dense morning mist. The Parliamentarian infantry regiments of Colonel Denzil Holles and Lord Brooke (both of which had served at Edgehill in Essex's forces) holding fortified positions, were all but destroyed during the fierce fighting. Holles' redcoats had three of their company commanders killed and at least 249 men taken prisoner, and ceased to exist a month later, while Brooke's regiment was disbanded on 10 December.[38] During the stand off between the main field armies at Turnham Green the next day, the King's forces faced Essex's army, backed up by the Trained Band regiments of the City of London. On the left flank of the Parliamentarian positions, musketeers and dragoons were placed in the gardens of Chiswick House. The enclosed fields were described as 'thick enclosures, with strong hedges

33 TNA, SP28/2B, f.438r.
34 TNA, SP28/4, f.189v.
35 TNA, SP28/4, f.291r.
36 BL, Ms Add 17062.
37 TNA, SP16/503/1, f.1v.
38 Young and Tucker (eds), *Military Memoirs*, p.46; Peachey, *Edgehill Campaign*, pp.10–11.

and ditches, so lined with men as they could well stand one by another.'[39] It was during the skirmishing around these locations that two of the company commanders of Colonel Wardlaw's dragoon regiment, Captains Forbes and Archibald Hamilton, were reported to have been captured by the Royalists, suggesting that their men were involved in the action and perhaps suffered some casualties.[40]

Complicating the picture is the formation of a third regiment of dragoons in Essex's army under the command of Lord Brooke. By August 1642 he had raised a troop of 60 harquebusiers and on the 12th received £30 to purchase their scarves.[41] Brooke was also commissioned Colonel and raised a foot regiment of 1,000 men in purple coats in London that joined Essex's army in time to serve at Edgehill. As commander-in-chief of Parliament's Midlands Association, he placed a garrison into Warwick Castle, whilst on 6 October he received pay for 370 men and a further two weeks' pay for the officers of a regiment of dragoons. He was also furnished with £100 towards buying saddles and to transport horses to Worcester, and on 10 December received £150 for more saddles.[42] It remains unclear if Brooke's regiment was an entirely new command, or if he simply inherited parts of another formation.

Lord Brooke, a popular and effective commander, was shot and killed by a marksman whilst besieging Lichfield Close in February 1643, but his dragoon unit continued for another three months. One of the captains of a company of dragoons was Anthony Otway. He served in this capacity between 6 April to 3 June 1643, when his unit was transformed into a troop of Horse in Colonel Purefoy's regiment, although in 1644–5 it operated alongside other cavalry units in Warwickshire.[43] An undated warrant for pay to 'several soldiers which were in Captain Otway's troop and company of dragoons, and in arrears for both' includes the names of 26 men 'with divers others', who were to receive a month's pay at 1s 8d per day 'as dragoons before the assignations.'[44] Such a reduction in numbers must reflect the high level of 'wastage' among Otway's ranks. By comparison, Sergeant-Major Joseph Hawkesworth's cavalry troop of Colonel Purefoy's Warwickshire regiment, raised as a troop of 80 Horse on 25 April 1643, mustered 46 troopers in January 1644, 62 in December 1644 and 56 in August 1645, thus suggesting a much higher retention rate during a period of eighteen months.[45]

Captain Anthony Otway later alleged that he should not suffer the charges involved in the raising of the troop, which were the responsibility of the clerk employed by the gentleman who raised it.[46] The unit, which mustered 42

39 Young and Tucker (eds), *Military Memoirs*, p.47.

40 *A [sic.] Exact and True Relation of the Battell fought on Saturday last at Acton, between the Kings Army, and the Earle of Essex his forces: With the number that were slain on both sides* (London: 14 November 1642). TT, E.127 [8]; *Certaine Speciall and Remarkable Passages*, 12–18 November 1642.

41 TNA, SP28/1A, f.102r.

42 TNA, SP28/2A, ff.326r, 328r–329v, 339r; SP28/143, ff.28v, 59v.

43 TNA, SP28/136/33, unfol.

44 TNA, SP28/124/1, unfol.

45 TNA, SP28/121A, ff.167r.–167v, 178r; SP28/122, f.225r.

46 TNA, SP28/253B, ff.75v–76r.

troopers in January 1644, 44 in September 1644 and 48 in March 1646, was one of the most disorderly troops in the county due, perhaps in part, to its origins as a dragoon company.[47]

Following the capture of Lichfield by Rupert's forces after the second siege of the Close on 20 April 1643, among those mentioned as marching out of the surrendered garrison was 'the Minister's commander of the dragoons, under command of Captain Otway; [and] a commander of dragoons from Killingworth under command of Captain Peter Hunt.'[48] Otway's accounts record the levying and purchase of dragoon and cavalry horses from Warwick as well as various townships in the county in early 1643.[49] The Earl of Denbigh was appointed commander-in-chief of the Associated counties of Warwickshire, Staffordshire, Shropshire and Worcestershire in June 1643, and some references to contributions made towards dragoon mounts for his forces suggest that a formation survived, or was reconstituted after the conversion of Captain Otway and his company to a cavalry troop. Hence, Captain Walter Scott was paid as Captain of dragoons in Denbigh's regiment of horse from 11 December 1643 to 30 March 1645. Scott's lieutenant was William Smith.[50]

A further regiment of dragoons established in the Earl of Essex's field army in 1642 was commanded by Colonel John Middleton, a Scottish professional soldier with Continental experience, and by all accounts an energetic and capable officer. The unit consisted predominantly of the three firelock companies of Essex's own foot regiment, and the resulting dragoon regiment itself was never any greater than four companies strong. The three companies described as firelocks were likely armed with bastard, or lighter, muskets, because their numbers equate to the 300 weapons of this type issued to Essex's regiment from the Tower stores and received by Captain Ambrose Tyndall (one of the captains) on 3 September 1642.[51] These three companies may also have worn tawny orange coats, which had been supplied to Essex's foot regiment in September 1642. John Middleton was commissioned Colonel and Captain of dragoons on 3 September.[52] His regiment served during the Edgehill campaign, but on, or soon after, 22 December it was disbanded.[53] Following the mediocre performance of the Earl of Essex's horse at Edgehill, on 9 November Middleton received a commission to take command of the regiment of horse formerly of Lord Fielding. Middleton's dragoons were referred to in a pay warrant of 11 November as 'lately Colonel Middleton's.'[54] A warrant, dated 24 October 1642, was to pay 'Colonel John Middleton, colonel of a regiment of dragoons for 20 days' pay as well as the general officers of the field (the colonel excepted) £61 14s 11d, and also for

47 TNA, SP28/121A, ff.228r, 349v; SP28/123, ff.268r–268v.
48 WSL, Ms Salt 596.
49 TNA, SP28/136/33, unfol. ; SP28/136/28, unfol.
50 TNA, SP28/131/12, ff.14r–14v.
51 TNA, WO55/1937.
52 TNA, SP28/2B, ff.336r; SP28/3B, f.359r.
53 TNA, SP28/2B, f.420r; SP28/3B, f.335r; SP28/36, f.489v.
54 TNA, SP28/4, f.323r; SP28/3B, f.335r.

the pay of the officers and 90 soldiers belonging to his own troop for the same time £139 10s 0d, in all the sum of £198 4s 6d.'[55]

On 17 November, Middleton received £100 for mounting himself, and £120 as an allowance for three wagons, in addition to the sum of £170 'for and towards his pay as colonel and captain of the said dragoons from 3 September, being the date of his commission, to 24 October … for all amounting to the sum of £340 upon account.'[56] In late October 1642, the regiment mustered 331 dragoons, excluding commissioned and non-commissioned officers. The regimental officers paid in late October 1642 were: Surgeon Thomas Cooke, Quartermaster Richard Greville, Provost Marshall Phillip Cotton and Wagon-master William Bickerton.[57] According to a warrant of 18 October 1642 Cooke, 'surgeon of that regiment whereof Colonel John Middleton is colonel for so much to him advanced for the furnishing of his chest' was paid the sum of £15, while he was also advanced £12 'to furnish himself and two mates with horses'.[58] Middleton's company commanders received similar disbursements. Colonel Nicholas Devereux, Colonel of a regiment of foot in Gloucestershire, stated on 29 July 1646, that he had served as Lieutenant-Colonel and Captain of firelocks, then dragoons, by virtue of a commission the Earl of Essex (his kinsman) dated 15 April 1643; and under Colonel Arthur Forbes for five months and 14 days, with pay arrears (at £56 per month) amounting to £300.[59] However, a warrant signed by Essex reveals that Devereux had previously served as a Captain in the dragoon regiment of Colonel John Middleton during the Edgehill campaign, receiving pay for himself and his officers for their service between 14 and 26 October 1642, amounting to £35 5s 0d.[60]

On 18 October 1642, Captain Devereux received a the further sum of £81 0s 0d 'for the pay of his company of 72 dragoons in the regiment of Colonel John Middleton for 15 days to end the twenty-eighth day of this instant October.'[61] These details are confirmed by entries in the account book of Francis Vernon, one of the treasurers to the Earl of Essex's army, as well as other warrants that record disbursements to Lieutenant Thomas Lawrence and Cornet John Clayton, both of Nicholas Devereux's company.[62] Another company was commanded by Captain Ambrose Tyndall, an experienced officer who had previously been a lieutenant in Sir John Meyrick's regiment of foot in the Earl of Northumberland's forces against the Scots. In summer 1642. Tyndall was in Captain William Roberts's company of Charles Essex's regiment in the Parliamentary army designed for Ireland. He served in Charles Essex's foot, then in Middleton's regiment of dragoons from 13 October to 22 December 1642. A warrant, dated 19 October 1642, ordered fifteen days' pay for his company of 60 dragoons 'to end the twenty-eighth day of this

55 TNA, SP28/2B, ff.335r, 460r.
56 TNA, SP28/3B, ff.359r–359v.
57 TNA, SP28/3B, ff.335r–336r, 341r.
58 TNA, SP28/2B, f.420r.
59 TNA, SP28/154, unfol.
60 TNA, SP28/2B, f.412r.
61 TNA, SP28/2B, f.415r.
62 TNA, SP28/143, f.33r; SP28/2B, ff.305r–305v.

instant October' of £67 10s 0d.[63] Lieutenant Nicholas Halford and Cornet Thomas Sager were also paid with Tyndall's company.[64] Captain Robert Turner led the fourth formation. Like Devereux and Tyndall, he had formerly been a Captain of firelocks in Essex's own regiment of foot (in post by August 1642), but between October and November commanded a company of dragoons under Colonel John Middleton.[65] The firelock companies under Captains Devereux, Tyndall and Turner were converted to dragoons when the army reached Worcester on 24 September.[66] They participated in the fighting at Edgehill, possibly as part of Colonel John Middleton's regiment as they were paid with the unit during the weeks after the battle.

Another warrant, dated 19 October, was for the payment of £100 2s 6d to Tyndall 'for his company of 89 dragoons for fifteen days' service from 14 October 1642 onwards.' On 24 October Captain Robert Turner received £35 5s 0d for himself and the officers of his company for their service from 8 to 29 October. On 1 November, 48 dragoons from the same unit were paid the sum of £83.[67] Euseby Marbury is listed in various warrants during this period as lieutenant to Turner's company.[68] When Middleton's regiment stood down at the end of 1642 most of the dragoons returned with Captain Turner to the Earl of Essex's regiment of foot. Tyndall returned to the regiment on 22 December, taking over Captain John Skrimpshire's company, but he left in mid-1644 to become a reformado under Colonel Rowland Laugharne.[69] Devereux's men served under Colonel Thomas Essex in the West, before forming the nucleus of a foot regiment that garrisoned Gloucester and Malmesbury. Captain John Copley also commanded a company of dragoons in the Earl of Essex's army, though in which regiment is unclear.

Sir Richard Browne (1602-1669) From *A Survey Of Englands Champions*, Josiah Ricraft (London 1647) (Stephen Ede-Borrett collection)

63 TNA, SP28/4, f.314r–314v.; SP28/2B, ff.243r, 425r.
64 TNA, SP28/2B, f.305r.
65 TNA, SP28/1A, f.279r; SP28/2A, f.237r; SP 28/5, f.36v; *List of the Army*. TT, E117 [30].
66 TNA, SP28/36, f.482r.
67 TNA, SP28/2B, ff.337r, 424r., SP28/3B, f.299r.
68 TNA, SP28/143, ff.33r, 63r.
69 TNA, SP28/4, f.314, unfol.; SP28/17, f.66v.

On 1 June 1643 a Treasury warrant was made out for £50 for completing his company of 100 men.[70]

Sir Richard Browne raised and commanded a further regiment of dragoons associated with Essex's army. He was commissioned by Robert Earl of Warwick on 17 November 1642 to command all the companies of dragoons raised by the City of London and thereabouts, although one or two of the companies (probably those of Captain Francis Barker and Captain Salmon Nuttell) derived from Suffolk.[71] Browne was admitted to the Company of the Artillery Garden in 1622, and he became a wealthy merchant trading in timber and coal. As such, his Royalist adversaries sometimes referred to him as 'woodmonger'.[72] At the outbreak of war in 1642 Browne was the senior Captain in the Orange Regiment of the London Trained Bands. Although his regiment was raised and equipped as dragoons, it was converted to a foot formation on 14 February 1643, serving mainly as part of the garrison of Abingdon, of which Browne was Governor.[73] The dragoon regiment was established as seven companies of 100 men each, besides officers, but going by the 'Accounts of the Committee appointed to raise a regiment of dragoons to serve for the defence of the King and Parliament under the command of Colonel Richard Browne,' dated between 13 October 1642 and 6 January 1643, at least ten are listed:

Sergeant-Major Nathanial Whetham
Captain Joshua Browne
Captain John Bagshaw
Captain Salmon Nuttell
Captain William Jarman
Captain Henry Harbottle
Captain John Cluto
Captain Robert Terry
Captain John Gother
Captain John Okey[74]

An additional two – Captains Everett and Francis Barker – appear in early entries of the accounts for the raising of the regiment as commanding companies, but it is not obvious whether these officers were replaced by any of those listed above or transferred their companies elsewhere. A further question surrounds the existence of a colonel's company. The accounts mention that Richard Browne received the sum of £100 'for his advance money', whilst a further payment of £101 10s was made 'to Colonel Browne for his troop.'[75] This might actually refer to his own company of dragoons,

70 TNA, SP28/7, f.328r.

71 *CSPD 1641–43*, p.407.

72 For example, see *Mercurius Aulicus*, 17 February 1643; WSL, Ms Salt 477/13 (Letter from Sir Arthur Aston to Prince Rupert, 24 August 1644, mentioning 'Major-General Browne, the woodmonger, who lodges in Abingdon').

73 TNA, WO55/387, f.39r; SP28/144/2, ff.1r–7r, 28r–35v.

74 TNA, SP28/144/2, ff.1r–7r.

75 TNA, SP28/144/2,ff.30r, 33r.

although Browne's troop of horse is first mentioned on 13 November 1642 when a warrant was issued for 25 saddles towards its outfitting.[76] His cavalry regiment would not be formed until June 1644. Moreover, 'An Account of all the horse that marched forth with Major-General Browne from the 8th of June 1644, till the 8th of August 1646 and what hath been received by recruit,' contains details of the muster of six independent troops, seven troops of 'the Major General's regiment, three troops of Colonel Robert Martin's regiment and a troop of dragoons.'[77] The latter may have been the remains of Richard Browne's former dragoon unit that had converted to foot as part of his force based at Abingdon in late 1644 to 1645.

The accounts of Sir Richard Browne's dragoon regiment list the procurement of various items associated with the raising and equipping of such soldiers, ranging from mounts, saddles and furniture, swords and other accoutrements, halberds, footwear, hay for horses, horseshoes and the shoeing of horses, as well as the sum of £15 paid to Hugh Croxton, a London manufacturer, for regimental standards.[78] Browne's dragoons were formed too late for the Edgehill campaign, although it was reported in Parliament on 25 November that 'these dragoons, since 29 October, have absented themselves from their colours, and have refused to be mustered, and have sold their horses and their arms.'[79] Given the dates, these could have belonged to some of the earliest recruited companies, perhaps those brought from Suffolk. Captain Gilbert Barker had received £40 advance money and a pair of pistols on 13 October 1642. Other regimental officers paid in November 1642 were Surgeon Henry Meredith and Preacher John Leyton.[80]

Sir John Seaton's regiment of dragoons was also raised in the autumn of 1642. Seaton was a professional soldier, who had served in the Swedish army alongside his brother in the 1620s and 1630s. In 1620, 1,000 soldiers of the Scots-Dutch brigade under Colonel Seaton's command were sent to safeguard Elizabeth Stuart in Bohemia.[81] Sir John was described in October 1642 as 'a brave and valiant Scottish commander.'[82] His dragoon regiment, recruited partly in London from veterans from the Netherlands, where Seaton had previously served, originally comprised nine companies, although a tenth was added when Captain John Sparrow was commissioned to raise 120 dragoons around 30 November.[83] Seaton's regiment was certainly operational by early September 1642. However, despite Parliament's order of 6 August 'that all the soldiers shall have delivered unto them at their first marching, coats, shoes, shirts and caps in all to the value of 17s 0d for every man' some

76 TNA, SP28/262, f.19r.

77 TNA, SP28/144/2, ff.24r–25r; BL, Ms Add 5247, f.39v.

78 TNA, SP28/144/2, f.31r.

79 *CJ*, II, p.863.

80 TNA, SP28/144/2, ff.1r, 30r–31r.

81 Josef V. Polišenský, *Tragic Triangle: The Netherlands, Spain and Bohemia, 1617–1621* (Prague: Univerzita Karlova, 1991), p.181.

82 *England's Memorable Accidents*, 17–24 October1642; George Ormerod (ed.), *Tracts Relating to Military Proceedings in Lancashire during the Great Civil War* (Manchester: Chetham Society, 1844), p.60.

83 TNA, SP28/44, f.62r; SP28/4, ff.359r, 361v; SP28/5, ff.115r, 204v–206v, 334r, 340v, 452r; SP28/7, ff.92r–92v, 452r.

of the regiments left the city without their clothing issue.[84] It is difficult to know whether this included any of the dragoons in Essex's army, however. Although still in the early weeks of the conflict, Seaton's officers and soldiers appear to have undertaken the tasks and operational methods that would later become synonymous with the dragoons of both sides. Colonel Seaton was sent from London to Oxford to demonstrate Parliamentarian authority. According to one Parliamentarian newsbook, on Thursday 8 September:

> Captain Lee, Captain Stackhouse, and Captain Mason, towards the evening marched out of the City of London with two pieces of ordnance, and wagons of ammunition to Acton, and there took up their quarter that night. Captain Wilson with his company marching after them in the night rode to Uxbridge and quartered his men there, Acton not being able to contain them; and Colonel [John] Brown with his dragoons being to march the same way, wanting lodging there at Acton, crossed over from Acton [and] rode to Brentford to quarter there.

The following day, the writer continued, 'Captain Wilson marched from Uxbridge and quartered at Amersham, and in that afternoon drew his men into a body, and exercised them, and Captain Lee, Captain Mason, and the company of Captain Stackhouse did lodge at Chalfont St Peter, with their ordnance and ammunition.' On 10 September Wilson's company marched to Aylesbury, 'and there in the way met divers cavaliers that were conveyed up in carts towards London, being taken in the north, and guarded up by the High Sheriff's men of Buckinghamshire.' However:

> Captain Wilson hearing that they were coming drew up his men into a broad place in the rode that so they might have room to pass by his troop; and passing on further he drew up his men in battalia in a great cornfield on this side [of] Wendover, and so exercised his men on horseback, to see how his men could do execution on horseback if they should be set upon in a place that might be disadvantageous to them on foot; at last, having exercised his men, and hearing the other companies and the ordnance were coming he set forward towards Aylesbury, and half a mile on this side the town made a stand, that so all four companies might march into the town together, where they were received with much acclamation. Colonel Browne's dragoons coming about two hours after, there being no room in the town, they were constrained to go further to lodge themselves[85]

Two days later, Captain Lee's dragoons continued to Amersham, where they guarded a wagon containing money *en route* to Aylesbury. Similarly, Captain Mason's company marched to Missenden, upon which they searched the property of a suspected delinquent. We are also told that 'Captain Wilson he exercised his men this day twice, both morning and evening', whilst at

84 *CSPD 1642*, p.367.

85 *True Relation of the late proceedings of the London Dragoneers, sent down to Oxford, consisting of foure Companies under the command of Sir John Seaton* (London: 1642). TT, E118[39], pp.3–4.

Aylesbury Captain Stackhouse's company received a whole venison from the Countess of Caernarfon.

As Lord Saye neared Oxford in September 1642 Sir John Byron's Royalist troops, including 150 dragoons, left the city. When the Parliamentarian soldiers entered, they arrested Vice-Chancellor of the University, before demolishing the fortifications, confiscating the college plate (though later returning it) and searching the houses of recusants. According to *True Relation*, on 13 September:

> Sir John Seton came and commanded the dragoons to march towards Oxford, who was appointed under my Lord Saye to lead them, Captain Wilson's company being first drawn up into a body, Sir John marched away with them, and a mile or two on this side Oxford Captain Stackhouse his company overtook them, and there in a plain field Sir John commanded them to be drawn up in one body, and gave them some instructions which he would have them observe, and so marched forward with them, to Oxford. At one o'clock at night an alarm was given, and there came messengers running to one of the sentinels set without the town, telling him he had a discovery to make known, and that the enemy was coming; upon this, some horse went out, and before they could ride a mile and return with their discovery, Captain Wilson's company was drawn up into a body, and he stood at the head thereof, without the North Gate, expecting to give the enemy a salutation with a volley of lead, That night having set his sentinels, and given the corporals their charge, he marched about the city, to see how the townsmen did their duty in the managing their watch, at last returning towards his own court of guard, the sentinels knew their duty so well that they would not let him come within their army, but made him stand till the corporal came with his sword drawn, and pointed at his breast and took the word from his captain. And it being then morning they were all dismissed, and every of his soldiers repaired to his lodging.[86]

On 21 September, leaving Captain Bestney Mason's company in Oxford, Seaton's dragoons returned to London, Captain Lee's command foremost, with Captain Stackhouse 'being in the midst, and Captain Wilson with his company, marching in the rear.'

After Seaton's return to London, he was called upon to employ his professional expertise during a rapid move against Royalists in Kent, before he and the newly promoted Sparrow, 'two expert commanders', were ordered to Lancashire 'both to see their soldiers taught the use of their arms as also to encourage, direct and counsel them.'[87] On 29 September 1642 it was ordered that:

> the Lords and Commons in Parliament do conceive and find it so necessary that 1,000 dragoons, with some troops of horse should be raised speedily, and be set forth for the suppressing of the Malignant Party in Lancashire, and such other

86 *Ibid.*, p.5.

87 William Beamont (ed.), Edward Robinson, *A Discourse of the War in Lancashire*, Chetham Society, Old Series, 62 (1864), p.23.

> parts, as my Lord General shall appoint for protecting the well-affected people, and preventing of foreign power from landing, that it will not only be taken and resented by the House for an acceptable service in a time of great need, if any the well-affected and disposed persons of the City of London shall advance the sum of £16,000, for setting forth of such a power. But do declare, that such advancers shall have the public faith for the repayment of such moneys so to be advanced with interest after eight pound per cent. As also shall be taken into consideration by the House, for a further recompense of their so forward and pious act in a time of so great necessity and danger.[88]

These dragoons were to be raised in London and Southwark for service in the county. Hence, Parliament instructed that for their enlistment, 'All persons who are willing to go [as] soldiers in the service under Colonel Sir John Seaton as dragoons, are to report to Captain Henry Leigh at the sign of the Swan in Cripplegate, and Captain William Stackhouse at his house in Thomas Apostles, and there are to be listed for that service.' As Lancashire possessed a large number of Catholics, the county was a suspected invasion target for the Irish. It is likely that the reason for the use of the dragoons was to undertake coastal patrols to prevent the landing of Irish rebel forces on the long coastline of the County. On 8 October the sum of £15 15s was paid for 'nine dragoon colours with staves, belts, boots and swivels, and nine pairs of tassels and strings' for the regiment, although going by other evidence they may have been delivered some time earlier.[89] By 20 October, the force had begun its march to the relief of Manchester; in the face of Royalist threats to London, Seaton was diverted into the Earl of Warwick's force. Even so, by the end of the year he had continued his northwards dash, reaching Lancashire, where he took command at Manchester and was given a three-month commission.

The company commanders in Seaton's dragoon regiment in October 1642 were:

Colonel Sir John Seaton
Captain Jeremy Baines
Captain John Sparrow
Captain Peter Marrow
Captain Robert Hardy
Captain Richard Fincher
Captain William Stackhouse
Captain Bestney Mason
Captain Thomas Ayloffe[90]

When Sir John Seaton departed to Lancashire, his regiment remained behind under the command of Colonel George Melve as part of Essex's army. Pay warrants were issued for Melve as a Colonel and General adjutant

88 *LJ*, V, p.377.
89 TNA, SP28/2B, f.674r.
90 TNA, SP28/5, ff.204v., 225v., 334r., 340r.

for the army, before being given command of the regiment of dragoons on 19 November 1642.[91] By then the unit consisted at least five companies, and on 29 April 1643 it mustered 397 men, besides commissioned and non-commissioned officers, in ten companies.[92] The company commanders were:

Colonel George Melve
Sergeant-Major Jeremy Baines
Captain John Sparrow
Captain Peter Marrow
Captain Robert Hardy
Captain Francis Middleton
Captain Thomas Melve
Captain Thomas Maynard
Captain Hercules Langrish
Captain Simon Matthews

Jeremy Baines was a Captain in Sir John Seaton's regiment of dragoons between November and December 1642, and Sergeant-Major in the same regiment, now commanded by George Melve, by March 1643 and he was still with the regiment on 22 June 1643.[93] William Stackhouse had previously served as a lieutenant in the Green Regiment of the London Trained Bands during the summer of 1642. He was a Captain in Sir John Seaton's dragoons and was one of the officers identified in Parliament's commission of 29 September as one of the recruiters for raising the regiment.[94] Captain John Sparrow, evidently a professional soldier, led a company of Seaton's/Melve's regiment by 30 November 1642 until at least March 1643.[95] Peter Marrow was Captain from 30 November 1642 to at least early March 1643, whilst Robert Hardy served in Seaton's/Melve's dragoons in the Earl of Essex's army from late November 1642 until at least June 1643.[96] Likewise, Francis Middleton was in both regiments, remaining under Melve until at least June 1643.[97] Thomas Maynard by early March 1643 until at least late June 1643. Thomas Ayloffe was a Captain in Sir John Seaton's regiment, presumably enlisting when the dragoons briefly came under the authority of the Earl of Warwick in October 1642. He stayed in the regiment when it passed to Colonel Melve, until 25 March 1643, when he received a commission as Colonel of a regiment of foot in the Eastern Association Army.[98] Ayloffe was succeeded as Captain of dragoons by Hercules Langrish, who served up to June 1643, but during the following month he transferred to Colonel John Middleton's regiment of dragoons.[99]

91 TNA, SP28/3B, f.406r.
92 TNA, SP28/7, ff.320r., 452r.
93 TNA, SP28/5, f.204v; SP28/7, f.444r.
94 Ormerod, (ed.), *Military Proceedings*, pp.40–1.
95 TNA, SP28/4, f.359r; SP28/5, ff.204v–206r, 340r.
96 TNA, SP28/4, f.361r; SP28/5, f.205r–206r, 334v, 452r.
97 TNA, SP28/5, f.206r, 452r.
98 TNA, SP28/4, f.362r; SP28/5, ff.204v–206r.
99 TNA, SP28/5, ff.205r–206r.; SP28/7, f.320v, 452r.; SP28/9, f.216r.

Captain Richard Fincher received the sum of £100 on account for his company on 24 January 1643, when it was recorded that all his men were without horses. By 5 July, Fincher was a troop commander in Sir William Waller's regiment of horse, and later became Quartermaster-General of horse in Waller's army.[100] Thomas Melve was a Captain in the regiment commanded by Sir John Seaton and then under Colonel George Melve (possibly a kinsman) from late 1642 until the disbandment of the unit in summer 1643, but continued as a dragoon Captain in Essex's Army until at least February 1644.[101] Additionally, Simon Matthew signed several vouchers for the receipt of payments to Colonel John Middleton's dragoon regiment of Essex's army on 24 October 1642, and was himself paid on 19 November as 'captain of a company of dragoons for one half month, pay for the officers and his company, consisting of 37 men, amounting to £64 8s 0d.' The warrant for this is among those pertaining to Middleton's unit, and Matthew also signed vouchers for other payments to the unit. Matthew is the same officer who appears in pay warrants, dated 23 January and 25 May 1643, as commanding a company in Melve's regiment.[102] In addition to these officers, John Joyner was a lieutenant in Sergeant-Major Baines's company in Colonel Melve's regiment of dragoons, as confirmed by a pay warrant of 22 June 1643. Promoted to Captain and Lieutenant-Colonel respectively, Joyner and Baines transferred to Colonel Samuel Jones's regiment of foot at Farnham Castle on 5 July 1643.[103] Robert Fogge was chaplain to Seaton's and Melve's dragoons from at least late 1642 to 25 May 1643, and Isaac Smithers was the regimental surgeon.[104] According to a testimony of his service, another officer, Captain John Wood, 'did serve in the army under the Earl of Essex with the regiment of Colonel George Melve, as reformado captain to dragoons, from 24 February 1643 until 26 July 1643, during which time he behaved himself faithfully like a soldier.'[105]

During the Earl of Essex's Reading campaign in April 1643, the Lord General deployed a combined mounted force of cavalry and dragoons as a reconnaissance in force, to assess the strength and intentions of the King's army at Oxford. One Parliamentarian newsbook reported:

> That very night [23 April 1643] we sent a party of horse under the command of Colonel Middleton, and a regiment of dragoons under the command of Colonel Melve, to pursue Prince Rupert and make discovery of the enemy, who in the night time marched towards Dorchester [on Thames], where a great party of the enemy was quartered, and with intention only to give them alarm, but the scouts that were abroad were took, their sentinels slain, and our forces entered the town, killed forty at least, of which there were eight commanders slain in one house, who discharged pistols out of windows against our men, yet without hurry,

100 TNA, SP28/4, f.350r; SP28/5, ff.151r, 271v–272r.

101 TNA, SP28/5, f.171r, 205r–206v.; SP28/7, f.93r; SP28/8, f.139r; SP28/12, f.125v.

102 TNA, SP28/2B, ff.335r–336r, 460r; SP28/3B, f.500r; SP28/5, f.115r; SP28/7, f.92r.

103 TNA, SP28/7, f.444r; SP28/135, f.1v.

104 TNA, SP28/5, ff.206v–207r; SP28/7, f.79v; SP28/19, f.216r; Anne Laurence, *Parliamentary Army Chaplains, 1642–51* (Woodbridge: Royal Historical Society, 1990), p.126.

105 *CSPD 1645–7*, p.298.

> we took 140 horses, some of £50 price, and divers prisoners, some officers, and harbingers to the King, and plundered a little, and so retreated.[106]

The Lord General's letter to the Speaker of the House of Commons, written on 24 April 1643 read (in part):

> I hold it my duty to acquaint the Parliament with some passages that happened yesterday morning, and this last night: In the morning, about two of the clock, Captain Carr that commands Sir William Balfour's troop, with two troops more, being upon the guard at Caversham, to take care that no provisions should be put into the town, the General Ruthven, with some 2,500 Horse and dragoons, namely, seven regiments of horse, and two or three hundred dragoons, surprised two sentinels; but, having the alarm, our troops charged with 40 horse, and so retreated to Colonel Barclay's regiment, that was drawn over the bridge. The enemy charging, the musketeers gave fire (having Colonel Holborne with his musketeers) so resolutely, that they wheeled about and went away, our few horse following them three miles, their intention was to put in 40 barrels of powder.
>
> That evening, I sent out Colonel Middleton and Colonel Meldrum with horse, and Colonel Melve with four troops of his dragoons, to find out the enemy; they fell in about eleven at night at Dorchester, where the King's Lifeguard of Foot lay, and the King's Standard, which they knew not of till afterwards. If the soldiers could have been kept from plundering, they might have done much more; but, there being four troops of horse there, besides the regiment, and in danger of having Wallingford cut the passage between them and us, they only routed most of that regiment, took the Captain-Lieutenant to the guards, one other lieutenant, two of the King's harbingers, 40 prisoners, 150 horse, one cornet, which they say was Sir Thomas Aston's[107]

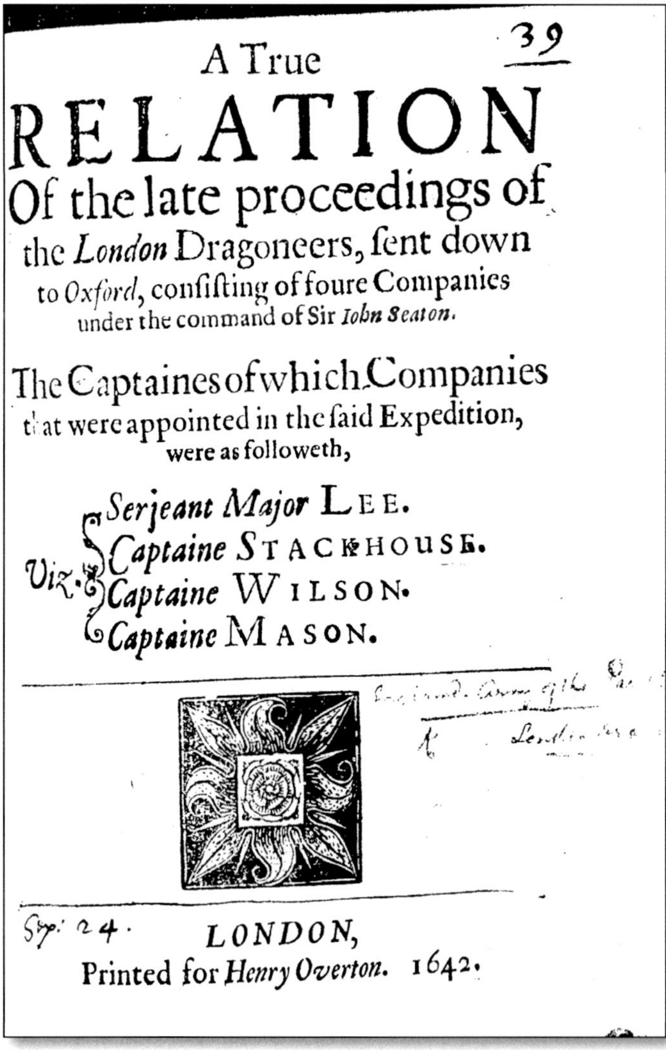

A True RELATION Of the late proceedings of the *London* Dragoneers, ſent down to *Oxford*, conſiſting of foure Companies under the command of Sir *Iohn Seaton*.

The Captaines of which Companies that were appointed in the ſaid Expedition, were as followeth,

Viz. *Serjeant Major* LEE. *Captaine* STACKHOUSE. *Captaine* WILSON. *Captaine* MASON.

LONDON, Printed for *Henry Overton*. 1642.

A True Relation of the Late Proceedings of the London Dragooners (1642) (Open source)

106 *Kingdomes Weekly Intelligencer*, 25–27 May 1643.
107 *LJ*, VI, p.17.

Colonel George Melve's dragoons were once more in action during the Chalgrove campaign of June 1643. Having captured Reading in late April the Earl of Essex allowed the defeated Royalist garrison to march out to unite with the King at Oxford, but sickness (probably in the form of typhus) exacerbated by chronic desertion, had devastated Essex's army and consequently prevented any follow-up strategic operations. On 7 June, the Earl wrote to the Essex Parliamentary Committee at Chelmsford, thanking them for supplying arms for the public service, but he also urged them to mount as many cavalry troopers and dragoons as they could, and send them to the army as quickly as possible.[108] During the evening of 17 June 1643, Prince Rupert led a raiding force, composed of 1,000 horse, 500 dragoons and 500 foot, from Oxford with the intention of intercepting a Parliamentarian convoy and generally harassing any enemy outposts to the southeast of Oxford. In the early hours of the following day, Rupert's forces overran the enemy quarters at Postcombe and Chinnor, and in the ensuing struggle the Parliamentarian troops were overwhelmed, losing around 200 casualties. According to *A True Relation of a Great Fight Between the Kings Forces and the Parliaments, at Chinner neer Tame on Saturday last*:

> Within lay some 200 dragoons of Sir Samuel Luke's Bedfordshire regiment, under their Sergeant Major Edwards. These, though, but new levied men, yet had already actually appeared in rebellion as being of that strong party, which the day before had marched out against Islip ... Almost all their horses and arms were taken, with three of Sir Samuel Luke's dragoon cornets. Their field or ground was black, with one, two, three, four, or five bibles, bossed and buffed, depainted in them.[109]

The Parliamentarian reaction to the raid was swift. As Essex's letter from Thame to the Speaker of the House of Commons – written on 19 June, partly to disguise the extent of the subsequent Parliamentarian setback at Chalgrove – detailed:

> Sir Philip Stapleton, who had the watch here that night at Thame, when he discovered the fire there, to know the occasion of it, he likewise sent one troop of dragoons under the command of Captain Dundas, who came up to them. There were likewise some few of Colonel Melve's dragoons that came up to them: at length our men pressed them so near, that being in a large pasture ground they drew up, and notwithstanding the inequality of the numbers, we not having above 300 Horse, our men charged them very gallantly, and slew divers of them; but while they were in fight, the enemy being so very strong, kept a body of Horse for his reserve, and with that body wheeled about and charged our men in the rear, so that being encompassed and overborne with multitude, they broke and fled, though it was not very far.

108 BL, Ms Egerton 2476, f.136r; HMC, *Seventh Report*, p.551.

109 *A True Relation of a Great Fight Between the Kings Forces and the Parliaments, at Chinner neer Tame on Saturday last* (London: 1643).TT, E.55 [11].

The primary Royalist account of the fight, generally thought to have been written by Prince Rupert's engineer, Bernard de Gomme, provides a detailed picture of events, and in particular, the deployment of dragoons:

> His Highness was now making halt in Chalgrove cornfield: about a mile and half [*sic.*] short of Chiselhampton Bridge. Just at this time (being now about nine o'clock) we discerned several great bodies of the rebels' horse and dragoons, coming down Golder Hill towards us from Easington and Tame, who (together with those that had before skirmished with our rear) drew down to the bottom of a great close, or pasture, ordering themselves there among the trees beyond a great hedge, which parted that close from our field … [There] marched some 350 under my Lord Wentworth, their Sergeant-Major-General, drawn altogether out of his lordship's own troop, Prince Rupert's regiment, commanded by Colonel Innes, Sir Robert Howard's and Colonel Washington's regiments … the van of this great party was a lesser party commanded by Sergeant-Major Legge, made up of the Prince of Wales his regiment, under Lieutenant-Colonel Lisle. These marched like a forlone-hope, a distance before the greater party.[110]

At about 8:45 am, Essex's horse and dragoons advanced towards a feature known as 'the Great Hedge', a double line of thick, shoulder-high hedgerows used to mark parish boundaries, and prevent cattle from straying. Colonel John Dalbier, a German professional soldier, in command of the Parliamentarian dragoons ordered them up to the hedge, where they opened fire on the Royalist cavalry, prompting Rupert into an attack. The Prince's troops successfully cleared the hedge line as his Lifeguard 'jumbled over after him.' Dalbier's dragoons initially held their ground but were greatly outnumbered:

> The better to entice them on, the Prince with his horse made show of a retreat, whereupon the rebels advanced cheerfully, doubling their march for eagerness, and coming up close to us. Then we discerned them to be eight cornets of horse, besides about 100 commanded horse, and as many dragoons of Colonel Mills (Melves, my Lord's *Relation* writes him) his regiment, now led by Captain Middleton. We were now parted by a hedge, close to the midst whereof the rebels brought on their dragoons; and to the end of it came their forlorn hope of horse.[111]

Although Rupert's intention might have been to fight initially with his cavalry, he nevertheless included a significant dragoon force in his strategy. It was reported:

> His Highness perceiving this great body, took care first of all how to secure the pass over Chiselhampton Bridge, for making good the retreat to us, lest other enemies as yet undiscovered, might cut it off from us. For this purpose Colonel

110 *His Highnesse Prince Ruperts Late Beating up the Rebels Quarters At Post-comb and Chinner in Oxfordshire And his Victory in Chalgrove Feild [sic], on Sunday morning June 18 1643* (Oxford: 1643).

111 *True Relation of a Great Fight.*

> Lunsford and Colonel Washington being sent with all the foot to lie on both ends [of] the bridge, the Prince's next design was to line the hedges along the lanes that led thither. For this purpose my Lord Wentworth and his Lieutenant Colonel, Mr John Russell were sent beforehand with their dragoons, for his Highness well hoped the rebels might be trained into that ambush.[112]

The Parliamentarian cavalry engaged Rupert's troopers with pistol and carbine fire, but they were driven from the field after sustaining a not inconsiderable number of losses in killed, wounded and captured. How many of these were among the dragoons remains unclear. One of the Parliamentarian casualties was Colonel John Hampden, who during the fighting was badly wounded, either shot in the shoulder or incapacitated when his own pistol exploded, and he died of his wounds a week later. Colonel George Melve's regiment was broken up before the Gloucester campaign of summer 1643. Nonetheless some of its soldiers remained in service for some months longer, some being transferred to Waller's army, and others attached to various regiments of horse in Essex's army.[113]

On 1 August 1643 the Deputy Lieutenants of the County wrote to the Lord General that the 'vast charges on the well-affected in Essex' prevented any large scale recruitment among the trained band regiments that had served previously with the Earl's army during the Reading campaign. They implored him that:

> the broken companies of these forces may be completed by putting many into one, so as to make up full numbers, to be commanded by such of their country captains as the earl shall find fit. This will save the expense of officers in command of a smaller number of men. They wish to have one regiment formed of all the foot that were sent out of their three regiments there, and who marched up so distinguished, all of which are only equal to one regiment. They ask also that the earl will order that the dragoons may all be contracted into such companies only as may be completed[114]

Equally, one of the greatest impediments in raising and retaining soldiers was the lack of available pay. When, in April 1643, Lord Grey's brigade rendezvoused with Essex's forces besieging Reading, troops deserted due to mounting arrears of pay. A number of these were 'freshwater soldiers' and needed to be reinforced by Essex's veterans, but during July Sir Thomas Barrington's regiment of foot had been reduced to 200.[115] Additionally, among accusations of plundering, Sir Thomas Martin's Cambridgeshire cavalry troop lost 29 troopers through desertion. The strength of the dragoon companies in the Eastern Association Army was equally depleted.[116] In the following July the collectors for the Essex Committee had reported that they

---

112 *His Highnesse Prince Ruperts Late Beating up.*

113 TNA, SP28/5, ff.204r–206v; SP28/7, f.444r; SP28/9, f.216r.

114 BL, Ms Egerton 2646, f.138r; HMC, *Seventh Report*, p.557.

115 *Certaine Informations*, 8–15 May 1643; *Kingdom's Weekly Intelligencer*, 7–14 May 1643.

116 BL, MSS Egerton 2646, ff.269r; 2647, ff.45r, 47r, 49v, 87v, 118r; TNA,SP28/5, f.171r, 205r–206v.

had gathered 'many dragoons and foot, who are willing to return to the army, if they may have their pay due; some would be content only with advance and assurance of their pay when they come there.'[117]

As Parliament's New Model Army was forming in the spring of 1645, Major-General Richard Browne was placed in command of the siege operations at Oxford while Sir Thomas Fairfax, its commander-in-chief, drew his regiments away from the city in pursuit of the King, who was advancing towards Leicestershire. Browne was in London in early June 1645 to speed up the sending out of troops to him, and when he came back to Abingdon on 4 June it was proclaimed that 'the Auxiliaries of Southwark and Westminster are speedily to be completed and in a readiness for that purpose.' The preceding campaigns had revealed increasing difficulty in bringing the London Militia regiments up to strength and coaxing or compelling them to march out of the city. On this occasion, however, the Southwark and Westminster men did not leave London at all, and nothing more was heard of the plan. In its place though, the Commons passed an Ordinance on 18 July 1645 to authorise the recruitment of dragoons in the City of London and Middlesex for service in 'the three associated counties of Oxfordshire, Berkshire and Buckinghamshire.'[118] These were raised by voluntary subscriptions in the capital. This company of London dragoons was commanded by Captain Francis Hanson, previously a captain in Colonel Samuel Jones'/John Fielding's regiment of Surrey foot, which had been disbanded in April 1645.[119] The financial accounts of Captain Hanson record that upon his company's first muster on 15 August 1645 there was one Captain, one lieutenant, one cornet, a quartermaster, two sergeants, three corporals, two drummers and 50 dragoons.[120]

A muster roll dated 6 September lists only 21 dragoons. The appearance of only 21 dragoons here may not have been particularly significant, for the accounts mention, slightly confusingly, that the commissioned officers, non-commissioned officers and soldiers listed on 15 August remained on the strength of the unit until 14 September. A further twelve dragoons were paid between 19 August to 30 September 1645; whereas there was another payment for eight 'private soldiers' from 15 August 1645 to 22 May 1646. In all the company was paid the sum of £798 17s 0d, of which £105 0s 0d was derived from 'the three associated counties of Oxfordshire, Berkshire and Buckinghamshire.' When the company mustered at Henley-on-Thames on 15 September 1645 it received fourteen days' pay, amounting to £105 0s 0d. At this point Hanson described his command as containing 70 dragoons 'all mounted and armed.'

The raising of dragoons from the capital at this juncture may have been related to the realisation that in what was increasingly becoming a war of movement, such troops would be more useful than the auxiliaries, which were foot. On 8 September 1645, Parliament passed an Ordinance,

117 BL, Ms Egerton 2646, f.137v; HMC, *Seventh Report*, p.555.

118 *LJ*, VII, p.501.

119 TNA, SP28/131/1, unfol.

120 TNA, SP28/131/8, ff.1r–7r; E179/253/12, f.35r.

authorising the raising of 500 horse and 500 dragoons in London and the suburbs. These units served with Colonel-General Sydenham Poyntz's forces in the Midlands.

10

The Eastern Association Army

On 20 December 1642, the Lords and Commons in Parliament passed an Ordinance which invited Norfolk, Suffolk, Cambridgeshire, Essex, and Hertfordshire 'to join in Association with the adjacent counties, for the mutual defence each of other county.'[1] This was under the overall command of William, Lord Grey of Wark. In 1643 Huntingdonshire and Lincolnshire were brought into the Association. The counties which composed the Eastern Association were among the wealthiest agricultural regions of England, so the material base of the army allowed it to become the largest, best supported and best paid in Parliament's service.[2] Grey's forces formed a brigade in Essex's army between April and July 1643. On 9 August Edward Montagu, 2nd Earl of Manchester was appointed 'Serjeant Major General of all the Forces of the Six associated Counties Eastern Association' in place of Lord Grey.[3] He restructured the army and strove to improve the organisation and funding of the Association from his base at Cambridge. The Ordinance appointing Manchester also made it possible to raise new cavalry and dragoon regiments in the Eastern Association, as well as remounting and expanding existing units. At the core of the army were the Earl of Manchester's own regiments of horse and foot, as well as the increasingly potent cavalry under Colonel Oliver Cromwell.

Manchester's own regiment of horse was raised in late summer 1643 and fought at the battles of Winceby and Marston Moor (where it possessed eleven troops), before going into the New Model Army in spring 1645 under the command of Colonel Nathaniel Rich. Likewise, the Earl's foot regiment was initially mustered on 26 August 1643 and by any standards was a large unit, consisting of as many as 20 companies. In May 1644 Manchester's foot mustered 1,628 soldiers, besides officers; 1,053 in July 1644; 1,111 in September 1644; and 984 in January 1645.[4] The regiment served in all the major operations of the Eastern Association Army, including the siege of

1 *LJ*, V, pp.331, 340, 384; *A&O*, I, p.51.

2 Holmes, *Eastern Association*, pp.76–7; Alan Everitt (ed.), *Suffolk and the Great Rebellion, 1640–1660* (Suffolk Records Society, 1960), pp.40–1.

3 *CJ*, III, pp.198–200; *LJ*, V, p.145.

4 TNA, SP28/15, ff.255r–57v; SP28/17, ff.183r–203r; SP28/25, ff.1r–5r.

Lincoln, Marston Moor and Second Newbury, and was disbanded on 25 March 1645.[5] On 1 February 1643, Manchester commissioned the Scots Presbyterian, Lawrence Crawford as Sergeant-Major-General of the horse and foot, Commissary-General of the Horse, Colonel of a regiment of horse and captain of a troop of horse in the Eastern Association Army. Crawford was a highly experienced professional, having served in the armies of Christian IV of Denmark, Gustav II Adolf of Sweden and the Duke of Ormond's forces in Ireland in 1641.[6] He was instrumental in making the foot of Manchester's army, which he led at Marston Moor, an effective fighting force.

As a result of the reorganisation of the Earl of Manchester's army in spring 1644 his dragoon regiment, which was raised in Essex in August 1643, was consolidated and reorganised from ten weak companies into five full strength ones. The original companies were in a poor state, with less men and even fewer horses. Though some companies maintained a reasonable strength, numbers in the regiment were increasingly low.

Edward Montagu, 2nd Earl of Manchester, 1602-1671 Contemporary Engraving, c1646 (Stephen Ede-Borrett collection)

Between 1 January and 25 March 1644:

Captain William Miller's command consisted of a Captain, one lieutenant, one cornet, one sergeant, two corporals, one drummer, 20 dragoons with mounts, and a further 18 without.

Captain John Holcroft's company mustered a captain, one lieutenant, one cornet, one muster-master, one sergeant, two corporals, one drummer, eleven dragoons with horses, 31 men were without them during the whole period; five lacked horses between 1 and 25 March, whereas from 20–25 March six more went unmounted.

Captain Goddard's company for the period 20–25 March 1644 comprised one captain, one lieutenant, one cornet, three sergeants, three corporals, two drummers and 79 dragoons, each of them in possession of a horse.

Captain Carter's company mustered, from 1 January to 25 January, a captain, one lieutenant, one cornet, one quartermaster, three sergeants, three corporals, two drummers and 72 mounted dragoons, although another sixteen dragoons were in want of horses.[7]

5 Spring, *Eastern Association*, pp.60–2; Holmes, *Eastern Association*, pp.162–3.

6 *CJ*, III, pp.387, 396, 427–8; *CSPD 1644*, pp.11, 404, 423.

7 TNA, SP28/13, ff.61v, 564r–565v; SP28/25/2, ff.296r, 212r, 305r, 442r, 445r.

Partly because of the increasingly religious purge of the commissioned officers in Manchester's army in early 1644, preferring Independents over Presbyterians, only two of the previous eight dragoon captains retained their posts, and the vacancies were allocated to three outsiders. Captain Henry Cannon reportedly commanded a company of Cambridgeshire dragoons, but on 13 July 1644, he and his men were transferred to Major-General James Holborne's regiment of dragoons in Waller's western army, in which Cannon continued until April the following year when he became an officer in Sir Hardress Waller's foot regiment in the New Model.[8] Captain William Miller was Captain of dragoons, though he later served in Colonel John Pickering's, then the Earl of Manchester's regiments of dragoons in the Eastern Association.[9]

During the first three months of 1644, Manchester's army remained in winter quarters, but as it assembled for the campaigning season it was larger, better equipped and remunerated than it had ever been. However, unlike Waller's and Essex's armies, Manchester's was increasingly divided by religious tensions between Independents and Presbyterians. Yet it held together enough to operate successfully against the northern Royalists during 1643 to secure Lincolnshire for Parliament, and win important victories at Gainsborough and Winceby. The following May the army participated in the siege of Lincoln, before combining with the Anglo-Scottish army outside York. At Marston Moor on 2 July 1644, the Eastern Association Army played the major part in the crushing victory over Rupert, although its regiments remained inactive in the north for some months afterwards. However, during the four-week campaign culminating in the Second Battle of Newbury, fought on 27 October, the forces of Waller, Essex and Manchester adopted a defensive approach, thus squandering the chance to defeat the last of the King's field armies, and effectively bringing an end to the war. Cromwell, leading the Association's horse, principally blamed Manchester for the strategic and tactical failings of the Parliamentarian armies, whose commanders had avoided tremendous opportunities to engage with the enemy. Such failures had immense political and military consequences for the Parliamentarian war effort, and largely brought about the birth of the New Model Army in 1645.[10]

By the late summer of 1644, eleven regiments of foot had been raised in the eastern counties for service with Manchester, although four of these were on permanent garrison duty. But, during the year there was a dramatic decline in the strength of the Association's foot, caused by a combination of losses incurred the York campaign, sickness, desertion, and by the diversion of levies and recruits reallocated to the hastily formed force in the vicinity of Oxford under Major-General Richard Browne.[11]

---

8 BL, Ms Harley 427, f.146r; TNA, E121/2/2; E121/3/4; E121/4/1/130; Wanklyn, *Reconstructing*, I, pp.44, 63.

9 TNA, E121/1/5.

10 Abbott, *Writings and Speeches*, p.307; *CSPD 1644–5*, pp.149–50, 159–60.

11 *CSPD 1644*, pp.266–267, 281–282, 383; *CJ*, III, pp.582, 589; *LJ*, VI, pp.663, 677.

The extent of the losses to the army's dragoons is unclear. A Parliamentary Ordinance, dated 12 July 1644, ordered that as part of the reorganisation of the army, recruits for the foot and dragoons (the numbers for the horse are not supplied) were to be raised in the following counties and cities. In Essex, 2,112 foot and 360 dragoons; in Norfolk, the same; in Norwich, 124 foot and 20 dragoons; in Hertfordshire, 704 foot and 120 dragoons; in Huntingdonshire, 642 foot and 50 dragoons; in Cambridgeshire, 697 foot and 119 dragoons; and in the Isle of Ely, 342 foot and 58 dragoons. The total, including Suffolk, whose numbers are not specified but must be the remainder, was 8,545 foot and 1,445 dragoons.[12]

It was further ordered by Parliament that:

> the said respective committees, or any three of them, are men for this hereby authorized in their respective counties, cities, and service, to impress fit and able men for this service, and to imprison such persons as shall refuse to give obedience, until they reform thereunto. [They were also authorised] to reduce the said foot forces respectively into companies and regiments, and the horse and dragoons into troops, and nominate and place over them colonels, captains, and other officers, except the majors of the said regiments, whose several and respective companies are to be commanded by the respective lieutenants thereof to the place of rendezvous. Provided that no regiment of foot shall consist of less than 1,000 foot, besides officers, and no troop of horse or dragoons of less than 100, besides officers, and where any county is hereby to raise a less number of men then will make up an entire regiment, the several and respective committees of such counties and places are to meet together with what convenience they shall think most fit and to join their forces into regiments, as aforesaid

By January 1645, Manchester's army still contained a powerful cavalry arm of 44 troops of horse, the bulk of which had been raised prior to the commencement of the 1644 campaign.[13] Though some of the horse, including Cromwell's own regiment, had been raised in the early months of the war, the legislation passed at the time of Manchester's appointment of 25 July 1643, and a particular ordinance of 12 August for Essex, sanctioned him to raise an additional 6,500 horse in the Eastern, Southern, and Midland counties, and from London and Middlesex.[14] However, the poor showing of Manchester's army after the summer of 1644, a product of the Earl's altered conduct towards the war and his resulting refusal to perform the military role consigned to him, caused significant disenchantment among its political backers in Westminster. On 19 November, the Association announced that it could no longer shoulder the cost of maintaining its army and hence, in April 1645 it was incorporated into the New Model Army, of which it formed the largest constituent part. Four cavalry and four infantry regiments, and most of its dragoons became the pattern on which most of the others were established

12 BL, Ms Egerton 2651, f.201r; *A&O*, I, pp.472–4.

13 Holmes, *Eastern Association*, p.170.

14 *CJ*, III, pp.171–2, 177; *LJ*, V, p.446.

Most of the dragoons of the Earl of Manchester's army were recruited in Essex by the ordinances of 4 and 12 August 1643, which charged the county with mobilising 1,000 dragoons for service with Sir William Waller but raised in the Eastern Association.[15] Waller's own regiment of dragoons was formed from dragoons in the Earl of Essex's army of 1642 and was initially commanded by Colonel George Melve, but by spring 1643 Waller had taken command and the following year put it under the command of Colonel James Holborne.[16] After Edgehill, Parliament had appealed to the eastern counties' authorities to produce 1,000 dragoon horses with all speed, 'for god's sake'. The county of Essex responded eagerly, though Suffolk, which had received a similar request took a week longer to dispatch only one-third of the requested number.[17] Nevertheless, in August 1643, the Association mustered 8,545 foot and 1,445 dragoons (each figure being given besides officers); of these, the Essex Committee was liable for the maintenance of 2,100 foot and 360 dragoons.[18] However, by the following month their neighbours in Suffolk were still struggling to raise their allotted quotas. On 21 September, the Association Committee notified the deputy lieutenants of Essex that a contract for the raising of two companies, previously assigned to Suffolk was to be given to Norfolk, the former being 'far from it'. The Committee added, 'we hear this day that the dragoons are with Lord Manchester at Lynn.'[19]

Although the greatest part of Manchester's dragoons was recruited in Essex by the ordinances of August 1643, they were subsequently assigned to other counties for the purposes of payment until the centralisation of the finance of the army within the Association in January 1644. In July 1643, Sir John Meldrum and Colonel Oliver Cromwell were ordered to relieve the town of Gainsborough in Lincolnshire, which had recently been pressed by Royalist forces, and was a key link in their lines of communication between Newark and the Earl of Newcastle's headquarters in Yorkshire. During the military crisis of mid–1643, dragoon units belonging to the Eastern Association Army participated in key military operations in the region. Here Meldrum's and Cromwell's troops met on 27 July and inflicted a severe defeat on the Royalists threatening the town. Three days before, Cromwell's 600 horse and dragoons, with three companies of Essex foot had, following a brief bombardment, stormed Burleigh House, just south of Stamford.[20] On 5 August 1643, a member of the County Committee of Essex reported, 'The dragoons are to be paid on this day, and on Monday next a fortnights' pay. The foot soldiers are to have three weeks' pay next week. We have paid all the

15 *CJ*, III, pp.199–200; ERO, LIB/PAM 1/10/10 – *An Ordinance of the Lords and Commons assembled in Parliament for the speedy raising of 1,000 dragoons to be levied according to ability in the several hundreds of the county of Essex, for the safety of the Kingdom* (London: 15 August 1643).

16 TNA, SP28/3B, f.406r; SP28/5, ff.204r, 225r, 334v, 340v; SP28/7, ff.79v, 94r–94v, 348r, 401r.

17 TNA, SP28/263, f.63v.

18 HMC, *Seventh Report*, p.578.

19 *Ibid*., p.564.

20 *A True Relation of Collonell Cromwells Proceedings against the Cavaliers, 28 July 1643* (London: 1643); *Certaine Informations*, 25–31 July 1643.

captains of dragoons three months' pay, except Captain Rossiter, who, as I am informed, has not above eight or ten dragoons there.'[21]

It was originally intended that the companies should be filled with volunteers, but these were not forthcoming, and the Essex Committee was compelled to recruit more widely and use impressed men to make up the numbers.[22] By February 1644, the Eastern Association Army was due for a major reorganisation, which would enable it to take the field. Consequently, one newsbook reported, 'We hear that the Lord Manchester is at Cambridge, and Colonel Cromwell, recruiting apace, he will be 3,000 horse, 2,000 dragoons, and 10,000 foot, which army expect to march the first this summer into the field, and it may be, before the enemy is ready, though not before he is aware, and to be a formidable army of the southern powers.'[23] However, the projected force of 2,000 dragoons never materialised, and at the spring muster of the horse numerous existing companies were in a poor condition, with few men and less horses.

As a result of such deficiencies, in April and May Manchester's dragoon regiment was consolidated and reorganised into five full strength companies. However, this involved the dismissal of some officers from their posts and the appointment of various Independents. Just two of the previous eight dragoon captains were preserved, and the vacant posts were allocated to three outsiders, two of whom were Independents – Captain Christopher Mercer, whose religious opinions are unknown, and Sergeant-Major Isaac Ewer, the later regicide.

On 14 January 1643 Cromwell, with his own cavalry troop and some dragoons broke up a pro-Royalist meeting in the marketplace at St Albans. After a brief mêlée around the gates of the *Great Red Lion* Inn, the dragoons 'dashed suddenly' upon Sir Thomas Coningsby, the High Sheriff of Hertfordshire, who had been attempting to read a Royalist proclamation, before he was arrested.[24] When on 28 July 1643, Cromwell was made Governor of the Isle of Ely, the Cambridgeshire Trained Band was mobilised to garrison the city. This was probably an auxiliary regiment of the trained band, which served up until 1647. On 26 May 1645, Cromwell was instructed to leave the siege of Oxford and to reinforce Ely, to bar any Royalist approaches to the borderland between the Eastern Association and disputed territory to the north.[25] On 12 August 1645, the Committee of Both Kingdoms ordered Colonel Francis Russell, who had replaced Cromwell as Governor of Ely, to maintain a garrison of 500 foot and 100 dragoons at a charge of £250 per week. In common with other garrison formations, the dragoons were led by various officers. Captain Francis Underwood, who is known to have commanded a company of foot by 1 April 1644, also led the dragoons at Ely and during the successful Parliamentarian operations

21 BL, Ms Egerton 2647, f.139v; HMC, *Seventh Report*, p.558.

22 TNA, SP28/26, f.335r.; SP28/27, f.86r.; BL, Ms Egerton 2647, f.166v.

23 *Parliament Scout*, 23 February–1 March 1644, pp.302–3.

24 *CJ*, II, pp.1000–1; John Vickers, *God's Ark overtopping the World's Waves* (London, 1646), p.246.

25 *CSPD, 1644–45*, p.530.

against Crowland Abbey.[26] The presence of such Eastern Association troops enabled not just a defensive posture to be maintained in Cambridgeshire and Huntingdonshire but made it possible to conduct offensive operations in southern Lincolnshire. Cromwell commanded some 'loose troops of dragoons' as Lieutenant-General of the Eastern Association Army, a term which might have referred to the Cambridgeshire trained band unit, or other more temporary and less recognised dragoon units, which are known to have served under him.

At least one company of dragoons was led by Captain Isaac Ewer of Sir Miles Hobart's regiment in the Association army. It accompanied this formation at the Parliamentarian siege of Reading in April 1643.[27] Captain Henry Cannon is reported to have commanded another company, although on 13 July 1644 he and his soldiers transferred to Major-General James Holborne's regiment of dragoons in Waller's western army. He continued in this role until April the following year when he became an officer in Sir Hardress Waller's regiment of foot in the New Model.[28] At some point, Captain William Miller was also a captain of dragoons, though he later served in Colonel John Pickering's, then the Earl of Manchester's regiments of dragoons in the Eastern Association.[29] When Colonel Edward Aldrich acted as Parliamentarian governor of Aylesbury, he had a small number of horse and dragoons under him. The latter, commanded by Captain Edmund Phipps (who claimed pay as Captain of a company of dragoons between 3 August 1643 and 13 May 1644) numbered 59 soldiers, besides officers on 16 November 1643. Phipps later served as Captain of a troop of horse in Buckinghamshire.[30] Three days prior to the Battle of Naseby in June 1645, the Hertfordshire horse and dragoons received orders to advance to Bedford, and there at the rendezvous appointed to meet the cavalry and dragoons commanded by Cromwell, marching from Cambridgeshire.[31]

On 6 June 1645 the Eastern Association Committee to the deputy lieutenants of Suffolk:

> The cloud of the enemy's army hanging still upon the borders, and drawing towards [Market] Harborough, make some supposals that they aim at the Association. In regard whereof, we have information that the army about Oxford was not yesterday advanced, albeit it was ordered so to do, we thought meet to give you intelligence thereof, and therewith earnestly to propound to your consideration, that you will have in readiness what horse and foot may be had, that so a proportion may be drawn forth for this service, such as may be expedient. And because we conceive that the exigence may require Horse and dragoons, we desire that all your Horse and dragoons may hasten to Newmarket, where they

26 TNA, E121/2/10; *Speciall Passages and Certain Informations*, 18–25 April 1643; *Certain Informations*,1–8 May 1643.

27 TNA, E121/2/9, unfol.

28 BL, Ms Harley 427, f.146r; TNA, E121/2/2; E121/3/4; E121/4/1/130; Wanklyn, *Reconstructing*, I, pp.44, 63.

29 TNA, E121/1/5; Spring, *Eastern Association*, p.69.

30 TNA, SP28/253A, ff.106r–106v; SP28/266/1, f.73r; SP 28/219, f.182r; SP 28/220/6, f.121r.

31 *Perfect Occurrences*, 11–17 June 1645; *Mercurius Civicus*, 11–17 June 1645.

> will receive orders for farther advance, according as the motion of the enemy and of our army shall require. And to allow both the several troops of dragoons and horse one week's pay, to be laid down by the owner, which shall be repaid out of the public money out of the county; the pay of each trooper being 14s per week, and of a dragoon 10s 6d per week. The place of rendezvous for the Horse and Dragoons to be at Newmarket; and for the Foot, Bury. Since the writing hereof, we received intelligence that the enemy's body with 60 carriages was upon his march towards the Association, three miles on this side of Harborough.[32]

When the Earl of Manchester's regiment of dragoons was reduced on 2 April 1644, effective command of the unit passed to Lieutenant-Colonel John Lilburne. Born around 1615, John was the elder brother of Henry Lilburne and younger brother of Robert, both Parliamentarian commanders in the north and, Robert subsequently in the New Model Army. John Lilburne, however, is better known for his religious and political activism, and his later role as a Leveller and radical. When the First Civil War began, he received a commission as Captain in the regiment of foot raised by Robert Greville, Lord Brooke. At Brentford on 12 November 1642, as the Royalists advanced on London, Captain Lilburne was the senior officer in the regiment in the absence of Brooke. With Colonel Holles' regiment it stood its ground and saved Essex's army. However, both were badly mauled and Lilburne was taken as a prisoner to Oxford. The Royalists planned to try him, as the first prominent Parliamentarian captured in the war, for high treason, but Parliament threatened to retaliate by executing Royalist prisoners, and an exchange was arranged. A later warrant records the payment of £49 10s 0d to 'John Lilburne, Captain of a company of foot late under the command of the right honourable Robert, Lord Brooke' from 11 February 1642 (being the day after the disbanding of the said regiment) to 15 February 1643, being two months' and ten days' pay.'[33]

On 7 October 1643 Lilburne's friend, Oliver Cromwell, offered him a commission as Sergeant-Major in Colonel Edward King's regiment of foot of the Earl of Manchester's Army of the Eastern Association. Cromwell was hostile towards King, a Presbyterian, and directed Lilburne to watch and report on him. Lilburne subsequently engaged in a lengthy religious dispute with the Colonel, while one of the regiment's captains Richard Beaumont, like Lilburne, was a radical dissenter with Anabaptist tendencies. On 16 May 1644, Lilburne was given command of Manchester's own regiment of dragoons with the rank of lieutenant-Colonel.[34] Of the circumstances of the receipt of his commission in the Eastern Association Army, he reported:

> After all these broiles with Colonel King, I ceased to be his major, and was afterwards made lieutenant colonel to the Earl of Manchester's regiment of dragoons, my commission bearing date the 16 May 1644, with whom I served faithfully and honestly, and being over active, his Lordship (in a manner) spoiled

32 Abbott (ed.), *Writings and Speeches* pp.198–9.
33 TNA, SP28/263, f.240r.
34 TNA, SP28/16, f.212v; SP28/29, f.330r.

> a soldier of me, by his abusing of me about the taking in of Tickhill Castle; which made me many times and often desirous to throw up my commission before ever the New Model was mentioned: but Lieutenant General Cromwell's persuasions of me to the contrary, made me hold it, much against my own mind, and then when the New Model came, he would have had me to continue, but I told him, I could not, in regard the Parliament had voted that all the officers in that model must take the Covenant, which I told him I could not do, and besides, I told him that I had served the Parliament faithfully out of a principle of conscience, (which to me was a greater tie then all the human Covenants in the world,) and never to my knowledge had given them just cause to distrust me: and if now after so much experience of my faithfulness they distrusted me, I was resolved not to serve a jealous master: so I was totally left out.[35]

The theoretical strength of a company in Lilburne's dragoon regiment was one captain, one lieutenant, one guidon, two sergeants, three corporals, two drummers and 95 dragoons. This was identical to the establishment in Colonel John Okey's New Model Army regiment in 1645, many of the officers and dragoons having derived from Lilburne's command. From February to March 1644 Lilburne's dragoons fought well at Newark, though he was plundered of all his possessions during Rupert's relief of the garrison on 22 March 1644. On 20 April, the Eastern Association Army was assembled at Huntingdon, from where they advanced towards Lincoln (which they seized after storming the city's defences and castle on 6 May), Stamford and Grantham.[36] The army then turned northwards, passing though Gainsborough, where it crossed the Trent on a bridge of boats. By 21 May, it had reached Doncaster, and following more than a week of atrocious weather, Manchester's regiments joined the Army of the Fairfaxes and the Earl of Leven's Scottish Army besieging York. On 3 June, Lieutenant-Colonel John Lilburne was shot through the arm during the storming of Sir Francis Wortley's manor house at Tankersley, near Wakefield. Shortly afterwards Lilburne sought permission to attack the Royalist stronghold at Tickhill Castle, as he had intelligence that the garrison was willing to surrender, but the Earl of Manchester refused. Against orders, Lilburne captured the castle with 200 dragoons without a shot being fired; he accepted the garrison's surrender on 26 July. In describing such events, he wrote:

> the day before the Lord Manchester quartered at Doncaster [20 May], at our rendezvous of the other side of the town next to York, I received orders from Lieutenant General Cromwell (from whom constantly I did receive my orders), to go and quarter with four of my troops of dragoons in Tickhill town, and to do the best we could, with our own security, to keep the enemy in, that they should not sally out, to do any mischief, in any of the quarters of the army: and accordingly I marched with four of my troops, and at the next town to it, we got the best guides

35 John Lilburne, *Innocency and Truth Justified* (London: 1646), p.46; *The Resolved Man's Resolution* (London: 1647), p.65.

36 Bod Lib., Ms Carte 74, f.159r; John Vicars, *Magnalia Dei Anglicana. Or, England's Parliamentary Chronicle* (London: 1646), III, pp.124, 217–9.

> we could, to inform us how the castle and town lay, and when we came to the town's end, I ordered Captain Beaumont, with a party on horseback, to care are into the town, and get betwixt their draw bridge and the town; to stop those that were in the town, from getting into the castle and sent to second him a party of musketeers afore, commanded by my lieutenant: and afterwards followed them with all the rest; by means of which we took divers horses and prisoners, and that night we all past upon the guard, and the next day being informed, that the mill dam, and the moat, might easily be drawn, if we could possess ourselves of the mill which stood close by their moat as soon as it grew dark, myself led down a guard of musketeers, and possessed the mill, and fell to work, to let out the mill dam, which was accordingly done, which when I had set in a good forwardness, I left Captain Beaumont's lieutenant to command that guard, who I knew to be a careful man, and walked the rounds to visit all the other guards myself, and being the next morning informed by some of the soldiers that the enemy's sentinels, called over the wall to mine, and wished they would speak to their commander to fall on, and they professed, they would not shoot a bullet against them, for their commanders used them basely, and kept their pay from them: upon which information, I inquired of my landlord, who I understood used to go into the castle, what store of powder, he conceived they had in the castle, and he told me, he did believe four barrels was the most they had, and withal told me, he was confident, they would upon easy terms surrender the castle, for the gentlemen within (said he) were no soldiers, nor no great fighters but were altogether given to their pleasures, and about 12 o'clock that day or the next, Colonel King, and a Captain of the Lord Fairfax's, came and desired me, to grant them liberty, to call to some of the gentlemen over the wall, which I granted: and they accordingly did, upon which by consent, we on both sides ceased shooting, and they talked very freely each to other, upon which the gentlemen in the castle, desired me to come into them; and be merry with them, an hour or two, and they would engage their honours, I should safely and peaceably come out at my desire, unto which I answered, I durst not, having no such commission from my general so to do, then they entreated me to give them leave to come out to me, to be merrie at the alehouse a little, and they would take my own engagement for their safe return, upon which discourse I presently conceived these gentlemen had no mind to fight, but were rather desirous, upon reasonable terms to be rid of the castle.

Of his regiment's more general conduct, Lilburne reported in the same document:

> during all the time we were in Yorkshire, I and my regiment of dragoons, constantly quartered in the van of the whole army; always nigh the enemy's garrisons, where constantly in a manner, we both fought for both horse meat and man's meat, or else with a great deal of vigilance, stood upon our guard, also our soldiers being so poor for want of pay, that many times myself and other of my officers, were several times forced to lend them money to shoe their horses, and I am confident to this day, have fallen short of the payment of it again, and yet I dare say, I kept the regiment in as good order, as ever it was from the day it was raised, and passed as readily and cheerfully upon their duty: And I dare be bold to aver it, I and they passed upon as hard and difficult services, and were in as

> many engagements, hazards and perils, for that time, the last summer, as ever any regiment of dragoons in England, raised by this Parliament, of the like number was[37]

Some dragoons were attached to the infantry brigade commanded by Major-General Laurence Crawford of the Eastern Association that assaulted the breach made near St Mary's Tower on 16 June 1644. Although at the end of the month, the Parliamentarians were compelled to raise the siege because of the approach of Prince Rupert's army, which was pressing forward to relieve the city. On 1 July, the Royalist cavalry surprised and drove off Lilburne's dragoons, who had been deployed to guard the bridge of boats over the River Ouse at Poppleton, which had been constructed to expedite troops to the eastern bank of the river and to establish communication between the allied armies. Rupert's troops thus crossed without opposition as they relieved York in their attempt to fulfil the King's orders to seek out and destroy the enemy as rapidly as possible.[38] Although outnumbered, the following day Rupert encountered the allied Parliamentarian and Covenanter armies at Marston Moor. Colonel Hugh Fraser's Scottish dragoons were positioned on the left flank of the Allied armies, but in his plan of the battle the Parliamentarian officer, Major-General Sir James Lumsden, mentioned the presence of a further 500 dragoons, being five companies of the Earl of Manchester's regiment of dragoons, commanded by Lieutenant-Colonel John Lilburne. Lumsden placed these to the right of Sir Thomas Fairfax's mounted front line.[39]

The presence of Lilburne's dragoons at the battle is confirmed by two troop lists produced shortly afterwards. The first, dated 11 July 1644, cites money distributed to the army's surgeons and mates for the treatment of wounded soldiers, and locates the companies of Lieutenant-Colonel Lilburne, Sergeant-Major Ewer, Captain Abbot and Captain Beaumont among cavalry troops belonging to Colonel Oliver Cromwell's and Colonel Charles Fleetwood's regiments of horse (both of the Eastern Association). Another schedule, drawn up for the purpose of paying a gratuity of a week's pay for service at Marston Moor, lists the same dragoon companies, in addition to Captain Mercer's.[40] The payment was made towards the end of the month, possibly on 23 July when the army reached Doncaster. An entry from the accounts of Sergeant-Major John Alford of the Earl of Manchester's regiment of horse states:

> July 1644: Also at Doncaster there was a week's pay given to all the troop excepting to the officers in commission by my Lord of Manchester as gratuity for their extraordinary good service at York fight, but what the sum was I cannot

37 Lilburne, *Innocency*, pp.22–23, 25.

38 Bod Lib., Ms Clarendon 28, f.135r; Parsons, *Diary of Sir Henry Slingsby*, pp.116–7.

39 Reproduced in Peter Young, *Marston Moor 1644: The Campaign and the Battle* (Kineton: Roundwood Press, 1970), plates 21–2; David Cooke, *The Road to Marston Moor* (Barnsley: Pen and Sword, 2007), pp.111–114.

40 TNA, SP28/17, ff.162r–174v; SP28/125/3, ff.419r–420r.

> directly tell but it was immediately paid out to the soldiers according to my Lord of Manchester's order.[41]

When the Earl of Manchester's dragoons were consolidated in spring 1644, Holcroft's company was taken over by Lieutenant-Colonel Lilburne as his own, and commanded by Captain-Lieutenant William Neale. Another officer dismissed from the regiment was Lieutenant-Colonel James Gordon, who petitioned Parliament on 30 June 1645, testifying that he had 'served as Lieutenant Colonel of dragoons under the Earl of Manchester, from 9 January 1644 until the reduction, when I was excluded, lately moved that his accounts should be audited, in order that he might receive satisfaction for his arrears, as other Scotch officers.'[42] After leaving the army of the Association, Sergeant-Major Sackville Moore and Captain Holcroft both received commissions in the force raised by the county of Essex in July – Moore seems to have been financially dependent upon military employment.[43] The dragoons were not mustered with the rest of Manchester's army after the Yorkshire campaign of 1644, instead remaining in the counties of the Eastern Association, where they rested and were re-equipped. On 12 September the Association's treasurer received a letter from the Sheriff of Northamptonshire, requesting instructions 'with respect to the disposal of 100 horses, which had been sent for Lieutenant Colonel Lilburne's recruits, and on which musketeers had not been mounted, as promised by Lieutenant-General Cromwell.'[44] The regiment was also active in local military operations throughout this time.

On 29 November, the Committee of Both Kingdoms informed the Eastern Association Committee at Cambridge:

> We need not urge on you how much the whole Association is concerned in the safety of the Isle of Ely, and how impossible it is for the men employed in its defence to subsist without supplies. We would therefore earnestly recommend to you that those forces under Colonels Rainborowe and Lilburne be forthwith supplied with money for their subsistence while they endeavour the reduction of Crowland and security of the Isle of Ely, and thereby the safety of the Association. We desire so ready a compliance with these directions that we may not either be obliged to give new orders or the Association be endangered by the neglect of these.[45]

Surviving muster rolls and Treasury warrants record that on 16 January 1645 Lilburne's regiment mustered 263 soldiers, besides officers, vizt:

> The lieutenant-Colonel's own company mustered one lieutenant, one cornet, one quartermaster, two sergeants, three corporals, one drummer, a drum-major, and 47 dragoons.

41 TNA, SP28/267/1, f.58v.

42 HLRO, HL/PO/JO/10/1/189; *LJ*, VII, p.466; HMC, *Sixth Report*, p.66.

43 BL, Ms Egerton 2467, f.212r; Holmes, *Eastern Association*, p.201.

44 TNA, PRO 30/15/3, no. 544; HMC, *Eighth Report*, App. II, p.61.

45 *CSPD 1644–45*, pp.155.

> Captain Burkett's command had one lieutenant, one cornet, one quartermaster, two sergeants, three corporals, and 55 dragoons.
>
> Captain Mercer mustered one lieutenant, one cornet, one quartermaster, two sergeants, three corporals, two drummers, and 74 men.
>
> Captain Beaumont's company consisted of one lieutenant, one cornet, one quartermaster, two sergeants, three corporals, one drummer, and 43 dragoons.
>
> Captain Tobias Bridge's commissioned and non-commissioned offers are unlisted, though 43 dragoons mustered for duty.[46]
>
> Disease and desertion may have taken their toll. Lilburne's own account of his men's service, being 'constantly quartered in the van of the whole army; where constantly in a manner, we fought for both horse meat and man's meat, or else with a great deal of vigilancy stood upon our guard' suggests the likelihood of a proportionally higher casualty rate than in the horse or foot.[47]

In early 1645, it was proposed by the Committee of Both Kingdoms that a combined military formation, made up of cavalry and dragoons from Essex's and the Eastern Association's armies, should rendezvous at Bedford to march to the assistance of Sir William Brereton's forces besieging Chester. The intention was that they would also be joined by troops from Lord Fairfax's army in Yorkshire and Parliamentarian troops from the Midlands. Thus, on 6 March 1645, the Committee of Both Kingdoms wrote to Manchester to request:

> Major-General Crawford with the 200 horse now quartered about Huntingdon, and the 200 from Northampton, besides two companies of dragoons under Major Ewer and Captain Abbott now about Newport Pagnell, and as many of Captains Mercer's, Beaumont's, and Lilburne's dragoons as he can speedily draw together, do march towards Coventry, where he shall receive into his charge such of the Lord General's horse as shall come thither under the command of Colonel Sheffield; as also such as shall come unto him from county Worcester, and from Colonel Fox, all which are to march under Crawford's command to the assistance of Sir William Brereton.[48]

Though Brereton was confident of capturing Chester, the arrival of Prince Maurice in the city in mid-February and Rupert in mid-March, frustrated all Parliamentarian operations in the locality. On 11 March, the Committee informed Sir William in a coded letter, 'On information that Rupert is marching towards you and doubting also that Langdale's forces may also [not] draw towards you, we have ordered forces from [Essex], [Manchester] and [Fairfax] to march to your assistance.' From a correspondent in London, Brereton was also informed:

---

46 TNA, SP28/18, f.256v; SP28/26, ff.160r–160v; SP28/27, ff.101r–103v, 129v, 144r; E121/2/1, unfol.

47 Lilburne, *Innocency and Truth*, p.25.

48 *CSPD 1644–5*, pp.336–7.

> I think the Committee of Both Kingdoms will let you know what they have done for the addition of forces to yours. They have ordered about 1,800 Horse and dragoons under Major-General Crawford to march unto you and, if Langdale marches to join Rupert, they have ordered the Yorkshire horse, Colonel Rossiter and some others to follow him. Today the Commons recommended to this Committee to treat with the Scots Commissioners about the speedy dispatch of the Scots army into the parts about Chester.[49]

Lieutenant Colonel John Lilburne at his trial (Open source)

Crawford's advance proceeded slowly and by 29 March he was still in Northamptonshire, but by now the Committee of Both Kingdoms, fearful of the movements of Princes Rupert and Maurice, informed him, 'We have received intelligence of the princes' retreat with their army out of Cheshire, and their drawing this way. We conceive that the [Eastern] Association may be in danger if you should march up to join Sir William Brereton, leaving the princes' forces between you and these parts'. The Major-General was thus ordered to march towards Aylesbury, from where his troops could defend the Eastern Association and ultimately bring the Association's forces under the authority of Sir Thomas Fairfax.[50]

A surviving warrant sheds some light on the final days of the Earl of Manchester's dragoons before the absorption of most of its numbers into Colonel John Okey's regiment of the New Model Army. The document authorised payments to the inhabitants of St Neots in Huntingdonshire for the quartering of the companies of Lieutenant-Colonel John Lilburne, and Captains Beaumont, Mercer and Sparrow, in addition to Sergeant-Major Montgomery's company of Manchester's foot regiment, for fourteen days between 19 March and 15 April 1645.[51] Captain Sparrow also quartered the 65 horses of his dragoons. The entire cost amounted to £88 3s 2d, with an extra

49 CRO, DDX/428, ff.15v–16r; *BLB*, I, 28–9.
50 *CSPD 1644–45*, pp.370–371, 378, 390–1.
51 TNA, SP28/29/2, ff.330r–331v.

£1 2s 4d paid out for stabling the mounts. An endorsement appended to the warrant, signed by Major-General Phillip Skippon, implies that Manchester's dragoons were formally reduced in mid-April 1645, although the sum for their quarter had been discharged at Reading on 8 April.

In April 1645, Lieutenant-Colonel Lilburne resigned his commission after refusing to sign the Solemn League and Covenant, which was required of New Model Army officers following the alliance between Parliament and the Scots. Whether he was ever considered to lead the New Model's dragoon regiment is unclear, but it remains a distinct possibility. Lilburne's pay arrears when he left the army amounted to £880 0s 0d.[52] Of the pay and commissions of his dragoons in Manchester's army, he wrote in his tract *The Resolved Man's Resolution*:

> And now in the second place, for money received by me when I was lieutenant colonel of dragoons, in which service I am sure I spent divers months and never received a penny, no not so much as to buy me a horse shoe, being forced to lend my soldiers money divers times to shoe their horses, part of which I lost for my reward, and I am sure that from February 1643 [*sic*. 1644] to September 1644, which was seven months' time, I received not 6d pay, and then as we marched to Banbury Leaguer, at Daventry town, I and other of my officers received at the hands of the Northampton Committee £800 as part of six weeks' pay, £215 of which Major Evers, my major had for his troop, and Captain Beaumont £185 for his troop, and Captain Abbot £180 for his troop, and myself for my troop £220, which then by my muster roll and debits dated from 25 March to 26 August 1644 exclusive, being 22 weeks, consisted of myself, lieutenant, cornet, quartermaster, two sergeants, three corporals, two drummers, and 85 common soldiers, which said money at that town's end was immediately paid to the troop, every common soldier having out of it six weeks' pay to pacify the mutiny they were in, and I am sure there was not one soldier in the muster roll but had it to a penny, and the officers slaid for theirs tell we came to Banbury, where I sent my quartermaster and other quartermasters to Mr Golson, the Treasurer for the rest of the six weeks' pay, which every troop then and there received; and I am sure mine was faithfully disposed of according to the muster roll to a penny, only as I remember, one or two had lost their lives at the castle before the last money came, and then after that siege we marched to the siege of Crowland, a service hard and difficult enough, where my cornet received £100 of the Cambridge Committee, in part of the foresaid debts, out of which I paid my officers and all my soldiers, then in being 14 days' pay, which according to the rules and practice of war I think is more than justified in strictness to have done, for 14 days' pay according to the forementioned debits comes to almost £130, all the slain and dead-pays of which tell the next muster, I might if I would justly have made my own, and then in my absence at Stamford as I remember my lieutenant made a new muster, from whom I received three weeks' pay, and he himself paid the soldiers their pay, I think justly, for when I came down to them at Sir Richard Stone's, near Huntington, heard no complaints from any of them. Where I paid them 14

52 Lilburne, *Innocency*, pp.25, 43, 46, 69; *Resolved Man's Resolution*, p.32.

days' pay I had received for them at London, and they having lately at Melton Mowbray had a skirmish with Sir Marmaduke Langdale, some of my soldiers were wanting, which my lieutenant told me he did confidently believe were slain, upon which at his desire, as I remember he paid three soldiers that he had listed since the last muster, but I was a looser by the bargain, for the soldiers supposed to be slain were only prisoners, whose pay after their deliverance I faithfully in Gloucestershire paid unto them, and this is all the pay to a penny I received as an officer of dragoons, being in all 91 days' pay, which for me, comes to £91. And from before Newark business, till we marched to Banbury, I never received a penny for myself, either of him, or my Lord Manchester, which then was but six weeks' half pay, and because my soldiers were promised six weeks' pay, as the rest of the army had, and had but three weeks' pay sent them, which set them all in a mutiny at Northampton, in the appeasing of which, I had almost lost my life amongst them, and was necessitated at Daventry (to get them to march) to pay the common soldiers all my own pay, and all my officers, and to engage my credit to them for their money, which we received at Banbury. And after this, there was at several times paid to myself and officers, seven weeks' pay.[53]

Other dragoon units raised from the Eastern Association Counties:

Colonel Oliver Cromwell's Regiment of Dragoons

When, on 28 July 1643, Cromwell was made Governor of the Isle of Ely, the Cambridgeshire Trained Bands were summoned to garrison the city. This was probably an auxiliary unit, which served until 1647. He led some 'loose troops of dragoons' as Lieutenant-General of the Eastern Association Army, a phrase which could have denoted this Cambridgeshire trained band formation, or other more temporary and less well-documented dragoon units, which are known to have served under him. In 1638, the Cambridge Trained Band contained 1,000 foot and 80 mounted soldiers, the latter being 30 harquebusiers and 50 dragoons. With other East Anglian militia units, they were selected for service in the First Bishops' War in Sir Simon Harcourt's regiment of foot, and in June 1640, they were transported to Newcastle for service against the Scots.[54] In common with other garrison formations the copious dragoon units were led by various officers at different times under the auspices of the Eastern Association. One such officer was Captain Henry Cannon. Although he reportedly served in Cromwell's regiment, on 13 July 1644 he was transferred to Major-General James Holborne's dragoons in Waller's army, in which Cannon continued until 30 April 1645.[55]

53 *Resolved Man's Resolution*, pp.35, 69.

54 Rushworth, *Historical Collections*, III, pp.1085–6.

55 BL, Ms Harley 427, f.146r; TNA, E121/2/2; E121/3/4; E121/4/1/130; Wanklyn, *Reconstructing*, I, pp.44, 63.

Captain Francis Underwood's Independent Company of Dragoons

Underwood commanded a company of foot in Cromwell's regiment of foot in the garrison of Ely by 1 April 1644. In 1646, he was promoted to major and lieutenant-Colonel, probably in the same regiment. He also led the dragoons within the garrison, and during the Parliamentarian operations against Crowland Abbey.[56] The following officers and non-commissioned officers are known to have served in Underwood's dragoons:

Cornet Edward Durdayne
Sergeant George Johnson
Corporal Ambrose John
Corporal John Haselwood
Corporal Thomas Lock
Corporal George Wright
Corporal Robert Cross

Colonel John Pickering's Regiment of Dragoons

Born in Titchmarsh, Northamptonshire, Pickering served as Parliamentary emissary and diplomat in its dealings with the Scots in 1641–3. In October 1642, he was employed by the Cambridgeshire Committee in the collecting of military intelligence on the advance of Royalist forces.[57] In August 1643, Pickering was appointed Commissary-General of the Musters for the Eastern Association Army. During the winter of 1643–4 he was commissioned Colonel of a regiment of dragoons, and though little is known of the unit, which existed by late December 1643, it may have been raised partly in Essex, like the majority of the Association's dragoons.[58] The majority of payments to Colonel Pickering's dragoons were made by the County Committee of Norfolk, though disbursements rendered by the Suffolk Committee at Bury St Edmunds on 28 January and 2 February 1644 might imply funding for the recruitment of his regiment in that county.[59] Following the reorganisation of the army in September 1643, several new regiments were formed by the Eastern Association, partially in response to Royalist threats to both London and the eastern counties. Pickering was selected, it might be assumed, due to the influence of Cromwell, who chose commanders and regimental officers principally for their military abilities, godliness, discipline and dedication to the Parliamentarian cause, rather from the local gentry of the county within which particular regiments were raised.

At the end of March 1644, Pickering's regiment of dragoons saw action during the storming of Hillesden House in Buckinghamshire, but it was reduced soon afterwards, perhaps into Manchester's own regiment. It is probable that Pickering's men were largely conscripted into service, and

56 TNA, E121/2/10; Spring, *Eastern Association*, I, p.28.
57 Holmes, *Eastern Association*, pp.163, 176; Glenn Foard, *Colonel John Pickering's Regiment of Foot, 1644–45* (Whitstable: Pryor Publications, 1994), pp.15–16.
58 TNA, SP28/143, f.17v; *LJ*, VI, p.415.
59 TNA, SP28/24, ff.519r–519v; SP28/128/1, f.118r; SP28/243, unfol.

this could have contributed to the short existence of the regiment. Besides, a contemporary Royalist source described them at Hillesden as 'a rude multitude, most of them pressed into service' because they fired their muskets at the church, instead of at the house itself.[60] The casualties during the siege amounted to about 40 on the side of the defenders and not above 6 of the attacking side, which included, according to the account of the action by the Parliamentarian governor of Newport Pagnell, Sir Samuel Luke, 'no officer killed or hurt save only Colonel Pickering and it only a little chock under the chin with a musket ball, but thanks be to god that he was dressed before I came away, and was very merry and cheerful.'[61] On 25 March 1644, Colonel Pickering received a commission to raise a regiment in what was the second phase of expansion of Manchester's army. The regiment consisted of ten companies and was first mustered in early April, yet although it fought at Marston Moor and other engagements in 1644, by the following spring it was well below strength through sickness and desertion, at the point of being transferred into the New Model Army.[62]

Like much of the foot and dragoons of Manchester's army Pickering's dragoons may have been issued with red soldiers' coats. On 14 September 1644 Samuel Moody of Bury St Edmunds received £350 for supplying 1,400 red coats lined blue to Pickering's and Russell's regiments of foot.[63] The following commissioned officers are recorded as serving in Pickering's dragoons:

Captain or Captain-Lieutenant Thomas Norris.
Serving in the regiment by 12 April 1644. Formerly a trooper in Colonel Cromwell's troop, then a corporal in Colonel Nathaniel Fiennes' regiment of horse.[64]

Captain William Miller
He commanded a company of dragoons by 28 August 1643, although the regiment is not known for certain, being variously reported to be Manchester's, Cromwell's, and Pickering's regiments. He was discharged from the army on 2 April 1644, but later served in the Lord Lieutenant of Ireland's Lifeguard.[65]

Captain James Birkin
He led a company of Cambridgeshire dragoons in January 1644, which may have been part of this regiment. His cornet was Samuel Wendis.[66]

60 HMC, *Seventh Report*, pp.446–7; Verney, *Memoirs*, II, pp.196–7.
61 Luke, *Letter Books*, pp.74–5.
62 TNA, SP28/25, ff.52r–95v; Holmes, *Eastern Association*, pp.163, 176; Foard, *Pickering's Regiment*, pp.40–1.
63 TNA, SP28/26, f.330r; E121/4/2, f.10r.
64 Spring, *Eastern Association*, II, p.82; Wanklyn, *Reconstructing*, I, p.157.
65 TNA, E121/1/5; SP28/227/1, f.9r.
66 TNA, SP28/152/20, f.17r.

Colonel Sir John Norwich's Regiment of Dragoons

The unit was raised in Buckinghamshire and Hertfordshire like Norwich's regiment of horse. In November 1643, the dragoons were transferred to Lord Grey of Groby to support his campaign in Nottinghamshire and served in the East Midlands Association in late 1643 and early 1644.[67] The brief regimental accounts of Colonel Norwich's dragoons record the regiment's receipt of pay 'for one month and 26 days' between 19 September and 11 November 1642. The total amount disbursed 'for the said regiment, consisting of 1,000 dragoons, besides officers' during this period was £1,416. The outstanding pay owing to Sir John between 15 November 1642 and 13 April 1643, being 148 days at £1 19s 10d per day as Colonel and Captain for himself and his allowable six horses, amounted to £238 12s. The regiment probably never reached anywhere near the 1,000 dragoons accounted for in autumn 1642. Muster rolls taken in November 1643 record the presence of 13 commissioned officers, 24 non-commissioned officers and 229 men in four companies, although at least one other company under Captain Gilbert Barker was raised. The companies mustered:

Colonel Sir John Norwich's Company

One Captain-Lieutenant (Thompson), one lieutenant, one cornet, two sergeants, three corporals, one drummer and 62 dragoons.

Sergeant-Major Layfield's Company

One lieutenant, one cornet, two sergeants, three corporals, one drummer and 58 dragoons.

Captain Smith's Company

One lieutenant, one cornet, two sergeants, three corporals, one drummer and 11 dragoons.

Captain Farmer's Company

One lieutenant, one cornet, two sergeants, three corporals, one drummer and 98 seamen.[68]

Colonel Edward Rossiter's Regiment of Dragoons

Colonel Edward Rossiter of Somerby, Lincolnshire commanded a probably short-lived regiment of dragoons. It is likely to have been raised in his native county from where his better known regiment of horse – which was originally established in September 1642 for the Earl of Lincoln for the defence of the county – was recruited.[69] Lincolnshire was officially brought into the Eastern Association in September 1643. In a letter of 23 June 1644 from the Nottinghamshire Committee, Colonel Rossiter was referred to as

67 Spring, *Eastern Association*, II, p.73; Holmes, *Eastern Association*, p.99.

68 TNA, SP28/133/2, unfol.

69 *CJ*, II, p.893; Holmes, *Eastern Association*, pp.135 & 213; Spring, *Eastern Association*, II, p.91; Wanklyn, *Reconstructing*, I, pp.52 & 62.

'commander-in-chief of the Lincolnshire horse.'[70] Two undated pay warrants, which mention sums apportioned to Samuel Bough, Burton and Buckany, list them as captains of dragoons under him.[71] However, when Rossiter enlisted in Lincoln's regiment of horse in December 1642, he vowed to raise at least 40 dragoons within fifteen days or return his £20 advance from Parliament. A further company was led by Captain Henry Fabian, although this company left the regiment in July 1643 to join Colonel Robert Russell's regiment of foot on the island of Guernsey, where it remained until its disbandment on 26 June 1646.[72] Such details suggest that, at least during the early part of the war, these dragoon units were raised as part of the same cavalry regiment, of which Rossiter took command as Colonel in April 1643. Nevertheless, he did not join Manchester's army on its march to York and was not at Marston Moor, although when the Eastern Association forces were disbanded in early 1645 Rossiter's cavalry regiment – possibly with his dragoons attached to it – joined Cromwell as part of the Associated Horse and fought on the New Model Army's right wing at Naseby. For most of 1644–6, Rossiter's command was deployed in the East Midlands observing and attempting to contain the Royalist garrison of Newark.[73]

Colonel Sir Miles Hobart's Regiment of Dragoons

A dragoon unit probably drawn from Norfolk, which served at the Parliamentarian siege of Reading in April 1643. Sergeant-Major Isaac Ewer, who was Captain in the regiment by 15 July 1643, later served in the Earl of Manchester's regiment of dragoons and subsequently in Okey's regiment in the New Model Army, so it seems likely that Hobart's dragoons passed into the same units.[74]

Sir Anthony Irby's Regiment of Dragoons

On 10 August 1642 Sir Anthony Irby of Whaplode, Lincolnshire, MP for Boston, received a commission from Robert, Earl of Essex 'to raise a troop of 100 dragoons in county of Lincoln, and to be captain of the said troop.' A commission, to Thomas Welby, 'appointing him Provost-Marshal of the regiment of dragoons of which Sir Anthony Irby is colonel' was issued on the same date.[75] Irby subsequently claimed pay as Captain of a company of dragoons and Colonel of a regiment of dragoons from 10 August 1642 to 2 May 1643.[76] Sir Anthony Irby's dragoons were attached to Colonel John Browne's regiment in the Earl of Essex's Parliamentarian army during the Edgehill campaign, before becoming an independent regiment of one company in 1643. Browne's dragoon regiment had an establishment of seven companies, each of 100 dragoons besides officers. Part of the formation

70 WA, CR 2017/C9/136; HMC, *Fourth Report*, p.267.

71 TNA, E121/3/1; E121/4/2.

72 TNA, SP28/42, f.435r.

73 TNA, SP28/173, unfol.; Sprigge, *Anglia Rediviva*, pp.36–8, 48–9.

74 TNA, E121/2/9; Spring, *Eastern Association*, I, pp.39, 57; Wanklyn, *Reconstructing*, I, pp.45, 56, 66.

75 *CSPD 1641–43*, p.369.

76 TNA, SP28/31, ff.575r–575v.

participated in the skirmish at Powick Bridge, where Browne was mortally wounded. However, the regiment retained its cohesion and fought at Edgehill, although it was reported in Parliament on 25 November that 'these dragoons, since 29 October, have absented themselves from their colours, and have refused to be mustered, and have sold their horses and their arms.'[77] Muster rolls pertaining to Irby's dragoons, dated 2 November 1642, 8 December 1642, and 1 March 1643 list 172, 134 and 100 men respectively, besides commissioned and non-commissioned officers.[78]

On 8 December 1642, Irby's men were ordered to Hull in support of Lord Fairfax's army in Yorkshire. As the Fairfaxes consolidated their grip on the clothing districts, they also undertook offensive operations against various Royalist-held towns. In this, Lord Fairfax expected to be reinforced by 500 Lincolnshire dragoons and other troops, but instead found himself lamenting that 'only 120 dragoons of Sir Anthony Irby's regiment are come hither, which I sent to Bradford with my son.'[79] These soldiers may have been at the storming of Leeds on 23 January 1643 as part of the force led by Sir Thomas Fairfax. During a heavy snowstorm, he detached a company of dismounted dragoons and five companies of foot from his main force, which worked southwards along a trench towards the River Aire and attacked the Royalist positions near Briggate. Here they engaged in a firefight with the defenders, and some of the dragoons poured so much musket fire on one defensive sconce that the Royalists were obliged to abandon it.[80] Irby's men were still in Yorkshire on 22 March when Lord Fairfax, whose army at Selby was unpaid and short of supplies, reported to Parliament that the Lincolnshire dragoons had deserted, and that without instant supplies of money, all his remaining troops would follow them.[81] The unit participated in the siege of Crowland on 25 April 1643, and after Irby's commission as Captain of horse, the unit was taken over on 10 May 1643 by Captain Thomas Atkin, who had previously been his cornet.[82]

Colonel Francis Lord Willoughby of Parham's Regiment of Dragoons

Sometime between 1642 and spring 1644, Willoughby commanded a possibly short-lived regiment of dragoons in the Eastern Association Army. Like other short-lived units, few details survive for it, although the regiment's officers and men could have been raised in Lincolnshire in conjunction with Willoughby's regiment of horse. Willoughby also led a regiment of foot in the army of the Eastern Association, which formed part of his garrison at Gainsborough in summer 1643 and participated in the botched operation

77 *CJ*, II, p.863.

78 TNA, SP28/120, ff.1245r–1245v.

79 *Perfect Diurnall*, 20–27 February 1643; *Parliamentary or Constitutional History of England*, XII, p.113.

80 *A True and Plenary Relation of the Great Defeat given by my Lord Fairfax forces unto my Lord Newcastles forces in Yorkshire, by Thomas Crompton* (London: 23 January 1643). TT, E88[19]; *A Relation of the taking of Leeds and Wakefield by Sir Thomas Fairfax* (London: 23–24 January 1643). TT, E88[23].

81 BL, Ms Add31116, f.53v.

82 TNA, SP28/298, f.326r.

against Newark in spring 1644. Both cavalry and infantry regiments were disbanded soon afterwards. Willoughby's dragoons may have possessed four companies, of whom the following were commanders:

Captain Thomas Estcourt. (He had previously served in the Earl of Lincoln's regiment of horse and was paid as captain in Willoughby's dragoons.[83])
Captain William Dickens
Cornet John Kersey
Quartermaster Brian Cosens[84]

Captain George Vernon (served in the regiment from 1 May 1643 until 24 August 1643. Between November 1643 and spring 1644, he was a captain in Manchester's regiment of dragoons.[85])

Captain Cornelius Vanderhurst (A Dutchman, he was originally a Lieutenant of foot under Sir Hugh Cholmley in Yorkshire. He went to Lincolnshire where he served as Captain of dragoons under Lord Willoughby of Parham from 27 May 1643 until his discharge on 19 August 1643. Vanderhurst then served as a reformado captain under Lord Fairfax in Yorkshire from 1 December 1643 until 20 May 1644, when he was commissioned captain in Colonel John Alured's regiment of horse. He resigned his commission on 1 May 1645.[86])

83 TNA, E121/3/3; Spring, *Eastern Association*, II, p.110.
84 Spring, *Eastern Association*, II, p.110.
85 TNA, SP28/265, unfol.; Spring, *Eastern Association*, I, p.58; II, p.111.
86 TNA, SP28/267/4, f.70r; Jones, 'War in the North', p.405.

11

The New Model Army

The New Model Army was created out of the chaos, missed opportunities and recriminations of autumn of 1644 when the armies of the Eastern Association, the Earl of Essex and Sir William Waller failed to crush the numerically inferior Royalist army at the Second Battle of Newbury. A Parliamentary Ordinance, dated 17 February 1645, establishing the New Model permitted Sir Thomas Fairfax, its commander-in-chief to choose his own officers 'out of any forces under the command of Parliament', although – except for two exceptions – these came from the armies of Manchester, Essex and Waller.[1] The first mention of the strength of the projected army in December 1644 gave it an establishment of 8,000 horse, 16,000 foot and 1,000 dragoons.[2] This was quickly revised however, and the establishment voted by the Commons on 11 January 1645 reduced the numbers to 6,000 horse, 14,000 foot and 1,000 dragoons – the latter were to consist of ten companies.[3] The New Model Army, whose formation in March and April 1645 was a considerable military and administrative achievement, defeated Charles I's Oxford Army at Naseby on 14 June 1645, and undertook a successful campaign in the West. In June 1646, Fairfax accepted the surrender of the Royalist garrison of Oxford, which hastened the end of the First Civil War.

While the initial list of colonels for the army was passed by Parliament on 21 January 1645, this included neither a Colonel of dragoons, nor a dragoon regiment. It is possible that in the first establishment the individual companies of dragoons were meant to be either attached to each regiment of horse or would operate as independent units. Nevertheless, among the proposals sent to the Commons by Sir Thomas Fairfax on 1 March was that such companies be fashioned into a regiment. Two days later it was resolved that 'the dragoons shall be formed into a regiment. The colonel and officers of dragoons were all reported and approved.'[4] Possibly Fairfax initially considered Lieutenant-Colonel John Lilburne, who had previously commanded the Earl of Manchester's dragoons, as Colonel of the regiment,

1 *LJ*, VII, p.209.
2 *CSPD 1644–1645*, p.205.
3 *CJ*, IV, pp.16–17.
4 *CJ*, IV, pp.65–7.

but in April 1645, Lilburne refused to sign the Solemn League and Covenant, which was required of New Model Army officers following the alliance between Parliament and the Scots. The colonelcy of the dragoons, there was only one dragoon regiment in the New Model, went to John Okey, a London drayman and stoker, though his family occupied property in and around the capital. In 1642–3, Okey served as a Captain in Colonel Richard Browne's regiment of dragoons, in Lord Brooke's troop or regiment of cavalry, then in Sir Arthur Haselrig's regiment of horse, where he was promoted and remained until spring 1645.[5]

The first list of company commanders of Okey's regiment, passed on 18 March 1645 and doubtless identical to that passed by the Commons on 3 March, was an heterogeneous mix of officers, some of whom had been in cavalry regiments and others in dragoon units. The second was produced by Sprigge in his *Anglia Rediviva*. Both are given below, with notes on each officer's previous service:

Sir Thomas Fairfax, c1646 John Vicars, *England's Champions* (Open source)

5 TNA, SP28/144/2, ff.1r–7r; SP28/143/1, f.27r; E121/2/3/43A/1; Wanklyn, *Reconstructing*, I, pp.50, 60, 71.

Table 3: Company commanders in Colonel John Okey's regiment of dragoons, 18 March 1645 (LJ, VII, pp. 277-9)

Rank	Name	Military career/army
Colonel	John Okey	Captain in Colonel Richard Browne's dragoons; Lord Brooke's troop or regiment of Horse; captain and sergeant major in Colonel Arthur Haselrige's regiment of Horse, Waller's Army[6]
Sergeant Major	William Gwilliam	Captain in Waller's regiment of Horse, Waller's Army; transferred to Ireton's NMA Horse 5/5/45[7]
Captain	John Farmer	Captain in Sir William Balfour's regiment of Horse, Essex's Army to c. 6/44[8]
Captain	Nathaniel Butler	Probably captain of Kentish dragoons under Waller's command in 1644[9]
Captain	Christopher Mercer	Captain in Manchester's/Lilburne's regiment of dragoons, Eastern Association Army[10]
Captain	Daniel Abbot	Captain in Manchester's/Lilburne's regiment of dragoons, Eastern Association Army[11]
Captain	Larken	Possibly captain in Colonel Valentine Walton's regiment of foot, Eastern Association Army[12]
Captain	Ralph Farr	Lieutenant to Sergeant-Major Okey in Haselrig's Horse, Waller's Army[13]
Captain	Burkett	Captain in Manchester's/Lilburne's regiment of dragoons, Eastern Association Army[14]
Captain	Tobias Bridge	Captain in Manchester's/Lilburne's regiment of dragoons, Eastern Association Army[15]

6 TNA, SP28/144/2, fols 1r.-7r.; SP28/143/1, fol. 27r.; E121/2/3/43A/1.
7 WSL, MS Salt 463, unfol.
8 TNA, SP28/2B, fol. 490r.; SP28/11, fol. 67r.
9 *CSPD 1644*, pp. 375, 469.
10 TNA, SP28/27, fols 101r.-3v., 129v.
11 TNA, SP28/125/3, fols 419r.-420r.; *Resolved Man's Resolution*, pp. 35, 69.
12 Spring, *Eastern Association*, II, p. 105.
13 TNA, E121/2/3/43A/1.
14 TNA, SP28/26, fols 160r.-v.
15 TNA, SP28/27, fol. 144r.; E121/2/1, unfol.

Table 4: Company commanders in Colonel John Okey's regiment of dragoons (Sprigge, Anglia Rediviva, p. 331)

Rank	Name	Military career/army
Colonel	John Okey	
Sergeant Major	Nicholas Moore	Captain in Waller's regiment of foot/dragoons; succeeded Gwilliam by 2/5/45[16]
Captain	John Farmer	
Captain	Christopher Mercer	
Captain	Daniel Abbot	
Captain	Ralph Farr	
Captain	Tobias Bridge	
Captain	Edward Wogan	Captain in Waller's regiment of foot/dragoons; company commander in Okey's by 14/5/45[17]
Captain	Harold Skirmager	Captain in Waller's regiment of foot/dragoons; company commander in Okey's by 13/5/45[18]
Captain	William Turpin, since Captain Neale	Captain in Waller's/Holborne's regiment of dragoons between at least September 1643 and December 1644; replaced by Neale, who had been lieutenant to Lieutenant Colonel Lilburne's company in Eastern Association Army, in or before 12/45, and captain-lieutenant to Okey's NMA company[19]

These lists differ markedly, and it is evident that by the beginning of the Naseby campaign there had been a change in half of the senior officer personnel of the regiment. The reason for this may have been to employ more suitable captains who were experienced in dragoon service. Four of Okey's original captains (Mercer, Abbot, Burkett and Bridge) – and possibly most of their soldiers, including those who would serve in the Colonel's company, although not the new Colonel – came from the Earl of Manchester's army. In January 1645, Lilburne's dragoons had mustered 263 officers and soldiers in five companies, so it appears that the nucleus of the new regiment all transferred together from this formation. In his biography of Colonel

16 TNA, SP28/30, fol. 143r.; SP28/31/1, fol. 19r.

17 TNA, SP28/31/1, fols 26r.-27r.

18 TNA, SP28/30, fol. 199r.; SP28/31/1, fol. 47r.

19 TNA, E121/1/4/56/74; SP28/33/3, fol. 420r.; SP28/31/1, fols 38r., 286r.

John Okey, H. G. Tibbutt contended that Nicholas Moore was Sergeant-Major to Lilburne's regiment, and he transferred with his company into Okey's New Model regiment.[20] Stephen Ede-Borrett lists Moore as 'Capt., Lilburne's dragoons, or (just possibly) Capt., Holborne's dragoons', though he suggests tentatively that 'the officer from Lilburne's regiment seems to be the more likely of the two.'[21] Nevertheless, Clive Holmes identifies the former as Sergeant-Major Sackville Moore, who left Lilburne's regiment and Manchester's army in early 1645. Both he and Captain Holcroft (another dragoon officer) took commissions in the force raised in Essex in July, and in a certificate of his service Moore does not indicate that he served in Okey's regiment.[22] Conversely, the Nicholas Moore listed by Sprigge had formerly been a Captain in Waller's regiment of foot/dragoons and by 5 May 1645 at the latest, replaced William Gwilliam as Sergeant-Major to Okey's dragoons when that officer transferred to Commissary-General Henry Ireton's New Model Army cavalry regiment.[23]

In making the regiment operational, Captain Farmer received 100 dragoon saddles and 100 snaphaunce muskets from the stores of the Tower on 7 April 1645, whereas ten days later Captain Mercer had delivered to him the same quantity of saddles and firelocks 'for his company of dragoons'. On 22 April Mercer further received '100 dragoon saddles with furniture and 100 muskets out of the stores provided for Sir Thomas Fairfax his army, for the recruiting of Colonel Okey's, Sergeant Major Gwilliam's and the said Captain Mercer's troops'. Additionally, whilst in the West Country, on 14 July Farmer was issued with a further 200 snaphaunce muskets, saddles and cartridges, 'being for the recruiting of Colonel Okey's regiment.'[24] Given that Farmer's company was raised from scratch for service in the New Model, it seems likely that at least half of these items were destined for its soldiers.

A further four companies (under Wogan, Turpin, Skirmager and Moore) came from Waller's forces. How many musketeers Waller succeeded in converting to dragoons in 1644 is not clear, as horses were in very short supply, but he had 1,500 of these soldiers in early September and no foot with him the following month.[25] The tenth company in Okey's regiment was recruited as new and commanded by Captain John Farmer, formerly a Captain in Sir William Balfour's regiment of horse in Essex's army until about mid–1644.[26] Two warrants, authorised by Fairfax, refer directly to the recruitment and pay of this company. On 5 April 1645, the New Model Army's treasurers were ordered to disburse 'unto Captain John Farmer towards the raising of a company of dragoons for service under Sir Thomas Fairfax the sum of £20 0s 0d.' Five days later another warrant sanctioned the treasurers to 'pay unto

20 H. G. Tibbutt, *Colonel John Okey, 1606–1662* (Bedford: Bedfordshire Historical Record Society, 1954), p.6, n. See also Wanklyn, *Reconstructing*, I, p.60.

21 Stephen Ede-Borrett, 'Some Notes on the Raising and Origins of Colonel John Okey's Regiment of Dragoons, March to June, 1645', *JSAHR*, 87 (2009), pp.206–13, (p. 209).

22 BL, Ms Egerton 2467, ff.140r, 212r.; Holmes, *Eastern Association*, p.201.

23 TNA, SP28/30/1, f.143r; SP28/31/1, f.19r.

24 WSL, Ms Salt 463, unfol.

25 *CSPD 1644*, pp.485, 495, 521, 523.

26 TNA, SP28/2B, f.490r; SP28/11, f.67r.

Captain John Farmer, Captain of a company of dragoons in the regiment of Colonel John Okey the sum of £128 2s 0d in full for fourteen days' pay for himself, officers, and soldiers in the said regiment.'[27]

Other than the assumption that a quantity of commissioned officers and men had formerly served as dragoons in other Parliamentarian forces, such as the Eastern Association Army, specific evidence for how new recruits were obtained for Okey's regiment is slight. Between February and April 1645, 7,226 foot soldiers and most of the required 6,600 cavalry were voluntarily recruited into the New Model Army from the now-obsolete armies of Essex, Manchester and Waller.[28] Sir Thomas Fairfax's authority to conscript recruits stemmed from an impressment bill passed by the House of Lords on 28 February 1645, with responsibilities for its enactment placed on the shoulders of the London Militia Committee and others.[29] Thus, on 19 March, the Committee of Both Kingdoms ordered the deputy lieutenants and Committee of Essex:

> Whereas the Parliament have ... authorized you to raise, levy, and impress such number of soldiers for the defence of the King, Parliament, and Kingdom as shall be appointed by us ... we, finding it expedient that the army under Sir Thomas Fairfax should be forthwith completed to the full numbers, do by these presents appoint you to cause 1,000 able and serviceable men to be levied within Essex for that employment [and] that especial care be taken in the choice of able, full grown, and well clothed men meet for this employment; that the new recruits be brought from the place of their levying by their conductors unto the rendezvous at St Albans, there to be delivered to such officers as Sir Thomas shall appoint to receive them, by 6 April; that care be taken in the choice of conductors and assistance afforded them to keep their men from straggling and pilfering the country as they go, or from departing from their colours; that the men so impressed be commodiously provided, as has formerly been the practice, with 1,000 red coats faced with blue.[30]

During early May 1645, with Charles I's forces now in the field, the Committee of Both Kingdoms urged Fairfax and the various county committees of London and the southeast 'for the recruits to be hastened and go forthwith to the army.' On 8 May the Committee of Cambridge was informed that 'the recruits from your county for Colonel Montague's regiment are not yet come up, so we desire that they be hastened away to St Albans, where there are officers appointed by the colonel to receive and conduct them. It is high time the regiments were full, the enemy being now in motion.' Similarly, the following day the Committee of Both Kingdoms informed the Committee of Kent:

27 TNA, SP28/29/1, ff.13r–13v, 187r.

28 HMC, *Thirteenth Report, App. I*, p.215.

29 *LJ*, VII, p.256.

30 *CSPD 1644–5*, pp.358–9.

> We have received yours of the 5th from Alresford, concerning your troop of dragoons, of whom we hear that they have done very good service, and may yet be of very good use in the army, and therefore we are very loath they should be disbanded. Such of the men as are of your trained bands you may retain at home, but the rest, with some others to be mounted, you are to furnish with money to carry them to the army, where they may be utilized as recruits[31]

Impressment was expensive, while recruits necessitated mustering, equipping and clothing, in addition to being guarded until they were delivered to the army's assembly point at Reading.[32] In an effort to bring the New Model up to its targeted strength of 22,000 and to replace the large quantity of deserters, in July, September and October 1645 several thousand new men were recruited. This included 127 soldiers for Colonel Richard Fortescue's regiment, two drummers and 156 private sentinels into Colonel William Herbert's (ex the Regiment of Walter Lloyd who had been killed at Taunton in June), and 310 for Colonel Hardress Waller's regiment. Moreover, amongst the New Model's horse, 42 troopers enlisted in Colonel John Butler's regiment on 2 July 1645 and given 26 days' pay as per a muster of 16 July. Similarly, a warrant for the disbursement of £90 17s 0d was issued for the payment of 54 recruits for Commissary-General Henry Ireton's regiment, according to a muster taken on 25 July, although it seems likely that these and Butler's soldiers were not conscripted, given that quotas for cavalry troopers were almost always reached by voluntary means.[33]

The strength of the New Model Army's dragoon regiment remained a concern to Sir Thomas Fairfax because he continued to find ways of reinforcing it. On 19 April 1645, the army's treasurers received the following warrant:

> These are to desire you to pay out of the treasury remaining in your hands the sum of one hundred three score and eight pounds and fifteen shillings; being thirty-two days' pay for 57 dragoons mounted and 24 on foot late in Captain Gorges' company in the service of Taunton and now reduced, to muster them with the rest of Colonel Okey's regiment, commencing 29 May 1645.[34]

By mid-April 1645, as the nascent New Model was beginning to take the field, the hard-pressed garrison of Taunton which had been under siege from July 1644 was on the verge of capture by Royalist forces commanded by Lord Goring. Taunton, a vulnerable and unwalled town, was the lynchpin for Parliamentarian opposition to Royalist control of the West Country. Sir Thomas Fairfax was therefore ordered to march to the aid of the garrison. On 30 April, he advanced from Reading with 9,000 men, but by 8 May, when

31 *CSPD 1644–5*, pp.447–8, 458–9, 464–8.

32 See, for example, warrants for the payment for the conducting of recruits in July and August 1645, including the disbursement of £1,000 0s 0d to Colonel Thomas Rainborowe 'towards the payment of the recruits upon their march from Reading towards the army and for such officers as command those recruits' (TNA, SP28/31/5, ff.471r, 541r, 576r).

33 TNA, SP28/31/6, ff.187r, 189r–190r, 197r, 234r, 239r, 244r, 246r; SP28/32/3, f.394r.

34 TNA, SP28/29/1, f.35r; SP28/30/1, f.143r.

he reached Blandford, the Committee of Both Kingdoms decided that he should return northwards now that the King's army had taken the field. Fairfax, however, dispatched a brigade of 3,000 foot, 1,500 horse and 600 dragoons under the command of Colonel Ralph Weldon – described by a participant in the campaign as '[the] eldest colonel, a gallant, wise, and brave gentleman' – to the relief of Taunton.[35] The remainder of the New Model Army quartered in the Thames Valley. Captain John Gorges's company of dragoons had initially been under the command of Captain Douglas of Sir William Waller's regiment of foot, a regiment that had been converted to dragoons on 13 July 1644. In December, it was part of James Holborne's force at the relief of Taunton and must have transferred to the garrison at around that time.[36] Waller's regiment was officially disbanded at Windsor in April 1645. After the relief of Taunton Captain Gorges transferred to Colonel Edward Cooke's regiment in Massey's brigade. In his later claim for outstanding pay, Gorges testified that he had been in Colonel Edward Cooke's regiment of foot until mid–1644, but on no occasion did he serve in the New Model, having been sent to the relief of Taunton.[37]

In the first week of July 1645, the New Model Army advanced quickly into the West Country. Fairfax's soldiers marched sixty-one miles in four days and reached the Somerset border, whereupon Goring, hearing of the army's rapid progress and fearful of being trapped between it and Taunton, abandoned the siege. Captain Gorges' dragoons evidently joined Colonel Okey's regiment in the West at this time, perhaps at Burrough Hill Fort, where on 13 July a Royalist garrison surrendered to the Colonel following a brief siege and assault.[38] A warrant, endorsed by Colonel Ralph Weldon, commander of the brigade sent by Fairfax, on 19 July 1645 was for the pay of 'such forces as were lately under my command at Taunton unto Colonel Okey the sum of £75 17s 0d in full for fourteen days' pay for 57 dragoons mounted and 24 on foot which have been lately in service with Captain Gorges at Taunton, and have reduced into Colonel John Okey's regiment of dragoons.'[39] On 18 and 19 July 1645, as Fairfax's forces were besieging Bridgewater, the officers and soldiers of the regiment – Okey's, Moore's, Farmer's, Mercer's, Abbot's, Farr's, Bridge's, Wogan's, Skirmager's and Turpin's companies – received fourteen days' pay for 'according to a muster taken on 16 June last.'[40]

The following day the regiment benefitted from the mustering of 200 recruits, raised principally by the efforts of Captain John Farmer. Hence, Farmer received the sum of £100 0s 0d, whilst on 25 August 1645 a warrant was issued for the payment of £210 0s 0d for a fortnight's pay for the 200 new

35 *A Narration of the Expedition to Taunton: The Raising the Siege before it, and the Condition of our Forces, and the Enemies, at this present in the West. Sent from a Commander in the Army, and dated at Chard, May 18. 1645*. TT. E.285 [10].

36 TNA, SP28/43, f.829v.; Wanklyn, *Reconstructing*, I, pp.44, 60.

37 TNA, E121/3/4/66; SP28/29/1, f.143r; SP28/253/A, f.66v.

38 *A Letter sent to the Right Honourable William Lenthall Esquire, Speaker to the Honourable House of Commons: concerning the routing of Col: Gorings army neer Bridgewater* (London: 22 July 1645). TT. E293 [17]; Sprigge, *Anglia Rediviva*, p.68.

39 TNA, SP28/31/4, f.285r.

40 TNA, SP28/31/1, ff.19r–20r, 22r, 26r–27r, 38r–41r, 47r.

recruits.[41] Given that, on Sir Thomas Fairfax's own admission, the quality of the New Model Army's foot was increased following the absorption of Royalist prisoners after Naseby and Bridgewater in particular, it remains a possibility that some of these experienced soldiers were also taken into Okey's dragoon regiment. The identities of most of the junior commissioned officers who served in Colonel Okey's regiment between1645 and 1647 can be identified from contemporary sources, such as pay warrants:

Table 5: Junior commissioned officers in Colonel John Okey's regiment of dragoons, April 1645-1647

Company commander	Capt.-Lt/Lieutenant	Cornet	Quartermaster
John Okey	William Neale	Thomas Okey[42]	
Nicholas Moore	Peter Evans[43]	William Phillips[44]	Richard Norris[45]
John Farmer	John Toplady[46]	William Tinge[47]	Christopher Dobbs[48]
Christopher Mercer	John Ross[49]	Adam Casse[50]	
Daniel Abbot	Francis Bolton[51]		
Ralph Farr	William Bowler[52]	Christopher Purslow[53]	
Tobias Bridge	John Barrow[54]		
Harold Skirmager	Henry Fulcher	John Scrooby[55]	Henry Baker[56]
William Neale	John Copless[57]	Roger Carr[58]	
Edward Wogan	Edward Herbert[59]	Stephen Page[60]	

41 TNA, SP28/31/3, ff.286r, 529r.
42 TNA, E121/1/1/2B/188. He was still serving in mid-1648.
43 TNA, SP28/45, fol. 428v.
44 TNA, SP28/30/1, fol. 98v.
45 TNA, SP28/44, fol. 412v.
46 TNA, SP28/29/1, fol. 179r.; SP28/186/2, fol. 4v.
47 TNA, SP28/140/7, fols 288v.-9r.
48 TNA, SP28/41, fol. 291r.
49 TNA, SP28/36, fol. 616; Rushworth, *Historical Collections*, VII, p. 937.
50 TNA, SP28/35, fol. 374r.
51 TNA, SP28/45, fol. 422v.
52 TNA, SP28/45, fol. 420v.; E121/2/3/43B/2.
53 TNA, SP28/41, fol. 374r.
54 TNA, SP28/44, fol.134r.
55 TNA, E121/3/3/62/1.
56 TNA, SP28/39/1, fol. 47v.
57 TNA, SP28/31/1, fol. 26r.; SP28/39/1, fol. 39r.; SP28/47, fol. 340v.
58 TNA, E121/1/1/26B/96; SP28/140/7, fol. 288v.
59 TNA, SP28/124, fol. 335r.
60 TNA, SP28/124, fol. 335r.

On 7 May 1645, Charles I left Oxford and concentrated his force of 11,000 men at Stow-in-the-Wold in Gloucestershire. Critically, Sir Thomas Fairfax immediately abandoned the siege of the city and marched rapidly to seek out and destroy the King's forces in a single decisive engagement. The movement of the Royalist's main field force compelled Sir William Brereton in Cheshire to abandon the siege of Chester and prompted Parliament to warn its principal garrisons from Leicester to York to prepare for a possible attack. At Uttoxeter, on 24 May, Charles I had with him 4,000 horse and 5,000 foot. Moving from Uttoxeter, the King captured Leicester by storm and for the first ten days of June quartered his troops in the Daventry area whilst anticipating news from Lieutenant-General George Goring that the Royalist siege of Taunton had come to a successful conclusion. Charles now called for reinforcements for his field army to be drawn from garrisons in the Midlands, although components of the New Model Army had by this time begun to establish a siege at Oxford.[61] Of the difficulties faced by the army in breaking the siege in pursuit of the King's forces, Fairfax complained to his father on 4 June 1645:

> I am very sorry we should spend our time unprofitably before the town whilst the King has time to strengthen himself and by terror to force obedience of all places where he comes … it is the earnest desire of this army to follow the King, but the endeavours of others to prevent it have so much prevailed.[62]

However, on learning that Leicester had been stormed, the New Model Army abandoned Oxford and advanced northwards to meet the Royalist army, which had reached Market Harborough.[63]

During the opening weeks of the campaign Okey's regiment of dragoons actively participated in the New Model Army's operations. Sums claimed by householders for quartering 'Captain Farmer's dragoons of Colonel Okey's regiment', along with others of the fledgling formation, indicate that in April and early May 1645 elements of the regiment were stationed in the Warwickshire parishes of Salford Priors, Rugby and Stratford-upon-Avon.[64] During the same period, Captain John Farmer's company of 70 dragoons was quartered on Burton Hastings. Whilst there, Farmer's lieutenant, John Toplady was supplied with a gelding and a mare by local inhabitants, worth £10 0s 0d.[65] Believing that Charles I's ultimate objective following the breakout of his army from Oxford was to relieve Chester and reconquer the north, Cromwell was commanded by the Committee of Both Kingdoms on 13 May 1645, to send Colonel Bartholomew Vermuyden, a cavalry officer who had served in the Eastern Association forces, to effect a link-up with the Scottish forces under the Earl of Leven in the Midlands

61 Symonds, *Diary*, p.169; Parsons, *Diary of Sir Henry Slingsby*, p.148.

62 Robert Bell (ed.), *Memorials of the Civil War: Comprising the Correspondence of the Fairfax Family with the Most Distinguished Personages Engaged in that Memorable Contest* (London: Robert Bentley, 1849), I, p.288.

63 Carte, *Letters*, I, pp.127–128; Sprigge, *Anglia Rediviva*, pp.23, 27.

64 TNA, SP28/184/5, f.32r; SP28/185/1, ff.38v–39r; SP28/186/4/51, f.2r.

65 TNA, SP28/186/2, ff.3v–4r.

The Scots were low on cavalry, so Vermuyden's mounted brigade of 2,000 horse and 400 dragoons – consisting of his own, Colonels Nathaniel Rich's, John Fiennes's, Robert Pye's and John Okey's regiments – began its march. If the King, who had departed from Oxford on 8 May, changed direction and marched into Yorkshire, then Vermuyden possessed the authority to purse him. Thus, on 15 May he was ordered to 'march northward and lie about Leicester and Ashby to wait further orders from Leven.'[66] The same day, whilst residing at Aylesbury the sum of £5,000 was disbursed by the New Model's treasurers 'unto Lieutenant General Cromwell or his assigns by warrant under his hand for the payment of such part of Sir Thomas Fairfax's Army as are now with Lieutenant General Cromwell.' Likewise, on 20 May, the dragoon companies of Colonel Okey, and Captains Abbot and Farr, in addition to Colonel Vermuyden's own troop of horse, were mustered, and two days later received fourteen days' pay.[67] By the next day, the brigade was at Sutton Coldfield, and on 24 May, it was quartered at Derby and the adjacent area. On 27 May Vermuyden's troops were reported by the Derbyshire Committee to be 'in our county betwixt Nottingham and Derby', and the following day Sir William Brereton in Cheshire, imparting his intelligence, wrote to the Colonel, 'I understand by some letters from Derby that with the forces under your command you are gone towards Sheffield.'[68]

Colonel John Okey Late 18th Century copy of a contemporary print (Stephen Ede-Borrett collection)

On 1 June 1645, the Committee of Both Kingdoms instructed Colonel Bartholomew Vermuyden 'to stay in those parts where he is in case the King's forces continue where they are. If the King's army should come southward or towards Sir Thomas Fairfax, who is now ordered to draw his forces toward Buckingham, that [then] he join with Sir Thomas, but in case the King's army go northward, that he do according to former orders.' How many of Okey's dragoon companies were with the brigade at this point is

66 *CSPD 1644–5*, pp.486, 504, 515.

67 TNA, SP28/30/3, ff.311r, 319r, 327r; SP28/30/4, f.346r.

68 BL, Ms Add 11331, ff.150v, 161r, 165v, 170r; *BLB*, I, 621, 643, 645, 649; Luke, *Letter Book*, p.540.

unclear, however. On 3 June 1645, two companies were at Aylesbury awaiting mounts. Captain Daniel Abbot received £24 12s 4d, being seven days' pay at Aylesbury whilst waiting for 34 horses 'to come into service towards the completing of his own and Captain Bridge's troops of dragoons according to the muster held at Aylesbury the third of June instant.'[69] 'Captain Farmer's dragoons of Colonel Okey's regiment' were still receiving quarter in the Warwickshire parishes of Salford Priors and Rugby on 9 June 1645 and must have rendezvoused with the rest of the unit during the next few days.[70]

By 6 June, the only significant Parliamentarian forces between the Royalist army and the Eastern Association were the garrison of Rockingham and Vermuyden's mounted troops. But having briefly reinforced the horse and dragoons of the Association the latter moved southward to shadow Charles I's movements. During the night of 6 June, Vermuyden's brigade arrived at Newport Pagnell, where his men quartered in the nearby villages of Western Underwood and Lavendon. On 10 June 1645, they rendezvoused with Fairfax's regiments, although Vermuyden's units were said 'to have been wearied by their long marches and in need of recruiting.'[71] Thus, some of Okey's dragoons had undertaken two weeks of arduous marches and near continuous movement. From this point onwards, the regiment rode in the vanguard of the New Model Army's march to Naseby and occupied the village the night before the battle.

Despite the frequent assumption that Colonel John Okey's regiment consisted of 1,000 dragoons at Naseby – based upon the prescribed establishment of ten companies, each of 100 dragoons – contemporary accounts mention substantially lower numbers during the weeks before the battle. The newsbook *Mercurius Civicus*, for the final week of April 1645 stated, 'At the last muster of Sir Thomas Fairfax his forces, the number was about 15,000 foot, 400 and odd dragoons, between 4,000 and 5,000 horse besides four regiments employed abroad in service.'[72] Similarly, on 13 May the Committee of Both Kingdoms ordered that '2,500 Horse and dragoons shall forthwith march under the command of Colonel Vermuyden'; this figure was made more specific with the remark that he should go northwards 'with a party of 2,000 horse and 500 dragoons.'[73] Such numbers tend to correspond with those in army pay warrants issued in the weeks immediately before Naseby.

David Blackmore's calculations of the all-ranks strengths Okey's companies as presented in surviving pay warrants, and based on the theoretical rates of pay for officers and soldiers, as well as the assumption – largely from the army's establishment – that each unit contained ten commissioned officers in its ranks, arrive at the following numbers being present at the battle:

69 TNA, SP28/30/5, f.443r.

70 TNA, SP28/185/1, ff.38v–39r, 47v–49v.

71 *CSPD 1644–5*, pp.532, 539, 557, 581–2; Luke, *Letter Books*, pp.302–7; Rushworth, *Historical Collections*, VI, pp.37–9.

72 *Mercurius Civicus*, 24 April–1 May 1645.

73 *CSPD 1644–5*, p.504.

Colonel Okey's company (under Captain-Lieutenant Neale) – 78
Sergeant-Major Moore's – 65
Captain Mercer's – 82
Captain Abbot's – 60
Captain Farr's – 55
Captain Bridge's – 46
Captain Wogan's – 72
Captain Skirmager's – 52
Captain Turpin's – 61
Captain Farmer's, new-raised and paid (the only company at full strength) – 105
Total for Colonel Okey's regiment of dragoons, including commissioned and non-commissioned officers, as 676 men.[74]

This suggests also that 571 officers and dragoons could trace their origins to the armies of Manchester, Essex and Waller. Nonetheless, an unusual warrant, issued on 19 July 1645, was drawn up to provide pay:

> to Captain Turpin £327 4s 0d being 32 days' pay for the officers and soldiers of his company of dragoons, also several other soldiers in Sergeant-Major Moore's and Captain Skirmager's companies that marched with him to Taunton, according to an attestation given in under the hand of Captain Turpin on 12 July instant last, covering 9 and 12 May last to make them even with the rest of the regiment.[75]

The suggestion here is that Turpin marched to Taunton in mid-April 1645, accompanied by an unspecified number of dragoons belonging to Moore's and Skirmager's companies. If so, not only did both he and these soldiers miss the fighting at Naseby, but the strength also (as given previously for these companies) may have been more depleted than assumed

During the morning of 14 June 1645, as both armies were deploying prior to the Battle of Naseby, Colonel John Okey was ordered by Oliver Cromwell, the commander of New Model Army's horse, to deploy his regiment of dragoons to secure the left flank of the army by occupying a series of hedges, thick features at right angles to the two forces, which marked a parish boundary. Hence, this was a critical deployment in protecting the New Model Army from any outflanking moves by Prince Rupert's Horse and commanded musketeers and enabling the Parliamentarians to fire on the advancing cavalry before it charged the front line divisions of Commissary-General Henry Ireton's regiments of horse. Foard suggests that Cromwell ordered Okey to the New Model Army's left flank so quickly, and to such a forward position, because it was realised that there were so many musketeers amongst Rupert's cavalry units.[76] Sir Bernard de Gomme's plan depicts them, while Okey's account mentions the presence of the musketeers and

74 TNA, SP28/29/1, f.13r–13v, 59r.–59v, 107r, 187r; SP28/30/3, ff.293r, 311r, 319r, 327r; David Blackmore, 'Counting the New Model Army', *ECWT*, 58 (2004), pp.3–5; Ede-Borrett, 'Some Notes', pp.206–13.

75 TNA, SP28/31/1, f.26r.

76 Foard, *Naseby*, p.203.

the intermixing of 'commanded shot' among cavalry brigades had been increasingly used by the Prince during the war. The task allotted to Okey's regiment was well within the remit of civil war dragoons, and the Earl of Essex had deployed some of his in similar fashion at Edgehill. In his account of the battle, penned shortly afterwards, Colonel Okey wrote:

> I was half a mile behind in a meadow giving my men ammunition, and had not the lieutenant general come presently, and caused me with all speed to mount my men, and flank our left wing, which was the King's right wing of horse; where was Prince Maurice, who charged at the head of his regiment, and the King himself in the next reserve charged at the head of his men, but by that time I could get my men to light, and deliver up their horses, in a little close, the enemy drew towards us.[77]

This deployment of Okey's dragoons is confirmed by two first-hand accounts; Captain Thomas Wogan of the regiment, who said that the unit 'was on the left-hand of all our horse and lined the hedges, which did mightily annoy the King's right wing of horse, as they advanced towards us.'[78] Sir Henry Slingsby, who served at the battle with the remnants of Sir Marmaduke Langdale's Northern horse, described from his position on the opposite flank of the King's army:

> Besides they possessed a hedge upon our right wing which they lined with musketeers to gall our horse (as indeed they did) before we could come to charge theirs. It fell upon Prince Rupert to charge at that disadvantage, and many of the regiment were wounded by shot from the hedge before we could join with theirs on that wing. But he did so behave himself in the charge that he beat them up upon that wing beyond the hills, and had our success been the like upon our left wing, in probability we might have had the day.[79]

Equally, Sprigge wrote that 'our dragoons begun the battle flanking the right wing of the enemy's horse as they charged our left wing of horse.'[80] Okey's men rode forward and took up their positions, where, in their Colonel's words 'by that time I could get my men to light, and deliver up their horses, in a little close.'[81] Foard argues persuasively (from written descriptions and his interpretation of musket bullet scatter patterns) that the majority of the dragoons occupied Archwong Close – Okey's 'little close' – and 'other adjacent closes', located to the northeast of the Sulby Hedge area.[82] This corresponds with Colonel Okey's description of his position being 'encompassed on the one side with the King's Horse and on the other side with the foot and horse to get the close; but it pleased God that we beat off both the horse and the foot

77 *A More Particular and Exact Relation of the Victory obtained by the Parliament's forces under the command of Sir Thomas Fairfax* (London: Richard Cotes, 1645), p.5.
78 Carte, *Letters*, I, p.129.
79 Parsons, *Diary of Sir Henry Slingsby*, pp.151–152.
80 Sprigge, *Anglia Rediviva*, p.39.
81 *More Particular and Exact Relation*, p.5.
82 For Foard's analysis see his *Naseby*, pp.245–8.

on the left, and the right wing, and cleared the field, and kept our ground.' There is convincing documentary and archaeological evidence to indicate that this area was in fact Archwong Close, an enclosed feature located to the northeast of the Sulby Hedge range and some 200m south south-east of the modern Naseby Battlefield Project's 'Sulby Viewpoint'. This was also behind and to the left of the Royalist position at the start of the battle. Archwong Close seems have been the most advanced (and most fiercely contested) position held by Okey's dragoons.

In his map of the battle, included in Sprigge's history of the New Model Army, *Anglia Rediviva*, published in 1647, Streeter depicted 'Lantford Hedge lined with dragoons', although he foreshortened the distance between the two forces at the beginning of the battle. This was the part of the hedge on the parish boundary with Sulby to the bottom of Broadmoor adjacent to Lantford Furlong.[83] Here, small groups of horses can be seen, set slightly back from the action. These are held by one of the riders, while the other dragoons (in files of four) march to line the hedgerow, where they are firing on Rupert's troopers as they were enveloped on both sides. In relation to Archwong Close, Streeter's depiction of Lantford Hedge could merely be a schematic representation of a further firing line or stopping off position where most, if not all of the horses were kept, established not only to engage Rupert's rapidly advancing horse as it swept by, but to provide a position to safeguard an extraction route either out of the Sulby Hedges or a line of retreat if so required. Hence, this could merely represent a further firing line or 'forlorn hope' established not only to engage Rupert's rapidly advancing horse, but to provide, in modern military terms, a covered rearguard or 'rendezvous' position.

As Okey continued:

> Which my men perceiving, they with shooting and rejoicing received them, although they were encompassed on the one side with the King's Horse, and on the other side with foot and horse to get the close; but it pleased God that we beat off both the horse and the foot on the left, and the right wing, and cleared the field, and kept our ground. When as the King's Horse had driven our men a mile before them on the left wing at their first coming on; then we discovered many of the King's regiment, by reason that they came somewhat near unto us; before ever they discharged a pistol at any horse; and had not we by God's providence been there, there had been but few of Colonel Butler's regiment left, after this we gave up ourselves for lost men, but we resolved every man to stand to the last.[84]

During this action, the dragoons were for some time separated from the rest of the army, and fully expected to be defeated in detail by the attacking Royalist cavalry and musketeers. But as Okey, who had for more than an hour resisted all attempts to dislodge him witnessed the consolidated regiments of foot drive back the King's infantry, he ordered his regiment to attack the now exposed Royalist right flank.

83 Foard, *Naseby*, p.246.
84 *More Particular and Exact Relation*, pp.5–6.

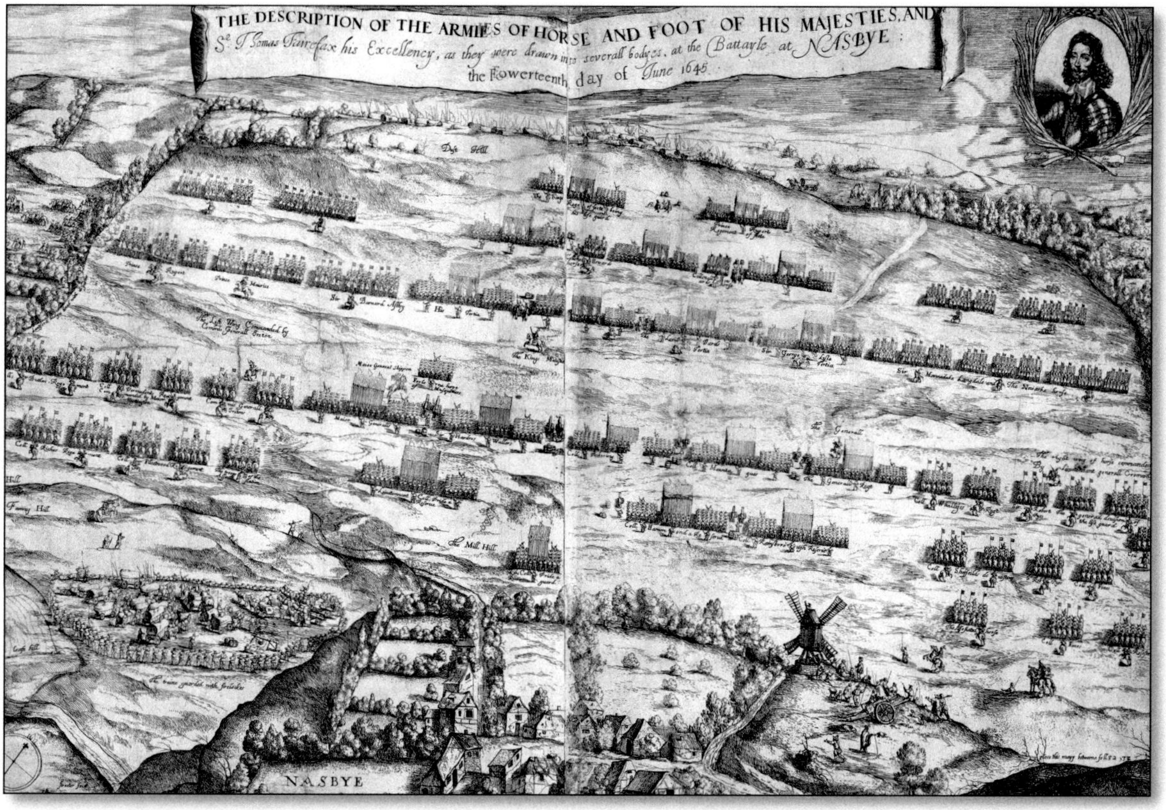

Robert Streeter's plan of the Battle of Naseby (Open source)

How Okey's men went about this is unclear, but the southern end of Archwong Close is contiguous with Lanford/Sulby Hedges and only 200m from the main Lanford position. It might be then, that given their experience and leadership, when the order came from their officers to reform or remount occurred, those in Archwong, if still in contact with the enemy covered each other in 'skirmishing order' either in pairs or by file, as they withdrew southwards towards where their mounts were waiting. Alternatively, if they were no longer in contact with the enemy (as it appears from Okey's account), the dragoons could have withdrawn by companies or files and perhaps employed some of their number as a tactical rearguard. Describing the closing stages of the fight at Naseby, Sprigge wrote:

> our dragoons having already begun to fire upon their horse, they not willing to abide a second shock upon so great disadvantage as this was like to be, immediately ran away, both fronts and reserves, without standing one stroke more. Our horse had chase of them from that place, within two miles of Leicester (being the space of fourteen miles) took many prisoners, and had the execution of them all that way.[85]

85 Sprigge, *Anglia Rediviva*, pp.39–40.

The rout and pursuit of Charles I's army is well described by Okey himself:

> I perceiving (after one hour's battle) caused all my men to mount and to charge into their foot, which accordingly they did, and took all their colours, and 500 prisoners, besides what we killed, and all their arms. After this the King his horse drew up into a body again. And then I drew up my dragoons, and charged the King's regiment of horse, and they faced about and run away, and never made any stay till they came to Leicester, and we pursued them within three miles and a half of Leicester, which was about 15 miles from the place where we fought. We took, as near as we can guess, between 4 and 5,000 men, with many horse, all their ordnance, bag and baggage; and there was as we were informed, but two foot men went into Leicester; the King himself very hardly escaped.[86]

It has generally been assumed from the specific comments by Sprigge ('our dragoons having already begun to fire upon their horse'), and Okey ('I … caused all my men to mount and to charge into their foot' and 'I drew up my dragoons, and charged the King's regiment of horse') that the New Model dragoons participated in the army's counter-attack on its left wing by remounting and charging as pseudo-cavalry.[87] Thus, Peter Young expressly stated:

> The charge of Okey's dragoons at the end of the day calls for comment. In those days dragoons were supposed to act simply as mounted infantry. They were not encouraged to regard themselves as the equal of horse. It may be that Okey's was the first mounted charge made by a dragoon regiment. Certainly, no other episode of the sort occurs in the annals of our civil war.[88]

Such conjectures can be questioned, however. Writing in 1988, Barry Denton declared:

> Surely what is being described [by contemporary remarks] is the New Model's use of firepower, not a cavalry action. Okey's men would have ridden to within 200 yards of the enemy, dismounted, and charged forward firing every 50 yards or so to build up a firefight. In support, the horse would prevent a counter charge, and within two or three minutes the shot from the dragoon weapons would force a fall back if not a full-scale retreat.[89]

The probability, therefore, that Okey's mounted attack involved firing at the Royalist cavalry, (either by dismounting to deliver salvees or from horseback) rather than a charge to contact, is fairly high. Rather than simply mounting up as cavalry – which they were not trained to do – the dragoons undertook a mounted deployment. This would be entirely in keeping with

86 *More Particular and Exact Relation*, p.6.
87 Peter Young, Naseby 1645: The Campaign and the Battle (London: Century, 1985), pp.275–6; Foard, *Naseby*, p.277; Hutton, *Making of Oliver Cromwell*, p.263.
88 Young, *Naseby*, pp.275–6.
89 Denton, *Naseby Fight*, p.50.

the practice of combined arms mounted operations employed by armies of the British Civil Wars, which included units of dragoons being officially or informally attached to cavalry regiments. This provided additional firepower and assisted movement, particularly during the opening and closing phases of combat, harassing operations and the covering of retreats. Moreover, assuming that 'Sulby Hedges' or the Close were impenetrable to the Royalist Horse, as they seem to have been, then they were also impenetrable the other way. Thus, any offensive action by Okey's dragoons would only have been possible by them moving down to the southern end of the hedge line and then changing direction northward again to attack the King's troops. Such a movement would also place them behind much of Ireton's cavalry regiments, so a mounted charge appears unlikely.

Close up of part of Okey's deployment at Sulby Hedges from Streeter (Open source)

In the case of the New Model Army dragoons at Naseby, there also remains the possibility that rather than dismounting to fire – a method of operating advocated by Cruso and Burt – they 'fired from horseback' instead. This would make perfect sense if that was in support of some of Ireton's horse, as previously mentioned. During the expedition of the relief of Gloucester by the Earl of Essex's army in September 1643, it was reported that in conjunction with a body of 200 musketeers and the cavalry regiments of Lord Grey and the Earl of Essex's (under the command of Sir Philip Stapleton), Captain Jeremiah Abercrombie's dragoons 'marching directly upon the enemy, and skirmishing with them, made their whole body to retreat; and though they still appeared before us, we marched on, and drove them seven miles.'[90]

90 Washbourne (ed.), *Bibliotheca Gloucestrensis*, p.239.

Fulfilling its mobile mounted role, Colonel John Okey's regiment of dragoons operated at the forefront of the New Model Army's campaign in the Southwest in 1645–6. As Fairfax's troops began their pursuit of the King's vanquished forces from Leicester towards the Midlands on 20 June Okey's men were somewhat ahead of them. Sprigge noted, 'No sooner had the Army done the work that God had for them thereabouts, but they marched towards Warwick, solicitous in nothing so much, as which way they might advance the public service.'[91]

The extensive 'Warwickshire Parish Civil War Loss Accounts' contain claims for quartering Colonel Okey's regiment for a single night. At Stratford-upon-Avon, for instance, one householder claimed the sum of £2 15s 0d for being charged 'with Captain Farmer under Colonel Okey and 17 men and horses when Sir Thomas Fairfax passed by.' The townspeople of Rugby, who had previously provided free quarter to the regiment, included another who, 'After Naseby fight I quartered Captain Mercer and his two men and their horses one night.' Between them sixteen householders were responsible for accommodating the lieutenant, cornet and 137 dragoons, along with their mounts under Captain Abbot for 'one night, it being a week after Naseby fight.'[92] Moreover, one inhabitant of Stratford-upon-Avon provided quarter for 'Captain Skirmager under Colonel Okey seven men and eight horses [for] two days and two nights', whereas Robert Shalcrosse of Kenilworth Augmentation in Kenilworth Parish billeted '100 men and officers of a troop of Captain Mercer's dragoons a day and a night', which he claimed, cost him £24 0s 10d.[93]

In addition to acting as part of the New Model Army's mobile advance guard during the ensuing South-western Campaign, Colonel John Okey's dragoons were instrumental in bringing about the surrender of the Royalist garrison of Bath, where, during a surprise dawn attack on 31 July 1645, they employed their resourcefulness and bravado in seizing the bridge into the city. As Sprigge recounted, when the New Model brigade commanded by Sir Hardress Waller arrived at Crediton, 'the next morning being Monday 8 December the dragoons were there by daybreak, but by reason of the extremity of the weather, the foot could not get to [the place] till Tuesday 9 December, on which day the horse and dragoons gave them possession of the town.' Likewise, at 9pm (last light) on 14 December, Captain Richard Deane, the army's Comptroller of the Ordnance, led a party of 200 foot and dragoons across the River Exe in an attempt to seize Powderham Castle, the fortified residence of the Royalist Sir William Courtenay.

Nevertheless, the castle had been reinforced in anticipation of such an attack, and they were forced to occupy the adjacent parish church. The following day they were assaulted by attackers who threw in many hand grenades, but the defenders managed to repulse them. Of the conduct of Okey's troops during the fight Sprigge, who was present at the events, later recounted:

91 Sprigge, *Anglia Rediviva*, p.53.

92 TNA, SP28/184/5, f.27r.; SP28/185/1, f.113r.; SP28/186/4/51, f.2r ; SP28/186/5, ff.3v, 13v, 18v, 20v, 26v, 28v, 30r, 32v, 42v, 45v, 47v, 49v, 52v, 97r, 101v, 105r, 120v, 122v.

93 TNA, SP28/136/51, f.27v; SP28/182/1, f.1v.

> In this service Captain Farmer (captain of dragoons) commanded our men, who as they were beyond expectation happy in their success (not one man being lost in the storm) so they were resolved to continue in their duty; and notwithstanding the extremity of the cold, by reason of the great frost and snow, and want of all means to resist or qualify the same in the church, having no firing there, they would not quit the same until they received orders so to do.[94]

Amidst horrendous weather conditions in the Southwest, with almost impassable roads, and the army afflicted by sickness and low morale, Fairfax (who himself was quite ill) had received instructions from the Committee of Both Kingdoms to draw off a substantial portion of his troops for service in the Midlands. Although Sir Thomas informed the Lords that he might be able to spare 7,000 or 8,000 men, the Commons rescinded the order.

However, on 25 November he was compelled to send four regiments of horse – initially those of Colonels Whalley and Fleetwood, and Commissary-General Henry Ireton, but later joined by Fairfax's own under Sergeant-Major Disbrowe – with six companies of Okey's dragoons to Buckinghamshire, to prevent forays by the King's Horse from Oxford into the surrounding area.[95] A rare set of lists in the form of pay schedules (calculated from now lost muster rolls) for these New Model cavalry regiments for providing 28 days' pay, dated 23 December 1645, survives among the Commonwealth Exchequer Papers and provides a troop-by-troop breakdown of unit composition and strengths. Hence, the General's regiment mustered 78 officers and 533 troopers; Ireton's had 71 officers and 510 troopers; Fleetwood's 71 officers and 445 troopers, while Whalley's regiment mustered 66 officers and 533 troopers. For some unknown reason there are no lists for Colonel Okey's soldiers among this document.[96]

Reunited with the rest of their regiment in Devon, the dragoons displayed their initiative during the New Model's assault in the early phase of the fighting against Goring's forces at Torrington on 16 February 1646, although Goring himself had already fled abroad prior to this. Here they were sent as an advance guard through narrow lanes lined with dense hedges, and in heavy rain and with night falling to 'steal up to the barricades to see what the enemy was a doing.' This action, however, inadvertently triggered a full-scale attack by Fairfax's army. During the main assault on the town Sir Ralph Hopton's foot fought with great tenacity, and before the barricades could be scaled these soldiers had to be driven off at push of pike and butt-end of musket.[97] After two hours' close quarter fighting the New Model foot managed to scale the obstacles and clear a pathway for the horse to enter and bring about the end of a particularly bloody battle. The Parliamentarian victory delivered a fatal blow to the King's forces in the West. Hopton, with his infantry force

94 Sprigge, *Anglia Rediviva*, pp.158–9.

95 Bell (ed.), *Memorials*, I, p.289; *CSPD 1645–7*, pp.221, 269–70, 283–4; *Perfect Passages*, 26 November–3 December 1645.

96 TNA, SP28/34/4, ff.490r–498v.

97 Sprigge, *Anglia Rediviva*, pp.173, 195, 198; *A Fuller Relation of Sir Thomas Fairfax's Routing of all the King's Armies in the West ... at Torrington* (London: 1642). TT, E324 [6].

demolished, escaped into Cornwall, where at Truro on 14 March 1646, he surrendered to Sir Thomas Fairfax after agreeing to disband the western army and to go into exile. With the reduction of Chester already achieved, only Charles I's headquarters at Oxford remained in Royalist hands

There is some evidence to indicate that during the significant recruitment of the New Model Army in September and October 1645 Colonel John Okey's regiment received some modest benefits. A warrant signed by Fairfax and dated 13 September ordered the delivery 'to Captain Abbot, eight state horses for the recruits of his troop.'[98] Furthermore, warrants issued for the payment of eight of Okey's companies (Bridge's and Turpin's are seemingly absent) in mid-October 1645 for 21 days' service allow the following computations to be made of the approximate strength of each company and of the regiment overall:

Colonel Okey's company – 97
Sergeant-Major Moore's –111
Captain Mercer's – 87
Captain Abbot's – 86
Captain Farr's – 130
Captain Wogan's – 98
Captain Skirmager's – 89
Captain Farmer's – 87

Total for Colonel Okey's regiment of dragoons, including commissioned and non-commissioned officers, as 783 men.[99]

Table 6: Company commanders in Colonel John Okey's regiment of dragoons, December 1646 (Wanklyn, Reconstructing, I, p. 71)

Rank	Name	Military career/army
Colonel	John Okey	
Sergeant Major	Nicholas Moore	
Captain	John Farmer	
Captain	Christopher Mercer	
Captain	Daniel Abbot	
Captain	Ralph Farr	
Captain	Tobias Bridge	
Captain	Harold Skirmager	
Captain	Edward Wogan	
Captain	William Neale	

98 TNA, SP28/32/3, f.410r.
99 TNA, SP28/32/2, ff.160r, 162r–163r, 165r, 168r, 187r, 191r.

Table 7: Company commanders in Colonel John Okey's regiment of dragoons, 31 May 1647

Rank	Name	Military career/army
Colonel	John Okey	
Sergeant Major	Nicholas Moore	Left regiment in 6/47; later sergeant major in Colonel Henry Ingoldsby's Horse in Ireland[100]
Captain	Christopher Mercer	
Captain	John Farmer	Left regiment in 6/47; returned to army in 1651[101]
Captain	Daniel Abbot	
Captain	Ralph Farr	Left regiment in 6/47[102]
Captain	Tobias Bridge	
Captain	Harold Skirmager	Left regiment in 6/47; captain in Daniel Abbot's regiment in Ireland[103]
Captain	Edward Wogan	Left regiment in 6/47; defected to Royalists 2/48[104]
Captain	William Neale	

Table 8: Company commanders in Colonel John Okey's regiment of dragoons, 31 August 1647

Rank	Name	Military career/army
Colonel	John Okey	
Sergeant Major	Daniel Abbot	
Captain	Tobias Bridge	
Captain	Christopher Mercer	
Captain	William Neale	
Captain	John Garland	Previously capt.-lt in Colonel Robert Liburne's Horse; succeeded to Farmer's company[105]
Captain	Francis Bolton	Lieutenant to Captain Abbot by 3/47; took command of Captain Farr's company by 15/6/47[106]
Captain	Francis Barrington	Cornet to Captain Abbot 6/45; took over remnant of Captain Wogan's company[107]
Captain	Francis Freeman	Had taken over Moore's company by 6/46 when he conducted the siege of Dunster Castle; cashiered by Okey in 1650[108]
Captain	Henry Fulcher	Lieutenant to Captain Skirmager and succeeded him by 6/47[109]

100 Wanklyn, *Reconstructing*, I, p. 81.
101 *Ibid.*
102 *Ibid.*
103 TNA, SP28/83, fol. 25v.
104 Wanklyn, *Reconstructing*, I, p. 81.
105 TNA, SP28/122, fol. 390r.; SP28/43. fol. 129v.
106 TNA, SP28/47, fol. 422v.; SP28/51, fol. 1r.
107 TNA, SP28/30, fol. 319r.
108 TNA, E121/1/1/37.
109 TNA, SP28/43, fol. 176v.

Table 9: Junior commissioned officers in Colonel John Okey's regiment of dragoons, June 1647-June 1650 (Wanklyn, Reconstructing, I, p. 130)

Company commander	Capt.-Lt/ Lieutenant	Cornet	Quartermaster
John Okey	Baldwin		
Richard Nicholetts	James Pope		
John Sharpe	Henry Cross		
Daniel Abbot	Henry Crewkerne	Thomas Joyner	John Parker
Tobias Bridge	John Barrow	Samuel Adey	
Christopher Mercer	John Ross		
Thomas Okey?	Adam Casse		
William Neale	Charles Thompson		
William Cheese			
Francis Barrington	William Hixt	Stephen Elmes	
Stephen Clement			
Francis Bolton	Charles Cary	Robert Young	
William Dives			
Henry Fulcher	John Scrooby	John Gibbs	
Francis Freeman	Joseph Gilmore		
Peter Evans	Richard Colton	Gilmore	
John Garland			
John Dahorne	John Dahorne	William Tinge	
Robert Line			
Richard Pierce			

In April 1647, Colonel John Okey's regiment was listed as 115 commissioned officers and no-commissioned officers, and 803 dragoons.[110] On 26 April, several officers and men of the regiment engaged themselves for the service in Ireland recently proposed by the Committee for Irish Affairs for the suppression of the rebellion there. The initial list included the names of five company commanders: Sergeant-Major Moore, Captain Farmer, Captain Skirmager, Captain Farr and Captain Wogan. These were subsequently replaced with Captains Francis Freeman, Francis Barrington, Francis Bolton, John Garland and Henry Fulcher.[111] According to a 'List of the non-commissioned officers and private soldiers in several troops, lately come off from the army', dated 16 June 1647, five commissioned officers, six non-

110 *Clarke Papers*, I, p.18.

111 Rushworth, *Historical Collections*, VI, p.465; *CJ*, V, p.114.

commissioned officers and 143 dragoons from Okey's regiment volunteered for the service in Ireland:[112]

At the outbreak of the Second Civil War in 1648, Captain Edward Wogan turned his coat and made off to Scotland with one company of the regiment. At this time, however, Colonel Okey with six companies had joined Colonel Thomas Horton in South Wales. Horton, the New Model's most senior officer on the ground in the region, had advanced from Brecon but was forced back by rebel troops from Pembrokeshire near Carmarthen. Nonetheless, he quickly regrouped, and at the beginning of May set out again with the aim of intercepting and fighting the principal rebel formation in Glamorganshire. This was ahead of a larger force commanded by Cromwell, which had been ordered from London to South Wales to strengthen local Parliamentarian troops and defeat the rebellion there. At St Fagans, a village located south of the River Ely and on a direct route to Cardiff, Horton's brigade encountered numerically superior enemy forces commanded by Major-General Rowland Laugharne on the morning of 8 May. Colonel Okey commanded three of his dragoon companies on the right flank of the Parliamentarian army, his Sergeant-major the others, whilst Lieutenant John Godfrey led the forlorn hope. The dragoons on the right wing – seconded by three troops of horse led by Sergeant-Major Walter Bethel, traversed northwards along the Crofft-y-Genau Road and wheeled left to occupy the ridge overlooking the rolling terrains of the ensuing battlefield.

Of the encounter, Colonel Horton later reported:

> Colonel Okey's own troop of dragoons, mounted with some horse on the right wing, disputed the first encounter very hotly, where he showed much resolution, and beat the enemy out of two closes and over a little brook, and their maintained their ground under command of the enemy's shot, until the forlorn of foot commanded by Captain-Lieutenant Fann, and some horse from the left wing came to their relief; and then they beat the enemy from hedge to hedge before them, until they came to a bridge where the enemy's greatest body were placed. The horse all this while and dragoons following his first success with much vigour, were constrained to stand the enemy's shot for some time before the foot (though they made great haste) could come up to them.[113]

Additionally, Okey's own account, penned on the day of the battle and describing his regiment's part in the ensuing victory is given below in full:

> Hitherto, till this day I could not give you a good accompt of our Welsh expedition, we have had so many obstructions through unseasonable weather, rugged ways, want of necessaries, and other inconveniencies, that we may well say these things; except the Lord had been with us, they had swallowed us up

112 TNA, SP28/124/1, ff.335r–338r.

113 *A true confirmation of the great victory in Wales: sent in a letter to the Speaker of the Honorable House of Commons, from Colonel Thomas Horton from Bridge-end, May 13. 1648* (London, 1648). TT, E443 [15]. See also, Chrystal Davies, 'The Battle of St Fagans, 8 May 1648', *Cromwelliana* (1991), pp.15–27.

Position of Okey's dragoons on the right flank at St Fagans (photograph by Paul Wright)

quick. But besides this we had attending on us a numerous army before us, and behind us a great party. We divers ways sought an opportunity to fight with them, which till this instant we could never do, they before taking always the advantage of their Welsh ways, hills, and rivers. This posture they continued in, till divers of our soldiers were wearied out, and both foot and horse so far spent, as the enemy himself knew his great advantage over us; and out of that consideration, having mightily increased his army, and wee through all these inconveniences somewhat decreased ours, he upon the eighth of this instant about eight of the clock in the forenoon proffered us the battle. We seeing his number, and he being upon us before we were well aware of him, quitted our present station, which was at Saint Fagans, the enemy drew into the place of our guards; but we being very loth to retreat, upon a little hill near Saint Fagans, made good our ground, drew up our army, faced the enemy, a forlorn hope of Horse and dragoons were drawn up under the command of Lieutenant Godfrey. And another forlorn hope of foot under the command of a lieutenant of foot. Next them marched 160 firelocks under the command of Captain Garland In the rightwing marched Colonel Okey with three troops of horse and three troops of dragoons In the body marched Colonel Horton commander-in-chief. In the left flank marched the horse under the command of Major Barton, with some dragoons. The body being thus drawn up, our forlorn hope of horse advanced and fell immediately into a ground where [...] of the enemy's foot with some horse lined the hedges, Lieutenant Godfrey with a forlorn hope of horse immediately charged them, routed them, and killed some of them. Colonel Okey upon this taking the advantage of the enemy's running, commanded presently Captain Garland with the firelocks, Captain Mercer with a commanded party of dragoons and some horse to second the forlorn hope. These falling on into another ground where the enemy was a lining the hedges, drove them from hedge to hedge and pursued them. The enemy in this retreat having so many reserves of foot at every hedge, he makes a stay with a new party. Still Colonel Okey commanded the party both of firelocks, dragoons and horse to advance; the enemy having a numerous army of foot, still ever and anon sends fresh reserves; but at the end he was beaten by this party of foot and horse to a water, and from thence over a river [Nant Dowlais], where again he made good his ground. There the dispute lasted a long while, till our body of horse and foot advanced, where the horse with the foot making way, and charging with the foot upon their musketeers, through the goodness of God after an hour's dispute they were put to the rout. We pursued, took divers prisoners, the number as yet unknown, and the quality; we hear of some men of quality both killed and taken; this for present in brief. We can give you an accompt that there were far more prisoners taken than the number of our army was; so that we can well say, God hath done great things for us in mightily stirring up the spirits of officers and soldiers so as courageously each one in his place in this business doing his part. We can truly say that this was the hand of God, we being but a handful in comparison to their great army which might have been a sufficient motive to have caused us to have refused to fight. Yet the confident of the great disadvantage the retreat would have been to us in our future proceedings. These were motives notwithstanding all the former difficulties, to induce us to fight, where through the Lord we had an answerable success; in which let the glory be given to God, and not to man. Our victory being an absolute rout of them, with very little loss to ourselves, some few bymen we had killed; the smallness of the number causing great admiration both to us and the enemy; divers of the enemy were killed, forty to one, and about 2,500 taken. The chief of them that we can hear of was Major-General Stradling, but none of our party either killed or wounded Captain Nicholets and Cornet Okey were both shot through their hats, but free from any other hurt; there have been a few men of my troop killed, and some hurt, but not many. For which and all other mercies I desire God may have the glory; by the next post you shall hear more. This being done in haste in the field; in the meantime I refer you to Captain Mercer, who can fully resolve you. No more for present; I take my leave, and remain

Your servant to command,
John Okey
From the field by St Fagans this 8th of May 1648.[114]

Following the battle two further dragoon companies, which had accompanied Cromwell on his westward march, rejoined Colonel John Okey's regiment and with it performed good service at the siege of Pembroke between 31 May and 11 July 1648. Two companies (perhaps the same ones) subsequently went with Cromwell's forces to the north of England, where the following month they participated in operations against the Scottish Engager Army at Preston and Winwick. Okey's remaining companies were deployed to Devon and Cornwall to quash the Royalist rising there. In the spring of 1649, five dragoon companies were required for Ireland, but it appears that only three went. Daniel Abbot took his own company to form the nucleus of a new regiment of six companies, but Francis Bolton, who became his Sergeant-

114 *A True and particular relation of the late victory obtained by Colonel Horton and Col: Okey against the Welch Forces under Major Generall Langhorn: expressed in a letter from Colonel Okey to a friend of his in London* (London: Henry Overton, 1648).TT, E441 [36].

Major, did not. The other two companies known to have gone to Ireland were commanded by Captains Francis Barrington and Richard Nicholetts. They joined Henry Cromwell's regiment, but as cavalry rather than dragoons.[115] Thus, seven companies remained in England from September 1649 to early June 1650, at which time several new commands were being raised. However, when Cromwell invaded Scotland Okey's was in the process of being converting from a dragoon unit to a regiment of Horse. The troop commanders in the summer of 1650 are confirmed by a warrant issued in mid-August.[116] Another warrant of December 1650 for Captain Neale's troop describes it as belonging to Okey's Regiment of Horse 'newly established'.[117]

115 *CSPD 1649–50*, pp.406–7; C. H. Firth (ed.), *The Clarke Papers: Selections from the papers of William Clarke, secretary to the Council of the Army, 1647–1649, and to General Monck and the commanders of the army in Scotland, 1651–1660* (London: Longmans, Green & Co., 1891), II, p.209.

116 TNA, SP28/70, f.19r.

117 TNA, SP28/73, f.38r.

12

Regional Warfare: Cheshire and the Welsh Borders

Some writers on the civil wars in Britain have suggested that given the nature of many dragoon operations, these soldiers were highly suited to regional warfare. Part of the reason may be that such 'contested' areas contained relatively high numbers of opposing garrisons, while the fighting was often fluid and varied in nature. In the northwest of England and the Welsh borders, this appears to have been the situation, although in the case of the Royalists many recruits and units were drawn into the Oxford Army. In the region, where the conflict had begun by September 1642, the raising and equipping of dragoons was distinctly variable. Despite the presence of significant formations of horse and foot recruited for Parliament in Lancashire, no direct evidence of dragoon units during the First Civil War has emerged. As for their Royalist counterparts, one account of the siege of Manchester reckoned that among Lord Strange's troops were 200 dragoons.[1] Sir Gilbert Houghton, who had trained band experience in the 1630s, raised some dragoons in the autumn of 1642. They were, however, defeated near Blackburn soon afterwards, though part of the unit continued to serve in Lancashire. Houghton associated himself with Strange until the disintegration of Royalist power in the county in May 1643.[2] Evidence for the existence of a regiment under Colonel Sir Thomas Tyldesley comes from the commission issued by him to Captain William Blundell of Crosby, issued at Leigh on 22 December 1642, to raise a company of dragoons:

> By virtue of his Majesty's commission under his sign manual to me directed, I do hereby constitute, and appoint you William Blundell, esquire, to be captain of one company of dragoons in my regiment. And I do hereby give you full power and authority for his Majesty in his name to raise, impress and retain the said company, raised or to be raised by sound of drum or any other way (and in any of his Majesty's Dominions) for the defence of his Majesty's royal person, the two houses of Parliament, the Protestant Religion, the law of the land, the liberty and

1 Ormerod (ed.), *Military Proceedings in Lancashire*, pp.49–56.
2 LA, DDHO/352.

> property of the subject and privilege of Parliament, and when so raised to bring together and employ in his Majesty's service as you shall from time to time receive directions for. And I do hereby require all the inferior officers and soldiers of the company to obey you, as their captain, you likewise obeying your superior officers according to the discipline of war.[3]

Blundell was captured at Preston on 9 February 1643, but was released in time to march to Lancaster, where on 18 March his thigh was shattered by a musket bullet. He later claimed to have 'mustered the 100 dragoons which I was by commission raising.' Evidence is lacking as to whether any other dragoon formations were raised by Tyldesley during the civil wars in Lancashire or elsewhere.

Dragoons were used widely by the King's forces operating along the Welsh borders in 1643, though with varying levels of success. One company was raised in and around Shrewsbury by its governor, Sir Francis Ottley, and was 'to be employed in his Majesty's special service for the defence of this town.'[4] Ottley's commission from Charles I, dated 7 September 1642, is given below:

> Charles by the grace of God King of England, Scotland, France, and Ireland, defender of the Faith, etc. To our trusty and welbeloved Francis Ottley, Esquire, greeting. Whereas, out of our tender care of the peace and welfare of our good subjects within Our town of Shrewsbury, which we shall endeavour to preserve, we have thought good to commit to you your charge of a company of volunteers already raised, or to be raised, within Our said town, or elsewhere, for securing the same in these times of distraction, against all assaults, surprise, or attempt which may be made against the same. Our will and command, therefore, is, and we do hereby authorize you to take the said company of volunteers into your charge, and them to command, train, discipline, and exercise, as their captain and leader, willing and commanding the said soldiers to be obedient, and ready to receive and accomplish the directions, commandments and summons, of you, their captain, and of the officers you shall appoint under you in all things which shall concern, and be for the preservation of Our said town, and Our good subjects inhabiting there.[5]

A warrant issued in Ottley's name, possibly in March 1643, to muster the town dragoons under the command of Lieutenant John Allen:

> Sir Francis Ottley, Knight and governor of this town of Shrewsbury doth in his Majesty's name upon pain of imprisonment for three days, straightly charge and command all dragoons within this town and suburbs of Shrewsbury, with all their maintainers to be in readiness on foot with serviceable arms complete under the Cornmarket, this afternoon, betwixt the hours of two and five of the clock, to be employed in his Majesty's special service for the defence of this town, their own lives and estates from the danger of the rebels, who have entered Newport.

3 LA, DDB 2/1.
4 SA, 6000/13294; 'Ottley Papers' (1895), p.266.
5 'Ottley Papers' (1894), pp.42–3.

> And one that have only one dragoon piece must provide with them at the time and place aforesaid muskets for the service aforesaid under the command of Lieutenant John Allen, gentleman.[6]

By April 1643, the Corporation of Shrewsbury had overestimated its ability to raise and maintain a company of dragoons and 200 foot for the King's service. Lord Capel, the recently installed military commander in the Welsh borders, wrote to Ottley, 'divers of the dragoons listed and hitherto maintain in that troop, do not forbear to repair to their colours, now they are required for his Majesty's service and that divers maintainers do not pay, nor have not paid their maintenance undertaken.'[7] In his attempts to requisition horses and arms, on 13 June the Royalist commander reminded Ottley:

> you, amongst many others, have not sent in any horses for this service, are fit to send in two horses, man and horse arms, to be employed for his Majesty's present service and this country's safety. I therefore require you, that you send in such horses, and men and arms, to the town of Shrewsbury by Monday, which will be the 19th day of this instant June, to the *Red Lion*, there they shall be received and listed.[8]

However, by August 1643 the situation in the Welsh borders had become more difficult for the Royalists. On 10 August, the Parliamentarian garrison at Nantwich was reinforced by Sir Thomas Myddelton, who had returned from London, where he had been increasing his forces. Notwithstanding Capel's usual vigilance, he arrived safely with seven pieces of large ordnance, four cases of drakes, and about 40 carts of ammunition. Additionally, Myddelton and the Cheshire commander, Sir William Brereton, dispatched a force to besiege Eccleshall Castle, which was occupied by the Royalists, and Capel's intention was to muster a sufficient force to raise the siege. On 17 August, Sir Arthur Capel wrote to Sir Francis Ottley, the governor of Shrewsbury, requesting dragoons:

> I am solicited by the gentlemen of Staffordshire for those dragoons which are at Shrewsbury commanded by Captain Allen; I suppose them to be raised by the town and liberties, and formerly commanded by Captain Owen, I desire from you to be informed of their number, and condition for arms and horses, and as I shall receive information from you, I shall give further order … I desire further to be informed by you how the mounting of Colonel Crowe's dragoons is proceeded in, and what I expect to be done therein, and by what time.[9]

Following a lengthy blockade of the castle by Parliamentarian forces, its garrison deserted on 29 August. The Cheshire dragoon companies led by Captains John Bramhall, John Lea and John Cheswis took part in the siege,

6 SA, 6000/13294; 'Ottley Papers' (1895), p.266.
7 'Ottley Papers' (1895), p.311.
8 *Ibid.*, p.332.
9 *Ibid.*, pp.355–6.

and with other Cheshire and Staffordshire soldiers received a bounty from the sale of the goods of Eccleshall Castle, amounting overall to £5,000.[10] A small number of Royalists who had fled the skirmish in the town rode hastily to beckon the assistance of Colonel Hastings at Tutbury Castle. Not recognising that Eccleshall had been taken, he came to its aid, but was seen by Brereton's scouts. According to a contemporary report, 'Sir William understanding the whole design, made as speedy preparations to meet [Hastings], and upon notice of his near approach, placed his abuscades very secretly behind hedges, and afterwards faced the colonel with a small party of horse, skirmished a little with him, and then made a seeming retreat.'[11] The Royalist Horse continued its pursuit, only to encounter the Cheshire dragoons, who were waiting in ambush. Opening fire, they annihilated Hastings and his soldiers, who were 'put to an absolute rout, about 100 of his horse slain in the place, and about as many were taken prisoners; himself wounded, and with a few of his ragged troops escaped, and fled to Tutbury Castle.'[12] The loss of Eccleshall seriously curtailed the Royalist grip on Staffordshire in late summer 1643 and in turn exposed much of neighbouring Shropshire to Parliamentarian activity.

Various units of Royalist dragoons were raised and equipped in the Welsh Borders. Sir Thomas Hanmer of Hanmer, Flintshire, was commissioned by Charles I Nottingham on 7 September 1642 to raise a dragoon regiment from North Wales. He already commanded a troop of horse. In late December 1643, Hanmer acted as governor of Chirk Castle, and his dragoons were probably part of the garrison. His commission to raise 200 dragoons is given below:

> Charles, by the grace of God, King of England, Scotland, France, and Ireland, Defender of the Faith, &c. to our trusty and well-beloved Sir Thomas Hanmer, Baronet, greetings. Whereas by the subtilty, contrivance, and malicious practices of some persons, ill-affected to our government and the peace of this our kingdom, a most horrid rebellion is grown to a height in and about London, under the specious pretext of defence of our person, and of the common good, threatening the ruin and destruction of our subjects if timely care be not taken to put a stay to the rage and malice of these men; and whereas we may have some cause of jealousy that there is some design intended to disturb the peace and quiet of our well-affected subjects in the Counties of Chester, Salop, Flint, and Denbigh, we have thought good for the better strengthening of these parts to will and require you, and do by these presents grant unto you full power and authority, by yourself, and by such commanders and officers as you shall constitute and appoint, forthwith to levy in this our kingdom, by beating the drum, two hundred dragoons, of such persons as shall voluntarily undertake the said service, by accepting of pressed money, which said soldiers so raised you are to take charge of as their captain and leader, and to employ them for aid of the said several counties, or upon such other occasion, for our service, as we shall from time to time direct. Willing and

10 CRO, ZCR63/2/702, f.24r.; HMC, *Seventh Report*, p.121.
11 *Perfect Diurnall*, 7 September 1643.
12 Vicars, *Gods Ark*, p.63.

> commanding all our commissioners of array, sheriffs, mayors, justices of the peace, bailiffs, constables, and all other our officers, ministers, and subjects, to be aiding and assisting you and your officers, and they to be obedient and ready to accomplish your commands and directions in all things which shall concern the advancement of our service in the premises, as they and every of them will answer the contrary at their peril; and these our letters shall be to you and every of them sufficient warrant and authority. Given at our Court at Nottingham, the 7th day of September, in the 18th year of our reign.[13]

Likewise, in 1642 Sir Robert Howard of Clun Castle was appointed one of the Commissioners of Array for Shropshire. By January 1643, most of his locally raised regiment of dragoons joined the King's Oxford Army and participated in various operations until mid-1644 when it returned to Shropshire.[14] Howard's men participated in the defence of Bridgnorth in 1646, of which town he had been appointed governor in the place of Sir Lewis Kirke. When it capitulated to Parliament on 26 April, he with others signed the articles of surrender. Colonel Howard's dragoons were evidently armed with matchlock muskets. On 20 June 1643, the Earl of Forth requested Henry Percy, General of the King's artillery, to 'deliver to the bearer hereof, Edward Jones, lieutenant in the regiment of Sir Robert Howard's Dragoons, for the use of their regiment, 200cwt of powder, with match and shot proportional.'[15] The Assessment of Broad St and Castle wards for Ludlow for raising soldiers includes entries for Howard's dragoons:

> Whereas the said town was ordered to raise 25 soldiers under the command of Captain Blunden, we trust that such habitants of the said town to furnish all of them with money, horse, clothes, and arms each and every one of the said soldiers.
>
> For billeting of soldiers besides officers under the command of Captain Blunden now deceased, from 27 April 1643 until the first of this instance June 1643, being 33 days [at] £29 10s 6d.[16]

On 19 March 1643 Captain William Blunden wrote to the Royalist governor of Shrewsbury, Sir Francis Ottley, requesting guidance over the use of his company:

> I have this day sent a letter to our high sheriff to know his pleasure what [is] to be done concerning my company of dragoons, I desire you to do me that favour to have an answer by this bearer from the sheriff of his resolutions what [is] to be done, if that the sheriff be not in town I desire you to open the letter, and to have your resolution what is to be done, I pray you to afford your best advice

13 NLW, Ms Bettisfield 111; John Lord Hanmer, *Memorial of the Parish and Family of Hanmer in Flintshire* (London: Chiswick Press, 1877), pp.64–5.

14 SA, 6000/13288, 13291; 'Ottley Papers' (1895), pp.286–7; Warburton, *Memoirs*, II, pp.237, 314.

15 Bod Lib, Ms Rawlinson Misc. 395; William Macray (ed.), *Ruthven Correspondence: Letters and Papers of Patrick Ruthven, Earl of Forth and Brentford* (London: J.B. Nichols, 1868), p.78.

16 SA, LB7/1994.

> and furtherance what is to be done, and you shall command him, whom is your servant, I have not as yet received my colours from our colonel.

Blunden also informed Henry Bromley, the sheriff of Shropshire:

> This day I have a warrant from you to our high constables of Sleep Hundred for the summoning of all from 16 to 60 years to be at Bridgnorth on Wednesday next, which has put me to a pussel therein, for I was resolved with what force I had to have come to Salop the 20th day, being tomorrow, therefore, I desire to have your command whether I shall come for Salop, or else for Bridgnorth, forthwith. We are altogether destitute of powder, bullets, and match. If I go for Bridgnorth you must have a care to have all things there, otherwise we shall be all together unfurnished; so with my respects to you, desiring a speedy answer by this bearer, I shall ever rest, Bishops Castle, your friend[17]

These letters highlight what was a critical time in the locality, and there was perhaps some confusion arising from orders and counter-orders. On 4 March the City of Lichfield had been taken by the Parliamentary forces under Sir John Gell, whilst Prince Rupert had been recently repulsed at Bristol and the Royalists defeated at Middlewich. Furthermore, Shrewsbury and Bridgnorth had been stripped of soldiers, and Blunden's dragoons were without ammunition. On 26 March 1643, Arthur Lord Capel, who had recently been appointed Lieutenant-General of Shropshire, Cheshire, and North Wales by Charles I, reported from Bridgnorth to Viscount Falkland – the King's Secretary of State at Oxford – his preparations for Prince Maurice's coming down to Staffordshire, and emphasised the importance of Worcester and Tewkesbury to Royalist strategy in the Midland region. Capel duly requested Colonel Henry Hastings to advance to Stourbridge if possible, if necessary, to protect Worcester, where all the army's cannon ammunition was. He informed Falkland also that he had countermanded orders for the Shropshire trained bands and 100 Bridgnorth dragoons to rendezvous at Newport, 'but has commanded them to be ready at a sudden warning.'[18]

Sir Francis Ottley, an active Royalist commander in the region, in August 1642 had been the Captain of a militia company in Shrewsbury that was reported as 'new volunteers by the King's commission to him', and from mid-September, he raised a further 200 foot.[19] Such troops constituted the nucleus of a permanent garrison and the town militia regiment at Shrewsbury under Ottley's governorship. In 1644, the corporation reported that 'the inhabitants of the town were all soldiers or maintained soldiers under them (if they did not do their duty in their own persons)'.[20] From late December 1642, a company of dragoons was also raised in and around Shrewsbury under Sir Francis Ottley's governorship, and captained successively by Ottley and then two local men – Roger Owen and John Allen. The initial response was poor,

17 'Ottley Papers' (1895), pp.286–7.
18 WSL, Ms Salt 487.
19 FRO, D/G/3275, f.84r; 'Ottley Papers' (1894), pp.39–40.
20 'Ottley Papers' (1896), p.240.

however, with only about 60 enlisted, although the unit remained active into 1644.[21] A warrant issued by Sir Francis to muster the town dragoons at Shrewsbury under the command of Lieutenant John Allen, March 1643 reads:

> Sir Francis Ottley, Knight and governor of this town of Shrewsbury doth in his Majesty's name and upon pain of imprisonment for three days, straightly charge and command all dragooners within this town and suburbs of Shrewsbury which shall there be maintained to be in a readiness on foot with serviceable arms complete, under the corn market this afternoon, betwixt the hours of two and five of the clock, to be employed in his Majesty's special service for the defence of this town, their own lives and estates from the danger of the rebels, who have entered the confines of this county at the town of Newport. And those that have one dragoon provided, must provide and bring with them, and place aforesaid sufficient muskets for the service aforesaid under the command of Lieutenant John Allen, gentleman.[22]

Not everyone complied, however. Thomas Jones, a barrister and burgess of the town, held Parliamentarian sympathies, even though in 1644 Prince Rupert stayed in his house. When Shrewsbury was surprised by the Parliamentarians in February 1645 Jones was taken prisoner, but the commissioners for corporations later alleged that he had:

> declared himself against the commission of array in the time of the wars, which was the dispute between the King and the Parliament, and refused to find a dragoon for the King's service, for which he was committed by Sir Francis Ottley, then governor of Shrewsbury; which commitment Mr Jones [his cousin, the Parliamentarian Colonel Samuel Jones] afterwards brought two men to testify to before the Parliament's Committee in that town as an argument of his good affection to them. His brother, that was of the Parliament's party and recorder of the town in the time of the rebellion, declared him then publicly upon the bench at a quarter-sessions a man well-affected to the Parliament.[23]

By the autumn of 1643 Sir Francis Ottley was also Colonel of a regiment of horse, which was then operating from Ludlow. A troop of Ottley's horse was at Bridgnorth in October 1645, and some of the regiment fought at Denbigh that November.[24] Also known to have been raised in the Welsh borders on behalf of the King was Colonel Henry Crowe's dragoons. They operated with Lord Capel's forces in 1643, while Crowe was based at Ludlow by May 1643 and his men were also quartered in the Shrewsbury area.[25] Some dragoons, possibly from Shropshire, also appear to have been commanded by Colonel Francis Baker. In February 1643, he was commissioned to raise a regiment

21 'Ottley Papers' (1895) pp.266, 311, 355–356.
22 SA, 6001/13294.
23 'Ottley Papers' (1894), p.299; (1896), pp.214–16.
24 SA, LB7/2064; Symonds, *Diary*, p.252; 'Ottley Papers' (1896), pp.252–3, 272–3.
25 SA, LB8/1/163, f.4r; LB7/2320; 3355/2566; 'Ottley Papers' (1895), 327, 345–6.

of 1,200 foot and dragoons, feasibly as part of the Bishop's Castle garrison, although any further history of these troops is difficult to discern.[26] Another dragoon unit which contributed to the Royalist war effort in the borders operated from the garrison of Shrawardine under the command of a Captain Johnson. This company may have belonged to, or was attached to. Sir William Vaughan's regiment of horse, four troops of which had landed from Ireland at Beaumaris and Neston in February 1644. Whilst the regiment served at major actions, such as Marston Moor, Montgomery and Naseby, it was also stationed in various Shropshire garrisons, including Shrawardine of which Vaughan was governor until 1646.[27]

On 16 January 1643, the Cheshire Royalist commander Sir Thomas Aston was commissioned to raise 500 dragoons in Cheshire, possibly, like his cavalry, from Anglican officers and men.[28] Four companies were recruited from his tenants and volunteers in Cheshire and Lancashire, between January and March, although some of the dragoon officers were Chester men and there were links with the 'city regiment'. Captain Thomas Newland, for instance, 'brought in 60 foot ready raised' to form one unit. Sir Thomas Aston's dragoon formation seems to have operated largely with his horse in a larger, combined 'regiment', even though this often caused it to be obscured among its listings.[29] Sir Thomas' dragoons were not formed in time to take part in operations against Sir William Brereton's Parliamentarian forces in Cheshire in early 1643. But it may be the case that after Sir Thomas' defeat at Middlewich on 13 March, and the problems encountered by him in securing pay and provisions from the Commissioners of Array at Chester, plus the ensuing return of his cavalry to the Oxford Army, there was a scaling down of dragoon enrolment. Either way, although Sir Thomas initially enrolled 220 dragoons, the unit was mauled at Newbury in September 1643, losing about 100 men. In February 1643, while back at Chester, a number Aston's troopers received new clothing, while his new dragoons were equipped and clothed as they were recruited.

The problems encountered by commanders, such as Sir Thomas, in raising dragoons were not uncommon in the King's armies, especially in Cheshire and the Welsh borders, which after the onrush of 1642 were frequently beset by recruiting problems occasioned by lack of resources and potential recruits. Symonds described how the Royalist Colonel Samuel Sandys of Ombersley in Worcestershire (he was MP for Droitwich in the Short Parliament, a Commissioner of Array for Worcestershire, was appointed governor of Evesham by the King, and commanded a cavalry troop during the Edgehill campaign) 'raised three regiments: one of horse, one of foot, one of dragoons all at his own charge.'[30] The County persistently encountered

26 BL, Ms Add 18981 f.20r.

27 Symonds, *Diary*, p.181; CRO, DDX/428, ff.33v & 52r; BL, Ms Add 11331, f.89r; *BLB*, I, 99, 127, 479.

28 BL, Ms Harley 6852, f.98r.

29 BL, Ms Add 36913, ff.88r–94v, 101v, 105r, 107r–108v; BL, Ms Harley 6853, ff.149r–151v.

30 Symonds, *Diary*, p.12. See also WA, BA13825/1/1. Commission for Colonel Sandys to be Governor of Evesham, 20 January 1643; BA13825/1/3. Commission to Captain Samuel Sandys to have a regiment of foot, 20 November 1643; BA13825/1/4. Commission from Prince Rupert

problems in raising the basic Assessment, the monthly distribution of which was the source of the disagreement between Sandys and the governor of Worcester, Sir William Russell. This created disorder among Sandys' troops, who were left to furnish themselves from the civilian population as best they could, appropriating rations, clothing, and even bedding. A later statement of expenses made to the King's Commissioners of Array recounted that in August 1643, James Hill of Doddingtree was robbed by Sandys' dragoons, who took 'certain clothes, woollen and linen to the value of £5.'[31] Sandys' appeal to the restored Charles II for 'consideration of the war service' rendered by him related that in 1643 he:

> left the Parliament in order to serve his late Majesty of blessed memory, who was graciously pleased to send him a commission unlooked for, to command a troop of horse. That accordingly he commanded a troop at Wickfield, afterwards at Edgehill, and in the march to Brentford, under the command of the right honourable the now Earl of Bristol. That he offering to raise a regiment of foot at his own charge, and going into Worcestershire to discover the condition of the country, his troop of horse in such his absence was disposed of, but restored to him again. He was necessitated to arm his foot regiment at his own charge, being by fraud disappointed of the Trained Band arms (which by his Majesty's proclamation he ought to have had) while he was absent upon service by his Majesty's particular command In the same year he raised a regiment of horse, consisting of seven troops, and soon after a good part of a regiment of dragoons, to the number of eight-score at least, who after some time were scattered and broke, for want of pay. But shortly after he recruited both his regiments of horse and foot, without the least charge to his Majesty which kept up in constant service to the end of the war.[32]

Thus, the recruitment of Colonel Sandys' dragoons was never completed, and in late 1644 they were reformed as a troop of horse in his own regiment under Captain Thomas Symonds. Some commissions for the raising of troops, including dragoons, were either too ambitious in their expectations, and thus yielded few recruits, or for various reasons the units themselves failed to materialise. One example is, in March 1645 three commissions were issued by 'Prince Charles, Captain General of the Associated Western Army' to William Bull of Shapwick, Somerset, 'to raise and command a company of dragoons, a troop of horse, and a regiment of foot from the hundred of Whitley, the tithing of High Ham excepted.'[33] No evidence of the existence of such units has come to light, and so it must be assumed that they came to naught.

Whether commanders such as Sir Thomas Aston possessed any military experience prior to the civil wars is unknown – his brother John substituted

---

to Colonel Samuel Sandys regarding the raising of money to support Colonel Sandys' regiment of horse, 17 December 1643.

31 BCA, Ms 3312/18/29.

32 WA, BA13825/2/46/20.

33 Somerset A, DD/5G/61.

for him during the First Bishops War, although the reason for this is unknown. Sir Thomas's kinsman, Sir Arthur Aston, was a Catholic professional soldier of considerable experience, who had fought for the Polish-Lithuanian Commonwealth until the Truce of Altmarck in 1629.[34] It is claimed that Sir Arthur returned to England in 1639 with 'as many soldiers of note as he could bring', although the actual number remains unknown.[35] He was commissioned Sergeant-Major-General to Viscount Conway in the Second Bishops War.[36] Despite his religion, he led a brigade of Royalist dragoons at Edgehill; he raised at his own charge a regiment of horse, which served as part of the Oxford Army and the garrison of Oxford. Sir Arthur was also, on 22 November 1642, appointed governor of the strategically important town of Reading and commissioned by Prince Rupert on 17 March 1643 'as captain of a free company of dragoons to act as auxiliary to your regiment of horse, and to be raised from volunteers in any part of the Kingdom of England and dominion of Wales.'[37]

There is some evidence that in the period immediately after Edgehill, in October-November 1642, Aston advised his kinsman Sir Thomas, to raise dragoons only (rather than horse) and to clothe them in the same grey-green hue as that of his own troops. This is significant, given Sir Arthur's Continental experience, leadership of the Oxford Army's dragoon units during the Edgehill campaign, and, with Prince Rupert, a proponent of combined arms mounted operations. Despite his long-standing military standing, however, Aston's cantankerous and brutal nature was detested by his fellow officers, soldiers and civilians within the Reading garrison and elsewhere. After relinquishing command of the garrison when he was hit on the head by a roof tile, Clarendon, one of Aston's detractors, remarked 'there was then thought of great misfortune to the King, for there was not in his army an officer of greater reputation, and of whom the enemy had a greater dread.'[38] On 19 September 1644, Sir Arthur was thrown from his horse and fractured his leg, from which gangrene set in, and amputation was performed on 7 December. Thus, having become incapable of discharging the active duties of Governor of Oxford, to which he had succeeded on the death of Sir William Pennyman, the King removed him and conferred upon him a pension of £1,000 a year. According to the antiquary Anthony Wood, Aston was relieved 'to the great rejoicing of the soldiers and others in Oxford, having expressed himself very cruel and imperious while he executed that office.'[39]

It might follow, given that most Royalist and Parliamentarian commanders employed military professionals to train, organise and lead

34 Basil Morgan, 'Sir Arthur Aston', *ODNB* (2004); Robert Frost, 'Scottish soldiers, Poland-Lithuania and the Thirty Years' War', Steve Murdoch (ed.),*Scotland and the Thirty Years' War, 1618–1648* (Leiden: Brill, 2001), pp.191–213, (pp.204–9).

35 George Steinman, 'Memoir of Sir Arthur Aston', *The Gentleman's Magazine*, 155 (1834), pp.144–50, (p.145).

36 TNA, SP95/3, f.105r; PC 2/42, f.105r.

37 BL, Ms Add 18980, f.8v; BRO, R/Z10, 11–13.

38 Clarendon, *History*, IV, pp.27, 44.

39 Wood, *Life*, I, p.110.

their regiments and sub-units, Sir Thomas Aston may have followed suit. Even so, the earlier careers of his dragoon officers remain obscure, other than them being country gentlemen in Cheshire, Lancashire, and perhaps Shropshire. The army of Parliament raised and operating in Aston's native Cheshire, commanded by Sir William Brereton, was boosted from the start by the presence of experienced professionals, whose expertise was greatly in demand. James Lothian, an experienced Scotch officer accompanied him from London in 1642 to coordinate Brereton's foot and practice his considerable skills of siege-craft. The author of one Parliamentarian account of the fighting at Middlewich in March 1643 termed Lothian 'a right Scottish blade', and he was singled out by Sir Thomas Myddelton and others for his leadership of the Cheshire foot in Cheshire and the Welsh borders the following year.[40] Aston's closest Parliamentarian neighbour, Colonel Henry Brooke, employed professionals to command and train both his own troop of horse and company of foot, while at least three of Brereton's dragoon captains, including Captain Simon Finch, who had served in the army in Ireland in Sir Michael Earnley's regiment of foot before being captured at Nantwich in 1644, boasted previous military proficiency.[41]

The turncoat, William, Lord Paget raised a regiment of '1,200 foot for the defence of his Majesty's person' in Staffordshire. Though he put up the money for it and took a personal part in recruiting, on 16 August 1642 he wrote to the Royalist MP Sir Richard Leveson, 'I have sent one of my officers to beat up my drums in your part and about Newport, and do desire you to assist him in what you may for the encouragement of the people to King's service.'[42] In doing so, much reliance was placed upon the career soldier Richard Bolle and his deputy, Richard D'Ewes, for the training and enrolling of each of the regiment's companies. In the absence of much evidence for the source of the initial costs of recruiting, equipping, and paying of Royalist dragoons, it must be assumed that such sums were borne by local commissions of array, voluntary contributions, or individual officers. Thus, when sometime after 18 December 1642, Colonel Sir Richard Lloyd of Esclus, son of Evan Lloyd of Dulasau raised horse and dragoons for the King. He was at Oxford in 1643 and was Governor of Holt in 1645. Sir Richard wrote to Sir Francis Ottley, the Royalist governor of Shrewsbury, 'I must entreat you to stand my friend in this business of raising my regiment [of dragoons], I have left orders with Major Holland or [Captain] Jack Calveley for the receiving of them. I pray you further it what you may and speak to the rest of my good friends to do the like for the sooner I have them ready the sooner I shall be able to do the country service.' However, neither of these officers mentioned under him appear in the garrison of Holt.[43]

40 *Cheshire's Successe since their pious and truly valiant Colonel, Sir William Brereton, Baronet, came to their rescue, &c.* (London, 20 March 1643). TT, E94 [6]; *A Copy of a Letter sent from Sir Thomas Myddelton* (London, 10 July 1644). TT, E54 [16]; *The Success of Our Cheshire Forces, as they came Related by Sir William Brereton's own pen* (London: 26 August 1644). TT, E8 [8].

41 Abram, "Sufficiently Different', pp.228–29; 'Military Professionals', *TLCAS*, 112 (2020), pp.125–26.

42 SRO, D868/2/36b; HMC, *Fifth Report, App.*, p.142; HMC, *Thirteenth Report, App. I*, p.63.

43 Thanks to Will Hughes for this information.

His relative, Colonel Edward Lloyd acted as governor of Oswestry in 1644. According to the lost narrative of his 'actions and sufferings', Sir Richard 'gave the King all his plate and raised a troop of dragoons, and armed them at his own charge, advancing likewise a month's pay to every soldier out of his own purse.'[44] Another Welsh gentleman, Thomas Davies of Gwysaney, was commissioned by the King to raise 500 foot and dragoons in Flintshire and Denbighshire (probably from men of the Flintshire Trained Bands) to serve under Lord Capel in 1643. Capel's orders, issued at Oxford on 19 July, stated:

> Right trusty and well-beloved We greet you well. We having given our commission to our trusty and well-beloved Colonel Thomas Davies to raise one regiment of 500 foot and dragooners for our service, and the defence and security of our counties of Flint and Denbigh, have thought fit to recommend unto you, and to let you know that although other persons may have received commissions to raise forces in those parts who have thereby the precedency, yet we knowing the ability of Colonel Davies who hath served us, and our late royal father of blessed memory in all our expeditions, cannot but esteem him fit to have that respect as to be preferred to the priority of command (especially in the county of Flint), which our pleasure is your lordship see performed upon all occasions that may offer themselves for our service.[45]

Whether Davies raised this many men, both foot and dragoons, is unknown, although the former was predominantly drawn from the Flintshire Trained Bands

Sir Thomas Aston's horse and dragoons – recruited in Cheshire and parts of Lancashire – were paid for by the Oxford Colleges in 1642–3, but also by voluntary subscriptions and short-term loans. Even so, in early 1644, whilst quartering in the West Country, his combined command of seven troops and 300 troopers/dragoons was paid £319 13s per week out of the contributions allotted from six Wiltshire Hundreds.[46] Such a system, however, could be haphazard and greatly depended on the cooperation of the local gentry, as well as the effectiveness of the methods used to collect it. Depositions made against Dr George Snell, Laudian archdeacon of Chester, and pluralist rector of Wallasey and Waverton, in 1645 alleged that during the summer of 1642 he supported the Commission of Array in Cheshire, preached to Aston's soldiers, and marched about the county with him in possession of a sword and pistol. He also paid for 'a man, horse and arms' to serve in Sir Thomas's troop. The trooper had his mount killed at Edgehill and returned home to Cheshire.[47]

The experiences of Sir Vincent Corbet in Shropshire were not too dissimilar. He sat as MP in 1640, was Captain of the Shropshire Trained Band horse and Commissioner of Array in 1642. In December 1642 with the King's

44 'Ottely Papers' (1894), pp.52, 149.
45 NLW, 1595E/1 Gwysaney Letters (nineteenth century transcripts); CCC, III, 1718.
46 BL, Ms Add 36913, f.101v; WSHC, X3/119, unfol.
47 TNA, SP23/118, ff.505r, 509v; SP23/190, ff.642r–642v.

consent, thirty-three 'Principal gentlemen of Salop', headed by the sheriff, Henry Bromley, proposed:

Sir William Brereton (1604-1661) From *A Survey Of Englands Champions*, Josiah Ricraft (London 1647) (Stephen Ede-Borrett collection)

> We, whose names are hereunder written, do hereby engage ourselves, each to the other, and promise upon the faith and word of a gentleman, that we will do our utmost endeavours, both by ourselves and friends, to raise as well for the defence of our King and country, as our own particular safeties, one entire regiment of dragooners, and with our lives to defend those mens' fortunes and families, who shall be contributors herein to their abilities. And for the more speedy expedition of the said service, we have thought fit to entreat Sir Vincent Corbet, formerly captain of the horse for this county, to be our chief commander over the aforesaid regiment. And likewise, we have appointed the day of our appearance for bringing in of every man's proportion of his horse and money, according to the subscription of his undertaking, to be the twentieth day of December, all in the battlefield.[48]

Hence, Corbet's commission as Colonel of dragoons was authorised, 'for the defence of his Majesty and that county.'[49] The arrangement for raising these soldiers was extended to provide for their maintenance by a general tax on the county of Shropshire. Yet by the following month most of the subscriptions had failed to materialise. At their first muster, the dragoons numbered just 60 men, and by January 1643 still less than 300 men had been recruited. At least four of the dragoon regiment's captains were local men and most of its recruits appear to have been obtained from the area as well. Captain Edward Baldwin, for instance, acquired recruits in South Shropshire, including 26 from Ludlow, although an appeal was made for 'an officer to exercise these dragoons if you know one fit for service.'[50] Corbet's hastily raised and inexperienced men joined Sir Thomas Aston's troops

48 HMC, *Tenth Report,* App. IV, pp.403–4.

49 BL, Ms Harley 6851, ff.236r, 248r; SA, SRRU 6000/13291.

50 SA, LB7/2015; 'Ottley Papers' (1895), pp.259–60.

returning to Cheshire in January 1643, but they were overwhelmed during the brief action at Nantwich.

Sir William Brereton, the victorious Parliamentarian commander, later described how, during the skirmish, the body of dragoons sent to occupy the town was 50 in number, and 'were presently disordered and many of them ran away without ever giving fire.'[51] Moreover, John Harrington, a relative of the Royalist leader in Shropshire, Sir Francis Ottley, wrote, 'I was heartily sorry to see Sir Vincent Corbet so poorly furnished with raw soldiers and young commanders.'[52] Sir Thomas Aston, who had experienced these soldiers previously at Nantwich and Middlewich, described them at Whitchurch on 17 March 1643 as 'those few dragoons in fear of daily surprise.'[53] Even so, according to Brereton's account of the battle at Hopton Heath in Staffordshire two days later, where Corbet's Shropshire horse and dragoons fought with the Earl of Northampton's forces 'which was a great addition to their strength. These came on with great resolution and boldness, and in very good order. Some say there were six score, others judge there were 200 in front, when they came up and charged our horse.'[54] After the dragoons on each side had skirmished for the space of an hour, the Royalists attacked and defeated the greater part of the Parliamentarian horse, but the foot held firm.

Before 15 March 1643 Arthur, Lord Capel was appointed Lieutenant-General of North Wales and Shropshire by the King, and by 23 March he was in Shrewsbury to take up his command.[55] However, the area had been drained of military resources by the Royalist army and Capel's attempts to press recruits and money in Flintshire and Denbighshire were particularly unpopular. Hutton asserts that Capel 'possessed certain long-term advantages which might prove potent if he were an able leader.'[56] For some weeks Royalist patrols ranging from Capel's forward headquarters at Whitchurch – approximately 20 miles north of Shrewsbury and halfway to the Royalist garrison of Chester – harassed Sir William Brereton's forces in north Shropshire and the Nantwich area. On 13 April, at Ranmore Heath, near Malpas, Royalist mounted troops (probably including Sir Vincent Corbet's dragoons) attacked the Parliamentarians and pursued them back to Nantwich, the location of Brereton's headquarters. Following the fighting, Corbet wrote to Sir Francis Ottley at Shrewsbury:

> So it is that we are upon continual service and some of our men are daily hurt and cannot avoid much prejudice without a surgeon to apply present remedies. In regard whereof I pray you do me the favour to send young Shelvock, or some other good surgeon whom you will recommend me, with all speed to Malpas, where I and my regiment are now quartered; and let him bring with him his implements and all manner of necessaries, and he shall have a remuneration to his content.[57]

51 *Cheshire's Successe.*
52 'Ottley Papers' (1894), p.69.
53 BL, Ms Harley 2135, f.93r.
54 Greenslade and Baugh, *History and Antiquities of Staffordshire*, I, p.81.
55 *Certaine Informations*, 18 April 1643.
56 Hutton, *Royal War Effort*, p.60.
57 'Ottley Papers' (1894), p.150.

Reflecting the confused and fluid nature of operations in the region during this period, the pilfering of livestock and goods from several villages continued across the Cheshire border. While on 17 May 1643, with 'a great company of cavaliers both of Whitchurch and Shropshire, and other places to the number of 1,500 or more' Lord Capel made a perfunctory attack on Nantwich.[58] A few days later, Capel was ordered by Rupert to advance to the Royalist-held town of Warrington to secure supplies and to aid the garrison. However, as he marched he was unaware that it had recently laid down its arms. Forewarned of Capel's movements, Brereton sidestepped him and 'with the horse and all the foot in Nantwich' attacked his base at Whitchurch and another recently begun at Market Drayton. Following a two-hour night action and a fighting retreat on the part of the defending Royalists, on 30 May the Cheshire forces stormed the former. Malbon reported, 'The Nantwich foot soldiers firing very fiercely upon them, and they in the town did the like, maintaining their works and town very bravely.'[59] The Royalist garrison, commanded by Sergeant-Major Michael Woodhouse, was overcome and the town was seized with a substantial quantity of military supplies and additional plunder. For much of the remainder of 1643, detachments of Sir Vincent Corbet's dragoon regiment served in various garrisons in Shropshire, whilst in 1644 Corbet acted as governor of Morton Corbet Castle, and it could be that his dragoons operated out of the garrison there. Corbet's men later formed the garrison of High Ercall, and a detachment of dragoons reportedly participated in the fight at Denbigh Green on 1 November 1645.[60]

In 1642 some local gentlemen encountered difficulties in turning out bodies of dragoons, even though they had previously been levied. On 13 December it was reported that Sir Richard Hopton, who had been commissioned by the Earl of Essex to raise troops from the trained bands and volunteers of Herefordshire:

> had promised the Earl of Stamford that he had 1,000 dragoons at four days' warning to be ready for his service, came into Ledbury and brought with him his colours and his drum, and there in a commanding manner called all the countrymen in order to bring in their dragoons. The first man answered him that he had received His Majesty's book to the contrary, and that he durst not, lest he should be held a traitor. The others did answer alike, so that he went out of Ledbury, and his colours and drum were taken away from him. It is said that Hopton has since come to Worcester and turned to the King's part.[61]

The Parliamentarian army in Cheshire commanded by Sir William Brereton contained various dragoon units, which served at the forefront of operations as both specialist mounted soldiers and assault troops. Brereton himself received commissions as Colonel and Captain of foot from 20 September 1642

58 Hall (ed.), *Memorials*, p.55; Warburton, *Memoirs*, II, p.495.

59 Hall (ed.), *Memorials*, pp.56–60; HMC, *Twelfth Report*, App. IX, pp.39–40.

60 Symonds, *Diary*, p.259.

61 HMC, *Fifth Report*, App., p.142; Stuart Peachey and Alan Turton, *The Fall of the West* (Bristol: Stuart Press, 1994),VI, p.631.

to 24 June 1645, Captain of a troop of harquebusiers from 20 September 1642 to 24 June 1645, and Colonel of a regiment of harquebusiers from 16 April 1644 to 24 June 1645.[62] However, these were not all the military units that he led. On 3 November 1645, Sir William informed the Committee of Accounts, 'I raised and took down with me [to Cheshire] in December [1642] these companies of dragoons: Captain Bramhall, Captain Goldegay and Captain Lea which, together with my horse and all the force with me, were put upon service by the way and the first night after we came into Cheshire.'[63] In his accounts he further mentioned that he received no pay for commanding the 'good regiment of dragoons' from 'his first coming down into Cheshire until the time I returned to the Parliament on 24 June 1645', due to lack of a commission.[64]

Moreover, after Sir William had submitted his accounts, he wrote on 12 January 1646 to a friend: 'there is accounted for a regiment of horse from 16 April 1644, whereof I commanded a good regiment of horse from 1 March 1643 and another regiment of dragoons, both of which there hath been perfect lists given to the Committee of Accounts, the truth thereof I do attest upon oath.'[65] Similarly, when Brereton drew up a list of his army for the Committee of Both Kingdoms on 30 April 1645, the dragoons were unmistakably part of it and therefore had to be included, the regiment did not officially exist and therefore the companies were included in the strength of his infantry regiment. When on 18 October he produced another list merely of his own regiments, the dragoons were not included.[66] Evidently, the latter details were meant to support Brereton's accounts, in which he claimed no pay for leading them due to the lack of a commission.

Originally raised in London and Cheshire, the dragoons participated in the defence of London in November 1642. Upon their arrival in Cheshire in late January 1643, they fought against Sir Thomas Aston's troops at Nantwich and the First Battle of Middlewich, before participating in Sir William Brereton's operations in Staffordshire and the fight at Hopton Heath in March 1643. Three companies of Cheshire dragoons took part in the capture of Eccleshall Castle on 30 August, while the soldiers under the command of Captains John Bramhall, John Lea and John Cheswis benefitted from the sale of the goods of the garrison with other Cheshire and Staffordshire troops.[67] Despite some initial battlefield inexperience, the Cheshire dragoons developed into versatile and highly specialised troops who were accustomed to hazardous service. Furthermore, they were commanded by experienced and resourceful officers who were for the most part professional soldiers, and some of whom had previously served in the Irish wars.

According to later petitions submitted by disabled veterans in Cheshire and Stafford, John Bickerton of Crewe swore that he served under Sergeant-

62 JRRIL, TW/262; TNA, SP28/35, ff.164r–165v, 168r; SP28/152/7, f.20r; SP28/300, f.558v; BL, Ms Add 11332, f.43r; *BLB*, II, 809.
63 BL, Ms Add 11332, f.43v; *BLB*, II, 809.
64 TNA, SP28/152/7, f.20r.
65 CRO, ZCR/63/2/691, f.13r.
66 BL, Mss Add 11332, f.43v; 11333, f.3r; *BLB*, I, 385; II, 703.
67 CRO, ZCR/63/2/702, f.24r.

Major Bramhall and at Longford in Shropshire in 1644 he 'received by the enemy nineteen wounds, six whereof fell upon his right hand.' Bramhall himself testified that John Sillitoe 'was shot into the thigh at the storming of Cholmondeley House [on 8 July 1644], at which time he was in actual service under my command. And by reason of the said shot, is disabled from the getting of a livelihood by his labour and pains as formerly he was accustomed to do, he having had above 20 pieces of bones taken out of the wound.' Moreover, in an endorsement of a petition submitted by Robert Stevenson, Captain Godfrey Gimbert wrote on 9 March 1647:

> These may certify all whom it may concern that the bearer hereof ... has faithfully served the Parliament under my command three years last past as a common soldier and a corporal of firelocks. In which service, he was several times wounded. By which, he has lost his limbs and is altogether unable to get his living, having once the great bone in his arm severed in pieces and at another time upon a sally forth of Beeston Castle the great bone of his thigh shot in pieces, besides (as it may appear) has had divers other cuts and wounds.[68]

Like some of their Royalist counterparts, in terms of equipment, tactics and leadership Brereton's dragoons or firelocks seem to have been 'sufficiently different' to the rest of the army and towards the forefront of an evolution in the role of mounted warfare in seventeenth century warfare. Owing to battlefield attrition, the capture, reassignment and promotion of officers, and the influx of recruits from the Royalist army from Ireland, in 1644 Brereton's dragoons were reorganised into three companies, led by Captains Finch, Gilbert and Holt, although other commands and detachments are known from later in the war under different officers. Thus, Sir William spoke more than once of 'three to four' companies of dragoons under his command. Like other Parliamentarian forces in Shropshire and the borderlands of Wales, those of Cheshire were bolstered by soldiers from the English army in Ireland who had changed sides in 1644 after the Battle of Nantwich and the siege of Liverpool.

Maybe 600 of the 1,500 soldiers captured on 25 January took service with Brereton's army. Some of these might have served previously in the firelock companies of Captains Sandford and Francis Langley. Nothing is known of the latter's fate, but Sandford played a leading role in the capture of Hawarden Castle and with eight of his men took Beeston in a surprise operation. He was killed leading Sir John Byron's attack on Nantwich on 17 January 1644. According to Malbon, papers outlining plans for the assault were found in his pockets.[69] The range of operations undertaken by the dragoons belonging to the Cheshire Army of Parliament was extremely wide and varied, from

68 CRO, QJF 74/4, f.47r; QJF 78/1, f.37r; QJF 78/4, f.33r; SRO, Q/SR/274, f.4r.

69 HMC, *Fourteenth Report*, App. VII, pp.124, 131, 143; Hall (ed.), *Memorials*, pp.91–109. See also Lowe, 'The Campaign of the Irish Royalist Army', *THSLC*, 111 (1959), pp.62 & 65; Ian Ryder, *An English Army for Ireland* (Partizan Press, 1987), p.31; John Barratt, 'What Sanford's Firelocks Did Next', *ECWNQ*, 50 (Partizan Press, 1995), pp.18–21; Andrew Hopper, *Turncoats and Renegadoes: Changing Sides during the English Civil Wars* (Oxford University Press, 2012), pp.89–90.

small-scale raids, intelligence gathering, skirmishes and foraging operations (often in enclosed country) to full-scale assaults and combined arms warfare. In May 1645,as Charles I's army began manoeuvring northwards from its base at Oxford, Sir William Brereton was ordered by the Committee of Both Kingdoms to rendezvous his forces with those of Lords Fairfax and Leven, and the county of Lancashire at Barlow Moor, an open heath on the north bank of the Mersey, south of Manchester.[70] The prevaricating Committee had debated whether Sir Thomas Fairfax with the bulk of the New Model Army should besiege Oxford or follow the King.

Determining that the Scots, the northern Parliamentarians and forces of various Midland counties could deal with the Royalist threat, the Committee decided that Fairfax should stay put and instructed Cromwell, in command of a substantial body of horse, that if Charles continued northwards, he was to join Sir Thomas in besieging the Royalist capital. In a letter to Leven on 22 May, Brereton described his dragoons 'which were soldiers in Ireland' as 'very serviceable' and 'well-accommodated'. He added, 'I can bring no more foot than one regiment and some choice dragoons – firelocks which were soldiers in Ireland lately mounted.'[71] The following day the Cheshire commander informed the Committee of Both Kingdoms from Manchester, 'The Cheshire foot which I expect are not above 5–600. There are 8–9 troops of Cheshire horse and 3–4 very serviceable companies of dragoons, well-accommodated.' On 25 May he reported, 'In pursuance of Lord Leven's and Lord Fairfax's orders, I have continued on the outskirts of Lancashire and Cheshire betwixt Knutsford and Manchester and Stockport with my Horse and dragoons, and a regiment of foot ever since the day of rendezvous appointed by Lord Fairfax.' Moreover, writing two days afterwards to the Lancashire MP William Ashurst, after waiting at Barlow Moor for the agreed meeting to materialise, Brereton reiterated, 'I have brought up the Cheshire Horse and dragoons, and what foot could possibly be spared.'[72]

Sergeant-Major John Bramhall's Company

The son of widow Bramhall of Nantwich, John is likely to have been a mercer before the war. His first service was as Captain in Colonel John Hampden's infantry regiment in Essex's army, which had been formed in July and August 1642, fought at Edgehill, Brentford and Turnham Green. During November 1642 Bramhall joined Sir William Brereton as Captain of one of three companies of dragoons raised in the capital for the Cheshire forces. His detailed accounts begin with 'A particular of such moneys paid to my soldiers after I came out of my Lord General's army during my stay in London until I came upon the service in Cheshire.'[73] They provide much detail about Bramhall's service and expenditure, as well as the equipping, provisioning and activities of his command. John Bramhall held a commission as Captain

70 BL, Ms Add 11331, ff.127v, 158r, 133r–134v, 144r, 139v–140r; *BLB*, I, 572, 578–582, 597–599; *CSPD 1644–5*, pp.504, 506, 509, 512.

71 BL, Ms Add 11331, f.142v; *BLB*, I, 610; HMC, *Fourteenth Report*, App. IV, p.62.

72 BL, Ms Add 11331, ff.148v, 151r, 164r, 169r; *BLB*, I, 622, 631, 651.

73 BL, Ms Harley 2128, ff.20r.–35v.

of a company of dragoons from 21 November 1642 to 20 August 1643, as Sergeant-Major of dragoons from 20 August 1643 to 30 April 1644, and Sergeant-Major of a troop of horse from 30 April 1644 to 5 February 1645. He was an energetic and talented officer who was constantly in action with Brereton during the period November 1642 to autumn 1643, when Bramhall was captured.

Following his company's participation in the reduction of Eccleshall Castle in August, Captain Bramhall was captured with some of his junior officers and dragoons at Loppington in north Shropshire a month later.[74] Bramhall's accounts show that 30 firelocks and 24 mounts were also lost in the battle, suggesting that nearly half of his company was taken.[75] John was exchanged in April 1644, but by then Brereton's dragoons were beginning to be remodelled. He thus received command of a troop of horse, although with his former position as dragoon leader gone and being seemingly at odds with his commander-in-chief's war aims, Bramhall resigned his commission in early February 1645. This is borne out by his appearance as a signatory to the anti-Brereton petition three months later. In August 1650, Major John Bramhall was commissioned Sergeant-Major in Colonel Henry Brooke's militia regiment of foot.[76] Whether he saw action with the unit at the Battle of Worcester the following year remains unclear.

Bramhall's company was raised in London in November and December 1642, although going by the names present in its first complete muster roll, he is likely to have had some Cheshire men with him already. During the first recruitment period, between 21 November and 2 December, one captain, one lieutenant, one cornet, two sergeants, three corporals, one drummer, one clerk and 57 soldiers were mustered. The company officers were paid the sum of £19 10s in stages from 21 November to 15 December. Before departing from London in the first week of December, Captain John Bramhall purchased horsemeat for his soldiers at a cost of £15 7s 4d, with an additional 19s spent on 'the diet of my officers'. Leaving the capital for the march to Cheshire, 20 of Bramhall's soldiers reached Abbots Langley in Hertfordshire on 2 December, where they were paid £29 18s 6d. Between 11 and 15 December the remaining 37 dragoons received £2 15s 6d, having marched with Sir William Brereton's other forces to Watford. John Bramhall's accounts show his initial outlay in pay for his officers and men to have been £53 15s 0d. Having marched to Northampton, his cornet and two sergeants had £1 4s in pay, while 15s 8d 0d was laid out for hay and corn for their horses. The first complete muster of Bramhall's company dates from 24 January 1643:[77]

Bramhall further claimed pay for 53 dragoons between 24 January and 31 March 1643, and 60 between 31 March and 20 May 1643. On 20 May 1643 one captain, one lieutenant, one cornet, one quartermaster, two sergeants,

74 Hall (ed.), *Memorials*, pp.76–7; *Shropshires misery and mercie, Manifested in the defeat given to the Lord Capels ravenous and devouring Armie, by the forces of Cheshire and Shropshire* (November 1643), pp.2–3.

75 BL, Ms Harley 2128, ff.34r–34v. ('where my officers and soldiers [were] captured').

76 *CSPD, 1650*, p.509.

77 BL, Ms Harley 2128, ff.20v–21r, 31v.

three corporals, two drummers, one clerk and 80 men mustered for service. Among the junior and non-commissioned offers there had been some promotion from the ranks, perhaps due to casualties sustained during the early stages of the fighting in Cheshire and transfers to other commands. Between 20 August 1643 and 30 April 1644 (the date upon which it was disbanded) Bramhall's command mustered 60 soldiers.[78]

Captain Gwilliam Goldegay's Company

Goldegay, probably a professional soldier, commanded one of the companies of dragoons that Brereton brought from London to Cheshire during December 1642 and January 1643. He first appears in a warrant of November 1642, in which as quartermaster (perhaps in the army of the Earl of Essex) he was tasked to conduct three sakers from the Tower of London to Reading.[79] Goldegay was commissioned Captain of a company of Cheshire dragoons on 6 December 1642, and he with his men were listed in London where the unit was recruited. Lieutenant Monkes and Cornet John Marum were paid with the command on 15 April 1643, whilst a warrant for Captain Goldegay's pay from Ralph Judson is dated 19 August of the same year.[80] Goldegay's dragoons played an important part in winning the small victory outside Nantwich that allowed Brereton control of the town and enable him to establish his headquarters there. On the evening of 28 January 1643, a force sent ahead by Brereton, consisting of Sergeant-Major James Lothian, with 50 dragoons under Captains Bramhall and Goldegay, secured the town ahead of an attack from Sir Thomas Aston's Royalists. As Brereton's forces approached Nantwich after marching from Congleton and Sandbach, the town had already been secured for Parliament by a couple of dragoons that Brereton had sent ahead. Here they repulsed an attack by Sir Thomas Aston's troops. Clearing a lane of the enemy, 'Captain Goldegay dismounted his dragooners, and turned his horses upon them, which brought them into confusion, and charged upon them very sore.'[81]

Goldegay was wounded in the combat, and his lieutenant (Joseph Banbury) and two soldiers were killed. Perhaps in their inexperience, the dragoons neglected to leave anyone to hold their mounts, which were taken by the Royalists for charging cavalry. Aston, however, retreated and set an ambush for Brereton's main force in the fields either side of a local brook. Having been informed of this by locals, Brereton directed his soldiers into the fields on either side while their column of packhorses continued along the road. The main fighting outside Nantwich appears to have occurred in the fields and hedgerows, on both sides of the road, during which confused fight the Parliamentarians were left with the spoils.[82] Owing to his wounds, Captain Goldegay was absent from duty for most of the year, recovering from his wounds, but he reappeared under the command of the Shropshire

78 BL, Ms Harley 2128, ff.23v & 32r.

79 TNA, WO55/1937.

80 TNA, SP28/225/3, ff.865v–866r; SP28/208, f.20v; SP28/196/1, ff.16v & 12v.

81 *Cheshire's Successe*; Hall (ed.), *Memorials*, p.20.

82 Hall (ed.), *Memorials*, p.36; *Cheshire's Successe*.

Committee in October 1643, and claimed pay on 1 November. Although it is not clear if he had any troops under him, William was a Sergeant-Major at Wem in October 1644, and by November 1645 he had risen to lieutenant-Colonel, operating in North Wales with Mytton, and Cheshire forces under Jones and Lothian.[83] Goldegay's former dragoon company was probably dissolved in 1644, and its officers and soldiers dispersed to other commands.

Captain John Lea's Company

The certificate of John Lea, gentleman of Stafford states: 'Captain Lea hath been a very faithful servant to the parliament, engaging not only on several engagements, freely endangering his life (being once shot through the body). And also we further certify that the aforesaid Captain John Lea was in actual service from 7 November 1642 until 12 November 1643.' It further records that his pay arrears 'for the above service, for 370 days due £370. Paid £50 in London, total due to him £320.'[84] He evidently received his commission in London and must have raised his company in the city. In the words of Dore:

> he held it for the whole of that remarkable period after Brereton's return to the North-West when, against all the odds, the parliamentarians gained control of Lancashire, most of Cheshire, North Staffordshire and North Salop. Brereton's statement that Lea was with him [in a letter of 3 November 1645] 'the first night when we came into Cheshire' (which was when Aston was defeated and Nantwich captured), taken with the frequent mention of dragoons in the accounts of Malbon and others of the raids, surprises and minor battles that followed and the testimony of the certificate that Lea 'upon several engagements freely adventured his life' leave little doubt that Lea must have played a useful part.[85]

After the taking of Eccleshall Castle on 30 August 1643, Captain Lea and his soldiers were rewarded with £15 from the profits of the sale of its goods.[86] Lea's absence from the records after this, and the mention in his certificate of him being 'once shot through the body' (probably indicating a severe wound), suggests that he did not return to military service after November 1643. Captain Simon Finch, a Royalist officer who changed sides after the relief of Nantwich in February 1644, appears to have taken control of Lea's company.

Captain John Cheswis' Company

John Cheswis was commissioned Captain of dragoons by Sir George Booth on 5 November 1642.[87] His company was raised for service in Cheshire by the spring of 1643. Warrants dated 17 April, 10 May, 18 June and 8 August 1643 relate to his pay.[88] He was captured during operations in Shropshire (perhaps

---

83 BL, Ms Add 11332, ff.75r–75v.; *BLB*, II, 1224–5.
84 TNA, SP28/252/1, f.184v; SP28/265/1, ff.68r–68v, 70r.
85 *BLB*, II, 809, note 2.
86 CRO, ZCR/63/2/702, f.24r.
87 TNA, SP28/267/3, ff.112v–117r.
88 TNA, SP28/196/1, ff.6v, 14r, 18r, 21v.

at Loppington on 11 September 1643), although he is mentioned as being a prisoner-of-war in Shrewsbury in March 1644. On his release in April Captain Cheswis took command of a troop of horse (this may have been a new unit or his dragoons were upgraded). He was paid on five occasions around this time, which could have been associated with the paying and equipping of this new troop.[89] During the summer of 1644 he was involved with the Cheshire horse in numerous operations. According to Malbon, 'Upon Thursday 8 May 1644 Captain Cheswis, with a few horse, issued forth of the town [of Nantwich], and near Cholmondeley Hall he took five men and horse with their arms, and slew one, which five he brought prisoners to Nantwich.'[90] John Cheswis was killed in action at Oswestry on 20 July 1644, his widow, Lady Leigh being provided with a pension of £50 per annum on the authority of the Council of War and deputy lieutenants.[91] The following served in his dragoon company and possibly his later troop:

Lieutenant James Geirn
Corporal Jeremiah Clough
Corporal James Gibson[92]

Captain Gilbert Gerard's Company

Captain Gilbert Gerard raised a company of dragoons under the command of Captain Richard Littler in early 1643. It appears to have been recruited in northeast Cheshire (and probably more specifically, the town of Northwich and its environs). Littler may have been a local man, but going by Sir William Brereton's other dragoon captains, he was more likely a professional soldier. The company's role seems to have included the safeguarding of the strategically important area of upper-Bucklow Hundred, including the Parliamentarian garrisons of Halton and Norton, and in particular patrolling the various passes over the River Mersey at Runcorn, the Weaver at Frodsham Bridge, the ford on the salt marshes at Frodsham Ditch, and perhaps Acton Bridge and ford to the south. As such, Gerard's/Littler's dragoons received pay, mounts and equipment from local sources in particular. During late 1643 the constables of Mere laid out £2 9s 4d for 'a horse, men and arms under Captain Littler', while their colleagues at Dutton provided pay to the company.[93]

Similarly, two undated warrants relate to the supply of dragoon horses and food. Captain Richard Littler instructed Thomas Woollett, one of the constables of Aston township 'to provide Sergeant Hall [with] two horses, one of your own, the other from George Guest, for scout horses this night for our safeties and the safety of this township.' The constables of Bucklow Hundred also charged those of Aston and Aston Grange with bringing each day two horse-loads of oats to Great Budworth, presumably for the dragoon

89 TNA, SP28/31/4, f.431v; SP28/196/1, ff.3v–4r, 6v, 18r, 21r.
90 Hall (ed.), *Memorials*, p.128.
91 TNA, SP28/196/3, f.490v; SP28/267/3, f.115r; SP28/128/13, f.26r; BL: Ms Harley 2166, f.130r.
92 TNA, SP28/225/3, f.682v; E121/3/1, f.287v; E121/5/7/351, f.31r.
93 BL, Ms Harley 2128, ff.166r, 60v.

horses. The township of Aston was also responsible for finding pay for Littler's soldiers. A warrant issued by Colonel Henry Brooke on 2September 1643 informed the officials:

> I formerly sent out several leys to them for collecting of moneys for the dragoons and as you are, as appears, behind with your payment. These are henceforth to charge and command you that you are besides with and withal four weeks' pay more at 6s 6d per week, which you to supply at Norton before 7 [September] 1643 to my clerk.[94]

The command was taken over by Captain William Wright following Richard Littler's death on 2 February 1644. Wright had served as lieutenant to the company, being paid with Sergeant James Harwood on 25 November 1643.[95] The testament of Captain Wright, dated 12 August 1647, states that he received his commission on 11 April 1644, serving in command of the company until he was stood down by Sir William Brereton on 30 September 1644.[96] During the spring of 1644 the Bucklow Sequestration Committee disbursed the sum of £9 15s 3d to 'Captain Wright for the Northwich garrison', thus confirming his connection to Colonel John Leigh, Gilbert Gerard (by then lieutenant-Colonel) and the town itself.[97] During the period of its service, the dragoon company consisted of three officers, two sergeants, three corporals and thirty-six soldiers. John Witter, son of a Frodsham yeoman, acted as cornet before taking up a commission as ensign to Sergeant-Major John Trevis of Colonel Leigh's foot regiment, serving as lieutenant to Lieutenant-Colonel Richard Brooke in 1645, and to Captain John Brooke in early 1646.[98]

Captain Simon Finch's Company

Simon Finch came over to England with the Royalist army from Ireland in November 1643 as a Captain in Sir Michael Earnley's regiment of foot. He was captured on 25 January 1644 following the defeat at Nantwich and brought by Sir William Brereton to London where he was imprisoned at Southwark. Finch consequently joined the forces of Parliament, although his younger brothers continued to serve in the Royalist Anglo-Irish regiments A deposition of William Wilbraham (presumably a Parliamentary agent), dated 13 May 1644 states:

> that about a month since this examinant being in London fell into company with one Captain Finch as he informed this deponent was a captain in one of the regiments that came out of Ireland and was taken prisoner near Nantwich in service for His Majesty. Who told the examinant that he was taken prisoner near Nantwich and was brought to Acton Church where his money was taken from him from where he was brought prisoner to Nantwich, and that since he hath

94 Aston, unlisted warrants, dated 20 November 1643 x 2 February 1644, 2 September 1643.

95 TNA, SP28/152/9, f.15r.

96 BL, Ms Harley 2128, f.166r; TNA: SP28/208, f.33v; E121/351, ff.63r–63v.

97 BL, Ms Harley 2137, f.151r–151v.

98 TNA, SP28/224/1, f.24v; SP28/124/1, ff.40v–54r; E121/5/7/351, ff.63v–65v.; E121/5/7/43, f.44r.

> accepted of a commission to be captain of a troop of horse under Sir William Brereton, which Commission Captain Finch showed this deponent and further said not.

The following day Simon's brother, Captain John Finch signed a receipt for:

> the several goods hereafter named which said goods were left there in the custody of the said Elizabeth, being late the goods of Captain Simon Finch under Sir Michael Ernle's regiment; which said Simon was taken prisoner at Nantwich in the county of Chester, in His Majesty's service. But since that time hath forfeited the said goods by taking up arms against His Majesty under the command of Sir William Brereton as it doth appear upon oath taken before the said mayor and others, as also by good testimony to the right honourable Lord Byron, lord field marshal-general, who by his warrant under his hand and seal hereunto annexed, hath given to me the said John Finch all the said goods so remaining in their custody. An old pair of spurs, fifteen points, a little white pitcher, a plush jump with silver clasps, a taffeta doublet and cloth breeches, a cloak lined with plush, a pair of shammy sleeves, a red scarf, three coarse linen towels, an old trunk and £15 in money, which said goods were all praised to £3 8s 2d, besides the money, which made up in the whole £19 13s 2d All which said goods and money, I John Finch do acknowledge to have received, of the said Randle Holme, and Elizabeth his wife, by virtue of the said warrant from the said Lord Byron and thereof of every part and parcel thereof. I do hereby acquit and discharge them the said Randle Holme and Elizabeth his wife their and either of their executors and administrators from the said goods And I do promise and assume hereby, both for myself and Robert Finch, lieutenant under Captain Edmund Langley who is to have part thereof, both by my Lord Byron's direction and my promise to the said Lord Byron.[99]

Finch was a highly valued officer who distinguished himself on several occasions. On 31 January 1645 the Shropshire Committee wrote to Brereton from Wem, 'We desire Captain Finch and his company to be in the party you send, for he is well known to us.'[100] After the fall of Chester Finch led his dragoons into North Wales with the forces under Colonel Mytton. With Captain Gimbert's men they participated in the siege of Holt Castle, which proved an arduous task. Mytton clearly placed much value on the effectiveness of these experienced and skilled troops, hence reporting on 8 April 1646:

> The siege of Holt hath of late been of great difficulty and hazard to those few men I have there, for the drawing off of the Cheshire firelocks from that service without my privity gave the enemy an advantage to burn the guard the firelocks kept (which cost the country much to fortify), and about forty dwelling-houses more in the town, and exposed my men (who lay in open quarters, and fewer in

99 BL, Ms Harley 2135, ff.69v–71r.
100 BL, Ms Add 11331, f.137r; *BLB*, I, 1.

number than the enemy within were) to their power, which necessitated my men to be upon continual duty.[101]

By then the siege operations against Lichfield Close had begun. Companies of the Cheshire foot under Sir William Brereton's command at Lichfield were badly in arrears of pay, including an unpaid bounty promised for their part in the capture of Chester. On 14 April 1646 Captains Finch and Gimbert received between them £102 18s 'for pay for their companies that came upon service at Lichfield in discharge of the month's gratuity upon taking Chester.'[102] As Carr and Atherton suggest, 'These were the only companies where this money came from Brereton, although payment was made to other individuals, and may indicate some competition between Brereton and the Cheshire Committee for the service of these elite troops who had spearheaded most of the operations against Chester. The rest of the Cheshire foot were paid their gratuity by the County Committee and sent on their way to Lichfield piecemeal as it secured the money.'[103]

Sir William was in much need of the dragoons, who had served so effectively at various other sieges. On 1 April Lieutenant John Turner of Gimbert's company travelled from Holt to Lichfield 'on special service' and was reimbursed his expenses by Brereton. It is likely that Finch's and Gimbert's entire commands did not arrive until early May, however, as Captain Gimbert, six officers and ten of his dragoons were paid at Holt from Cheshire, while both captains received a month's wages there on 21 April from the same source.[104] On 13 May Finch signed a letter with Gimbert and the 'Cheshire Commanders at Lichfield' to Sir William Brereton, complaining about lack of pay. Even so, his company was evidently much involved in the siege operations. On 25 May Brereton had reported to John Swinfen, one of his associates in Westminster, the details of a recent 'desperate sally' by the Royalist garrison upon the Parliamentarian earthworks, during which (among others) 'five or six of Captain Finch's firelocks [were] wounded.' Moreover, its junior officers were described on 12 June as 'being upon guard.'[105] Among the muster rolls of the Cheshire forces at the siege, drawn up ten days later, present under Captain Finch were one lieutenant, one cornet, two sergeants, one drummer, three corporals and 76 dragoons. On 30 May, and 5 and 12 June 1646 payments were made to the following:[106]

Lieutenant Mather	Corporal James More
Cornet Sykes	Corporal Darby Malone
Sergeant Robert Lathom	Drummer Richard Hawkes
Sergeant Henry Davies	Drummer John Carter
Corporal Hugh Stanley	Clerk Henry Wilkes

101 *A Letter to the Speaker of the House of Commons, concerning the Surrender of Ruthin Castle to Thomas Mytton, Major General of North Wales* (London: 1646).

102 TNA, SP16/513/1, f.79v.

103 Carr and Atherton (eds), *Civil War in Staffordshire*, p.59.

104 TNA, SP28/37/639–40, unfol.

105 BCL, Ms 595611, p.231; TNA: SP16/513/1, f.91r.

106 BCL, Ms 595611, pp.203, 252–3; TNA: SP16/513/1, ff.70r, 72r, 87v.

It is probably unsurprising that the later military career of Simon Finch was an active one. He became an officer of the Chester garrison in 1647, commanding a company of foot that from the evidence of a contemporary muster roll contained some officers and dragoons formerly under his command[107]. On 22 August 1650 Finch received a commission as major in Colonel Robert Duckenfield's militia regiment of Cheshire foot, and at the Battle of Worcester, as its lieutenant-Colonel, he was singled out for his actions. When Duckenfield's militia regiment disbanded Simon took command of five companies to be posted to Ireland to reinforce Sir Hardress Waller's regiment of foot (four of which were led by officers who had previously served with Finch in Brereton's army). In 1651 he also sat at Lord Derby's court-martial. By December 1656 Finch was serving in Ireland and continued there until 1659.[108] The following also appear in undated (but possibly 1645) pay warrants as commissioned and non-commissioned officers of the company:

Cornet Walton	Corporal Thomas Wilson
Cornet Randle Hall	Corporal Hugh Stanley
Sergeant John Walker	Drummer John Normansell
Corporal Thomas Warren	Drummer John Berry[109]

Captain Godfrey Gimbert's Company

Captain Godfrey Gimbert was probably a professional soldier and may have previously served in Ireland. He began his service in Cheshire as cornet of dragoons, and had received a commission as Captain by December 1643 when he was paid in that rank by Richard Stelfox, Sir William Brereton's clerk. On 18 July 1644 Godfrey was paid the sum of £2 1s 6d for the completing of his company.[110] Gimbert is listed in command of 60 firelocks (dragoons) in April 1645, who early the following month were engaged in besieging Beeston Castle. As commander of 'Fort Royal', the Parliamentarian blockhouse situated opposite the fortress's outer gates, on 9 May Gimbert received a letter of defiance from the Royalist governor, Captain William Vallett. Lord Byron, the governor of Chester would later report of the officer:

> Beeston Castle, commanded by Captain Vallet, formerly an officer in my regiment of horse, both which places [Lathom House in Lancashire and Beeston] were defended with as much gallantry and resolution as possibly could be expected, and not rendered till forced thereunto by the uttermost of extremities.

Vallett's letter to Gimbert is reproduced below:

> I understand by the bearer that you intend to burn the house. Indeed it should not have been left for you to have done it, that I did commiserate a poor widow

107 TNA, E121/5/7/misc., ff.59r.-v.

108 *CSPD, 1650*, p.509; *1651–2*, pp.117–8; Ludlow, *Memoirs*, I, pp.357–8; II, p.446.

109 TNA, SP28/225/4, f.753v; E121/5/7/351, ff.46v, 52v.

110 TNA, SP28/196/1, f.13r; SP28/152/7, f.8v; E121/5/7/43, f.1r.

> and two poor orphans in so much that I was content rather to shew that extremity to suffer it to be a den of thieves and traitors But if you take this course you prevent that which I might, upon good reasons, do myself and I shall make it such a precedent as the surveyors of your works – Aldersey, Spurstow, Metcalf *cum multiisaliis* of your traitorous faction shall repent. And whereas you flatter yourself with hopes of taking this place, I scorn your threats and attempts, and the forces of your best general, for all his great ram's head[111]

Gimbert replied:

> From my royal fort which stands for the confusion of a den of traitors in Beeston Castle. Governor, I have received your civil expressions in a scandalous paper. You said you delighted in civility; it appears in your beastlike expressions. You told me you would not be tied to conditions And do you think to tie [me] that am at liberty, and that by you whom I keep close prisoner amongst your anti-Christian, Babylonian crew and will wait to expend my dearest blood upon the destruction of such traitors to King and state as that den of blasphemers are whereof you are chief. You cause me to burn the house by your expressions. For your scandals to my general, you put it upon him whose shoes you are not worthy to clean. But I suppose you take the counsel to write this letter with the asses whom you took prisoners

The 'house' that the two commanders were bickering over was evidently located between the castle and the siege-works, rather than Beeston Hall which Rupert had set fire to in March 1645. Malbon offers the most likely culprit in his description of how in November 1644 a sally from the garrison surprised the Parliamentarian guard, 'being in one Owen's house standing at the foot of the castle hill at dinner and very careless.'[112] On 12 November the sum of 11s was paid to Gimbert's lieutenant, John Turner, 'for extraordinary good service against Beeston Castle when it was beleaguered and hopes to have taken it.'[113]

Of Gimbert's later military career, he was an officer in the Chester garrison during the early months of 1647. In November of the following year, orders were given to pay him £20 towards his arrears from money owed for the Royalist Colonel Robert Werden's ransom. He had been captured defending Chester on 18 January 1645 and compounded for delinquency. However, the money was still unpaid on 9 July 1650 when Gimbert was recorded as dead. Colonel Robert Duckenfield wrote to the Committee for Compounding asking for the money to be paid to his widow, whom he described as 'very poor and having lost her husband in the service of the state.'[114] In spring 1646, Captain Gimbert's dragoons, with those of Finch's company, participated in besieging Holt Castle, but by mid-May they had joined the remaining Cheshire forces at Lichfield Close. Whilst at Holt on

111 BL, Ms Add 11331, ff.101r & 101v; *BLB*, I, 459–60.

112 Hall (ed.), *Memorials*, p.153.

113 TNA, SP28/152/7, f.24r.

114 TNA, SP28/224/2, f.267r; *CJ*, VII, p.39.

14 April, Gimbert's men received their Chester gratuity (their captain getting his bonus of £51 2s), and ten days afterwards they had a month's pay.[115] The company had arrived at Lichfield Close by 21 May 1646. Various military documents and eyewitness accounts indicate that during 1645 at the least, Captain Godfrey Gimbert's company was at the forefront of the fighting in Cheshire and beyond.

A warrant, drawn up by Colonel Henry Brooke in the absence of Sir William Brereton, and dated 14 July 1645 to the army's treasurer, James Croxton, includes detailed charges for the medical care of wounded soldiers by Widow Praterfelt. Such wounds may have been incurred during operations at Beeston Castle, where Gimbert's dragoons and other troops closely besieged the Royalist garrison until its surrender in November 1645:

> For diet, lodging, washing, poultices, fire and candlelight given to Robert Anglesey, a wounded soldier of Captain Gimbert's company for 9 weeks at 5s 0d per week – £2 5s 0d
>
> For diet, lodging, washing and poultices given to Lawrence Wood, a wounded soldier of Captain Gimbert's company for 10 weeks at 5s 0d per week – £2 10s 0d
>
> For Robert Sandford, a wounded soldier of Captain Gimbert's company, for diet, lodging, washing, poultices and attendance for 3 weeks at 5s 0d per week – 15s 0d
>
> For Robert Bramhall, a wounded soldier of Captain Gimbert's company, for diet, lodging, washing, poultices and attendance for 3 weeks and 3 days at 5s 0d per week – 17s 0d
>
> Sum of £6 7s 0d[116]

A company muster, taken on 21 November 1645, records some of the scars of the bitter fighting, presumably relating to their operations against the walls of Chester on 19 and 21 September. Besides the captain, lieutenant, one sergeant, two corporals, two drummers and 51 soldiers recorded present, there were ten soldiers listed either as 'absent upon wounds' or 'wounded'.[117]The status of three more dragoons (described as 'wounded and discharged') remains unclear.

On 23 May 1646, the company assembled with the rest of the Cheshire forces at the siege of Lichfield Close and mustered:

Lieutenant John Turner	Corporal Richard Osman
Cornet John Urmston	Corporal John Ball
Quartermaster Thomas Bentley	Corporal John Forshall
Sergeant Leigh	Drummer Richard Bradbury
Sergeant Arthur Dickinson	65 dragoons[118]

115 TNA, SP28/37, ff.639v & 640r; SP16/513/1, f.79v.

116 TNA, 28/31/4, f.369r.

117 TNA, SP28/224/1, ff.72r.–74v.

118 BCA, Ms 595611, pp.252–3.

Captain Joseph Holt's Company

Like other Parliamentarian dragoon commanders in Cheshire Joseph may have been a professional soldier. He was probably the Cornet Holt who received pay with Bramhall's dragoons on 22 July 1643. The Hugh Holt who was reimbursed for a payment of cloth whilst at Northampton in December is likely to have been the company's first quartermaster, and later received a commission as Captain of pioneers in the army.[119] A warrant for pay to Captain Joseph Holt dates from 22 June 1644, and it is conceivable that he took command of the dragoons of Gerard's company when the commission of its officer commanding, Captain William Wright ended on 30 September 1644.[120] On 10 February the sequestrators of Bucklow Hundred paid the sum of £1 6s 8d to Holt for pasturing two horses in Dutton Park.[121] Gerard's dragoons had previously been supplied with weapons, pay, provisions and mounts by the constables of the Bucklow townships of Mere, Dutton, Aston and Aston Grange, possibly in the form of standing orders.[122] On 30 April 1645 Holt was serving as Captain of a company of 80 dragoons in the Cheshire Parliamentarian army.

Captain Holt was further listed, on 27 May 1645, as leading a detachment of 25 dragoons, being part of a force of Cheshire soldiers assembled by Sergeant-Major James Lothian in readiness for a rendezvous with the New Model Army in Leicestershire following the Battle of Naseby.[123] His company saw action at Denbigh Green on 1 November 1645 against a Royalist force commanded by Sir William Vaughan. As Lancaster reported:

> they [the Parliamentarians] were in a lane flanked by the enemy's horse and dragoons, so that they were forced to make good that pass with the forlorn hope and Cheshire dragoons, under the command of Captains Finch and Holt, stout and resolute men. These with the forlorn hope behaved themselves gallantly and maintained the pass until the foot came up.[124]

On 18 December 1645 Captain Holt's soldiers received pay with the two other companies of Cheshire firelocks, and following the fall of Chester he and his company received gratuities for their part in the siege. Moreover, the total sum paid to 'Captain Joseph Holt, and his officers and soldiers' by Treasurer Croxton was £811 5s 10d.[125] The company was still drawing pay on 26 November 1646 when Lieutenant John Reading signed a receipt for

---

119 BL, Ms Harley 2128, ff.27v & 20r; Ms Add 11331, f.113.

120 TNA, SP28/225/3, f.673r.

121 BL, Ms Harley 2137, f.200r.

122 BL, Ms Harley 2128, ff.60v & 166r.

123 BL, Ms Add 11331, ff.45v, 165v; *BLB*, I, 385, 654.

124 *A True Relation of a Great Victory obtained by the Parliament Forces, &c., against the King's Forces, &c., near Denbigh*; BL, Ms Add 11332, f.76; *BLB*, II, 801.

125 TNA, SP28/224/1, ff.202v & 202r; SP28/128/13, f.18r; BL, Ms Add 11333, ff.30r, 118v; *BLB*, II, 1040, 1235.

it as 'Lieutenant to Captain Joseph Holt'.[126] Undated warrants also exist for Sergeant/Cornet Thomas Canary and Sergeant Hugh Jordaine.[127]

Captain Kempton's Company

On 15 and 24 July 1643, the Cheshire Parliamentarian collector Ralph Judson made payments to 'Captain Kempton's soldiers'.[128] Evidence that Kempton served as a Captain of dragoons in the Cheshire forces comes from references to his clerk, John Urmston, who had been involved in paying dragoons at the beginning of 1643 and listed as 'cornet to Captain Kempton' in warrants dated 15 July and December of the same year. Although Kempton is not directly stated to be a dragoon officer, Cornet Urmston later served in Captain Godfrey Gimbert's company at the siege of Holt Castle in April 1646 and later with the Cheshire forces at Lichfield Close.[129] However, a list of pensioners made at Stockport on 8 December 1653 includes Randle Cartwright, 'a soldier under Captain Kempton, wounded in the right arm at Hanmer.'[130] The action in question occurred on 20 June 1643 when according to Malbon, 'Colonel Brereton's troop, Captain Bulkeley and many other troopers and dragoons' from Nantwich were ambushed and defeated by Royalist forces with the loss of a number of officers and men. Although it is evident that Captain John Bramhall's company were present (losing 8 horses and 14 firearms), such references suggest that Captain Kempton commanded the remaining dragoons in Flintshire.[131]

Captain/Captain-Lieutenant James Stockport's Company

Two references associate this officer with Brereton's dragoons. A pay warrant to John Berry describes him as 'drummer in Captain James Stockport's company of dragoons in Colonel Michael Jones's regiment.'[132] In June 1645, Jones succeeded Sir William Brereton as Colonel of his regiment of horse following his recall to Parliament. It seems that he retained his colonelcy when Sir William returned to active military service later in the year. This included the short campaign in North Wales that culminated in the victory at Denbigh Green on 1 November. Drummer Berry had previously served in Captain Joseph Holt's company, so Stockport may have briefly taken command of the unit between the wounding of Holt at Chester on 21 September 1645 and his recovery by Denbigh Green, when he was commended for his conduct.

Nevertheless, on 12 January 1646 the county treasurer disbursed the sum of £466 6s 'to the Cheshire dragoons as appears under the hands of Captains Finch, Gimbert and Holt, with £50 paid to Captain Stockport for his dragoons.'[133] This implies that the latter had a company, or at the least a detachment under his command, although this might have been a

126 TNA, SP28/224/1, f.184v.
127 TNA, E121/5/7/351, ff.33r, 39r, 55v.
128 TNA, SP28/196/1, f.11v.
129 TNA, E121/5/7/351, ff.28v–29r; BCL, Ms 595611, pp.252–3.
130 BL, Ms Harley 2128, f.69v.
131 Hall (ed.), *Memorials*, pp.62–3; BL, Ms Harley 2128, ff.34r–35r.
132 TNA, E121/5/7/351, f.53r.
133 BL, Ms Add 11333, f.118v; *BLB*, II, 1236.

temporary appointment as he appears nowhere else in this role. As no other officer of that name is known to have served with the Cheshire army, this must have been Captain-Lieutenant James Stockport, who spent much of the war leading Colonel Henry Mainwaring's own company of foot and, in early 1645, probably the remains of his regiment during fighting at Farndon Bridge against troops under Prince Maurice, who were attempting to relieve Chester. If so, his record shows that he was a highly experienced and trusted officer.

Captain Collinson's Company

A payment of £8 10s 0d was made by one of the army's treasurers on 12 March 1643 to 'Captain Collinson's dragoons'.[134] Nothing more is known of this officer, although it is possible that he had interim command of Captain William Goldegay's company following his absence from duty for most of the year due to wounds received at Nantwich in January.

Sergeant-Major Morris's Company

On 23 December 1644, Sir William Brereton paid the sum of £20 'to Sergeant Major Morris for his company of firelocks.'[135] The identity of this officer is puzzling as he appears in no other references in connection with the Cheshire forces. A John Morris served in the Royal army in Ireland, then came to England, but defected to Parliament after the fall of Liverpool on 1 November 1644. He joined the Northern Army as Sergeant-Major and was promoted to lieutenant-Colonel in May 1645 during the siege of Pontefract, only to change sides again three years later.[136] If it was him, he may have been (like Captain Finch and others) an able and experienced officer whose services Brereton was keen to retain, if only briefly.

Lieutenant-Colonel Michael Jones' Company

Jones, who commanded his own cavalry troop and was appointed commander of the Cheshire horse when Sir William Brereton went back to London in June 1645 following the Self-Denying Ordinance, also raised a dragoon unit. An entry in Sir William Brereton's accounts, dated 11 December 1644, details a payment of £5 14s 'to Lieutenant Colonel Michael Jones to pay for shoes bought for some of his company of firelocks.'[137] There can be no doubt that these were dragoons, given Brereton's common use of the term 'firelocks' for these soldiers, as well as Jones' role among mounted forces. Formed, perhaps, to operate in conjunction with his cavalry troop, or at least in more general dragoon tasks, the company originated in October 1644 with the 'fifty foot who came voluntarily from the enemy at Liverpool, and brought their arms to serve under him under whom they served in Ireland and took the Covenant.'[138] These soldiers are likely to previously have been with Jones

134 TNA, SP28/196/3, f.4r.
135 TNA, SP28/152/7, f.16r.
136 Jones, 'War in the North', pp.394–5.
137 TNA, SP28/152/7, f.26v.
138 *Ibid.*, ff 22v, 25r.

in the Earl of Kildare's Regiment, and thus like others from the Protestant forces in Ireland, were veterans, and, as such, were highly sought after by the Parliamentarian armies on the mainland of Britain. Jones' dragoon company may have been a short-lived unit – it is not listed among Brereton's army list of 30 April 1645 (although other known troops and companies were not either) – a warrant signed by Sir William and dated 2 June 1645 ordered Treasurer Croxton to expend the sum of £30 0s 0d for the employment of intelligencers 'during the time that he [Jones] is out with his party of Horse and dragoons.'[139] The dragoons under Jones' command were possibly disbanded, or more likely, absorbed into a pre-existing dragoon or cavalry formation.

139 TNA, SP28/30/7, f.654r.

Bibliography

Manuscript Sources

Aberystwyth, The National Library of Wales
Clenennau Letters and Papers 539
MS 1595E/1 Gwysaney Letters (19th century transcripts)
MS Bettisfield 111 Sir Thomas Hanmer's commission
MS Chirk Castle 1/B3 Book of Indictments at the Quarter Sessions for Denbighshire, 1670–90

Aston, Cheshire
Dispersed accounts of Sir Thomas Aston and unlisted warrants, 1642–6

Beverley, East Riding Archives
BC/II/7/4 Minute book of the Governors and Beverley Corporation, 1597–1660

Birmingham, City Archives
MS 3312 Hanley Court Estate Archive
MS 595611 Letter Book of Sir William Brereton

Chelmsford, Essex Record Office
ERO, D/Y 2/7/50 Letter from Cromwell to the Borough of Colchester

Chester, Cheshire Archives
DCC/14 Crewe (Cowper) Collection
DCC/47/22–40 Condover (Cowper) Collection
DDX/428 Letter Book of Sir William Brereton
ZCR/63/2/691 Letter from Sir William Brereton
ZCR/63/2/702 Eccleshall Castle sale of goods

Chippenham, Wiltshire and Swindon History Centre
X3/119 Letters and papers of Sir Thomas Aston, Rupert, Hopton and Charles I
413/444/A Prince Rupert's Diary

Gloucester, Gloucestershire Archives
D2510/11–12 Orders for the raising, equipping and payment of dragoons in Cirencester
D7115/2/47; D2510/26 Instructions to the Collectors of Gloucestershire for raising dragoons

Hawarden, Flintshire Record Office
D/G/3275 Letter from the Flintshire Commission of Array

Ipswich, Suffolk Record Office
FB/130/I/1/8 Instructions to the Constables of Suffolk

Kew, The National Archives
E121; E179; SP16/251; SP16/492; SP16/494; SP16/494; SP16/503; SP28/1A; SP28/2A; SP28/2B; SP28/3B; SP28/4; SP28/5; SP28/7; SP28/8; SP28/9; SP28/11; SP28/13; SP28/15; SP28/16; SP28/17; SP28/18; SP28/19; SP28/22; SP28/24; SP28/25; SP28/26; SP28/27; SP28/29; SP28/30; SP28/31; SP28/33; SP28/36; SP28/37; SP28/41; SP28/43; SP28/44; SP28/45; SP28/51; SP28/70; SP28/73; SP28/120; SP28/121A; SP28/123; SP28/124; SP28/125; SP28/131; SP28/133; SP28/136; SP28/138; SP28/139; SP28/143; SP28/144; SP28/149; SP28/150; SP28/151; SP28/152; SP28/154; SP28/204; SP28/220; SP28/243; SP28/253A; SP28/253B; SP28/261; SP28/262; SP28/263;SP28/266; SP28/267; SP28/298; SP28/299; SP28/300; SP28/313; SP95/3;PRO 30/15/3; WO49 (Ordnance Office Debenture Books); WO55 (Miscellaneous Ordnance Papers)

Leeds, West Yorkshire Archives
WYL100Sir William Savile's letters to the city of York
WYL150/5810 (T/32/46) Survey of Colonel Sir John Mallory's regiment
WYW1352/1/1/12/23/127; WYW1352/1/1/12/23/130 Advancement of money for dragoons

Leeds, University of Leeds, Special Collections
BC CW 1642/39A

Lexington, Massachusetts, Scottish Rite Masonic Museum & Library
USM 009 Sir Thomas Aston's commission

Lichfield Cathedral Library
MS Lichfield 24 Account of Colonel Richard Bagot, governor of Lichfield

Lincoln, Lincolnshire Archives
8ANC8/47 Letter from Sir Edward Walker to the Earl of Lindsey, 12 December 1642

London, Dr Williams Library
Modern MS Folio 7

London, House of Lords Record Office
Main Papers

London, National Army Museum
1993-10–112–1 Commission of Lord Willoughby D'Eresby

London, Society of Antiquaries
MS 138, fol.130r. Commission of Lieutenant-Colonel John Warcup

London, The British Library
MSS Add 11331–3 Letter Books of Sir William Brereton
MS Add 17062 Diary of Richard Symonds
MS Add 18980–1 Civil War Letters Various
MSS Add 36913–19 Aston Correspondence and Papers
MS Egerton 2646–7 Correspondence of the Cambridgeshire Committee
MS Harley 2128 Accounts of Captain John Bramhall
MSS Harley 6804, 6851–2 Civil War Documents Various

Manchester, John Rylands Research Institute and Library
TW/262 Commission of Sir William Brereton

Matlock, Derbyshire Record Office
D3287/1043/4, D252/60/26c

Museum of London
46–78/709

Nottingham, Nottinghamshire Archives
C/QSM Nottinghamshire Quarter Sessions records

Oxford, Bodleian Library
MS Fairfax 36 Sir Thomas Fairfax Papers
MSS Carte 66, 118 Correspondence of the 1st Duke of Ormond
MS Carte 74 Journal of Colonel Edward Montague
MS Eng. Hist. C53
MS Eng. Misc. B. 433 Draft commission from Charles I to Rupert
MS Rawlinson D395
MS Rawlinson D924
MSS Tanner 62, 64

Preston, Lancashire Archives
DDB 2/1 Commission of Captain William Blundell
DDHO/352

Reading, Berkshire Record Office
R/Z10–12;R/Z3/27/1–7; R/Z3/29; R/Z3/33; R/Z3/35–6; R/Z3/38/1; R/Z3/39; R/Z3/42

Shrewsbury, Shropshire Archives
3365/2570 Bills for soldiers' billets, 1642–3
6000/13291 Commission of Sir Vincent Corbet
6000/13294 Commission of Sir Francis Ottley
LB7/1994 Ludlow Borough. Assessment of Broad St and Castle wards for raising soldiers

Stafford, Staffordshire Record Office
D868/2/36b Letter of William, Lord Paget

Stafford, William Salt Library
MS Salt 402 Letter from the Corporation of Stafford to Charles I
MS Salt 46 Certificate of Sergeant Major William Gwilliam
MS Salt 477/4 Letter from Sir Arthur Aston to Rupert
MS Salt 482 Letter from Colonel Bagot to Rupert
MS Salt 487 Letter from Lord Capel to Viscount Falkland
MS Salt 518/2 Letter from Sir Gilbert Gerard to Rupert
MS Salt 596 Letter of Thomas Ellis

Taunton, Somerset Archives
DD/5G/6 Commissions of William Bull

York, Minster Library
CWT Civil War Tracts

Wakefield, West Yorkshire History Centre
QS, 1/14/5/6/1 Petition of Samuel Constantine of Kettlewell

Warwick, Warwickshire Archives
CR2017/C9–10 Letter Books of the Earl of Denbigh
CR2017/C176 Letter from Charles I to the Sheriff of Shropshire

Wigston, Leicestershire and Rutland Record Office
QS6Leicestershire Quarter Sessions records

Worcester, Worcestershire Archives
BA13825Sandys of Omberley Archive
1714/899/192Diary of Henry Townshend
3762/8Transcriptions of Droitwich Corporation Accounts

Printed Primary Sources

Contemporary Newsbooks
A Continuation of our Weekly Intelligence from His Majesties Army (London)
A Perfect Diurnal of the Passages in Parliament (London)
A True and Perfect Diurnal (London)
A True and Perfect Diurnall of all the Chief Passages in Lancashire from the 3 July to the 9 July 1642 (London)
Certaine Informations from Severall Parts of the Kingdom (London)
Certaine Speciall and Remarkable Passages (London)
England's Memorable Accidents (London)
Mercurius Aulicus (Oxford)
Speciall Passages and Certain Information from Speciall Places (London)
The Moderate Intelligencer (London)
The Parliament Scout (London)

Contemporary Tracts and Pamphlets
A Continuation of true intelligence from the English and Scottish forces in the north in the services of King and Parliament, 13 July 1644 (London: 1644). TT, E2 [14]
A Copy of a Letter sent from Sir Thomas Myddelton (London, 10 July 1644). TT, E54 [16]
A Full and True Relation of the Battle between the King's Army and the Earle of Essex, in a letter from Captain Edward Kightley (London: 1642). TT, E126 [24]
A full Relation of the Desperate charge of the malignants for the betraying of Monmouth, also how Lieut.-Col. Kyrle fell into the enemy's quarters near Hereford, likewise a copy of Col. Sandys' letter of the manner of taking Shelford House (London: 4 November 1645). TT, E308 [19]
A Full Relation of the Late Victory obtained (through Gods providence) by the forces under the command of General Lesley, the Lord Fairfax, and the Earl of Manchester (London: 11 July 1644).TT, E54 [19]
A Fuller Relation of Sir Thomas Fairfax's Routing of all the King's Armies in the West ... at Torrington (London: 1642). TT, E324 [6]
A Letter sent to the Right Honourable William Lenthall Esquire, Speaker to the Honourable House of Commons: concerning the routing of Col: Gorings army neer Bridgewater (London: 22 July 1645). TT, E293 [17]
A Letter to the Speaker of the House of Commons, concerning the Surrender of Ruthin Castle to Thomas Mytton, Major General of North Wales (London: 1646)
A More Particular and Exact Relation of the Victory obtained by the Parliament's forces under the command of Sir Thomas Fairfax (London: Richard Cotes, 1645). TT, E288 [38]
A Most True Relation of the Battell fought by Capt. Hotham against the Earl of New-Castle, neer Tollerton in Yorkshire (London: 3 December 1642). TT, E129 [9]
A Most True Relation of the Present State of His Majesties Army: Wherein Also the Truth of that Declaration Published by the Parliament, of Their Happy Victory in the Battaile at Keynton, is Both Justly Asserted and Abundantly Proved, Humbly Presented by the Author who was Personally Present, to the Honourable the Lords and Commons in Parliament Assembled (London: 3 December 1642). TT, E244 [2]

A Relation of the Battel fought between Keynton and Edgehill, by His Majesty's Army and that of the Rebels (Oxford: 1642). TT, E126 [24]
A Relation of the taking of Leeds and Wakefield by Sir Thomas Fairfax (London: 23–24 January 1643). TT, E88 [23]
A Second Letter from the Right Honourable the Lord Fairfax, of his late prosperous proceedings against the Earl of Newcastle and his Popish Army in Yorkshire (London: 1643). UL, BC CW 1642/39A
A True and Impartiall relation of the battaile betwixt, His Majesties Army, and that of the rebells neare Newbery in Berkshire, Sept. 20, 1643 (Oxford: L. Lichfield 1643). TT, E69 [10]
A True and particular relation of the late victory obtained by Colonel Horton and Col: Okey against the Welch Forces under Major Generall Langhorn: expressed in a letter from Colonel Okey to a friend of his in London (London: Henry Overton, 1648). TT, E441 [36]
A True and Plenary Relation of the Great Defeat given by my Lord Fairfax forces unto my Lord Newcastles forces in Yorkshire, by Thomas Crompton (London: 23 January 1643). TT, E88 [19]
A true confirmation of the great victory in Wales: sent in a letter to the Speaker of the Honorable House of Commons, from Colonel Thomas Horton from Bridge-end, May 13. 1648(London: 1648. TT, E443 [15]
A True Relation of a Great Fight Between the Kings Forces and the Parliaments, at Chinner neer Tame on Saturday last (London: 1643). TT, E55 [11]
A True Relation of a Great Victory obtained by the Parliament Forces in Cheshire, under Sir William Brereton, against the King's Forces, under the command of Sir William Vaughan, near Denbigh, November 1. 1645 (London: 5 November 1645). TT, E308 [14]
A True Relation of the Late Battell Neere Newbury (London: 26 September 1643). TT, E69 [2]
A True Relation of the Late Fight Betweene the Right Honourable The Earle of Manchester's Forces, and the Marquesse of Newcastles Forces, 11 Oct., neere Home Castle in Lincolnshire (London: 11 October 1643). TT, E71 [5]
A True Relation of the Lord Brooke's Settling of the Militia in Warwickshire (1642). TT, E669. [50]
A True Relation of the Proceedings of the Scottish Army, from 12th March to the 25th, dated from his Excellency the Lord Generall Lesley's Quarters, neare Sunderland, 25 March 1644 (Edinburgh: James Lindesay, 1644). NU, GNM SANT
An Exact and True Relation of the Dangerous and Bloody Fight Between His Majesties Army, and the Parliaments Forces, neere Kyneton in the County of Warwick, the 23.,of this instant October. Sent in a Letter to John Pym Esquire (London: 28 October 1642). TT, E124 [26]
An Exact Diarie or a brief Relation of the progress of Sir William Waller's Army since the joining of the London Auxilliaries with his forces (London: 19 July 1644).TT, E2 [20]
An Ordinance of the Lords and Commons … with two exact Relations of the said Victory Obtained against the Kings forces, nere Knasby in Northampton-shire the fourteenth of this instant Iune (London: Edward Husband, 17 June 1645). TT, E288 [26]
Cheshire's Successe since their pious and truly valiant Colonel, Sir William Brereton, Baronet, came to their rescue, &c. (London, 20 March 1643). TT, E94 [6]
His Highnesse Prince Ruperts Late Beating up the Rebels Quarters At Post-comb & Chinner in Oxfordshire And his Victory in Chalgrove Feild [sic], on Sunday morning June 18 1643 (Oxford: 1643)
Terrible News From York sent in a letter to London (London: 1642). ML, CWT, 42-04-08
The Last Intelligence from his Excellency his Quarters at Reading, since the surrendering of the town (London: 27 April 1643). TT, E100 [5]
The Last Weeks Proceedings of the Lord Brooke (London: 1643). TT, E91[19]
The Manner how the Prisoners are to be brought into the City of London (London: T. F.and J. Coe, 1645). TT, E288 [45]

The Success of Our Cheshire Forces, as they came Related by Sir William Brereton's own pen (London: 26 August 1644). TT, E8 [8]
True Proceedings from York, and a True Relation of the Manner of his Majesties setting up of his standard at Nottingham (London: 22 August 1642). TT, E115 [4]

Books and Edited Collections

Abbott, W. C. (ed), *Writings and Speeches of Oliver Cromwell*, 4 vols (Oxford: Clarendon Press, 1988)
Anderson, Archibald, et al (eds), *The Acts of the Parliaments of Scotland, AD MCXXIV-AD MDCCVII*, 11 vols (Edinburgh: 1814–44)
Ashcroft, M. Y. (ed), *Scarborough Records, 1641–60* (Northallerton: North Yorkshire Record Office, 1991)
Barriffe, William, *Military Discipline: or, the Young Artillery Man* (London: John Dawson, 3rd edn, 1643)
Beamont, William (ed), Robinson, Edward, *A Discourse of the War in Lancashire*, Chetham Society, Old Series, 62 (1864)
Bell, Robert (ed),*Memorials of the Civil War: Comprising the Correspondence of the Fairfax Family with the Most Distinguished Personages Engaged in that Memorable Contest*, 2 vols (London: Robert Bentley, 1849)
Blount, J. T., *The Art of Making Devises* (London: 2nd edn, 1655)
Boyle, Roger, Earl of Orrery, *A Treatise of the Art of War dedicated to the King's Most Excellent Majesty* (1677)
Bulstrode, Richard, *Memoirs and Reflections upon the reign and government of King Charles the 1st and K. Charles the 2nd* (London: N. Mist, 1721)
Bund, J. Willis (ed), *Diary of Henry Townshend of Elmley Lovett, 1640–1663*, 2 vols (London: Worcestershire Historical Society, 1920)
Burt, Nathaniel, *Military Instructions, or the Soldier tried for the use of the Dragoon* (London: 1644)
Calendar of the Manuscripts of the Marquess of Ormonde, K. P., preserved at Kilkenny Castle, 2 vols (London: HMSO, 1902)
Carr, Ivor and Atherton, Ian (eds), *The Civil War in Staffordshire in the Spring of 1646: Sir William Brereton's Letter Book, April-May 1646*, Collections for a History of Staffordshire, Fourth Series, 21 (Staffordshire Record Society, 2007)
Carte, Thomas, *A Collection of Original Letters and Papers, concerning the affairs of England, from the year 1641 to 1660, found among the Duke of Ormonde's Papers*, 2 vols (London: 1735)
Carte, Thomas, *The Life of James, Duke of Ormond*, 5 vols (Oxford: Oxford University Press, 1851)
Clarke, T. S (ed), *The Life of James the Second, King of England*, 2 vols (London: Longman, 1816)
Collins, Arthur (ed), *Letters and Memorials of State*, 2 vols (London: T. Osborne, 1746)
Cruso, John, *Militarie Instructions for the Cavallrie* (Cambridge: 1632)
Day, William Ansell (ed), *The Pythouse Papers: Correspondence Concerning the Civil War* (London: Bickers and Sons, 1879)
Dick, Oliver L. (ed), *Aubrey's Brief Lives* (London: Secker and Warburg, 1950)
Dore, R. N. (ed), *The Letter Books of Sir William Brereton*, 2 vols, RSLC, 123, 128 (1984, 1990).
Duc de Rohan, Henri, *The Complete Captain* (London: 1631)
Firth, C.H. (ed), *The Clarke Papers: Selections from the papers of William Clarke, secretary to the Council of the Army, 1647–1649, and to General Monck and the commanders of the army in Scotland, 1651–1660*, 4 vols (London: Longmans, Green & Co., 1891–1901)
Firth, C.H. (ed), *The Memoirs of Edmund Ludlow, Lieutenant General of the Horse in the army of the Commonwealth of England, 1625–1672*, 2 vols (Oxford: Clarendon Press, 1894)

Firth, C. H. and Rait, R. S (eds), *Acts and Ordinances of the Interregnum, 1642–1660*, 3 vols (London: HMSO, 1911)
Foure Paradoxes, or Politique Discourses: 2 concerning militarie discipline, written long since by Thomas Digges Esquire. 2 of the worthinesse of warre and warriors, by Dudly Digges, his sonne (London, 1604)
Generall Lesley's Direction and Order for the Exercising of Horse and Foot (London: 1642)
Goldney, Frederick H., *Records of Chippenham Relating to the Borough* (London: Diprose, Bateman & Co., 1889)
Grosart, Alexander B. (ed), The Lismore Papers: Autobiographical notes, remembrances and diaries of Sir Richard Boyle, first and 'great' Earl of Cork, 5 volumes (Privately printed, 1886)
Hall, James, (ed), *Memorials of the Civil War in Cheshire and the adjacent counties by Thomas Malbon, of Nantwich, Gent., and Providence improved by Edward Burghall*, Lancashire and Cheshire Record Society, 19 (1889)
Hahlweg, Werner, *Die Heeresreform der Oranier, Das Kriegsbuch des Grafen Johann von Nassau-Siegen* (Wiesbeden: Selbstverlag der Historischen Kommission, 1973)
Hamilton, W. D and Bruce, J. (eds), *Calendar of State Papers Domestic: Charles I, 1625–49*, 23 volumes (London: HMSO, 1858)
Hexham, Henry, *The First Part of the Principles of the Art Military practiced in the Warres of the United Netherlands* (Delft: 1642)
Hutchinson, Lucy, *Memoirs of the life of Colonel Hutchinson* (London: H. G. Bohn, 1863)
J. B., *Some Brief Instructions for the Exercising of the Horse-Troops* (London: 1661)
Journals of the House of Commons, 1547–1687, 9 vols (London, 1742)
Journals of the House of Lords, 1509–1681, 13 vols (London, 1771)
Lacy, Thomas, *The Old Troop, or, Monsieur Raggou: as it was acted at the Theatre-Royal* (London: 1672)
Lang, David, (ed), *A Diary of the Public Correspondence of Sir Thomas Hope of Craighall, 1633–1645*(Edinburgh: Bannatyne Club, 1843)
Lang, David, (ed), *The Letters and Journals of Robert Baillie, 1637–1662*, 3 volumes (Edinburgh: Bannatyne Club, 1841)
Lewis, John (ed), *The Siege of Chester: Nathaniel Lancaster's Narrative* (Nottingham: Raider Books, 1987)
Lilburne, John, *Innocency and Truth Justified* (London: 1646)
Lilburne, John, *The Copy of a Letter from .... a friend* (London: 1645)
Long, C. E. (ed), *Diary of the Marches of the Royal Army during the Great Civil War; kept by Richard Symonds*, Camden Society, Old Series, 74 (1859)
Lupton, Donald, *A Warre-like Treatise of the Pike* (London: 1642)
Macray, W. D (ed), *Beaumont Papers: Letters Relating to the Family of Beaumont of Whitley, Yorkshire* (London: Nichols, 1884)
Macray, W. D (ed), Clarendon, Edward, Earl of, *The History of the Rebellion and Civil Wars in England*, 6 volumes (Oxford: Clarendon Press, 1888)
Macray, W. D (ed), *Ruthven Correspondence: Letters and Papers of Patrick Ruthven, Earl of Forth and Brentford* (London: Nichols, 1868)
Markham, Francis, *Five Decades of Epistles of Warre* (London: 1622)
Markham, Gervase, *The Soldier's Accidence* (London: 1625)
Monck, George, *Observations upon Military and Political Affairs* (London: 1671)
Owen, G. Dyfnallt (ed), *Calendar of the Cecil Papers in Hatfield House*, 22 volumes (London: HMSO, 1971)
Pafford, J. H. P. (ed), *Accounts of the Parliamentary Garrisons of Great Chalfield and Malmesbury, 1645–1646*, Wiltshire Archaeological and Natural History Society, Records Series, 2 (Brussels: J. Adam, 1966)
Parsons, Daniel, *The Diary of Sir Henry Slingsby* (London: Longman, 1836)
Pennington, D H. and Roots, I. A. (eds and intro.), *The Committee at Stafford, 1643–1645* (Manchester: Manchester University Press, 1957)
Philip, I. G. (ed), *Journal of Sir Samuel Luke*, 3 volumes (Oxford: Oxfordshire Record Society, 1947–53)

Phillips, W. (ed), 'The Ottley Papers Relating to the Civil War', *TSANHS*, 2nd Series, VI (1894), pp.27–78; VII (1895), pp.241–360; VIII (1896), pp.1–38
Roy, Ian (trans and ed), *The Royalist Ordnance Papers 1642–1646*, 2 vols (Oxford: Oxfordshire Record Society, 1964 and 1969)
Rushworth, John, *Historical Collections of Private Passages of State*, 8 vols (London: D Browne, 1721)
Sprigge, Joshua, *Anglia Rediviva or England's Recovery* (London: 1647)
Stanning, J.H. (ed), *The Royalist Composition Papers: being the proceedings of the Committee for Compounding, A.D 1643–1660, so far as they relate to the County of Lancaster*, 6 volumes (Manchester:1891–1942)
Terry, C. S (ed & intro.), *Papers Relating to the Army of the Solemn League and Covenant 1643–1647*, 2 volumes (Edinburgh: Scottish History Society, 1917)
Turner, Sir James, *Pallas Armata: Military Essays of the Ancient Grecian, Roman, and modern art of war written in the years 1670 and 1671*(London: 1683)
Underwood, J. A. (trans), Johan Jakob Christoffel von Grimmelshausen, *The Adventures of Simplicius Simplicissimus* (Harmondsworth: Penguin, 2018)
Vickers, John, *God's Ark overtopping the World's Waves* (London: 1646)
Vicars, John, *Magnalia Dei Anglicana. Or, England's Parliamentary Chronicle*, 4 volumes (London: 1646)
Venn, Thomas, *Military and Maritine [sic] Discipline in Three Books* (London: E. Tyler, et al., 1672)
Verney, Frances P., *Memoirs of Verney Family during the Civil War*, 2 vols(London: Longmans, Green & Co., 1892)
Vernon, John, *The Young Horse-Man or, the Honest Plain-Dealing Cavalier* (London: 1644)
Walker, Sir Edward, *Historical Discourses upon Several Occasions* (London: W. B., 1705)
Wallhausen, Johann Jacobi von, *Kriegskunst zu Fuß* (Oppenheim: 1615)
Wallhausen, Johann Jacobi von, *Kriegskunst zu Pferd* (Frankfurt: 1616)
Warburton, Eliot, *Memoirs of Prince Rupert and the Cavaliers*, 3 volumes (London: S & J. Bentley and Henry Fley, 1849)
Ward, Robert, *Animadversions of Warre* (London: John Dawson, 1639)
Washbourne, John (ed), *Bibliotheca Gloucestrensis: A Collection of Scarce and Curious Tracts Relating to the County and City of Gloucester* (Gloucester, 1825)
Webb, John and T. W. (eds), *Memorials of the Civil War Between King Charles I and the Parliament of England, as it Affected Herefordshire and the Adjacent Counties*, 2 Volumes (London: Spottiswoode, 1879)
Wicks, Alan (ed), *Bellum Civile: Sir Ralph Hopton's Memoirs of the Campaign in the West, 1642–1644* (Leigh-on-Sea: Partizan Press, 1988)
Wilson, John, *Buckinghamshire Contributions for Ireland 1642 and Richard Grenville's Military Accounts 1642–1645* (Buckinghamshire Record Society, 1983)
Whitelocke, Bulstrode, *Memorials of the English Affairs* (London: Nathaniel Ponder, 1682)
Wood, Anthony, *The Life and Times of Anthony Wood, antiquary, of Oxford, 1632–1695, described by Himself*, 3 vols (Oxford: Oxford Historical Society, 1891–2)
Young, Alan R. (ed), *The English Emblem Tradition: Volume 3: Emblematic Flag Devices of the English Civil Wars, 1642–1660*(Toronto: University of Toronto Press, 1995)
Young, Peter and Tucker, Norman (eds), *Military Memoirs of the Civil War: Richard Atkyns and John Gwyn* (London: Longmans, 1967)

Reports of the Historical Manuscripts Commission

Thirteenth Report, App. I (1891)
Fourteenth Report, App. VII-VIII (1895)
Fifth Report, I (1876)
Seventh Report (1879)
Hastings MSS, II (1928)

Secondary Sources

Books and reports

Abram, Andrew, *More Like Lions than Men: Sir William Brereton and the Cheshire Army of Parliament, 1642–46* (Solihull: Helion & Co., 2020)
Atkin, Malcolm, *Worcestershire Under Arms: An English County During the Civil Wars* (Barnsley: Pen & Sword, 2004)
Barratt, John, *Cavaliers: The Royalist Army at War 1642–1646* (Stroud: Sutton, 2000)
Barratt, John, *'The King's Irish': The Royalist Anglo-Irish Foot of the English Civil War* (Solihull: Helion & Co., 2019)
Bennett, Martyn, *In the Midst of the Kingdom: The Royalist War Effort in the North Midlands, 1642–1646 (Warwick: Helion & Co., 2021)*
Binns, Jack, *A Place of Great Importance: Scarborough in the Civil Wars, 1640–60* (Lancaster: Carnegie, 1996)
Bowden, Peter J., *The Wool Trade in Tudor and Stuart England* (London: Palgrave Macmillan, 1962)
Denton, Barry, *Naseby Fight* (Leigh-on-Sea: Partizan Press, 1988)
Donagan, Barbara, *War in England 1642–1649* (Oxford: Oxford University Press, 2008)
Edwards, Peter, *Dealing in Death: The Arms Trade and the British Civil Wars, 1638–52* (Stroud: Sutton, 2000)
Everitt, Alan (ed), *Suffolk and the Great Rebellion, 1640–1660* (Suffolk Records Society, 1960)
Firth, C. H. and Davies, Godfrey, *The Regimental History of Cromwell's Army, 2 vols* (Oxford: Clarendon Press, 1991 edn)
Foard, Glenn, *Colonel John Pickering's Regiment of Foot, 1644–45* (Whitstable: Pryor Publications, 1994)
Foard, Glenn, *Naseby: The Decisive Campaign (Barnsley: Pen & Sword, 2004 edn)*
Furgol, Edward, *A Regimental History of the Covenanting Armies* (Edinburgh: John Donald, 2nd edn, 2021)
Gentles, Ian, *The New Model Army in England, Ireland, and Scotland, 1645–1653* (Oxford: Blackwell, 1992)
Greenslade, M. W. and Baugh, G. C. (intro.), *The History and Antiquities of Staffordshire, by Stebbing Shaw*, 2 vols (East Ardsley: E. P. Publishing, 1976)
Hazell, Martin, *Fidelity and Fortitude: Lord Capel his regiments and the English Civil War* (Leigh-on-Sea: Partizan Press, 1987)
Holmes, Clive, *The Eastern Association in the English Civil War* (Cambridge: Cambridge University Press, 2008)
Hopper, Andrew, *Black Tom: Sir Thomas Fairfax and the English Revolution* (Manchester: Manchester University Press, 2007)
Hughes, Ann, *Politics, Society and Civil War in Warwickshire, 1620–1660* (Cambridge: Cambridge University Press, revised edn, 2002)
Hutton, Ronald, *The Making of Oliver Cromwell (New Haven and London: Yale University Press, 2021)*
Hutton, Ronald, *The Royalist War Effort, 1642–46 (*Upper Saddle River, NJ: Prentice Hall Press, 1984)
Jones, Archer, *The Art of War in the Western World* (New York: Oxford University Press, 1987)
Jones, Serena, *No Armour But Courage: Colonel Sir George Lisle, 1615–1648* (Solihull: Helion & Co., 2016)
Lawrence, David R., *The Complete Soldier: Military Books and Military Culture in Early Stuart England, 1603–1645 (Leiden: Brill, 2008)*
Manning, Roger B., *An Apprenticeship in Arms: The Origins of the British Army 1585–1702* (Oxford: Oxford University Press, 2006)
Money, Walter, *The First and Second Battles of Newbury and the Siege of Donnington Castle during the Civil War, 1643–6* (London: Simpkin, Marshall & Co., 1881)

Ogier, Charles, *Dziennik podróży do Polski, 1635–1636* (Gdańsk: Biblioteka Miejska, 1950)

Peachey, Stuart, *The Edgehill Campaign and the Letters of Nehemiah Wharton* (Leigh-on-Sea: Partisan Press, 1997)

Peachey, Stuart and Turton, Alan, *The Fall of the West*, 8 vols (Bristol: Stuart Press, 1994)

Phillips, J. R., *Memoirs of the Civil War in Wales and the Marches, 1642–1649*, 2 volumes (London: Longmans, 1874)

Reid, Stuart, *Scots Armies of the Seventeenth Century I: The Army of the Covenant 1639–51* (Leigh-on-Sea: Partizan Press, 1988)

Reid, Stuart, *The Finest Knight in England* (Leigh-on-Sea: Partizan Press, 1987)

Robinson, Gavin, *Horses, People and Parliament in the English Civil War: Extracting Resources and Constructing Allegiance* (Farnham: Ashgate, 2012)

Ryder, Ian, *An English Army for Ireland* (Leigh-on-Sea: Partizan Press, 1987)

Scott, Christopher L. and Turton, Alan, *Hey for Old Robin!: The Campaigns And Armies Of The Earl Of Essex During The First Civil War, 1642–44* (Solihull: Helion & Co., 2017)

Scott, Christopher L., Turton, Alan and von Arni, Eric Gruber, *Edgehill: The Battle Reinterpreted* (Barnsley: Pen & Sword, 2004)

Somerville, James, *Memorie of the Somervilles*, 2 vols (Edinburgh: James Ballantyne and Co., 1815)

Spence, Richard T., *Skipton Castle in the Great Civil War 1642–1645* (Skipton Castle, 1991)

Spring, Laurence, *In the Emperor's Service: Wallenstein's Army, 1625–1634* (Solihull: Helion & Co., 2019)

Spring, Laurence, *The Army of the Eastern Association: Officers and Regiments* (Pike & Shot Society, 2016)

Spring, Laurence, *Waller's Army: The Regiments of Sir William Waller's Southern Association* (Pike & Shot Society, 2007)

Tibbutt, H. G., *Colonel John Okey, 1606–1662*(Bedford: Bedfordshire Historical Record Society, 1954)

Terry, C. S, *The Life and Campaigns of Alexander Leslie, First Earl of Leven* (London and New York: Longmans, Green and Co., 1899)

Turton, Alan, *The Chief Strength of the Army: Essex's Horse (1642–1645)* (Leigh-on-Sea: Partizan Press, 1992)

Tylden, G., *Horses and Saddlery: An Account of the Animals Used by the British and Commonwealth Armies from the Seventeenth Century to the Present Day* (London: J. A. Allen, 1965)

Wanklyn, Malcolm, *Reconstructing the New Model Army Volume 1: Regimental Lists April 1645 to May 1649* (Solihull: Helion and Co., 2015)

Young, Peter, *Edgehill 1642: The Campaign and the Battle* (Kineton: Roundwood Press, 1967)

Young, Peter, *Naseby 1645: The Campaign and the Battle* (London: Century, 1985)

Articles and Chapters

Abram, Andrew, "Sufficiently Different to the Rest of the Army': The Cheshire Parliamentarian Dragoons in the First Civil War', *JSAHR*, 98 (2020), pp.220–38

Abram, Andrew, 'The Influence of Military Professionals and Trained Band Officers in Lancashire and Cheshire during the British Civil Wars', *TLCAS*, 112 (2020), pp.113–34

Atherton, Ian, 'Royalist Finances in the English Civil War: The Case of Lichfield Garrison, 1643–5', *MH*, 33 (2008), pp.43–67

Barratt, John, 'What Sanford's Firelocks Did Next', *ECWNQ*, 50 (Partizan Press, 1995), pp.18–21

Blackmore, David, 'Counting the New Model Army', *ECWT*, 58 (2004), pp.3–5

Bonsall, James, 'The Study of Small Finds at the 1644 Battle of Cheriton', *JCA*, 3 (2007), pp.29–52

Bradley, Nigel B., 'Sir William Constable's Regiment 1642–1655: A study of the Civil War commander and his officers', *JSAHR*, 55 (1977), pp.215–43

Claxton, Kevin M., 'The Battle of Cheriton: The analysis of artefacts from an English Civil War Battlefield', *JCA*, 13 (2018), pp.80–96

Davies, Chrystal, 'The Battle of St Fagans, 8 May 1648', *Cromwelliana* (1991), pp.15–27

Davies, Godfrey, 'The Army of the Eastern Association, 1644–5', *EHR*, 46 (1931), pp.88–96

Davies, Godfrey, 'The Parliamentary Army under the Earl of Essex, 1642–5', *EHR*, 49(1934), pp.32–54

Donegan, Barbara, 'Halcyon Days and the Literature War: England's Military Education before 1642', *P&P*, 147 (1995), 65–100

Ede-Borrett, Stephen, 'Some Notes on the Raising and Origins of Colonel John Okey's Regiment of Dragoons, March to June, 1645', *JSAHR*, 87 (2009), pp.206–13

Edwards, Peter, 'The Supply of Horses to the Parliamentarian and Royalist Armies in the English Civil War', *HR*, 68 (1995), pp.49–66

Edwards, Peter, 'Turning Ploughshares into Swords: The Arms and Military Equipment Industries in Staffordshire in the First Civil War, 1642–1646', *MH, 27 (2002),* pp.52–79

Frost, Robert, 'Scottish soldiers, Poland-Lithuania and the Thirty Years' War', Steve Murdoch (ed), *Scotland and the Thirty Years' War, 1618–1648* (Leiden: Brill, 2001), pp.191–213

Gaunt, Peter, 'Learning the Ropes in 'His Own Fields': Cromwell's Early Sieges in the East Midlands', *Cromwelliana* (2003), pp.27–39

Graham, Aaron, 'Finance, Localism and Military Representation in the army of the Earl of Essex (June-November 1642)', *HJ*, 52 (2009), pp.879–98

Graham, Aaron, 'The Earl of Essex and Parliament's Army at the Battle of Edgehill: A Reassessment', *WH*, 17(2010), pp.276–93

Gilbert, C. D, 'A Dramatic Incident in Royalist Worcestershire: 'Tinker' Fox's Raid on Bewdley of May 1644', *MH*, 35 (2010), pp.129–35

Hopper, Andrew, "Tinker' Fox and the Politics of Garrison Warfare in the West Midlands, 1643–50', *MH*, 24 (1999), pp.98–113

Kelenik, Joseph, 'The Military Revolution in Hungary', Dávid Géza and Pál Fodor (eds), *Ottomans, Hungarians, and Habsburgs in Central Europe* (Leiden: Brill, 2000), pp.117–62

Kurrelmeyer, W., 'The Etymology of Dragoon', *TPMLAA*, 57 (1942), pp.421–34

Leadbetter, Peter, 'Extracts from The Earl of Denbigh's Letter Book', *Arquebusier*, XXXVIII/II (2022), pp.22–28

Love, Ronald S, '"All the King's Horsemen": The Equestrian Army of Henri IV, 1585–1598', *SCJ*, 22 (1991), pp.511–33

Lowe, John, 'The Campaign of the Irish Royalist Army in Cheshire, November 1643-January 1644', *THSLC*, 111 (1959), pp.49–76

Malcolm, Joyce, 'All the King's Men: The Impact of the Crown's Irish Soldiers on the English Civil War', *IHS*, 21 (1979), pp.239–64

Mungeam, Gerald I., 'Contracts of the Supply of Equipment to the New Model Army in 1645', *JAAS*, 6 (1968–70), pp.53–114

Pearse, Richard, 'The Use of the Matchlock when Mounted', *JSAHR*, 44(1966), pp.201–204

Robinson, Gavin, 'Horse Supply and the Development of the New Model Army, 1642–1646', *WH*, 15 (2008), pp.121–40

Slack, Ron, 'Colonel Gell and Major Sanders: Internal feuding among the Parliamentary forces in Derbyshire during the Civil Wars of 1642–1646', *DM*, 16 (2) (2001), pp, 34–48

Steinman, George, 'Memoir of Sir Arthur Aston', *TGM*, 155 (1834), pp.144–50

Stevenson, John and Carter, Andrew, 'The Raid on Chinnor and the Fight at Chalgrove Field, June 17th and 18th, 1643', *Oxoniensia*, 38 (1973), pp.346–56

Terry, C. S, 'The Scottish Campaigns in Northumberland and Durham between January and June 1644', *AA*, 2nd Series, 21 (1899), pp.146–79

Young, Peter, 'King Charles I's Army of 1642', *JSAHR*, 17 (1938), pp.102–109

Unpublished Theses

Crawshaw, Thomas, 'Military Finance and the Earl of Essex's Regular Army: 1642–1644', PhD thesis (York University, Toronto, 2013)

Gratton, Malcolm, 'The Parliamentarian and Royalist War Effort in Lancashire 1642–1651', PhD thesis (University of Manchester, 1998)

Harrison, George Anthony, 'Royalist Organisation in Wiltshire, 1642–1646',PhD thesis (University of London, 1963)

Jones, Jennifer, 'The War in the North: The Northern Parliamentary Army in the English Civil War, 1642–1645', PhD thesis (York University, Toronto, 1994)

Newman, P. R., 'The Royalist Army in Northern England, 1642–45', PhD thesis (University of York, 1978)

Robinson, Gavin, 'Horse supply in the English Civil War 1642–1646', PhD thesis (University of Reading, 2001)

Roy, Ian, 'The Royalist Army in the First Civil War', PhD thesis (University of Oxford, 1963)